THE CAMBRIDGE COMPANION TO
THOMAS REID

Each volume of this series of companions to major philosophers contains specially commissioned essays by an international team of scholars, together with a substantial bibliography, and will serve as a reference work for students and
nonspecialists. One aim of the series is to dispel the intimi-
dation such readers often feel when faced with the work of a
difficult and challenging thinker.

Widely acknowledged as the principal architect of Scottish common sense philosophy, Thomas Reid is increasingly
recognized today as one of the finest philosophers of the 18th
century. Combining a sophisticated response to the skeptical and idealist views of his day with a robust realism about
mind, world, and value, Reid's thought stands as an important alternative to Humean skepticism, Kantian idealism,
and Cartesian rationalism. This volume is the first compre-
hensive overview of Reid's output and covers not only his
philosophy in detail but also his scientific work and his extensive historical influence.

New readers will find this the most convenient and ac-
cessible guide to Reid currently available. Advanced students
and specialists will find a conspectus of recent developments
in the interpretation of Reid.

Terence Cuneo is Assistant Professor of Philosophy at Calvin
College, Grand Rapids, Michigan

René van Woudenberg is Professor of Philosophy at the Vrije
Universiteit, Amsterdam

The Cambridge Companion to
THOMAS REID

Edited by

Terence Cuneo
Calvin College, Grand Rapids, Michigan

René van Woudenberg
Vrije Universiteit, Amsterdam

CAMBRIDGE
UNIVERSITY PRESS

PUBLISHED BY THE PRESS SYNDICATE OF THE UNIVERSITY OF
CAMBRIDGE
The Pitt Building, Trumpington Street, Cambridge, United Kingdom

CAMBRIDGE UNIVERSITY PRESS
The Edinburgh Building, Cambridge CB2 2RU, UK
40 West 20th Street, New York, NY 10011-4211, USA
477 Williamstown Road, Port Melbourne, VIC 3207, Australia
Ruiz de Alarcón 13, 28014 Madrid, Spain
Dock House, The Waterfront, Cape Town 8001, South Africa

http://www.cambridge.org

First published 2004

Printed in the United States of America

Typeface Trump Medieval 10/13 pt.   *System* LaTeX 2_ε [TB]

A catalog record for this book is available from the British Library.

Library of Congress Cataloging in Publication Data
The Cambridge companion to Thomas Reid/edited by Terence Cuneo,
    René van Woudenberg
        p.   cm. – (Cambridge companions to philosophy)
    Includes bibliographical references and index.
    ISBN 0-521-81270-4 (hc) – ISBN 0-521-01208-2 (pbk)
        1. Reid, Thomas, 1710–1796.   I. Cuneo, Terence, 1969–
II. Woudenberg, René van.   III. Series.
    B1537.C36 2004
    192–dc21   2003051249

ISBN 0 521 81270 4 hardback
ISBN 0 521 01208 2 paperback

CONTENTS

vii

CONTRIBUTORS

ALEXANDER BROADIE is Professor of Philosophy and Chair of Logic and Rhetoric at the University of Glasgow, Scotland. He has published extensively in medieval philosophy and the history of Scottish philosophy. His books include *The Circle of John Mair: Logic and Logicians in Pre-Reformation Scotland* (1994), *The Shadow of Scotus: Philosophy and Faith in Pre-Reformation Scotland* (1999), and *The Scottish Enlightenment: The Historical Age of the Historical Nation* (2002). He is also the editor of *The Cambridge Companion to the Scottish Enlightenment* (2003).

C. A. J. COADY is an ARC Senior Research Fellow and the Deputy Director of the ARC Special Research Centre for Applied Philosophy and Public Ethics at the University of Melbourne, Australia. He has published numerous articles in epistemology, philosophy of language, philosophy of mind, ethics, and political philosophy. He is the author of *Testimony: A Philosophical Study* (1992) and *Morality and Political Violence* (forthcoming).

TERENCE CUNEO is Assistant Professor of Philosophy at Calvin College, Michigan. The author of several articles on Reid's moral philosophy and in contemporary metaethics, he is also the editor of *Religion in the Liberal Polity* (forthcoming).

LORNE FALKENSTEIN is Professor of Philosophy at the University of Western Ontario. He has published widely in the history of early modern philosophy and is the author of *Kant's Intuitionism: A Commentary on the Transcendental Aesthetic* (1995).

JOHN GRECO is Associate Professor of Philosophy at Fordham University, New York. In addition to having published numerous articles in epistemology, he is the author of *Putting Skeptics in Their Place* (2000) and the editor of *Reading Sosa* (forthcoming) and the coeditor (with Ernest Sosa) of *The Blackwell Guide to Epistemology* (1999).

PETER KIVY is Professor of Philosophy, Rutgers University, New Jersey. Among his many books are *Music Alone: Philosophical Reflections on the Purely Musical Experience* (1991), *Authenticities: Philosophical Reflections on Musical Performance* (1998), *New Essays on Musical Understanding* (2001), *The Possessor and the Possessed: Handel, Mozart, Beethoven, and the Idea of Musical Genius* (2001), and *Introduction to a Philosophy of Music* (2002).

BENJAMIN W. REDEKOP is Associate Professor of Liberal Studies at Kettering University, Michigan. In addition to having authored several articles on Reid, he is the author of *Enlightenment and Community: Lessing, Abbt, Herder, and the Quest for a German Public* (1999) and the editor of *Power, Authority, and the Anabaptist Tradition* (2001).

WILLIAM L. ROWE is Professor of Philosophy at Purdue University, Indiana. He has published numerous articles in philosophy of religion, action theory and the history of philosophy. He is the author of *Thomas Reid on Freedom and Morality* (1991), *The Cosmological Argument* (1998), and *Philosophy of Religion: An Introduction* (2001, 3rd edition) and is the editor of *God and the Problem of Evil* (2002).

DALE TUGGY is Assistant Professor of Philosophy at the State University of New York, Fredonia. His publications include articles on Thomas Reid and in the philosophy of religion.

JAMES VAN CLEVE is Professor of Philosophy at Brown University, Rhode Island. He is the author of numerous articles in metaphysics, epistemology, philosophy of mind, philosophy of language, and the history of modern philosophy as well as *Problems from Kant* (1999).

RENÉ VAN WOUDENBERG is Professor of Philosophy at the Vrije Universiteit, Amsterdam, The Netherlands. In addition to publishing articles in epistemology, history of philosophy, and philosophy of language, he has written several books including *Gelovend denken* (1992), *Het mysterie van de identiteit* (2000), and *Filosofie van taal en tekst* (2002).

NICHOLAS WOLTERSTORFF is Noah Porter Professor of Philosophical Theology, Yale University, Connecticut. He is the author of, inter alia, *On Universals* (1970), *Works and Worlds of Art* (1980), *Until Justice and Peace Embrace* (1983), *Reason within the Bounds of Religion* (1984, 2nd edition), *Divine Discourse* (1995), *John Locke and the Ethics of Belief* (1996), and *Thomas Reid and the Story of Epistemology* (2001).

PAUL WOOD is Professor of History at the University of Victoria, Canada. He has published widely in the intellectual history of early modern Europe and is the editor of *Thomas Reid on the Animate Creation: Papers Relating to the Life Sciences* (1995) and *The Correspondence of Thomas Reid* (2002).

NOTE ON CITATIONS

References to editions of or sources for Reid's published works use an abbreviated title of work or source as indicated below:

LIST OF ABBREVIATIONS FOR WORKS BY THOMAS REID

C   *The Correspondence of Thomas Reid*, ed. Paul Wood. Edinburgh: Edinburgh University Press, 2002.

EAP   *Essays on the Active Powers of Man*. In *The Works of Thomas Reid*, 6th ed., ed. Sir William Hamilton. Edinburgh: MacLachlan and Stewart, 1863. Reprint Bristol: Thoemmes Press, 1994.

EIP   *Essays on the Intellectual Powers of Man*, ed. Derek R. Brookes, with annotations by Derek R. Brookes and Knud Haakonssen. Edinburgh: Edinburgh University Press, 2002.

EQ   "An Essay on Quantity; occasioned by reading a Treatise, in which Simple and Compound Ratios are applied to Virtue and Merit," *Philosophical Transactions of the Royal Society of London* 45 (1748): 505–20. Reprinted in *The Works of Thomas Reid*: 715–19.

IHM   *An Inquiry into the Human Mind on the Principles of Common Sense*, ed. Derek R. Brookes. Edinburgh: Edinburgh University Press, 1997.

LFA   *Lectures on the Fine Arts*, ed. Peter Kivy. The Hague: Martinus Nijhoff, 1973.

LNT   *Lectures on Natural Theology (1780)*, ed. Elmer Duncan. Washington: University Press of America, 1981.

LRF   *Thomas Reid on Logic, Rhetoric, and the Fine Arts*, ed.
      Alexander Broadie. Edinburgh: Edinburgh University Press,
      forthcoming.
OP   "On Power," ed. John Haldane. *Philosophical Quarterly* 51,
      no. 202 (January 2001): 3–12.
PE   *Practical Ethics*, ed. Knud Haakonssen. Princeton: Princeton
      University Press, 1990.
PO   *The Philosophical Orations of Thomas Reid*, ed. D. D. Todd.
      Carbondale: Southern Illinois University Press, 1989.
PRLS *Thomas Reid on the Animate Creation: Papers Relating to
      the Life Sciences*, ed. Paul Wood. Edinburgh: Edinburgh University Press, 1995.
SP   *Reid on Society and Politics*, ed. Knud Haakonssen and Paul
      Wood. Edinburgh: Edinburgh University Press, forthcoming.
W   *The Works of Thomas Reid*, 6th ed., ed. Sir William Hamilton.
      Edinburgh: MacLachlan and Stewart, 1863. Reprint Bristol:
      Thoemmes Press, 1994.

Reid engaged extensively with the work of Locke and Hume, and
several of the essays included in this volume make numerous references to this work. Thus, a similar abbreviation scheme is used when
referring to Locke's *An Essay Concerning Human Understanding*
and Hume's *An Enquiry concerning the Principles of Morals, An Enquiry concerning Human Understanding*, and *A Treatise of Human
Nature*.

LIST OF ABBREVIATIONS FOR WORKS BY JOHN LOCKE

E   *An Essay Concerning Human Understanding*, ed. Peter H. Nidditch. Oxford: Clarendon Press, 1975.

LIST OF ABBREVIATIONS FOR WORKS BY DAVID HUME

EHU   *An Enquiry concerning Human Understanding*, ed. Tom L.
      Beauchamp. Oxford: Oxford University Press, 1999.
EPM   *An Enquiry concerning the Principles of Morals*, ed. Tom L.
      Beauchamp. Oxford: Oxford University Press, 1998.
THU   *A Treatise of Human Nature*, ed. David Fate Norton and Mary
      J. Norton. Oxford: Oxford University Press, reprinted with
      corrections, 2001.

In the case of references to the first two books published in Reid's lifetime (IHM and EIP), the abbreviated title is followed by two Roman numerals that indicate essay and chapter, and then a page number (if necessary), preceded by a colon. Thus a reference to Essay II, Chapter v, page 97 of *Essays on the Intellectual Powers of Man* is made as follows: EIP II.v: 97. Occasionally, an author may also include the line numbers on the page cited. In this case, the line numbers follow the page number preceded by a forward slash. Thus a reference to Essay II, Chapter v, page 97, lines 5 through 10 of *Essays on the Intellectual Powers of Man* is made as follows: EIP II.v: 97/5–10. With a single exception, references to *Essays on the Active Powers of Man* are made thus: The abbreviated title is followed by two Roman numerals that indicate essay and chapter, a page number (if necessary), preceded by a colon that is followed by the letter "a" or "b," which indicates the left-hand and right-hand column respectively of the page in the Hamilton edition. Thus a reference to Essay II, Chapter i, page 637, column a of *Essays on the Active Powers of Man* is made as follows: EAP II.i: 637a. The exception to this is the references to Essay III of the *Essays on the Active Powers of Man*, which Reid divided into three parts with chapters. In the case of references to Essay III, then, the abbreviated title is followed by three Roman numerals that indicate essay, part, and chapter, respectively, followed by a page number (if necessary), preceded by a colon, that is followed by the letter "a" or "b." Thus, a citation to Essay III, part iii, Chapter ii, page 581, column b of *Essays on the Active Powers of Man* is made as follows: EAP III.iii.ii: 581b.

References to works by Reid published after his lifetime conform to the following format: The abbreviated title is given followed by a page number, preceded by a colon. Thus a reference to page 82 of *Thomas Reid on the Animate Creation: Papers Relating to the Life Sciences* is made as follows: PRLS: 82.

Several of the essays contained in this volume cite Reid's unpublished manuscripts contained in Aberdeen University Library (AUL) and elsewhere. Unless indicated otherwise, references to the general collection designated AUL MS 2131 are given by the aforementioned general collection title, followed by an Arabic numeral designating the box number, a Roman numeral designating the envelope number, another Arabic numeral designating the item number (all separated by forward slashes) and then (if necessary) either a page number preceded by a colon or a folio number followed by "v" (verso) or "r" (recto) preceded by a comma. Thus a reference to page 11 of item 3 in envelope II, box 3 of AUS MS 2131 is made thus: AUL MS 2131/3/II/3: 11. By contrast, a reference to folio 2 verso of item 3 in envelope II, box 3 of AUL MS 2131 is made thus: AUL MS 2131/3/II/3, fol. 2v. References to the general collection designated AUL MS 3061 are given by the aforementioned general collection title, followed by an Arabic numeral that indicates the item number, separated by a forward slash, and followed by a page number (if necessary), preceded by a colon. Thus a reference to page 5 of item 6 of AUL MS 3061 is made thus: AUL MS 3061/6: 5. Unless indicated otherwise, references to other manuscripts held in this collection and manuscripts held at other locations are referred to by their general designation number. Thus a reference to AUL MS 2343 is made thus: AUL MS 2343.

References to Locke's *An Essay on Human Understanding* take the following form: The abbreviated title is followed by two Roman numerals that indicate book and chapter, an Arabic numeral that indicates section, and then a page number (if necessary), preceded by a colon. Thus a reference to Book IV, Chapter 1, section 1, page 525 of *An Essay on Human Understanding* is made as follows: E IV.i.1: 525.

References to Hume's *An Enquiry concerning Human Understanding* and *An Enquiry concerning the Principles of Morals* are made as such: The abbreviated title is followed by an Arabic numeral that indicates section number, an Arabic numeral that indicates part number (if necessary) and page number (if necessary), preceded by a colon. Thus a reference to section IV, page 109 of *An Enquiry concerning Human Understanding* is made thus: EHU IV: 109. References to Hume's *Treatise on Human Nature* take the following form: The abbreviated title is followed by three Arabic numerals that indicate book, part and section, and then a page number (if necessary), preceded by a colon. Thus a reference to Book 3, part 3, section 1, page 367 of *A Treatise on Human Nature* is made as follows: THU 3.3.1: 367.

Unless indicated otherwise by the author of a particular essay, works by authors other than Reid (and the works by Locke and Hume mentioned above) are referred to by name of the author, the publication date of the work or edition cited (followed by "a," "b," "c," etc. to distinguish publications in the same year), and a page number (if necessary), preceded by a colon. For example, a reference to page 100 of Nicholas Wolterstorff's *Thomas Reid and the Story of Epistemology*, published in 2001, is made thus: Wolterstorff 2001: 100.

Full information about cited works and sources is given in the bibliography.

CHRONOLOGY OF EVENTS RELATING TO
THOMAS REID AND HIS CONTEXT

1731–70   David Skene
1732   Death of Margaret Gregory, Reid's mother
1733–6   Reid is librarian at Marischal College
1736   Reid and John Stewart visit Cambridge, London, and Oxford
1737   Reid ordained minister of New Machar, Aberdeenshire
1739–40   Hume's *A Treatise of Human Nature*
1740   Reid marries his cousin Elizabeth Reid in London
            George Turnbull's *Principles of Moral and Christian Philosophy*
1742   *George Turnbull's Observations upon Liberal Education*
1744   Birth of Martha, the only one of Reid's six children to survive him
1745–6   Jacobite Rising under Prince Charles Edward Stuart
1748   Hume's *Philosophical Essays concerning Human Understanding* (later titled *An Enquiry concerning Human Understanding*)
            Colin Maclaurin's *Account of Sir Isaac Newton's Philosophical Discoveries*
            Reid's "Essay on quantity" published in volume 45 of the *Philosophical Transactions of the Royal Society*
1751   Adam Smith appointed Professor of Logic and Rhetoric at Glasgow, becoming Professor of Moral Philosophy at Glasgow in 1752
            Reid appointed regent at King's College, Aberdeen
            Hume's *An Enquiry concerning the Principles of Morals*
1753–1821   James Gregory
1753–1828   Dugald Stewart
1754   Reid becomes Honorary Burgess of Aberdeen
1755   Hutcheson's *A System of Moral Philosophy*
1757   Hume's *The Natural History of Religion*
1758   Founding of the Aberdeen Philosophical Society, the "Wise Club," of which Reid is founding member and first secretary
            Reid attends inaugural meeting of the Gordon's Mill Farming Club

1779	Hume's *Dialogues Concerning Natural Religion*
1780	Archibald Arthur elected as Reid's assistant and successor
1781	Immanuel Kant's *Critique of Pure Reason*
1783	Reid elected Fellow of the newly founded Royal Society of Edinburgh
1784	Reid appointed Vice-Rector of Glasgow University by the Rector Edmund Burke
1785	Reid's *Essays on the Intellectual Powers of Man*
	Fourth edition of Reid's *Inquiry*
	Reid reappointed Vice-Rector of Glasgow University by the Rector Edmund Burke
	Dugald Stewart appointed Professor of Moral Philosophy at Edinburgh
1788	Reid's *Essays on the Active Powers of Man*
	Immanuel Kant's *Critique of Practical Reason*
1789	French Revolution
1790	Reid is founding member and first president of the Glasgow Society of the Sons of Ministers of the Church of Scotland
1791	Reid joins the Glasgow Friends of Liberty and attends Bastille Day dinner
	Medallion of Reid struck by James Tassie
	Reid contributes money to the French National Assembly
	Death of Reid's wife Elizabeth
	James Gregory's *Philosophical and Literary Essays*
1794	Reid publishes "Observations on the dangers of political innovation" in *Glasgow Courier*, 18 December
1795	Adam Smith's *Essays on Philosophical Subjects*
1796	Reid's portrait painted by Raeburn
	Death of Reid, 7 October
1799	Reid's "University of Glasgow" published in John Sinclair's *Statistical Account of Scotland*, vol. 21
1805	Death of Reid's daughter Martha

Introduction

History can be a fickle judge. After enjoying enormous popularity in the United States, Great Britain, and France for almost one hundred years after his death, Thomas Reid (1710–96) disappeared from the philosophical canon. Reid's disappearance did not have the consequence that his thought failed to influence subsequent philosophers: One can discern, for example, distinctly Reidian themes and methodology at work in Moorean "ordinary language" philosophy. But it did mean that Reid made no appearance in the story that philosophers in the last century have told – and continue to tell – about the development of early modern philosophy. The basic shape of this story is familiar enough and goes something like this:[1]

Early modern philosophy was animated by two central worries: First, given its dismal history of disagreement and present state of faction, how could philosophy progress in the way and to the degree that the natural sciences had? And, second, how could traditional objects of philosophical inquiry such as free will, the soul, and God be fit into the world as described by the new science? The urgency of both these issues occasioned a crisis in modern philosophy. In their own way, and with varying degrees of success, rationalists such as Descartes and empiricists such as Hume grappled with these issues. But only in the figure of Immanuel Kant do we encounter a sustained and ingenious attempt to blend the rationalist and empiricist ways of addressing these problems.

A theme that emerges from this book is that this story needs to be retold. The story needs to be retold not so much because it is fundamentally misguided, but because it is incomplete. There is, in addition to the Kantian response to the crisis in modern philosophy, a Reidian response – a response of a different character, but of comparable sophistication and ingenuity.

I

One of the most striking features of Thomas Reid's thought is that the typically modern anxiety about what we might call the "progress" and "location" problems is absent. There is, in Reid's published work, no lamentation about the lack of progress in philosophy.[2] Nor is there complaint about how philosophy compares unfavorably with the new science. On the contrary, in the preface to the *Essays on the Intellectual Powers of Man*, Reid writes that whatever the current prejudices may be against philosophy,

About two hundred years ago, the opinions of men in natural philosophy were as various, and as contradictory, as they are now concerning the powers of the mind. GALILEO, TORRICELLI, KEPLER, BACON and NEWTON, had the same discouragement in their attempts to throw light upon the material system, as we have with regard to the intellectual. If they had been deterred by such prejudices, we should never have reaped the benefit of their discoveries, which do honour to human nature, and will make their names immortal....

The remains of ancient philosophy upon this subject [viz., the powers and operations of the mind], are venerable ruins, carrying the marks of genius and industry, sufficient to inflame, but not to satisfy, our curiosity. In later ages, DES CARTES was the first to point out the road we ought to take in those dark regions. MALEBRANCHE, ARNAULD, LOCKE, BERKELEY, BUFFIER, HUTCHESON, BUTLER, HUME, PRICE, Lord KAMES, have laboured to make discoveries; nor have they laboured in vain. For, however different and contrary their conclusions are, however skeptical some of them, they have all given new light, and cleared the way to those come after them.

We ought never to despair of human genius, but rather to hope, that, in time, it may produce a system of the powers and operations of the human mind, no less certain than those of optics or astronomy. (EIP Preface: 13–14)

This passage is remarkable for both its balanced assessment of philosophy's state and its high estimation of the philosophical tradition.[3] The tradition has given us insight concerning the powers and operations of the mind, by which Reid means both the intellectual and active powers of the mind such as "[t]he powers of memory, of imagination, of taste,[4] of reasoning, of moral perception, the will, the passions, the affections, and all the active powers of the soul" (IHM VII: 218). And there is, says Reid, hope for real progress on these matters – even when so much of recent thought has been "skeptical" in character.[5] In light of this measured optimism, it is natural to raise the question: Why is this characteristically modern theme of philosophy in crisis absent from Reid's thought?

It is not because Reid was ignorant of the history of philosophy or the success of the new science. Reid had a firm grip on the history of philosophy, as is evident in his extensive and detailed discussion of what he calls the "theory of ideas."[6] Moreover, Reid himself was a practicing scientist, and, among all the great eighteenth-century philosophers, Reid is arguably the most learned and expert concerning scientific issues.[7] Nor is the anxiety absent because Reid is dismissive of the new science. On the contrary, Reid repeatedly lauds the accomplishments of Newton and Bacon. Nor, finally, is it absent because Reid insisted on a sharp division between the methods of science and philosophy. Like Hume, Reid explicitly claims that philosophy should (in certain domains, at least) also employ the broadly inductive methods of Baconian science.[8] So, once again: Why this absence of anxiety in Reid's thought about the progress of philosophy?

Part of the answer lies in the fact that Reid took himself to have identified the root of why philosophy had failed to progress as it should. The Reidian diagnosis of what we've called the "progress problem" is conspicuously different from that of his contemporaries. Unlike Hume, Reid does not claim that the failure of philosophy to progress primarily consists in the fact that philosophers have failed to use the "experimental method" of the new science – although Reid emphasizes that it is partly due to this. Nor is his diagnosis the Kantian one, according to which philosophy's failure to progress is explained by the reach of theoretical reason having exceeded its grasp – although there are certainly echoes of Kant in what Reid says.[9] What Reid claims is

that the defects and blemishes in the received philosophy concerning the mind, which have most exposed it to the contempt and ridicule of sensible men, have chiefly been owing to this: That the votaries of this Philosophy, from a natural prejudice in her favour, have endeavored to extend her jurisdiction beyond its just limits, and to call to her bar the dictates of Common

Sense. But these decline this jurisdiction; they disdain the trial of reasoning, and disown its authority; they neither claim its aid, nor dread its attacks.

In this unequal contest betwixt Common Sense and Philosophy, the latter will always come off both with dishonour and loss.... Philosophy (if I may be permitted to change the metaphor) has no other root but the principles of Common Sense; it grows out of them, and draws its nourishment from them: severed from this root, its honours wither, its sap is dried up, it dies and rots. (IHM Introduction iv: 19)

So, in Reid's view, philosophy's lack of progress should mainly be attributed to its flouting the principles of common sense, by which Reid means (roughly) those propositions that properly functioning adult human beings at worlds like ours explicitly believe or take for granted in their ordinary activities and practices.[10] But why has philosophy disregarded the principles of common sense? And what exactly has been the consequence?

Reid's answer to the first question is that modern philosophers have almost universally embraced what he calls "the Cartesian system" (IHM: VII: 208).[11] The Cartesian system, as Reid describes it, has two main elements, the first of which is a particular version of what we now call "epistemological foundationalism." For our purposes, we can understand epistemological foundationalism to be a three-part thesis. In the first place, the foundationalist claims that our beliefs have various kinds of epistemic merit such as being warranted, entitled, reliably formed, certain, a case of knowledge, and so forth.[12] In the second place, the foundationalist maintains that beliefs that display a given epistemic merit come in two kinds – those that are evidentially based on some other belief that has that merit and those that are not. Finally, the foundationalist specifies the conditions under which a belief has that merit – conditions under which a belief may be "immediately" warranted, entitled, reliably formed, and so forth (i.e., not evidentially based on some other belief that has the merit in question) or "mediately" justified, warranted, entitled, and so forth (i.e., evidentially based on some other belief that has the merit in question). The dominant trend in modern philosophy, according to Reid, has been to claim that the former sorts of belief are few in number:

There is, no doubt, a beauty in raising a large fabric of knowledge upon a few first principles. The stately fabric of mathematical knowledge, raised upon the foundation of a few axioms and definitions, charms every beholder. DES CARTES, who was well acquainted with this beauty in the mathematical sciences, seems to have been ambitious to give the same beautiful simplicity to his system of philosophy; and therefore sought only one first principle as the foundation of all our knowledge, at least of contingent truths.

And so far has his authority prevailed, that those who came after him have almost universally followed him in this track. This, therefore, may be considered as the spirit of modern philosophy, to allow of no first principles of contingent truths but this one, that the thoughts and operations of our own minds, of which we are conscious, are self-evidently real and true; but that everything else that is contingent is to be proved by argument. (EIP VI.vii: 516)[13]

Reid's suggestion is that fundamental to the modern system is the thesis that the only beliefs that are immediately warranted, entitled, reliably formed, or a case of knowledge – Reid can, in various passages, be read as having different epistemic merits in mind[14] – are ones that concern "the thoughts and operations of our own minds, of which we are conscious." If an agent's belief concerning some contingent matter of fact other than the conscious thoughts and operations of her mind is warranted, entitled, reliably formed, or a case of knowledge, then it must be "proved by argument" from some belief concerning the conscious thoughts and operations of that agent's mind.

For ease of reference, we can call foundationalism of this kind "classically modern foundationalism."[15] The Cartesian system, according to Reid, links foundationalism of this variety with a methodological thesis that Reid calls the "way of analogy," which is a manner "in which men ... form their notions and opinions concerning the mind, and ... its powers and operations" (IHM VII: 203). According to Reid, the tendency of those who engage in the way of analogy is to think of the mind in crudely mechanistic terms. Descartes and his followers – by which Reid means nearly all modern philosophers –

have built upon the same foundation [viz., consciousness] and with the same materials. They acknowledge that nature hath given us very simple ideas: These are analogous to the matter of Des Cartes's physical system. They acknowledge likewise a natural power by which ideas are compounded, disjoined, associated, compared: This is analogous to the original quantity of motion in Des Cartes's physical system. From these principles they attempt to explain the phaenomena of the human understanding, just as in the physical system the phaenomena of nature were to be explained by matter and motion. (IHM VII: 212)

Although Reid does not single him out by name in this passage, Hume is perhaps the most egregious example of those who engage in the way of analogy. The Humean mind is the Newtonian universe writ small – a theater in which the "materials" are "particles" of impressions and ideas governed by the quasi-Newtonian laws of contiguity, resemblance, and causality.[16]

Reid was of the conviction that analogical reasoning of this sort led naturally to what he called "the way of ideas" or the thesis that

things which do not now exist in the mind itself, can only be perceived, remembered, or imagined, by means of ideas or images of them in the mind, which are the immediate objects of perception, remembrance, and imagination. This doctrine appears evidently to be borrowed from the old system [i.e., the Aristotelian system]; which taught, that the external things make impressions upon the mind, like impressions of the seal upon wax; that it is by means of these impressions that we perceive, remember, or imagine them; and that those impressions must resemble things from which they are taken. When we form our notions of the operations of the mind by analogy, this way of conceiving them seems to be very natural, and offers itself to our thoughts: for as every thing which is felt must make some impression upon the body, we are apt to think, that everything which is understood must make some impression upon the mind. (IHM VII: 216)[17]

The main reason that the espousal of the Cartesian system has made philosophy a "ridiculous figure in the eyes of sensible men" (EIP II.xv: 186), says Reid, is that it issues in epistemological skepticism concerning the external world. The path to skepticism from the first component of the system is fairly direct: "From the single principle of the existence of our own thoughts, very little, if any thing, can be deduced by just reasoning, especially if we suppose that all our other faculties may be fallacious" (EIP VI.vii: 518). To use one of Reid's own examples, from the mere belief that a person is having, say, a pain sensation, he cannot justifiably infer the existence of a pin whose sharpness occasioned this sensation. The proposition *that there is a sharp pin that is causing this sensation* is no more probable than not with respect to his belief that he is having a pain sensation of a certain kind: "Common sense may lead him to think that this pain has a cause; but whether this cause is body or spirit, extended or unextended, figured or not figured, he cannot possibly, from any principles he is supposed to have, form the least conjecture" (IHM V.vi: 65).[18]

One of the reasons that it is extraordinarily difficult to argue from beliefs about the content of our minds to the existence of external reality is that these beliefs are, according to advocates of the Cartesian system such as Hume, supposed to be about *images* in the mind that imagistically resemble external reality.[19] According to the Humean way of ideas theorist, we secure a mental grip on external reality by forming beliefs about images in the mind and inferring, on the basis of a resemblance between those images and the external world, entities in the external world that resemble those images.[20] But, as Reid tirelessly urges, we typically form no beliefs about our sensory experiences, and there is no significant resemblance between a sensory experience such as a pain sensation in one's finger and the sharpness of the instrument that occasioned it.[21] It makes no difference, moreover, if we think of that sensory experience as an awareness of an idea in the mind. There is no imagistic resemblance between an idea of pain in the mind that we are aware of when experiencing pain and the sharpness of the instrument that occasioned that idea, for the idea in question is not itself sharp, extended, and so forth. Accordingly, if what the way of ideas theorist says is true, there is no adequate inference from ideas in the mind to an external reality that resembles it. The "natural issue" of the way of ideas is also skepticism concerning the external world (IHM VII: 210). To which Reid adds that even if there were objects such as ideas, they would not explain how we get a mental grip on external reality:

We are at a loss to know how we perceive distant objects; how we remember things past; how we imagine things that have no existence. Ideas in the mind seem to account for all these operations: They are all by means of ideas reduced to one operation; to a kind of feeling, or immediate perception of things present, and in contact with the percipient; and feeling is an operation so familiar, that we think it needs no explication, but may serve to explain other operations.

But this feeling, or immediate perception, is as difficult to be comprehended, as the things which we pretend to explain by it. Two things may be in contact without any feeling or perception; there must therefore be in the percipient a power to feel or to perceive. How this power is produced, and how it operates, is quite beyond the reach of our knowledge....

This power of perceiving ideas is as inexplicable as any of the powers explained by it: And the contiguity of the object contributes nothing at all to make it better understood; because there appears no connection between contiguity and perception, but what is grounded on prejudices, drawn from some imagined similitude between mind and body.... (EIP II.xiv: 185)

In a move that both prefigures and has inspired major trends in contemporary epistemology and the philosophy of mind, Reid proposes jettisoning the Cartesian system. This means, first of all, repudiating a version of classically modern foundationalism in favor of a version of foundationalism that is (to use John Greco's terminology) "moderate and wide."[22] Reid's favored version of foundationalism is moderate because it tells us that a belief can be in excellent epistemic standing – say, be a case of knowledge or certain – without being indubitable or incorrigible.[23] And it is "wide" because it says that many of our beliefs about external objects, other minds, events in the past, moral truths, and the like are both (i) not inferred from other propositions and (ii) in excellent epistemic condition. Indeed, according to one reading of Reid's treatment of the "first principles of contingent truths," Reid's view is that it is a first principle of common sense that the particular deliverances of the faculties of perception, memory, consciousness, the moral sense, and so forth are immediately warranted, entitled, reliably formed, and so on.[24]

To fully divest ourselves of the Cartesian system, however, we must take a further step: We must also reject the way of analogy and its offspring, the way of ideas. Since ideas do not offer us any explanation of *how* we get a mental grip on reality, it would be better, claims Reid, to stick with our pre-reflective conviction that we apprehend entities of various kinds, but not by way of pictures in the head that imagistically resemble them.[25]

II

Hegel once quipped about the Kantian critical method that refusing to engage in philosophical reflection about substantive metaphysical issues until one had first examined the nature and limits of the understanding was akin to "refusing to enter the water until you have learnt to swim."[26] Hegel was no Reidian, but his comment in this case is decidedly Reidian in spirit. If philosophy had stumbled because it embraced the Cartesian system, the way forward, according to Reid, was not to begin with a critique of reason, but to begin in the thick of human experience by paying "due attention" to the use and structure of ordinary language, the principles taken for granted in the "course of human actions in conduct," and "the operations of our own minds" (EIP I.v: 56–7).

Of these three planks in his philosophical methodology, Reid himself grants special priority to the last: The "chief and proper source" of knowledge of the mind, says Reid, is accurate reflection upon the operations of our own minds, or introspection (ibid.). Ascribing this sort of authority to introspection is not, of course, likely to appeal to the post-Wittgensteinian philosopher or the contemporary psychologist. But Reid saw no particular reason to be suspicious of introspection. And it should be emphasized that he clearly recognized its limits. In the first place, introspective knowledge needs to be supplemented and guided by our best scientific knowledge of the nature of mind. That adherents to the way of ideas failed to pay close enough attention to the operations of mind, and thereby confounded distinct cognitive acts such as sensation and perception, is one of Reid's main objections to their views. But Reid also stressed that adherents to the way of ideas embraced scientifically suspect physiological hypotheses regarding the mechanisms involved in human perception.[27] And it should not be overlooked that Reid's work in the theory of vision and geometry plays a major part in his rejection of the way of ideas.[28] As Lorne Falkenstein has argued, Reid's work in the theory of vision and, in particular, his use of the Berkeleyan distinction between visible and real figure are fundamental to his rejection of Berkeley's claim that the objects of vision and touch exist only in the mind as radically different types of sensation.[29]

Secondly, Reid himself stresses that the introspective method is of limited use. Attending to the operations of our minds is extraordinarily difficult as "[t]he number and quick succession of the operations of the mind make it difficult to give due attention to them" (EIP I.vi: 60). Moreover, we are, among other things, habitually disposed to attend to the objects of the operations of mind and not the operations of mind themselves.[30] So, although accurately reflecting on the operations of mind is central to Reid's common sense philosophy, it is not itself a practice easily engaged in by the ordinary person. On the contrary, it requires the exercise of virtues such as attention, patience, and discernment that Reid suggests may be in short supply among the vulgar.[31]

It is not surprising, then, that both when criticizing the positions of others and when developing his own positive views, Reid leans heavily on the ways in which ordinary folk use language and the principles of common sense that they take for granted in their ordinary activities and practices. In this respect at least, Reid's philosophical method is one that foreshadows both American pragmatism and the "linguistic turn" in Anglo-American analytic philosophy. It is also, interestingly enough, that aspect of Reid's thought that has attracted the most criticism. To single out what is perhaps the most famous of such criticisms, Kant's invective in the introduction to the *Prolegomena* accused Reidian common sense of being an "appeal to the opinion of the multitude, of whose applause the philosopher is ashamed ... when no rational justification for one's position can be advanced ... when insight and science fail."[32]

Kant's criticism has been echoed by philosophers of rather different persuasions.[33] This is more than a little ironic, for Reid himself would not have denied that there is a sense in which appealing to common sense – to what it "is ridiculous to doubt" – *is* humiliating for the philosopher:

When I remember distinctly a past event, or see an object before my eyes, this commands my belief no less than an axiom. But when, as a Philosopher, I reflect upon this belief, and want to trace it to its origin, I am not able to resolve it into necessary and self-evident axioms, or conclusions that are necessarily consequent upon them. I seem to want that evidence which I can best comprehend, and which gives perfect satisfaction to an inquisitive mind; yet it is ridiculous to doubt, and I find it is not in my power. An attempt to throw off this belief, is like an attempt to fly, equally ridiculous and impracticable.

To a Philosopher, who has been accustomed to think that the treasure of his knowledge is the acquisition of that reasoning power of which he boasts, it is no doubt humiliating to find, that his reason can lay no claim to the greater part of it. (EIP II.xx: 233)

Reid's response to humiliation of this sort is that it is salutary for the philosopher: The philosopher's humiliation should beget philosophical humility. And philosophical humility or modesty does indeed pervade Reid's views on common sense and ordinary language; Reid is no less aware of the limitations of appeals to ordinary language and common sense than he is of the limits of appeals to introspection. We can, Reid emphasizes, be mistaken about what we take to be principles of common sense and, thus, should be "cautious, that we do not adopt opinions as first principles, which are not entitled to that character" (EIP I.ii: 46). And while philosophy must start from, and be guided by, ordinary language, Reid states that "all languages have their imperfections ... and can never be adequate to all the varieties of human thought" since "we can expect, in the structure of languages" only "those distinctions which all mankind in the common business of life have occasion to make" (EIP I.v: 56). Indeed, as Reid indicates in his discussion of the way in which we talk about the movement of the earth, ordinary language can lead us astray.[34] Finally, it should be noted that Reid himself is willing to deviate from ordinary language and what appears to be common sense, when the latter clashes with our best science. Perhaps the best example of this in Reid's own thought lies in his treatment of causality. Reid understood the best science of his day – that is, Newtonian science – to establish that matter was inert. Accordingly, Reid was willing to allow that, even though ordinary language and the beliefs of ordinary folk indicate otherwise, material objects are not causally efficacious: "In compliance with custom, or, perhaps, to gratify the avidity of knowing the causes of things," Reid writes, "we call the laws of nature causes and active powers. So we speak of the powers of gravitation, of magnetism, of electricity" (EAP IV.iii: 607a).[35] But "[t]he name of a *cause* ... is properly given to that being only, which, by its active power, produces some change in itself, or in some other being" (EAP IV.ii: 603a). As the latter passage indicates, by an "active power," Reid means the power of intelligent agents to bring about some change in itself or some other entity. All causation, according to Reid, is *agent* causation. All causation in nature, then, is ultimately the result of the exercise of God's agent power or the power of agents subordinate to God.[36]

In summary, then, the Reidian diagnosis of and solution to the progress problem is both revolutionary and modest. It is revolutionary insofar as it identifies a package of commitments – the Cartesian system – that philosophers had heretofore accepted uncritically, and proposes, on account of the unattractive consequences of those commitments, rejecting them. But it is modest insofar as both the diagnosis and the solution do not stray far from the principles of common sense. Philosophizing has to start *somewhere,* and Reid saw no reason that we should leave our commonsensical modes of discourse and convictions at the door when entering into the philosophical workplace. Admittedly, it is sometimes easy to identify modesty of this sort with lack of sophistication. But such an identification would be a mistake in Reid's case. Reid's positive philosophical methodology is complex: It should be viewed as the interplay between the deliverances of introspection, science, observations concerning the structure and use of ordinary language, and the principles of common sense. Reid certainly does ascribe a particular type of authority to common sense and ordinary language; until shown otherwise, they are presumed to be reliable guides to reality. But trade-offs between these different features sometimes need to be made, and the philosopher must exercise good judgment in making them.

III

Reid, then, offered a general strategy for addressing the progress problem – a strategy out of step with both the rationalist and empiricist thought of his day. Advocating a strategy of this sort, however, was only a first step toward adequately addressing the progress problem. A fully adequate response to the problem required exhibiting how one's favored philosophical methodology could shed light on the issue of how traditional objects of philosophical inquiry could be accommodated within the world as described by the best science. Reid's conviction – and here it is instructive to note a parallel with Kant – was that, among the various entities most in need of accommodation in the world as described by Newtonian science, human free choice had special priority: Without our having free will in a robustly libertarian sense, moral responsibility and, thus, traditional morality would be illusions.[37] For both Reid and Kant, other traditional issues such as personal identity through time were of secondary importance to this. Ascribing to agents strict identity through time was an important issue for Reid mainly insofar as it was necessary to underwrite our ordinary practices of holding agents morally responsible for their actions and character traits.[38]

Although Reid and Kant were agreed on this much, they adopted different strategies of locating free choice in the Newtonian universe, for they understood the nature of this universe rather differently. Kant advertised his project in the Introduction to the *Critique of Pure Reason* as one that (among other things) attempted to account for the possibility of synthetic a priori knowledge of necessary truths. And among the synthetic a priori propositions for which we have to account, says Kant, are Newton's laws of motion.[39] Although it is not entirely uncontroversial in what sense Kant held these laws to be "necessary and universal," the drift of Kant's thought appears to be that they are "transcendentally necessary" or metaphysically necessary at worlds in which human beings have experience. Understood thus, Kant was a necessitarian about these laws of nature inasmuch as he held it to be transcendentally necessary that, for example, for any action, there is always an opposite or equal reaction.[40] To this thesis Kant joined a broadly Leibnizian version of determinism: All the actions of the self in time are entirely determined by such natural laws. Of course Kant was perfectly aware that determinism is incompatible with libertarian freedom, and so he proposed dividing the world and the self in two: Insofar as we are inhabitants of the phenomenal realm, or the world of appearances, our actions are entirely determined. Insofar as we are inhabitants of the noumenal realm, or the world of things-in-themselves, we are free in the libertarian sense (and must be so for practical purposes).[41]

Viewed thus, Kant's strategy of addressing the location problem is one of avoidance: Rather than attempt to fit human free will into the Newtonian universe, his proposal is to place it in a different realm altogether – a nontemporal, nonspatial "noumenal" realm. Reid shared Kant's resolve to defend the claim that we have free will in a robustly libertarian sense, but did not share Kant's concern that free will of this sort has no place in the Newtonian universe. Fundamental to our existence, says Reid, is that "[w]e *have, by our constitution a natural conviction or belief that we act freely* – a conviction so early, so universal, and so necessary in most of our rational operations, that it must be the result of our constitution, and the work of Him that made us" (EAP IV.vi: 616b). Reid continues:

This natural conviction of our acting freely, which is acknowledged by many who hold the doctrine of necessity, ought to throw the whole burden of proof upon that side; for, by this, the side of liberty has what lawyers call a *jus quaesitum*, or a right of ancient possession, which ought to stand good till it be overturned. If it cannot be proved that we always act from necessity, there is no need of arguments on the other side, to convince us that we are free agents. (EAP IV.vi: 620a-b)

But then what about those features of the experimental method or the Newtonian universe that might threaten to overturn this native conviction concerning our freedom?

In Section VII of *An Enquiry concerning Human Understanding*, Hume argued that we have no conception of active power or the power of free choice because (i) we can see no dependence relation – let alone a necessary dependence relation – between the exercise of this power and its effects, and (ii) we have no idea how the exercise of this power could bring about behavior of certain kinds in the agent who exercised the power. Reid was unimpressed by this complaint:

To this [i.e., Hume's argument] I answer that if a man believed that in heat there was a will to melt ice, he would undoubtedly believe that there is in heat a real efficient[42] power to produce that effect, though he were ignorant how or by what latent process the effect is produced. So we, knowing that certain effects depend on our will, impute to ourselves the power of producing them, though there may be some latent process between the volition and the production which we do not know. So a child may know that a bell is rung by pulling a certain peg, though he does not yet know how that operation is connected with the ringing of the bell, and when he can move that peg he has a perfect conviction that he has power to ring the bell.

Supposing we were unable to give any account how we first got the conception of power, this would be no good reason for denying that we have it. One might as well prove that he had no eyes in his head for this reason[:] that neither he nor any other person could tell how they came there. (OP: 8, 5)

Reid's reply is that every person is convinced that certain events depend on the exercise of his active power, and it matters not a bit whether we can give an account of how the exercise of this power brings about these events. It should be noted that Reid does not leave the matter at this, but goes on to give an account of how we get a mental grip on active power. We do so not by way of being acquainted with some impression or idea, as Hume appeared to suggest we must if we had such a conception, but by what Reid calls a "relative conception." "Our conception of power is relative to its exertions or effects.... [P]ower... [is] something which has a certain relation to the effect" (EAP I.i: 514a).[43] To put Reid's point in the way we might nowadays couch it, we can get a mental grip on a particular power by way of the apprehensive use of the singular concept or definite description *the entity whose exercise brought about such and such effects.* Of course in so grasping a power, one must possess the notion of *some thing's bringing about another thing.* In Reid's view, however, there is nothing particularly problematic about acquiring such a concept; acquisition of this concept needn't come about by comparing ideas or hunting for an impression that corresponds to the concept. Rather, as the first passage quoted from the *Active Powers* above indicates, we acquire this concept by way of our "constitution." Given certain kinds of experiential inputs – namely, the "consciousness of our own activity" (EAP I.v: 523b) – we form, by a law of our constitution, the concept of something's causally bringing about something else.[44]

But to say this is not perforce to give an account of how we get a mental grip on the *necessary* connection that is supposed to obtain between cause and effect. Nor is it to address the claim that determinism is constitutive of the Newtonian universe and, thus, prohibits our thinking of human agents in space/time as being free in a robustly libertarian sense. The heart of Reid's response to these worries is expressed in the following passage, in which he claims that the laws of nature are contingent:

A law is a thing conceived in the mind of a rational being, not a thing that has real existence;[45] and, therefore, like a motive, it can neither act nor be acted upon....

The *physical laws of nature* are the rules according to which the Deity commonly acts in his natural government of the world; and whatever is done according to them, is not done by man, but by God, either immediately, or by instruments under his direction. These laws of nature neither restrain the power of the Author of nature, nor bring him under any obligation to do anything beyond their sphere. He has sometimes acted contrary to them, in the case of miracles, and, perhaps, often acts without regard to them, in the ordinary course of his providence. Neither miraculous events, which are contrary to the physical laws of nature, nor such ordinary acts of the Divine administration ... are ... impossible, nor are they *effects without a cause.* God is the cause of them, and to him only are they to be imputed. (EAP IV.ix: 628a-b)[46]

Reid is what we might call a "theistic non-necessitarian" about the laws of nature. Laws of nature are simply rules according to which God commonly acts. Theistic non-necessitarianism of this variety is crucial to Reid's strategy of addressing the location problem.

While it is not entirely clear what Hume is saying when he claims that there is a "necessary" connection between cause and effect, one plausible suggestion is this: Hume believed that nothing would count as an apprehension of a "must" between a particular cause and effect unless it carries with it implications of uniformity for the general case. In apprehending a necessary causal connection between two event tokens A and B, we also see that events could never transpire otherwise.[47] If this is Hume's thought, then Reid's answer is that grasping the dependence relation that obtains between cause and effect requires no such apprehension. One can grasp that a particular willing of type A brings about an event token of type B without being committed to the claim that all willings of type A bring about event tokens of type B.

Reid's non-necessitarianism is equally fundamental to his rejection of what he calls the "system of necessity," which can be viewed as the upshot of the combination of a pair of principles commonly embraced by its advocates. The first assumption is that human willings are events. The second is the necessitarian claim that

(N) Any event E is related to some other event E* in this way: Necessarily (as a law of nature) given E*, then E.

From these two principles it follows that our willings aren't in any sense up to us; given the laws of nature, none of us could have willed otherwise than we did.[48]

Reid not only believes we have no reason to accept (N) – (N) is not, for instance, a consequence of Newton's system – but that theistic non-necessitarianism gives us reason to reject it. If the laws of nature simply describe how God commonly acts in the world, there is no reason to believe that God cannot act differently from the way that God commonly does. And what holds for divine actions – namely, that they are not subject to natural laws – holds also for human actions. In a passage that has striking affinities with Kant, Reid writes that it is a mistake to think of voluntary human actions as falling under laws of nature at all:

> But it is to be observed, that the voluntary actions of man can in no case be called natural phaenomena, or be considered as regulated by the physical laws of Nature. Our voluntary actions are subjected to moral, but not to physical laws. The moral as well as the physical laws of Nature are enacted by the great Author of Nature, but they are essentially different. The physical laws of nature are the rules by which the Deity himself acts in his government of the world, and, therefore, they are never transgressed. Moral laws are the laws which as the supreme Lawgiver he prescribes to his reasonable creatures for their conduct, which, indeed, ought always to be obeyed, but, in fact, are often transgressed. . . .
>
> There are many important branches of human knowledge, to which Sir Isaac Newton's rules of Philosophizing have no relation, and to which they can with no propriety be applied. Such are Morals, Jurisprudence, Natural Theology, and the abstract Sciences of Mathematicks and Metaphysicks; because in none of the sciences do we investigate the physical laws of Nature. There is therefore no reason to regret that these branches of knowledge have been pursued without regard to them. (PRLS: 185–6)

Reid is one of Newton's greatest devotees. But, in Reid's view, embracing the Newtonian system needn't amount to claiming that its methods should be applied in every domain. The domain of voluntary human action is a domain of causality, to be sure. But it is not a domain of *natural* causality (although Reid is happy to admit that we are influenced by desires, moods, urges, etc.).[49] The causality at work in the domain of human voluntary action is that of human agents exercising their active power – where the exercise of active power is not one that falls under natural laws.[50]

There is a final implication of Reid's views about natural laws that is worth remarking on. Earlier it was pointed out that Kant viewed Newton's laws of motion as being synthetic a priori – "necessary and universal" in a robust sense of these terms. Since Kant could see no way by which we could grasp the necessity of these laws by ordinary inductive means, he proposed that we, in some sense, impart these laws to reality: Apart from our cognitive activity, there are no laws of nature of this sort, and it is we who confer their modal status on them. Our knowledge of the more particular laws of physics, moreover, is (according to one interpretation of Kant) to be deduced from these necessary general laws.[51]

Reid emphatically rejects this understanding of the laws of nature:

> The laws of Nature are not capable of demonstrative proof; but must be drawn from the phaenomena by just induction, like to that by which we deduce the grammatical rules of a language from the language itself. . . . [T]hat kind of induction . . . is the only proof we can have of a law of Nature. This is contrary to the rules of syllogism, and, indeed, is not demonstrative proof; but it is the only proof we can have; and it is such a proof as we rest upon with perfect security in the common affairs of life. (PRLS: 184, 190)

On this issue, as in so many others, Reid claims that when we dig into the deep nature of reality we find, not necessity, but contingency. God has created the world and our constitutions in certain ways, but God needn't have created them in those ways. Reid's proclivity to be impressed by the contingent character of the workings of nature and the human mind is, of course, one manner in which his thought stands sharply opposed to that in the German transcendental tradition. And it is, at least in part, one of the reasons that Reid would have found no inducement to accept idealism on account of the putative necessity of the laws of nature.

IV

The essays in this volume concern some of the topics on which Reid wrote and lectured that are likely to be of interest to philosophers. Given the wealth of these topics,[52] the choice as to which should be treated in such a book is difficult. But the hope is that the essays included here bring out some of the most philosophically important and interesting features of Reid's work.

The opening essay of the volume, Alexander Broadie's "Reid in Context," endeavors to throw light on Reid's thought by situating Reid in three different, albeit overlapping, contexts. The first is the religious, political, and social context. In contrast to a popularized portrayal of Reid, as a man of almost entirely academic interests, Broadie maintains Reid was deeply involved in the life of the Scottish Kirk (in which Reid was a minister) and in political debates such as the abolition of slavery, as well as in multiple literary and philosophical societies. The second context – the context to which Broadie devotes most of his attention – is Reid's intellectual context. Broadie singles out for special attention the marked influence that Reid's teacher at Marischal College, George Turnbull, had on Reid, and the importance of Reid's mature work in logic. The third and final context is the familial one, a context, Broadie suggests, that is perhaps the narrowest, but was nonetheless the most important to Reid.

Paul Wood's contribution, "Thomas Reid and the Culture of Science," attempts to correct the common misperception that Reid's mathematical and scientific endeavors were peripheral to the primary intellectual focus of his career, namely, his reply to Humean skepticism and analysis of the faculties of the human mind. From an early age to the end of his life, Wood argues, Reid was entrenched in debates regarding mathematics, chemistry, astronomy, physics, optics, and biology. Reid's expertise in these areas of science, Wood further contends, had a profound impact on his philosophical work in epistemology, metaphysics, and ethics. For example, Reid's attack on the way of ideas owes a deep debt to his work in optics, his account of general conception and natural kinds is plausibly viewed as a direct response to Buffon's *Histoire naturelle*, and his Newtonianism pervades his work on causality and ethics. To which Wood adds that the order of influence did not proceed in one direction: While Reid's expertise in science deeply influenced his philosophical work, his scientific work is also best viewed as set within the context of, and often motivated by, his epistemological, metaphysical, and moral concerns.

Reid is best known as the father of Scottish common sense philosophy. Nevertheless, Reid's doctrine of common sense has proved to be one of the most controversial and elusive features of his thought. Nicholas Wolterstorff contends in his essay, "Reid on Common Sense," that much of the confusion concerning Reid's doctrine of common sense stems from an ambiguity in Reid's own characterization of the view. The ambiguity is that between, the principles of common sense, on the one hand, as the first principles of reasoning and, on the other, as things that we all do and must take for granted in our ordinary activity and practices. These are, Wolterstorff argues, two importantly different ways of understanding the principles of common sense that Reid himself never managed to distinguish sharply. In an engagement with Reid's own texts as well as recent work on the topic of first principles, Wolterstorff suggests that the latter way of understanding the principles of common sense makes the best sense of Reid's position and that, thus understood, Reid's doctrine of common sense is of considerable importance and originality.

In both the *Inquiry* and *Essays on the Intellectual Powers*, Reid devotes a great deal of attention to the topic of perception. While it is fairly clear why Reid thinks that the mental representationalist views of his predecessors and contemporaries are flawed, there is a live controversy as to the nature of Reid's own views concerning perception. Most are agreed that Reid is a direct realist of some sort about perception. But the character of Reid's realism is unclear. In "Reid's Theory of Perception," James Van Cleve canvasses some of the reasons that Reid rejected rival views of perception, considers recent interpretations of Reid's view on perception, and distinguishes between three types of direct realism – what he terms "epistemological direct realism," "perceptual direct realism," and "presentational direct realism." Van Cleve argues that Reid is a direct realist in each sense. The claim that Reid is a presentational direct realist about perception (roughly, that he embraced the view that we have acquaintance with external objects in perception) is a controversial one. Against philosophers such as William Alston and Nicholas Wolterstorff, Van Cleve contends that this is nonetheless the most compelling interpretation of Reid's view.

In various places, Reid appears to claim that sufficient for replying to the skeptical arguments of Berkeley, Hume, and others is rejecting the theory of ideas that plays such a crucial role in these arguments. In "Reid's Reply to the Skeptic," John Greco argues that, Reid's official claim to the contrary, Reid's rejection of the way of ideas is only one component of his reply to the skeptic. There are, in addition to this rejection, three other important ingredients in Reid's reply. First among these is Reid's own positive theory of perception, according to which the beliefs formed in perception are noninferential. Second is Reid's theory of evidence, which Greco describes as a moderate and broad version of epistemological foundationalism. Third, and final, is a methodological thesis that tells us that we ought to begin our theorizing by trusting all of our cognitive faculties until we have reason to believe otherwise. According to Greco, these four components of Reid's reply jointly constitute a powerful and perhaps decisive response to the skeptic.

While Reid rarely missed the opportunity to polemicize against Hume, Hume himself wrote very little about Reid's work. What he did write, however, indicates that he thought that Reid had resurrected the doctrine of innate ideas.[53] In his essay, "Nativism and the Nature of Thought in Reid's Account of Our Knowledge of the External World," Lorne Falkenstein addresses the questions of in what sense Reid was a nativist who believed in innate thoughts, and what kind of philosophical work Reid's nativism does in his account of our knowledge of the external world. Falkenstein distinguishes several different ways in which a thought can be innate and contends that Reid's nativism should be distinguished from the kind that Locke attacked and Kant defended: It is at once more empiricist than Kant's position and more rationalist than Locke's or Hume's empiricist views. In its broadest outlines, Reid's moderate nativism is one according to which we are innately constituted directly to perceive objects as they are, provided that our sensory organs are stimulated in certain ways. According to Falkenstein, Reid's nativism, along with his work in non-Euclidean geometry and the theory of vision, plays a crucial role in Reid's rejection of Berkeleyan idealism and Humean skepticism – a rejection that is an important alternative to Kant's own response to these views.

René van Woudenberg's piece, "Reid on Memory and the Identity of Persons," explores Reid's views concerning the topics of memory and the identity of persons through time, and the way in which Reid saw these two subjects as being connected. In contrast to Locke and Hume, Reid denies that the objects of memory are ideas, claiming instead that they are actual events and states of affairs. When all goes well – or so Reid argues – the remembrance of these objects elicits true memory beliefs. Reid also rejected two influential views concerning personal identity through time, namely, the Lockean claim that a person's identity through time is constituted by that person's memory of past actions and events, and the Humean view that persons are simply bundles of impressions and ideas. In response to Locke, Reid says that memory plays the merely evidential role of furnishing evidence that an agent is the self-same person who did or experienced some thing at a previous time. In response to Hume, Reid claims that common sense dictates that persons are metaphysical simples and thus have perfect identity through time. Van Woudenberg examines Reid's rationale for making these claims and contends that it consists in Reid's commitment to certain principles of common sense, traditional theism, and the best science of his day.

The central topic of C. A. J. Coady's essay, "Reid and the Social Operations of Mind," is the philosophical import of the distinction that Reid makes between the "social" and "solitary" operations of mind. Initially put, the distinction is between those operations of the mind that require reference to other intelligent beings and those that do not. Reid's contention is that philosophers such as Hume have all but ignored the social operations of mind, and have thereby been forced to conclude that the obligations generated by promising and justice are the "creation of artifice."[54] Reid's account of the social operations of mind, Coady argues, allows Reid to develop an account of speech acts such as promising, entreating, and commanding according to which these acts are (in a sense Coady explains) natural phenomena. As such, the obligations that the performance of these speech acts generates are not grounded in convention. Thus understood, Coady suggests, Reid's views anticipate important aspects of contemporary speech act theory as well as theories of wide content in the philosophy of mind. The essay closes by considering the centrality of testimony to Reid's thought, and some of the puzzles of what Reid says on this issue.

Reid's *Essays on the Active Powers of Man* is dedicated to the topic of human freedom, and his work on this topic is widely regarded as one of his most enduring contributions to philosophy. In "Thomas Reid's Theory of Freedom and Responsibility," William Rowe offers an interpretation of Reid's agent causation account of human freedom and defends it against various objections. According to Rowe, it is Reid's position that an agent is free with respect to some action if she had the power to will that action or not to will that action. Contrary to what some philosophers have claimed, it is *not* Reid's view that in order for an agent to act freely she must have had the power to will the opposite of what she willed, or that she must have had the power to do otherwise, had she so willed otherwise. Rowe then canvases six objections to Reid's view – objections that claim that Reid's position entails an infinite regress of volitions, that it is subject to so-called Frankfurt-style counterexamples, that it is insufficiently robust to ground moral responsibility, and so forth. The upshot of Rowe's discussion is that, while not immune to doubt, Reid's position is sufficiently rich in resources to reply adequately to all of these objections.

Although Reid's views on freedom have attracted a fair amount of attention from philosophers, other features of his moral philosophy have been relatively neglected. Terence Cuneo's contribution to this volume, "Reid's Moral Philosophy," examines Reid's realist position in ethics. Cuneo argues that Reid raised important challenges to the moral antirealist positions of his day and that, contrary to some who portray Reid's view as unremittingly rationalist in character, his realist position in ethics is best viewed as a synthesis of various rationalist and sentimentalist strains of thought. Reid's moral ontology and account of moral thought and discourse is broadly rationalist in character: While rejecting the rationalist claim that moral facts consist in relations of "fittingness," Reid contends that there are moral facts that exist independent of convention or of our responding to nonmoral reality, and that a central function of moral discourse is to assert propositions that correspond to these facts. Reid's account of moral motivation and moral epistemology, however, owes a more obvious debt to the sentimentalists: We are ordinarily motivated to act morally, but by a multitude of different "principles," and not simply by reason. Moreover, we grasp moral reality by a "moral sense" – although Reid insists that a "sense" is a power of judgment, and not just a capacity to feel certain ways.

That Reid was one among only a few eighteenth-century philosophers who had a philosophy of art is the central claim of Peter Kivy's essay "Reid's Philosophy of Art." Reid, argues Kivy, was far ahead of his time inasmuch as he came very close to espousing an "expression theory" of the fine arts such as was later developed more fully by thinkers such as Collingwood and Dewey. Kivy lays down three criteria for what counts as a philosophy of art. First, it must have a firmly established concept of the fine arts; second, it must have an adequate analysis of what "art-relevant" features each of the major fine arts possesses; third, it must have a definition of art or an argument to the effect that such a definition is impossible. Kivy contends that Reid's theory satisfies all three criteria. Reid possessed a concept of the fine arts and included among them disciplines such as the visual arts, literature, landscape gardening, and, uncharacteristically for his day, instrumental music. He further claimed that the beauty of music, literature, and the visual arts consists, ultimately, in the expression of the artist's sublime or beautiful states of mind. In claiming this, Kivy suggests that Reid provides an account of the art-relevant features of (what we would call) the major fine arts, an account according to which the most important art-relevant features are their expressive properties – properties such as anger and sadness. Finally, and most controversially, Kivy maintains that by offering this account of the art-relevant features, Reid thereby offers us an expression theory of art: What makes it the case that something is a work of art, in Reid's view, is that it is appropriately expressive in character.

Those familiar with recent work in analytic philosophy of religion know that Reid's thought has played an important role in the formulation and defense of what is sometimes called "Reformed Epistemology."[55] In an essay that draws mostly on unpublished lectures, Dale Tuggy investigates Reid's philosophy of religion. Describing Reid as perhaps the last great Newtonian theist, Tuggy explores four features of Reid's philosophy of religion: his natural theology, his epistemology of religious belief, his account of the attributes of God, and his response to the problem of evil. Among other things, Tuggy argues that Reid develops an interesting version of the teleological argument, that his own epistemology of religion does not fit neatly with what some Reformed epistemologists have claimed, and that his treatment of the problem of evil exhibits an interesting blend of a keen sense of the limits of reason with a resolute nonfideism. Reid, Tuggy claims, may not have developed a full-blown philosophy of religion. But what Reid does say on this issue is a welcome perspective.

An unfortunate lacuna in Reid scholarship is that there is no general study of the influence of Reid or the commonsense school in the United States and Europe. Benjamin W. Redekop's essay, "Reid's Influence in Britain, Germany, France, and America," is an effort to remedy this situation.[56] In a historical survey of figures ranging from Dugald Stewart and Victor Cousin to C. S. Peirce, Redekop argues that the influence of Reid's thought in Britain, France, and America was, from the time of the publication of the *Inquiry* to the late nineteenth century, nothing short of enormous. Redekop contends that the popularity of Reid's work in the United States, Britain, and France can mostly be attributed to the fact that it promised to furnish a scientifically respectable position friendly to theism and resistant to the skeptical "acids of modernity." He further argues that the more tepid response to Reid in the Germanies in the eighteenth and nineteenth centuries was a function of the overtly rationalist tenor of German thought and the lack of a social "commons."

V

This book has been from its conception a collaborative project. As Reid himself notes, collaborative efforts generate obligations and responsibilities of various sorts. Indeed, Reid says that among the first principles of morals is the following:

No man is born for himself only. Every man, therefore, ought to consider himself as a member of the common society of mankind, and of those subordinate societies to which he belongs, such as family, friends, neighbourhood, country, and to do as much good as he can, and as little hurt to the societies of which he is a part. (EAP V.i: 638a-b)

As editors of this volume, we gratefully acknowledge that among the subordinate societies of which we are members is that of Reid scholars. In many ways, this book is the product of this society, and we offer our thanks for the advice and direction provided by those who have labored in the Reid vineyards far longer than we – especially Alexander Broadie, Knud Haakonssen, J-C. Smith, James Van Cleve, Nicholas Wolterstorff, and Paul Wood. (Wood was kind enough to provide references to *The Correspondence of Thomas Reid* prior to its publication and Broadie and Wood gracious enough to provide a dateline of important events in Reid's life and context.) We should also like to thank a group of younger Reid scholars for their help, in particular, Rebecca Copenhaver, James Harris, and Gideon Yaffe. Finally, we express our gratitude to the National Endowment of the Humanities, The Reid Society, The Reid Project at the University of Aberdeen, the Vrije Universiteit, The Netherlands, and Seattle Pacific University for the various kinds of support they provided.[57] Our hope is that this book will do as much good as possible, and as little hurt to the society of Reid scholars and the wider philosophical community as a whole.[58]

NOTES

1. Central elements of the story can be discerned in the introduction to Copleston 1985, Vol. IV.

2. In his earliest book, *An Inquiry into the Human Mind on the Principles of Common Sense*, Reid does comment on the "low state" of mental philosophy, but immediately adds that "however lame and imperfect the system [of the philosophers] may be, they have opened the way to future discoveries ... [and] put us in the right road ..."(IHM Introduction iii: 16, 18).

3. What Reid says about philosophy has its counterpart in what Immanuel Kant writes about "metaphysics" in the preface to the *Critique of Pure Reason*:

> There was a time when metaphysics was called the **queen** of all the sciences, and if the will be taken for the deed, it deserved this title of honor, on account of the preeminent importance of its object. Now, in accordance with the fashion of the age, the queen proves despised on all sides; and the matron, outcast and forsaken, mourns like Hecuba: *Modo maxima rerum, tot generis natisque potens, – nunc trahor exul, inops....* [Greatest of all by race and birth, I now am cast out, powerless (Ovid, *Metamorphoses* 13: 5018–10)]
>
> [M]etaphysics ... is rather a battlefield, and indeed one that appears to be especially determined for testing one's powers in mock combat; on this battlefield no combatant has ever gained the least bit of ground, nor has any been able to base any lasting possession on his victory. Hence there is no doubt that up to now the procedure of metaphysics has been a mere groping. (Kant 1998: 99, 109)

4. That is, the capacity of "discerning and relishing the beauties of Nature, and whatever is excellent in the fine arts" (EIP VIII.i: 573).

5. That Reid viewed skepticism as having great heuristic value is made clear in his abstract of the *Inquiry* sent to Hugh Blair on July 4, 1762: "Ever since the treatise of human Nature was published I respected Mr Hume as the greatest Metaphysician of the Age, and have learned more from his writings and manners of that kind than from all others put together" ("The Hume-Reid Exchange" in IHM: 257).

6. This is to echo Knud Haakonssen's comments in his introduction to *Essays on the Intellectual Powers of Man* (EIP Editor's Introduction: xiii). For Reid's own comments on the value of the history of philosophy, see EIP I.v: 57. Reid's interpretation of the way of ideas, it should be noted, has been challenged. See, for example, Yolton 1984.

7. The extent of Reid's involvement and expertise in the natural sciences has been a main theme of Paul Wood's work on Reid. See, for example, his contribution to this volume, his introduction to PRLS, and Wood 1984.

8. See EIP I.iii: 53. Section III will ask in what respects Reid thinks that the methodology is limited.

9. See, especially, EIP VI.viii: 534–6, in which Reid identifies as one of the *idola tribus* "the misapplication of our noblest intellectual power to purposes for which it is incompetent."

10. For more on the matter, see the essay by Wolterstorff in this volume. See also Wolterstorff 2001, Chap. IX, in which Wolterstorff highlights the similarities between Reidian common sense and what Wittgenstein calls our "shared world picture" in *On Certainty*.

11. See, also, EIP VI.vii: 525.

12. This is to indulge in a bit of anachronism: Descartes, Locke, Hume, and many other moderns did not view knowledge as a species of belief. (Interestingly, Reid is an outlier on this issue; see EIP VI.i: 411.) Nevertheless, Descartes and company can be said to be foundationalists of a sort with respect to knowledge, where knowledge is understood to be a nondoxastic direct awareness of reality.

13. See, also, IHM VII: 210–11. "First principles," as Reid uses the term, can be used to pick out propositions or states of believing. The present interpretation assumes that Reid is using it to pick out the latter phenomenon here.

14. As Alston 1985 notes, Reid's first principles appear to be principles of "veracity" or reliability. Elsewhere, however, Reid clearly has something more akin to entitlement or epistemic permissibility in mind. See, for example, Reid's discussion of Hume in EIP VII.iv: 568.

15. The term, as well as this characterization of the view, is borrowed from Wolterstorff 2001, Chap. VIII.

16. See Broadie 2000a: 61ff for more on this theme. Incidentally, Reid is adamant that Hume is a Cartesian of sorts, albeit of the skeptical variety. Hume, says Reid, "yields the antecedent of DES CARTES's enthymeme *cogito*, but denies the conclusion *ergo sum*, the mind being, according to him, nothing but that train of impressions and ideas of which we are conscious" (EIP VI.vii: 517–18).

17. See, also, IHM VII: 216 and EIP II. xiv: 177–8.

18. See PRLS: 179–80 for a crisp statement of the argument, as well as Greco's essay in this volume.

19. Assuming, that is, that Hume is not a phenomenalist or an idealist.

20. It should be noted, however, that this thesis concerning resemblance is not representative of all those thinkers whom Reid lumped under the Cartesian system. Descartes and Locke, for example, held more qualified versions of the view.

21. E.g., IHM V.ii: 56 and VI.xxi: 176.

22. See Greco's essay in this volume and de Bary 2001.
23. As Dale Tuggy points out in his essay in this volume, Reid worked with a concept of certainty more liberal than that of his contemporaries and predecessors. Says Reid, "many things are certain for which we have only the kind of evidence which Philosophers call probable" (EIP VII.iii: 562).
24. See Van Cleve 1999. Van Cleve maintains that only on such a "particularist" reading can Reid's foundationalism be viewed as being "wide" in character.
25. Although Reid is commonly interpreted as being a direct realist about perception (see, e.g., Copenhaver 2000), there is a lively controversy about the sense in which this is true. The issue is addressed in Van Cleve's essay in this volume.
26. Hegel 1975: 66.
27. This is brought out in Paul Wood's introduction to PRLS: 22–5.
28. See IHM VI in particular. For more on this subject, see the essay by Falkenstein in this volume and Daniels 1989.
29. See Falkenstein 2000b as well as his contribution to this volume.
30. See Reid's discussion "Of the Difficulty of attending to the Operations of our own Minds" (EIP I.vi).
31. Says Reid concerning the operations of the mind: "The habit of attending to them is necessary to make them distinct and steady; and this habit requires an exertion of mind to which many of our animal principles are unfriendly. The love of truth calls for it; but its still voice is often drowned by the louder call of some passion, or we are hindered from listening to it by laziness and desultoriness. Thus, men often remain through life ignorant of things which they needed but to open their eyes to see, and which they would have seen if their attention had been turned to them" (EAP V.ii: 641a).
32. Kant 1950: 7.
33. See MacIntyre 1966: 177, for example. In fairness to MacIntyre, Reid is given a much more sympathetic treatment in MacIntyre 1988.
34. See EIP II.xxii: 246.
35. See also EAP IV.iii and OP: 6, in which Reid speculates that our propensity to attribute causal powers to things has its roots in the animism of our ancestors. Reid says of the way our causal language has evolved: "By such changes, in the meaning of words, the language of every civilized nation resembles old furniture new-modeled, in which many things are put to uses for which they were not originally intended, and for which they are not perfectly fitted" (EAP IV.iii: 606a).
36. Tuggy 2000 provides an extensive discussion of Reid's views on causality.

37. J. B. Schneewind points out that Reid and Kant shared a further conviction about the character of morality: Both thinkers believed that morality is best thought of in terms of *self-governance*. In this respect, Schneewind contends, Reid and Kant stood out from among all their eighteenth-century cohorts. See Schneewind 1998: 6.

38. See, e.g., EIP III.v: 267.

39. See Kant 1998: 145.

40. For a detailed examination of Kant's views on this issue, see Friedman 1992.

41. This is to interpret Kant as a "two-world" theorist. Those who wish to interpret Kant as a "dual standpoint" theorist can translate what is said here and what follows accordingly.

42. It is important to note that, in contrast to contemporary philosophical usage, Reid uses "efficient" power as a synonym for "active" or "agent" power.

43. Reid's views concerning relative conceptions appear to have undergone revision from the time he wrote *Essays on the Intellectual Powers* to the time he wrote *Essays on the Active Powers*. In the former work, Reid writes (in a more Berkeleyan vein) that "a relative notion ... must be obscure, because it gives us no conception of what the thing is, but of what relation it bears to something else" (EIP II.xvii: 202). In the *Active Powers*, by contrast, Reid says: "From these instances, it appears that our relative conceptions of things are not always less distinct, nor less fit materials for accurate reasoning, than those that are direct; and that the contrary may happen in a remarkable degree" (EAP I.i: 514a). One wonders whether having seen the work that a relative conception must do in his scheme, Reid was forced to revise his views on this issue.

    Interestingly, both Edward Craig and Galen Strawson, who interpret Hume as a realist about causal connections, have claimed that Hume himself appeals to the idea of a relative notion in his discussion of causal connections. (See Craig 1987: 124 and Strawson 1989: Chap. 12.) For a reply that Hume did not do so, see Blackburn 1993.

44. See EIP VI.v: 479–80 for a more extensive discussion of this issue.

45. Reid thought of things that have "real" existence as being individuals in space/time. See EIP IV.ii: 323. For discussion of this issue, see Yaffe forthcoming, Chaps. 5 and 6.

46. See also PRLS: 183, 185, 221.

47. See Blackburn 1993: 99–100.

48. The implicit assumption here is that the laws of nature are not under our control.

49. Reid writes in his lecture notes on Natural Law and Natural Rights: "Physical laws apply not only to irrational natures, but also to rational

ones. Examples in our bodies and, in the mind, the association of ideas and passions; instincts; appetites" (PE: 189). Moreover, what Reid says in this passage should not be seen as being incompatible with the claim that there are laws describing human behavior of the sort that historians and social scientists traffic in.

50. For more on Reid's agent causation view of freedom, see the essay by Rowe in this volume.

51. See Friedman 1992.

52. Reid wrote and lectured on topics ranging from art, botany, epistemology, ethics, geometry, law, logic, metaphysics, natural theology, philosophy of mind, and politics to zoology. The eclectic nature of Reid's interests is understandable in light of the fact that, as a regent for thirteen years at Kings College, Aberdeen, and later as the Chair of moral philosophy at the University of Glasgow, Reid was required to teach, what is by today's standards, a staggeringly wide range of subjects. But it should also be added that Reid was an inherently curious man, concerned with the latest work in philosophy and science until his death at the age of eighty-four.

53. See the Hume-Reid correspondence in IHM: 256.

54. THN: 517.

55. Some of the work that explicitly bears Reid's influence is Alston 1991, Plantinga 1993 and 2000, and Wolterstorff 1983a.

56. Redekop's essay is a portion of a larger work in progress on this topic.

57. Seattle Pacific University, in particular, provided a Faculty Research Grant in the fall of 2002 that supported work on this project during its latter stages.

58. We thank Alexander Broadie, Lorne Falkenstein, James Harris, Steve Layman, Luke Reinsma, Paul Wood, and Nicholas Wolterstorff for their comments on previous drafts of this introduction.

1   Reid in Context

I. REID'S MANY CONTEXTS

In this chapter Thomas Reid (1710–1796) will be placed in context, with the aim of providing a perspective from which his thoughts can be better understood. Attention will therefore be focused primarily on the swirl of ideas, philosophical, theological, and scientific, to which he was exposed.

Intimately related to that swirl of ideas is the part played throughout Reid's life by the Kirk, Scotland's national church. His father, Lewis Reid (1676–1762), was a minister of the Kirk. Reid himself studied its theology at Marischal College, Aberdeen (1726–31), acted as a clerk of presbytery in the parish of Kincardine O'Neil (1732–3), and was parish minister (1737–51) in the parish of New Machar in Kincardineshire. Also, on several occasions he represented his university, first King's College, Aberdeen, and then Glasgow University, at the annual meeting of the General Assembly of the Church of Scotland, the Kirk's parliament. Late in life he was also a founding member of the Glasgow Society of the Sons of Ministers of the Church of Scotland.[1] Reid's views on religion and on the place of the Kirk in society were fully consistent with those of the Moderate party in the Kirk.[2] And what may be termed his "religious demeanor" was likewise on the side of moderation, as is indicated by his description of the people of Glasgow who have a "gloomy, Ent<h>usiastical Cast" (C: 38),[3] and are "fanatical in their Religion," though he continues in mitigation of their demeanor: "The Clergy encourage this fanaticism too much and find it the onely way to popularity. I often hear a Gospel here which you know nothing about, for you neither hear it from the pulpit nor will you find it in the Bible" (C: 40).[4]

31

Reid's opposition to the sort of cast of mind he found among the citizens of Glasgow went hand in hand with a profound faith that reveals itself repeatedly in his writings on human nature. Plainly the context provided by the Kirk was crucial to him. The Kirk's belief system and its institutions informed his soul, and therefore informed his philosophy also.

There are in addition the various political contexts. Here we should bear in mind academic politics, which played a part in each and every appointment to the professoriate in Enlightenment Scotland;[5] for example, Reid's appointment in 1764 to the Chair of Moral Philosophy at Glasgow with the help of Lord Deskford[6] and Lord Kames. Academic politics also played a part in Reid's earlier appointment in 1751 as regent at King's College, Aberdeen. National politics, as relating, for example, to the antislavery movement, were also part of Reid's context. An indication of the strength of his commitment to the antislavery movement is to be found in a letter to his cousin James Gregory: "Our University has sent a petition to the House of Commons, in favour of the African slaves. I hope yours will not be the last in this humane design; and that the Clergy of Scotland will likewise join in it. I comfort my grey hairs with the thoughts that the world is growing better, having long resolved to resist the common sentiment of old age, that it is always growing worse" (C: 197).[7] Reid was also committed to penal reform, and in particular gave strong support to the penal reformer John Howard.[8]

Reid was no less drawn to international politics, including the American Revolution and the French Revolution, on both of which he had strong views. Thus, for example, in summer 1791 he wrote: "Some few here think or affect to think, that to be a Friend to the Revolution of France is to be an Enemy to the Constitution of Britain, or at least to its present Administration. I know the contrary to be true in my self, & verily believe that most of my Acqu<a>intance who Rejoice in that Revolution agree with me in this" (C: 224).[9] Reid's attendance that year at a Bastille Day dinner fits ill with the common picture of him as an ivory-towered academic. He wrote on a range of political matters, including matters of lively public interest, and it should be recognized that those writings were by someone prepared to take a public stance on highly contentious public issues.[10]

In a variety of ways and at a variety of levels, therefore, Reid was active politically, and this despite the fact that he was clear-eyed about the disagreeable side of the political life:

When Gentlemen dip deep in the Politicks either of their County or of a larger Sphere, they meet with so many disagreable Rubbs, from jarring Interests, from the selfishness of some, the Ingratitude of others, & the Absurdity of many, that to be able to bear those things without being ruffled by them, a Man must be very Callous. The Employment of a Political Life for the most part is to Mine & Countermine in order to blow up the Designs of an Antagonist, or to advance ones own. This is but dirty & disagreable Work, and it is not easy for a Man who engages in it, to keep his hands clean and his Temper unruffled. (C: 165)[11]

Mention should also be made of the fact that Reid played a part in the life of several societies. First and especially important is the Aberdeen Philosophical Society, the "Wise Club," of which Reid was a founder, and whose membership included John Gregory, David Skene, Alexander Gerard, James Beattie, George Campbell, Robert Trail, James Dunbar, and others.[12] To this club, which was a vital part of Reid's intellectual context, he read a number of papers that later appeared in his first major work, *An Inquiry into the Human Mind on the Principles of Common Sense* (1764). Presentations by other members of the Society would also appear in print – for example, some parts of *The Philosophy of Rhetoric* (1776), the greatest work by George Campbell, principal of Marischal College and later the professor of divinity at the same college.[13]

Hume's philosophy was a major topic of the Society. In response to Hume's letter to Reid about a draft of part of the latter's *Inquiry into the Human Mind* Reid wrote to Hume:

Your Friendly Adversaries Drs Campbel & Gerard as well as Dr Gregory return their Compliments to you respectfully. A little Philosophical Society here of which all the three are members, is much indebted to you for its Entertainment. Your Company would, although we are all good Christians, be more acceptable than that of Saint Athanasius. And since we cannot have you upon the bench, you are brought oftner than any other man, to the bar, accused and defended with great Zeal but without bitterness. If you write no more in morals politicks or metaphysicks, I am affraid we shall be at a loss for Subjects. (C: 31)[14]

Besides the Aberdeen Philosophical Society Reid was also a member of the Glasgow Literary Society, whose membership list included Joseph Black, William Cullen, Adam Smith, David Hume, John

Millar, and James Watt. And he was elected to the fellowship of the Royal Society of Edinburgh in 1783, the year of the Society's foundation. Reid was active in both of these latter societies, especially the Glasgow Literary Society, to which he read many papers. The various societies in which he participated formed an important part of his context.

Without knowledge of Reid's complex environment we could have no understanding of the man nor therefore of how he came to be able to write the remarkable trilogy of works for which he is now best known, *An Inquiry into the Human Mind on the Principles of Common Sense* (1764), the *Essays on the Intellectual Powers of Man* (1785), and the *Essays on the Active Powers of Man* (1788). Not all elements in this rich diversity can be dealt with here, and since Reid's present-day fame and importance rest entirely on the fame and importance of his contributions to academic disciplines it is particularly his intellectual context that will be the focus of our attention. For this reason attention will be paid to Reid at Marischal College, Aberdeen, where he was a student and subsequently librarian, then to King's College, Aberdeen, where he was regent from 1751 until 1764, and finally to Glasgow University, where he was Professor of Moral Philosophy from 1764 until his death in 1796 (though he ceased to teach in 1780, in order to devote himself to his writing).[15]

Reid's post at King's was of a different kind from his post at Glasgow, and his lecture courses at the two universities were correspondingly different. While regent at King's he delivered four full cycles of courses, each cycle with a duration of three years, on, among other disciplines, mathematics, natural science, pneumatology (philosophy of mind), ethics, politics, natural theology, and rhetoric. In Glasgow the fact that Reid occupied the Chair of Moral Philosophy impacted directly on the subjects he covered, as did the further fact that Glasgow also had a Chair of Logic and Rhetoric, occupied in Reid's day first by James Clow[16] and then by George Jardine.[17] Though Reid had some latitude regarding the contents of his "public lectures" there were disciplines, especially logic, which he could not cover in them. Reid gave public lectures daily for a course that dealt with pneumatology, ethics, and politics, with most time paid to the first of these three; and thrice weekly he gave "private lectures" to an advanced class on the culture (that is, the cultivation) of the mind. These lectures were on logic, rhetoric, and the fine arts, though pneumatology was always on or just below the surface.[18]

Testimony to Reid's ability as a lecturer comes from his pupil and biographer Dugald Stewart, Professor of Moral Philosophy at Edinburgh University:

In his elocution and mode of instruction, there was nothing peculiarly attractive. He seldom, if ever, indulged himself in the warmth of extempore discourse; nor was his manner of reading calculated to increase the effect of what he had committed to writing. Such, however, was the simplicity and perspicuity of his style, such the gravity and authority of his character, and such the general interest of his young hearers in the doctrines which he taught, that, by the numerous audiences to which his instructions were addressed, he was heard uniformly with the most silent and respectful attention. On this subject, I speak from personal knowledge; having had the good fortune, during a considerable part of winter 1772, to be one of his pupils.[19]

One of the people to whom Reid was especially close was Henry Home, raised to the bench as Lord Kames,[20] who never occupied an academic post, but with whom Reid had countless conversations about the arts and sciences. We owe to Kames the fact that Reid wrote and published an important work on Aristotle's logic. The intellectual environment of this work will be discussed below.[21]

Since Reid's intellectual environment was exceptionally rich, the content of this chapter is the product of hard choices. I shall attend especially to things that impacted deeply on almost all that he wrote. Most especially I shall focus first on the lectures that George Turnbull (1698–1748) delivered to Reid's class at Marischal College from 1723 until 1726. Turnbull's philosophy of providential naturalism[22] shaped Reid's philosophical thought. And attention will be paid next to the background against which Reid wrote on logic and scientific methodology. Many other features of his intellectual environment will be taken up and developed in other chapters of this book. The features of his context that I have just mentioned form without question a central part of a much larger story.

One reason knowledge of Reid's contexts is important is that, in seeking to find our way into Reid's mind, it can only be helpful to know what problems and what solutions were being discussed in academic, legal, ecclesiastical, and other circles in Scotland in the eighteenth century, that is, during the Age of Enlightenment, and to know the terms, the idiom, in which the problems and solutions were being discussed.[23]

However, such an exercise in contextualization is limited in its usefulness, for though knowledge of what Reid's teachers taught him, what he read, and with whom he discussed things all contributes to a better understanding of his thought, he was his own man. As regards his philosophy, or his "inquiry" as he called it,[24] it is uniquely his, even though there were undoubtedly many intellectual influences operating on him from an early age. His uniqueness is hinted at in the phrase commonly used of him: "founder of the Scottish school of common sense philosophy." But that title is misleading, and this chapter will indicate the reason for this. The measure of philosophical consensus in the second half of the eighteenth century in Scotland might be sufficient to justify talk about a "Scottish school of common sense philosophy," but it is doubtful whether any one person founded it. Arguably, however, if it were appropriate to designate someone as *the* founder it would be Reid's teacher George Turnbull, in whose writings we find many statements of positions that we now think of as characteristically Reidian. In his extant writings, published and unpublished, Reid makes very few references to Turnbull; but for almost the whole of a three-year span during his student days Reid listened on an almost daily basis to Turnbull expounding his own and other people's ideas, and it is past belief that those countless hours of instruction would not have made a deep impression on Reid. The similarity of their views stands as testimony of sorts to the claim that the older man influenced his pupil. Turnbull must therefore figure significantly in any account of Reid's context.

However, not all the major influences on Reid are readily, or even at all, identifiable as on the side of "common sense." Most importantly, after the publication of *A Treatise of Human Nature* (1739–40) it was not possible to philosophize in Scotland as if there had been no Hume. Hume himself complained famously that the *Treatise* "fell dead-born from the press,"[25] but he was not quite right about that. Reid, for one, seems to have been jolted into thought by it almost immediately: "I never thought of calling in question the principles commonly received with regard to the human understanding, until the 'Treatise of Human Nature' was published in the year 1739" (IHM Dedication: 3). The impact on Reid was immense: "Ever since the treatise of human Nature was published I respected

Mr Hume as the greatest Metaphysician of the Age" (IHM "The
Hume–Reid Exchange": 257).[26] Thereafter Hume remained Reid's
chief target until the mid-1770s, when Reid began to be preoccupied
with Joseph Priestley's materialist philosophy. That Descartes, Malebranche, Locke, Berkeley, and Butler, who were also studied by Reid,
formed an important part of his intellectual context is evident from
explicit discussion of them in his writings. Emphasis, however, will
be placed here on lesser-known thinkers, men who are rarely mentioned by Reid though he was to a greater or lesser extent affected by
them.

    As well as Reid's intellectual context there was also that provided
by his family. However, these two are not mutually exclusive for he
was, through his mother, Margaret Gregory (1673–1732), a member
of the Gregory family, the most important intellectual dynasty that
Scotland has produced. Margaret had three brothers all of whom were
professors of mathematics: David, at Edinburgh and then Oxford;
James, at Edinburgh in succession to his brother David; and Charles,
at St. Andrews, to be followed in 1739 by his son David. Margaret
Gregory's uncle James Gregory had been Professor of Mathematics
first at St Andrews and then at Edinburgh. His son, also named James,
was Professor of Medicine at King's College, Aberdeen, and both his
(that is, James the elder's) grandson and his great grandson occupied
chairs of medicine at Edinburgh. Many others in the family distinguished themselves academically, and there is clear evidence both
that Reid took an active interest in his genealogy on the Gregory side
and also that the family was a major feature of Reid's self-image.[27]
He inherited the Gregory mantle and his life-long active interest in
the mathematical sciences[28] has to be seen in relation to this intellectual context provided by the family. The physical sciences, such
as astronomy, also attracted him and he reports astronomical observations that he made. The family interest in observational astronomy is no less important in this context. In particular Reid's great
uncle James Gregory was credited with the invention of the reflecting telescope.

    There is particular significance in this point regarding Reid's per-
ception of himself as a member of a family of scientists, for it calls
into question the common view of him as a man dedicated almost
exclusively to philosophy, in the modern sense of the term.[29] It is
not that philosophy was not at the heart of his endeavors, but that

his philosophical ideas cannot be considered in isolation from his scientific work without seriously diminishing his philosophy. The science was there with the philosophy at the core of his life.

II. PROVIDENTIAL NATURALISM: REID'S PHILOSOPHY CONTEXTUALIZED

As regards his educational context, after schooldays spent first at the parish school at Kincardine O'Neil (the village where he was later to become presbytery clerk) and then very briefly at Aberdeen Grammar School, Reid entered Marischal College, Aberdeen, in October 1722 when aged twelve, then a common age at which to begin university studies.[30] The faculty boasted men of formidable quality, including the mathematician Colin Maclaurin, friend, protégé, and expositor of Sir Isaac Newton, and the classicist Thomas Blackwell, who made major contributions to Homeric studies and under whom Reid studied Greek. One year before Reid's arrival at Marischal College George Turnbull took up a post as regent there. Starting in 1723 Reid studied under him for all but a few months of a three-year cycle of studies.[31] In the course of that cycle Turnbull expounded the ideas of Francis Bacon, Descartes, Newton, Locke, and the Earl of Shaftesbury. He also discussed rational religion and expounded the natural law tradition, as represented particularly by Hugo Grotius and Samuel Pufendorf. In his *The Principles of Moral and Christian Philosophy* (1740), Turnbull presents a number of ideas we now associate with Reid. The book appeared when Reid was minister of New Machar in Aberdeenshire and some fourteen years after he had ceased to be Turnbull's pupil, but we learn of the book that "it is (a few things taken from late authors excepted) the substance of several pneumatological discourses, (as they are called in the school language) read above a dozen years ago to students of Moral Philosophy, by way of preparative to a course of lectures, on the rights and duties of mankind."[32] Turnbull's reference is to the course that he delivered to Reid's class, and it may therefore reasonably be supposed that Reid learned those ideas during his early to mid-teens directly from Turnbull, and that Turnbull made a substantive contribution to Reid's philosophical development.

On the title page of volume 1 Turnbull quotes Newton: "And if natural philosophy, in all its parts, by pursuing this method, shall at length be perfected, the bounds of moral philosophy will also be enlarged." Turnbull does not quote Newton's next sentence, though it illuminates the one he does quote: "For so far as we can know by natural Philosophy what is the first Cause, what Power he has over us, and what Benefits we receive from him, so far our Duty towards him, as well as that towards one another, will appear to us by the Light of Nature."[33] In effect, therefore, Newton regards moral philosophy, and indeed natural theology also, as parts of natural philosophy, as extensions of natural philosophy into the fields of moral and theological enquiry. His view is not simply that the method and conclusions of natural philosophy are helpful or even essential to moral philosophy, but also that a moral philosophical enquiry is one kind of natural philosophical enquiry, for it is conducted within a distinct field of natural philosophy. The field in question is that concerning the human mind, its faculties, powers, appetites, principles of action including moral principles, and so on.

With respect to the concept of moral philosophy as a branch of natural philosophy Turnbull is a Newtonian:

Tho' not a few who are really lovers of, and great proficients in Natural Philosophy, be not ashamed of the deepest ignorance of the parts and proportions of the human mind, and their mutual relation, connexion and dependency.... Yet it is certain, that the order and symmetry of this inward part is in itself no less real and exact than that of the body. And that this moral anatomy is not only a part, but the most useful part of Natural Philosophy, rightly understood, is too evident to need any proof to those who will but take the trouble to consider what Natural Philosophy, in its full extent, must mean.[34]

Moral philosophy is a part of natural philosophy because it is an enquiry into "a real part of nature" and has to be pursued by the same means as are our enquiries into "our own bodily contexture, or into any other, whether vegetable or animal fabrick."[35] Or as Turnbull puts the point elsewhere: "the study of nature, whether in the constitution and oeconomy of the sensible world, or in the frame and government of the moral, must set out from the same principles, and be carried on in the same method of investigation, induction, and reasoning."[36]

Thus it is clear that Turnbull's affirmation "when natural philosophy is carried so far as to reduce phenomena to good general laws, it becomes moral philosophy,"[37] does not mean that when carried so far natural philosophy is transformed into something else, *viz.* moral philosophy, but rather that moral philosophy is the kind of natural philosophy that is being done when good general laws are being formulated. The moral part of the grand project of natural philosophy is identified as the most useful part because the moral enquiry, if well prosecuted, will yield knowledge on how to achieve or preserve our soundness of mind, and how to protect our inward state from being corrupted or otherwise damaged. Turnbull writes:

All true observations relative to the human mind, its powers and operations, and the connexions of moral objects . . . add to our moral dominion; to our empire over ourselves and others. Thus knowledge of the passions, and their natural bearings and dependencies encrease our power and skill in governing them, by shewing us how they may be strengthened or diminished; directed to proper objects, or taken off from the pursuit of improper ones; In short, how they may be variously regulated so as to answer certain ends.[38]

There is nothing in these positions not mirrored precisely in Reid's writings. He tells us at the start of the *Inquiry into the Human Mind*:

Wise men now agree, or ought to agree in this, that there is but one way to the knowledge of nature's works; the way of observation and experiment. By our constitution, we have a strong propensity to trace particular facts and observations to general rules, and to apply such general rules to account for other effects, or to direct us in the production of them. This procedure of the understanding is familiar to every human creature in the common affairs of life, and it is the only one by which any discovery in philosophy can be made. (IHM I.i: 11–12)

And it is Newton's methodology that is to be practiced, particularly as articulated in his *regulae philosophandi*, the rules for philosophizing: "he who philosophises by other rules, either concerning the material system, or concerning the mind, mistakes the aim" (IHM I.i: 12).[39] Further echoing Turnbull's phraseology Reid adds that "it must be by an anatomy of the mind that we can discover its powers and principles" (ibid.).

Newton is undoubtedly a crucial part of Reid's intellectual context; of the major philosophers (in the modern sense of "philosopher") of eighteenth-century Scotland Reid had the deepest understanding of Newtonian science. But it should be added that Reid makes it clear that as regards scientific methodology his special hero is not so much Newton as Francis Bacon (1561–1626):

Did not his Novum Organum give birth to the Art of Induction? Was there ever a Book in the World that delineated so important an Art so justly, & so minutely before that Art had an Existence? Has not Newton in his Opticks and in his Astronomy followed his precepts, step by step? . . . It seems to me that Newton & Locke since they came to be known abroad have contributed more to diffuse a true Spirit of Philosophy, than Lord Bacons Writings. His writings are forgotten & it is too little known that the Spirit of Newton and Locke descended from the Loins of Lord Bacon. (C: 211–12)[40]

This paean of praise to Bacon is in a manuscript note composed by Reid in response to a draft of part of Dugald Stewart's *Elements of the Philosophy of the Human Mind*. Bacon describes a properly scientific procedure for investigating the natural world, including human beings, and in the *Elements* Stewart, as Reid argues, fails in certain of his explanations because he does not follow Bacon's prescription. However, Newton remains special for Reid, not because Newton invented the true scientific methodology (which he did not) but because he applied it with such stunning success.

The methodology of Bacon, duly refined and formulated by Newton in his *Regulae philosophandi*, was at the heart of Turnbull's philosophical doctrine. That doctrine, now given the name "providential naturalism," is formed round four propositions. The first is that the *regulae* are the means to success in natural philosophy, where "natural philosophy" includes not only what we now think of as the natural sciences but also the scientific study of the human mind, a study that aims to discover the laws governing the working of the human mind.

The second proposition of providential naturalism is that the laws of nature are the product of a providential act of divine will, and that once the divine will is invoked in explanation of the laws there is no further principle of explanation that can be added. Their existence is necessary only in the sense that having been willed into existence by the creator, they could not, so to say, resist God's will that they exist. We can explain the behavior of natural things in terms of natural laws, and the natural laws of a lesser generality can be brought under natural laws of a greater. But the existence of the natural objects themselves and of the laws of the greatest generality is explicable only in terms of the fact that God created the natural order. When Turnbull refers to "inferences that respect the contriver, maker, and governor of the world" and speaks of the world's "wise, good and beautiful administration,"[41] he is invoking the heart of his philosophy. Let us say, then, that natural scientific questions can be asked of each new scientific discovery, but that at some point our natural scientific enquiry will not receive an answer at the same level as the question. The explanation moves to a different level because it is in terms not of yet another natural phenomenon or natural regulative principle but of an act of a freely engaged divine will. We have to accept that things are in the end thus and so because God willed that things be thus and so.

The third proposition is that the divine purpose for which the laws of nature were created is discoverable by a study of things that operate according to the laws. Thus it is plain that we were made to live virtuous lives, as witness the fact that:

The wisdom and goodness of nature likewise discovers itself, in giving us a rule to guide us in our moral conduct distinct from and antecedent to all our knowledge acquired by reasoning, which is a moral sense of beauty and deformity in affections, actions and characters, by means of which, an affection, action or character, no sooner presents itself to our mind, than it is necessarily approved or disapproved by us ... the Author of nature has much better furnished us for a virtuous conduct than many philosophers seem to imagine.[42]

Scientific study likewise reveals that we are naturally directed toward knowledge and progress in knowledge: "Every discovery we make; every glimpse of truth, as it begins to dawn upon the mind, gives high delight ... truth or knowledge is naturally as agreeable and satisfactory to the understanding, as light is to the eye."[43]

At which point we are on the edge of the fourth proposition of providential naturalism, that our cognitive faculties, which are of course part of the divine dispensation, have a scientifically determinable function, knowledge of which gives us some insight into the mind of God, at least to the extent that we can learn what God's purpose was in creating our faculties. In particular, scientific study of our cognitive faculties reveals that they were given us to be mechanisms for the formation of true beliefs. Our senses enable us to have true beliefs about the material world, and our moral sense and our sense of beauty likewise deliver up truths about the world and about our fellow creatures. The role of the faculty of imagination is crucial in our being directed toward the truth. Ideas are associated in the imagination, and without such operations we would make no cognitive progress. Turnbull has no doubt about God's purpose in giving us a natural tendency to associate ideas: "It is, indeed, in consequence of the law of association, that we learn any of the connections of nature; or that any appearance with its effects, is not as new to us at all times as at first ... without it we would plainly continue to be in old age, as great novices to the world as we are in our infancy; as incapable to foresee, and consequently as incapable to direct our conduct."[44]

All the propositions that form the doctrine of providential naturalism are readily extractable or at least constructible from Reid's writings also, but Reid does not follow Turnbull in all things. There appears to be a disagreement between the two men regarding a question of especial importance to Reid, namely, the nature of ideas. Turnbull raises the question of the location of power, and starts from the affirmation that though in common language we speak about the power of matter, matter is in fact absolutely inactive: "For did ever matter of itself change its state, whether of motion or rest, without some cause, to which the change is exactly proportioned?"[45] But it is not only material things that are powerless: "All our ideas also are no less evidently quite passive perceptions, which have no activity, or can produce nothing."[46] But as against Turnbull's affirmation that ideas have no activity, Reid holds that ideas *are* mental acts. To have an idea about X is to be thinking about, imagining, or conceiving X. The mind is the agent and its ideas are the acts that the mind *qua* agent engages in.[47] Nevertheless, there is no substantive dispute between Turnbull and Reid on this matter, for neither philosopher thinks that acts act; agents act, and no act is itself an agent. Turnbull sometimes speaks about the will as the only thing that is active, sometimes of mind as alone active. But his summary statement is this: "That whatever operates, acts, hath power, or produces in nature, is an intelligent conscious principle, capable of willing and of giving existence to effects by willing their existence, which kind of principle we shall henceforth, for brevity's sake, conformably to common language, call in one word, *mind*."[48] Reid could have penned this sentence; indeed, in respect of its content he did so several times.

It should be added that the phrase "conformably to common language" in the sentence just quoted, is not idle; it points to a crucial part of Turnbull's methodology. He writes: "Language, not being invented by philosophers, but contrived to express common sentiments, or what every one perceives, we may be morally sure, that where universally all languages make a distinction, there is really in nature a difference."[49] Precisely this methodological principle is invoked a thousand times by Reid,[50] both as a weapon against Hume, whom he accuses of systematic misuse of language, for example, of the terms "impression" and "idea," and also as a basis for developing his own positive philosophy of common sense.

Many of the ideas presented by Turnbull are to be found in other sources, and Turnbull himself found many of them elsewhere. Nevertheless his synthesis of these ideas, from whatever source, is unique to him. The ideas I have referred to are also to be found in Reid, who could also of course have found them in other places. But the fact that the youthful Reid heard Turnbull expound these ideas provides strong reason to hold that Turnbull made a significant contribution to the philosophy that Reid, the greater philosopher by far, was later to develop.

III. BACONIANISM: REID AND THE NEW LOGIC

While hardly leaving the question of Turnbull's influence on Reid, I turn now to a field of enquiry to which Reid made a significant contribution, namely, logic, and shall attend to aspects of the context within which he made his contribution. For Reid, a most important role for logic is to help us, through discovery of truths, to make our lives better. The study of logic, in itself a theoretical exercise, has therefore a practical justification to which Reid draws our attention. What was wrong with the old logic, that of Aristotle, was that it "did nothing considerable for the benefit of human life."[51] We should therefore seek a new logic, one which will be of benefit to us.

Throughout the Middle Ages and the Renaissance the preeminent logic was Aristotle's. But Francis Bacon criticized the doctrine at the heart of Aristotle's logic, namely, the account of the syllogism, because it was of little if any use to scientists investigating nature. Nevertheless Aristotle's logic remained center stage in the universities until at least well into the eighteenth century, by which time opinion had become deeply divided on the value of Aristotle's contribution to logic and to scientific methodology. Here I shall ask about those who were writing about logic in Scotland; we shall be dealing with men, close friends of Reid, who formed a significant part of the context within which he thought about these matters.

His most substantial contribution to the discipline was "A brief account of Aristotle's Logic, with remarks,"[52] written some time between 1767 and 1773 at the instigation of Lord Kames, and published in 1774 as an appendix to Kames's *Sketches of the History of Man*. On 31 October 1767 Reid wrote from Glasgow to his friend David Skene in Aberdeen: "I passed eight Days lately with Lord Kaims at Blair-Drummond. . . . I have been labouring at Barbara Celarent for three weeks bygone"(C: 62).[53] This is the earliest intimation we have of Kames's invitation to Reid to write the "Brief account," an invitation Reid received because "[n]o man is better acquainted with Aristotle's writings."[54] The work has several interesting features, which enable us to place Reid in relation to a number of people who knew him well. I particularly emphasize this "logical dimension" of Reid's context since his understanding of the proper function of logic entered into all his work. Reid's acceptance of the inductive, empirical method recommended by Francis Bacon is evident in his writings on physics, astronomy, and the life sciences,[55] as well as in the study of the human mind that he expounded in his three main works. For Reid the study of the human mind and its faculties was a contribution to natural science and hence required the employment of methods appropriate to the natural sciences.[56]

Reid was well read in logic, a field underpinning all academic disciplines. He was familiar not only with Francis Bacon but also with the seventeenth-century logicians Bartholomew Keckermann and Franco Burgersdijk, as well as with the Port-Royal logic of Antoine Arnaud and Pierre Nicole. The influence on him of John Locke was also profound. In addition there were thinkers with whom he was in personal contact and with whom he must have had endless conversations on logic. These included Lord Kames and George Campbell. The three friends had very similar views regarding the kind of logic that was appropriate to the modern age, a logic that could make a substantive contribution to the betterment of people's lives. Here I shall comment briefly on one aspect of what was in question. The point at issue is a defining feature of eighteenth-century thought, and Reid is in the thick of the debate.

In the course of his *Sketches of the History of Man* Kames focuses on the Aristotelian syllogism. He takes as an example the argument for the proposition that man has a power of self-motion: "All animals have a power of self-motion: man is an animal: ergo, man has a power of self-motion." But, argues Kames, if indeed every animal has a power of self-motion, then of course a man, being an animal, must have such a power. And yet, he objects, the proposition that men have a power of self-motion is not *inferred from* the premise that every animal has self-motion; instead it is *contained within* it. Furthermore, it is only by experience that we can know that men have a power of self-motion, and indeed the fact that men have such power is more clearly ascertained by experience than is the proposition that other animals have it. In that case it is absurd to argue that since all animals have the power, men also have it, for that is to derive what is certain from what is comparatively uncertain. The syllogism therefore does not record progress in knowledge as we move from premises to conclusion.

On this matter Kames's ideas are very similar to those of George Campbell.[57] Campbell notes the way that natural scientists operate; first they consider individual cases and then they rise by inductive reasoning to general principles, which both explain the observed instances and also permit us to speak about instances not yet observed. In this process the researcher begins with what is more certain, the individual instances, and proceeds to the less certain, the general principles. Syllogistic reasoning, however, moves in the opposite direction, from what is in fact less certain to what is in fact more. This much is acknowledged by Lord Kames also. Campbell emphasizes an important detail. Begging the question (the Latin technical term used by Campbell is *petitio principii*) is classified as a fallacy. Yet it seems to be one to which Aristotelian syllogisms are subject by their nature. Unless the conclusion (for example "man has self-motion") is contained in the premises (for example "all animals have self-motion and man is an animal") it cannot be validly drawn by syllogistic means from those premises.

Reid's essay, "A brief account of Aristotle's logic," should be seen in the context of such teachings as have just been expounded. During the Scottish Enlightenment all the scientists were Baconian and none more so than Reid, who praised Bacon's theory and followed him in practice no less than he criticized Aristotle's theory and did not follow him in practice. Reid affirms:

The art of syllogism produced numberless disputes, and numberless sects, who fought against each other with much animosity, without gaining or losing ground; but did nothing considerable for the benefit of human life. The art of induction, first delineated by Lord Bacon, produced numberless laboratories and observatories, in which Nature has been put to the question by thousands of experiments, and forced to confess many of her secrets, which before were hid from mortals. And by these, arts have been improved, and human knowledge wonderfully increased.[58]

The evidence here adduced indicates that Reid's views on logic must have met with a good deal of support among the enlightened writers of Scotland. Reid, it may be noted, had a Baconian approach even to deciding which sort of logic was to be commended to scientists. Baconian logic furthered the aims of natural science. But Aristotelian syllogistic logic cannot do that, for, on Reid's reading of Aristotle, a valid syllogism is circular. Unless we already know the truth of the conclusion we are in no position to affirm the premises. Plainly such logic neither advances human knowledge nor brings benefit to human life, in contrast to Baconian logic. It is therefore Baconian logic that should be adopted.

IV. CONCLUSION: THE WIDEST CONTEXT AND THE NARROWEST

Apart from two brief visits to England, one in 1736 to Oxford, Cambridge, and London with his friend the mathematician John Stewart,[59] and one in 1740 to London to marry his cousin Elizabeth, daughter of his uncle George Reid, Reid spent his whole life in Scotland. But there was nothing parochial about his outlook. Reid was a member of the international Republic of Letters. His ideas reached far beyond Scotland and he kept abreast of developments that other citizens in the Republic of Letters had achieved in the fields of mathematics, physics, chemistry, life sciences, linguistics, rhetoric, and many others. This international network of thinkers is the widest context within which Reid operated.

The narrowest was his own family. But he writes at times as if that smallest of contexts is also, for him and for everyone, the most important: "Of all the happiness that this World affords, I take Domestick Happiness to be the chief, and there cannot be too much care and Attention given to preserve it. It is a Delicate thing, & requires Prudence and Attention, as well as good Intention" (C: 164).[60] All the evidence suggests that Reid and his family bestowed due prudence, attention, and good intention on this "Delicate thing." Partly in consequence of this, Reid lived contentedly into old age. In May 1792 Reid summed up his situation in a letter prompted by the death of his wife Elizabeth:

By the loss of my bosom-friend, with whom I lived fifty-two years, I am brought into a kind of new world, at a time of life when old habits are not easily forgot, or new ones acquired. But every world is GOD's world, and I am thankful for the comforts he has left me.... I have more health than at my time of life I had any reason to expect. I walk about; entertain myself with reading what I soon forget; can converse with one person, if he articulates distinctly, and is within ten inches of my left ear; go to church, without hearing one word of what is said. You know, I never had any pretensions to vivacity, but I am still free from languor and *ennui*. (C: 230)[61]

NOTES

1. For reference to his membership of the Society's Council, see C: 230, datelined Glasgow, 24 July 1792.
2. For an account of the Moderate party, see Sher 1985. For discussion of Reid's religious views, see Dale Tuggy's chapter in this volume.
3. Letter to Reid's former colleague Andrew Skene, dated 14 November 1764. The letter is printed (inaccurately) in W: 40b.
4. Letter to David Skene, datelined Glasgow, 13 July 1765. See also W: 41b.
5. For examples of the exercise of political patronage in the Scottish universities, see Emerson 1992, 1994, 1995, and Wood 1997.
6. Lord Deskford, designated by his earlier title of James, Earl of Findlater and Seafield, was the dedicatee of Reid's first masterpiece, the *Inquiry into the Human Mind* (1764) – which was published in the year that Deskford campaigned on Reid's behalf in the battle for the Glasgow Chair of Moral Philosophy.
7. The letter is assignable to late February 1788. See also W: 72b.
8. See C: 186–7, datelined Glasgow, 28 August 1786.

9. The letter is assignable to July/August 1791. For discussion, see PE: 76, 80–5.

10. Among the many manuscripts relating to matters of lively public interest are AUL MS 3061/3 on the storage of foreign grain, and AUL MS 3061/5 on the regulation of interest charges. Regarding Reid's contribution to the debate on the French Revolution, see his paper "Some thoughts on the utopian system" (AUL MS 3061/6: 1–5), published in PE: 277–99. A revised version of this last paper will appear in SP.

11. The letter is datelined Glasgow College, 24 November 1783.

12. For details, see Ulman 1990 and Suderman 2002.

13. Campbell and Reid died in the same year after a friendship that spanned about sixty years during almost all of which they had lived in each other's intellectual pockets. See Broadie 2000b. They were both graduates of Marischal College, and indeed had overlapped there; they had both been ministers of the Kirk working in parishes near Aberdeen and had helped each other in the discharge of their ecclesiastical duties. Both were distinguished teachers in Aberdeen and they maintained close contact after Reid left to take up the Chair of Moral Philosophy in Glasgow in 1764.

14. The letter is datelined King's College, 18 March 1763. Reprinted in IHM: 264–5.

15. For details of Reid's life, see Wood 1984, 1985, 2000a, 2001.

16. In 1752, through a misjudgment of cosmic proportions, Clow was appointed to the Glasgow Chair of Logic and Rhetoric in preference to Hume.

17. Clow seems to have been a wholly derivative thinker on logic, as witness *A System of Logic by James Clow A. M., Professor of Logic in the University of Glasgow*, transcription by John Campbell dated 1773 (Edinburgh University Library). Jardine, favorite pupil of Adam Smith, friend of Reid and John Millar, and teacher of Sir William Hamilton, likewise made no contribution to logic, but he was famously innovative in his teaching methods. See Jardine 1825. For discussion of his ideas in their context, see Davie 1961.

18. See Wood 1997, 2000a.

19. W: 10b–11a. Dugald Stewart's "Account of the life and writings of Thomas Reid D. D." is in W: 3a–35b. Reid and Stewart remained close friends until Reid's death in 1796. It was at Stewart's instigation that, in 1796, during a visit to Edinburgh, Reid's portrait was painted by Henry Raeburn.

20. The close bond between the two men, which lasted for several decades, is indicated in the moving letter Reid wrote to Kames's widow shortly

after Kames's death: "I have lost in him one of the greatest Comforts of my Life" (C: 161). The letter is datelined Glasgow College, 30 January 1783. See also W: 61b.

21. Reid and his family were regular guests at Kames's family seat at Blair Drummond. It was during one of those visits that Kames invited Reid to write his "A brief account of Aristotle's logic, with remarks" (W: 681a–714).

22. The term "providential naturalism" was coined by David Fate Norton (1966, Chap. 6). See also IHM: xiv, xxi–xxiii.

23. For detailed discussion of all these matters, see Broadie 2003a.

24. Although "inquiry" is his own preferred description of his output, others have spoken of his accomplishment as a "system." He himself rejected the idea that he had a "system": "I have an Aversion to the having a System imputed to me especially by my Friend. It may be a Defect in a System to leave any part of the Subject untouched. Innumerable Defects of this kind may be found in my Book [sc. *An Inquiry into the Human Mind*], and therefore I neither call it a System nor would have it considered as a System but as what the title imports" (AUL MS 2131/3/II/3: 11). This is from a draft of a letter to Dugald Stewart. See C: 222. The letter is assignable to 1791.

25. See "My own life" in Greig 1932, I: 2.

26. From undated AUL MS 2131/2/III/1.

27. Reid's pride and close interest in his family background is evident in a letter of 24 August 1787 to his cousin James Gregory, Professor of the Theory of Medicine at Edinburgh. See C: 191–5. The letter is datelined 26 August 1787; also in W: 68a–70a.

28. For Reid as a scientist, see PRLS, Wood 1998 and Guicciardini 2001.

29. This point is spelled out in the chapter by Paul Wood.

30. For an account of Marischal College and King's College, Aberdeen, during the Enlightenment, see Wood 1993.

31. For information on what Turnbull taught, see Wood 2000a. For aspects of Turnbull's career at Marischal College, see Stewart 1987. More generally, see Stewart forthcoming.

32. Turnbull 1740. The *Principles* was originally written as two distinct books, the earlier titled *The Principles of Moral Philosophy*, and the later entitled *Christian Philosophy*; but the London publisher published them as respectively volume 1 and volume 2 of a single book, *The Principles of Moral and Christian Philosophy*, presumably motivated by the belief that he could thereby improve the sales prospects of the second book. He appears to have come belatedly to this idea, for volume 1 has two title pages, one with the title only of the second book, and the other

with the title *The Principles of Moral and Christian Philosophy. In Two Volumes*. The first book however, titled *The Principles of Moral Philosophy*, gives no indication that it is volume 1 of a two-volume book. It follows from these considerations that when Turnbull tells us at the start of volume 1 that "this enquiry" is the substance of several pneumatological discourses read above a dozen years earlier, the text to which he refers is only volume one. There is no good reason to believe that the contents of volume 2 also were delivered to Reid's class at Marischal College.

33. Newton 1952 Book 3, Query 31, final paragraph.

34. Turnbull 1740, I: i. The subtitle of Hume's *Treatise of Human Nature* is "*being an attempt to introduce the experimental method of reasoning into moral subjects.*" Plainly Hume was not the first to introduce the experimental method into moral subjects; Turnbull had already done so some fifteen years earlier on the authority of Newton.

35. Ibid.

36. Turnbull 1740, I: 2.

37. Turnbull 1740, I: 8.

38. Turnbull 1740, I: 29. Turnbull throws his net wide: "oratory, poetry, and all the fine arts which have it for their end and scope to touch the human heart agreeably, do no less depend than morality and politics, upon the science of the human affections, and their natural dependence and balance." Turnbull 1740, I: 29–30.

39. For Reid on the *regulae philosophandi*, see PRLS: 182–92.

40. From AUL MS 2131/3/II/3. See C: 211–12. The letter is assignable to 1791. For discussion of this manuscript, see Broadie 2003b. See also Robinson 1989. Elsewhere, writing on inductive reasoning, Reid is equally emphatic: "We owe all the Light we have got in this most important part of Logic to the great genius of Lord Bacon, who considering the low state of this part of Learning in his time hath done wonders." See AUL MS 2131/4/I/23, fol. 1v. There is an edition of this ms in LRF.

41. Turnbull 1740, I: 8. The *Principles* abounds in such phraseology.

42. Turnbull 1740, I: 39–40. The comment on "many philosophers" is a dig principally at Thomas Hobbes and Bernard Mandeville.

43. Turnbull 1740, I: 46.

44. Turnbull 1740, I: 90. For discussion of this quotation from Turnbull, and for its relation to Reid, see Broadie 2002a.

45. Turnbull 1740, II: 22.

46. Ibid.

47. See, e.g., EIP I.i: 31 and EIP II.xi: 160.

48. Turnbull 1740, II: 23.

49. Turnbull 1740, I: 118.
50. See, for example: "But the general principle – that every distinction which is found in the structure of a common language, is a real distinction, and is perceivable by the common sense of mankind – this I hold for certain, and have made frequent use of it. I wish it were more used than it has been; for I believe the whole system of metaphysicks, or the far greater part, may be brought out of it; and, next to accurate reflexion upon the operations of our own minds, I know nothing that can give so much light to the human faculties as a due consideration of the structure of language" (C: 185). See also W: 78b. The letter is assignable to spring 1786.
51. Thomas Reid, "Brief account," in Kames 1774, II: 236.
52. W: 681a–714. The "Brief account" is in LRF and follows the version that Kames published in the *Sketches*, not the substantially different edition in *The Works of Thomas Reid*. A further source of Reid's ideas on logic is a transcription of lecture notes of Reid's logic lectures delivered at King's College, Aberdeen, in 1763. See *A System of Logic Taught at Aberdeen, 1763 by Dr. T. Reid* (Edinburgh University Library, Shelf-mark Dk.3.2., 1–101). For discussion of this manuscript, see Michael 1999.
53. The letter is datelined Glasgow College, 31 October 1767 (inaccurately reproduced in W I: 49b). *Barbara* and *Celarent* are the traditional names of two forms of syllogistic reasoning, "Every B is C and every A is B, so every A is C" and "No B is C and every A is B, so no A is C," respectively.
54. Kames 1774, II: 165.
55. Examples abound in PRLS.
56. See Broadie 2003b.
57. It is likely that Campbell presented certain papers on logic to the Aberdeen Philosophical Society, the "Wise Club," quite early in its life. But whether or not the contents of "Of the nature and use of the scholastic art of syllogizing," the title of Bk. 1, Chap. 6 of Campbell's *Philosophy of Rhetoric*, were delivered by Campbell to the Wise Club, the ideas help to define Reid's environment.
58. "Brief account" in Kames 1774, II: 236.
59. Professor of mathematics at Marischal College, and formerly fellow student of Reid's under Turnbull.
60. The letter is to Mrs. Drummond of Blair Drummond, datelined Glasgow, 1 August 1783.
61. The letter is to Dugald Stewart and is assignable to May 1792. I wish to record my gratitude to Paul Wood for his generosity in allowing me full access to his edition of Reid's correspondence while his work on it was still in progress.

2   Thomas Reid and the Culture of Science

Around the time of Thomas Reid's death in October 1796, his contemporaries took stock of his accomplishments as a man of letters. One of the most challenging interpretations of Reid's life and career to appear came from the pen of his colleague, the Glasgow Professor of Mathematics, James Millar. Writing in an article devoted to the Gregory family (to which Reid was related), Millar commented that Reid was

peculiarly distinguished by his abilities and proficiency in mathematical learning. The objects of literary pursuit are often directed by accidental occurrences. An apprehension of the bad consequences which might result from the philosophy of the late Mr. Hume, induced Dr. Reid to combat the doctrines of that eminent author.... But it is well known to Dr. Reid's literary acquaintance, that these exertions have not diminished the original bent of his genius, nor blunted the edge of his inclination for mathematical researches; which, at a very advanced age, he still continues to prosecute with a youthful attachment, and with unremitting assiduity.[1]

Millar's portrait contrasts sharply with that found in what remains the most influential biography of Reid to date, Dugald Stewart's *Account of the Life and Writings of Thomas Reid*, first published in 1802. For whereas Millar saw the study of mathematics as the "original bent of [Reid's] genius," Stewart characterized Reid's mathematical and scientific pursuits as being incidental to, or recreational diversions from, the primary intellectual focus of his career, which for Stewart was the refutation of Humean skepticism and the construction of a truly scientific analysis of the faculties of the human mind.[2] Although Stewart's image of Reid was at odds with that of many of Reid's friends and associates, the *Account* gradually achieved

53

canonical status during the course of the nineteenth century (not least through its republication in Hamilton's edition of Reid's works) and it continues to shape our understanding of Reid today. However, the crucial historical question prompted by the disparity between the view of Reid advanced by his obituarists and that disseminated by Stewart remains, namely, who most accurately captured the "real" Thomas Reid?

If it is true that we cannot ascribe an unambiguous or fixed identity to any individual, past or present, then this question is, perhaps, unanswerable. Nevertheless, as I have argued elsewhere, the time has come to rethink the standard interpretation of Reid's intellectual identity derived from Dugald Stewart.[3] Thanks to the work initiated in the 1970s by David Fate Norton and Charles Stewart-Robertson on Reid's surviving manuscripts, and subsequently carried on largely by Knud Haakonssen and myself, we are now in a much better position to identify the limitations of, and lacunae in, Stewart's *Account*. One of the most notable revelations of this archival research has been that Reid's intellectual engagement with mathematics and the natural sciences was far more extensive and of much greater moment than Stewart acknowledged. The detailed study of Reid's manuscripts has, if anything, borne out the assessments of his competence and standing as a mathematician and natural philosopher made by Millar, and has therefore highlighted a major gap in Stewart's portrait of Reid. In this chapter, I will survey Reid's researches in mathematics and the natural sciences.[4] In doing so, I hope to provide a corrective to Stewart's comments on Reid's mathematical and scientific interests, and to show that Reid was deeply immersed in the scientific culture of the Enlightenment. To conclude I will identify some of the most important connections between Reid's investigations in mathematics and the natural sciences and the development of his philosophical outlook, and explore the interplay between his mathematical and scientific inquiries and his philosophical ideas. For it is my contention that we must take into account his life as both an Enlightenment man of science and a moralist in order to understand more fully his philosophical achievements.

I. THOMAS REID: MATHEMATICIAN

Even though he acknowledged that Reid had a predilection for mathematics when young, Dugald Stewart claimed that Reid abandoned his mathematical researches when he became preoccupied with Humean skepticism in the 1740s and only returned to them after his retirement from teaching in 1780 as a form of intellectual recreation.[5] Reid's surviving manuscripts tell a very different story, however. Papers dealing with mathematics date from all periods of his career, and they show that he was a practicing mathematician for most of his adult life.[6] Reid's youthful enthusiasm for mathematics is evident in the two earliest extant manuscripts in the Birkwood Collection, which were written in July and October 1729 while he was a divinity student at Marischal College, Aberdeen. The first deals with the concept of quantity in relation to multiplication. The second is a set of detailed reading notes on Newton's *Principia* that, as Niccoló Guicciardini has pointed out, displays considerable mathematical sophistication and acuity.[7] During the 1730s, Reid returned to the question of how best to define the notion of quantity, and his work on this topic ultimately bore fruit in his "An Essay on Quantity" (EQ), read before the Royal Society of London in November 1748.[8] Like other Scottish mathematicians such as Colin Maclaurin and John Stewart, Reid was prompted to reflect on the conceptual basis of Newton's fluxional calculus by George Berkeley's attack on the method of fluxions in *The Analyst* (1734).[9] But Reid's most sustained engagement with foundational issues focussed on the axioms and definitions of Euclidean geometry and, in particular, the vexed problem of Euclid's treatment of parallel lines.[10]

Although the evidence is circumstantial, it may be that Reid was initially motivated in the 1740s to consider critically Euclid's definitions of straight and parallel lines by David Hume's skeptical comments on the imprecision of basic mathematical and geometrical concepts in the *Treatise*.[11] What is more certain is that following his appointment as a regent at King's College, Aberdeen, Reid's experience of teaching the basics of geometry led him to think carefully about the logical cogency of the *Elements*, as did the publication in 1756 of Latin and English texts of the *Elements* edited by the distinguished Glasgow Professor of Mathematics, Robert Simson.[12] Reid distilled his thoughts in a discourse "On Euclid's definitions and axioms" that he delivered before the Aberdeen Philosophical Society on 26 January 1762 and, even though the text of this discourse does not survive, some idea of his argument can be gleaned from correspondence dating from the period 1763–4.[13] After initially thinking that the disputed eleventh axiom (upon which Euclid's demonstrations concerning parallel lines rest) could be derived from a suitably emended definition of parallel lines, Reid recognized that the problem with the logical structure of the *Elements* was much deeper and consequently endeavored to formulate definitions of right and parallel lines from which the eleventh axiom could be inferred. Reid was, however, unsuccessful in his search for such definitions. In May 1770, he was sufficiently frustrated to resolve "for the future to give up the Consideration of this Subject; having spent more time & thought in attempting to prove the simple properties of Streight lines from some one definition or Axiom than I can own without shame" (AUL MS 2131/5/I/1, fol. 1r). Yet Reid did not stick to his resolution, for on 13 September 1770 he made detailed reading notes from Gerolamo Saccheri's *Euclides ab omni naevo vindicatus*, in which Saccheri made an abortive attempt to demonstrate the truth of Euclid's eleventh axiom. It seems likely that Reid abandoned his researches at this point, but he returned to the question of Euclid's definitions and axioms in the early 1790s, when he summarized his work on the subject – which by then had spanned almost fifty years – in a discourse read before the Glasgow Literary Society.[14]

In *The Democratic Intellect*, George Davie argued that eighteenth-century Scottish mathematicians were concerned with the philosophical foundations of Euclidean geometry and Newtonian fluxions and that, following in the footsteps of Newton and Halley, they preferred geometry to algebra. Given Reid's engagement with foundational issues and his preoccupation with Euclid's *Elements*, he might therefore be taken as a representative of the tradition Davie dubbed "mathematical Hellenism."[15] When read against recent work on eighteenth-century British mathematics, however, Reid's mathematical papers tell a somewhat different story. For example, Davie's account of Scottish opposition to the use of algebra ignores the more nuanced attitudes of figures such as Colin Maclaurin. Whereas Robert Simson and his circle of mathematicians (who were the major exponents of mathematical Hellenism) may have believed that algebraical analysis was "little better than a kind of mechanical knack,"[16] both Maclaurin and Reid assessed the relative merits of algebra and geometry differently. Reid acknowledged in his teaching that the principles of algebra were just as self-evident as those of geometry, and showed his students how to apply algebraic reasoning in geometry. Moreover, following his move to Glasgow,

Reid was sharply critical of the geometrical approach to mathematical astronomy advocated by Simson's associate Matthew Stewart.[17] The mathematical topics that Reid investigated and the techniques he employed also differed from those characteristic of mathematical Hellenists like Simson. Consequently, Reid is better placed among the group of eighteenth-century British mathematicians that Niccoló Guicciardini has called "analytical fluxionists," who took Newton's mathematical legacy in a very different direction than Simson and his associates.[18] Reid's mathematical papers thus illuminate not only an important strand of his career largely ignored by Dugald Stewart, but also the broader debates within the British mathematical community in the age of Enlightenment.

II. THOMAS REID: NATURAL PHILOSOPHER

On his maternal side, Reid was descended from the Gregorys, a family that produced a remarkable succession of academics occupying university posts in Scotland and England, including a generation of mathematicians at the turn of the eighteenth century who helped to spread the Newtonian gospel across Britain. Reid himself followed in the Gregory family footsteps, in terms of being both a competent mathematician and a committed Newtonian. As a student at Marischal College in the 1720s, he was introduced to aspects of Newtonian natural philosophy by his regent, George Turnbull, and by the college's Professor of Mathematics, Colin Maclaurin. By 1729 he was deeply immersed in the study of the mathematical technicalities of Newton's *Principia* and, for the rest of his life, Reid investigated an array of empirical and theoretical problems set by Newton in astronomy, mechanics, and optics. During the course of his long career Reid also undertook researches in chemistry, while in the 1750s his teaching responsibilities at King's College led him to consider the science of electricity, and his enquiries in these two fields brought into sharp relief the limitations of the quantitative approach to natural philosophy that he had inherited from the *Principia*. Furthermore, like many other men of science, Reid grew increasingly skeptical of Newton's suggestion that all of the phenomena of nature could be explained in terms of the interactions of attractive and repulsive forces.[19] Consequently, even though Reid never questioned Newton's standing as the greatest of modern natural philosophers, he came to see that with the exception of the law of gravitation, much of what Newton had bequeathed to the Enlightenment was in need of refinement, revision, or replacement.

During the 1730s and 1740s, Reid's primary scientific collaborator was John Stewart, Colin Maclaurin's successor at Marischal College. After leaving Aberdeen for Edinburgh in 1725, Maclaurin gradually built up a network of observational astronomers in Scotland, which by 1737 included Stewart and most likely Reid. In February 1737 Reid was probably one of "Several Gentlemen" mentioned by Maclaurin who, along with Stewart, observed an eclipse of the sun, and in 1744 it seems that Reid tracked a comet. Reid and Stewart were again involved in observing an eclipse of the sun in July 1748, on this occasion as part of a group organized by Alexander Monro *primus*.[20] The two men also followed the dispute in physical astronomy between Cartesians and Newtonians over the shape of the earth, which was resolved in Newton's favor in 1738 with the publication of Maupertuis' *La figure de la terre*.[21]

Reid subsequently put his early work in astronomy to good use when teaching natural philosophy at King's College, for he devoted a significant proportion of his course to explaining such topics as the motions of the planets, eclipses of the sun and moon, the irregularities of the moon's motion, and the tides.[22] While at King's, he also continued to make telescopic observations, most notably in 1761, when he and some of his fellow members of the Wise Club observed the transit of Venus that occurred on 6 June.[23] In Glasgow, he shared his interest in astronomical matters with both the Professor of Practical Astronomy, Alexander Wilson, and Wilson's son Patrick, and he collaborated with his new colleagues in observing another transit of Venus in September 1769.[24] Furthermore, manuscripts dating from his Glasgow period show that he was reading various works on astronomy, and that he knew of William Herschel's telescopic discoveries.[25]

Reid's first sustained line of investigation in natural philosophy, however, addressed the question of the proper measure of the force of bodies in motion. In his correspondence with Samuel Clarke published in 1717, Leibniz contended that the true measure was mv^2 (*vis viva*), and not mv as Newton had claimed. A protracted debate between Leibnizians and Newtonians over *vis viva* then ensued, with the two camps trading salvos until the 1740s.[26] Apparently prompted by the first wave of exchanges in the 1720s, Reid began to formulate his own answer to the *vis viva* question in the 1730s in the context of his exploration of the issue of how best to define the nature of quantity, and he published his reflections on the debate in "An Essay on Quantity," probably in response to the appearance of further Newtonian polemics in the 1740s. But while Reid defended the Newtonian position, he did so in a manner that differed from his fellow Newtonians. For Reid rejected the claim commonly made by both parties in the dispute that the question could be resolved experimentally. Rather, he contended that mv was preferable to mv^2 as a definition of the force of moving bodies for two reasons, namely, that it was "clear and simple" and that it "agrees best with the Use of the Word Force in common Language" because "all Men agree, that the Force of the Body being the same, the Velocity must also be the same [and] the Force being increased or diminished, the Velocity must be so also" (EQ: 515).[27] Once the "Essay" was published, Reid seems to have lost interest in the debate, although one manuscript dating from 1781 survives in which he summarizes the arguments of Pieter van Musschenbroek in favor of the use of the measure mv^2.[28]

Of more lasting interest to Reid was the field of physical optics. Although it is unclear when he initially began to study optics seriously, his lectures on the subject at King's College demonstrate that he had mastered the basics of the theory of light set out in Newton's *Principia* and *Opticks*.[29] His reading notes taken in March 1757 from the recently published "Observations on Light and Colours" by the Scottish natural philosopher, Thomas Melvill, also show that he favored the view that light consisted of minute particles projected from luminous bodies. Melvill's paper also seems to have introduced him to the writings of Roger Joseph Boscovich, whose concept of point atoms fascinated him for the remainder of his career.[30] Reid subsequently hinted at the particulate nature of light in the *Inquiry* and, after he moved to Glasgow, his letters to David Skene document his interest in the achromatic telescopes constructed by John Dollond and the refractive powers of different kinds of glass and crystals.[31]

As the example of Dollond's telescope suggests, the sciences of optics and astronomy were closely related in the eighteenth century, and Reid's investigations during the 1770s and 1780s well illustrate the connections between them. Beginning in October 1770, he explored the phenomenon of the aberration of light, stimulated by Patrick Wilson's speculations on the subject.[32] Wilson wanted to understand this phenomenon primarily in order to eliminate errors from astronomical observations, but Reid considered its implications for optical theory more generally. Soon after his initial conversations with Wilson, he delivered a discourse to the Glasgow Literary Society in November 1770 "concerning the Velocity of Light shewing that this as deduced from Dr. Bradley's Theory of the Aberration of the fixed Stars is erroneous and a new Principle which affects that pointed out and examined," and their discussions continued through the 1770s, culminating in the publication in 1782 of a paper on aberration by Wilson in the *Philosophical Transactions*.[33]

Reid's exchanges with Wilson also raised questions regarding the behavior of light when meeting moving surfaces (including the eye), a subject which he believed previous writers on optics had largely ignored despite its theoretical significance. In a series of detailed and closely reasoned manuscripts dating from the 1780s he explored this issue, considering such related topics as the reflection and refraction of light in media that are in motion, the consequences of the progressive motion of light for our observation of objects such as the fixed stars, and Boscovich's assertion that aberration would occur if water telescopes were employed to observe terrestrial bodies.[34] The argument of two papers included in Boscovich's *Opera pertinentia ad opticam et astronomiam* (1785) was of considerable interest to Reid, as well as to Wilson and their mutual friend John Robison, because Boscovich claimed that the use of water telescopes in the manner he described provided a crucial experiment that would adjudicate the truth claims of Euler's wave and Newton's particulate theories of light.[35] Reid, Wilson, and Robison, however, all disagreed, and Robison went on to attack Boscovich's conclusions in a paper which Reid commented on favorably prior to its publication in the *Transactions of the Royal Society of Edinburgh* in 1790. Notwithstanding their disagreement with Boscovich, Reid encouraged Robison to devise an *experimentum crucis* to test the rival theories of Euler and Newton, and he was guardedly optimistic that it would "probably serve to confirm Newtons system & to detect the Error of Eulers" (C: 199).[36]

In sum, Reid's correspondence and his unpublished manscripts reveal that he was an able proponent of what Geoffrey Cantor has called "the projectile theory of light."[37] Derived primarily from Newton's *Principia* and *Opticks*, and developed in the first half of the eighteenth century, this theory affirmed, *inter alia*, that light consisted of exceedingly small particles, that it was subject to the laws of motion, and that it was acted on by the attractive and repulsive forces of ordinary matter. Reid's optical researches were framed in terms of these theoretical assumptions and he did not waver in his belief that the projectile theorists' interpretation of Newton was essentially correct. Yet he also recognized that Newton's legacy in optics had to be accommodated to new and sometimes anomalous phenomena, such as Dollond's construction of achromatic telescopes, and he was well aware of at least some of the problems raised by the supposition that light is particulate.[38] Reid was thus one of a small group of projectile theorists in eighteenth-century Britain who both disseminated publicly the principles of the theory in an academic setting and applied those principles in the context of original research.

Another branch of the natural sciences that Reid cultivated for much of his adult life was chemistry. While it is unclear when or why he first became interested in the study of chemistry, surviving sections of his natural history lectures at King's College and related documents indicate that by the 1750s he had acquired a working knowledge of the basics of chemical theory, and mastered a wide range of empirical information derived from the chemical analysis of the three kingdoms of nature.[39] At this stage in his career, he seems to have considered chemistry to be a largely practical science that was closely related to medicine, pharmacy, natural history, and the imperatives of economic improvement, especially with regard to agriculture.[40] But when he moved to Glasgow, he encountered the brand of philosophical chemistry forged there initially by William Cullen and then by Cullen's pupil, Joseph Black.[41] Shortly after leaving Aberdeen, Reid reported to David Skene that "Chemistry seems to be the onely branch of Philosophy that can be said to be in a progressive State here" (C: 39) and in the 1765–66 session he went so far as to attend Black's chemistry lectures in order to acquaint himself more fully with his new colleague's theory of latent heat.[42] As Dugald Stewart later observed, "In Dr BLACK ... REID acknowledged an instructor and a guide ... and ... attended the lectures of BLACK, with a juvenile curiosity and enthusiasm."[43] Reid was not, however, an uncritical auditor. He wrote to Skene that the "Doctrine of Latent Heat is the only thing I have yet heard that is altogether New," and said that while Black's theory gave "a great deal of Light to the Phanomena of heat that appear in Mixture, Solution, & Evaporation" it failed to illuminate the phenomena "which appear in Animal heat, Inflammation, & Friction" (C: 44).[44]

Despite such reservations, Reid continued to explore various aspects of Black's ideas over the course of the next two decades, largely in collaboration with Black's pupil William Irvine, who lectured on chemistry at Glasgow from 1769 until his death in 1787. For example, both Black and Irvine sought to justify theoretically the use of the thermometer as a measure of heat, and we find Reid reflecting on this issue in a manuscript dating from 1770.[45] Beginning in the mid-1760s, Irvine used Black's ideas to develop his own theory of heat, which centered on the concept of heat capacity. Reid duly attempted to get to grips with Irvine's ideas, but the surviving evidence is unfortunately too fragmentary to allow any firm conclusion about whether or not he accepted Irvine's as opposed to Black's theory of heat.[46] One other figure with whom Reid discussed chemical theory in the 1770s was Irvine's student Adair Crawford, who was one of the first to apply the theoretical insights of Black and Irvine to the question of animal heat. Crawford tells us that in the summer of 1777 he performed a series of experiments on combustion and animal heat and that he presented his results to Irvine, Reid, and Patrick Wilson "in the autumn of that year." We do not know what Reid thought of Crawford's theory, but it would seem that he helped Crawford to clarify certain mathematical aspects of the concept of temperature.[47]

One of the earliest Scottish converts to the revolutionary system of chemistry developed in France by Lavoisier and his associates was Thomas Charles Hope, and his election as Irvine's successor in 1787 marks a turning point in Reid's engagement with chemical theory. For it seems likely that Hope encouraged Reid to learn about French chemistry, and it may be that Hope recommended that he read William Nicholson's translation of Fourcroy's *Elemens d'histoire naturelle et de chimie* in the spring of 1789. Reid's lengthy and detailed reading notes survive, and they show that he closely scrutinized the sections of Fourcroy's text dealing with topics central to the Chemical Revolution, namely, the study of "airs," Lavoisier's theory of acids, and the rejection of phlogiston.[48] A second manuscript dating from 1790, "Of the Chemical Elements of Bodies," deals with another key feature of the Chemical Revolution

and attests to Reid's deepening knowledge of the theoretical inno-
vations of Lavoisier. While the latter part of this manuscript merely
summarizes or records random points from passages in Robert Kerr's
translation of Lavoisier's *Traité élémentaire de chimie*, the opening
pages represent a sustained attempt by Reid to state the essentials of
Lavoisier's concept of a chemical element and to identify the defining
properties of the five substances which Lavoisier judged to be "simple": light, caloric, oxygen, azote, and hydrogen.[49] What is perhaps
most noteworthy about this introductory material is Reid's willingness to countenance the existence of imponderable fluids such as
caloric. Although he is widely known as a critic of hypotheses involving unobservable entities such as vortices or etherial media, in
practice his attitude toward hypotheses and unobservable entities
was more complex than his published comments would indicate.[50]
As for caloric, he seemingly believed that the available experimental evidence confirmed the existence of such a fluid, and he may
well have been swayed by Lavoisier's methodological rhetoric and
quantitative methods. Moreover, theoretical chemistry in the eighteenth century routinely invoked the existence of etherial fluids in
a variety of guises, so that the conceptual fabric of the science was
woven out of unobservable explanatory mechanisms. Consequently,
Reid's flirtation with the concept of caloric should not surprise us,
given the weight of chemical tradition and the force of Lavoisier's
arguments.

While it cannot be claimed that Reid was an innovative or creative
chemist, his work in chemistry was neither superficial nor short-
lived. In terms of practical chemistry, he appears to have gained some
expertise in chemical analysis and, like many of his contemporaries,
he attempted to apply chemistry to the needs of improvement.[51]
Once in Glasgow, he became well versed in the research tradition in
the science of heat created by Cullen and Black, and he was closely
associated with the chemists who succeeded them, namely, John
Robison, Irvine, Hope, and Robert Cleghorn.[52] His predilection for
quantitative reasoning dovetailed with that of the Glasgow chemists,
and his recognition that chemical phenomena were not necessarily
explicable in terms of the attractive and repulsive forces posited by
Newton registers the vision of chemistry as an autonomous branch of
natural philosophy that was articulated by Cullen and Black.[53] Last,
his response to the French chemists displays a remarkable openness

to theoretical innovation, and his manuscripts on Fourcroy and Lavoisier shed important light on the reception of the new chemistry in Scotland at the end of the eighteenth century.

Like chemistry, the study of electricity was transformed during the age of Enlightenment, and for roughly two decades Reid kept track of the major advances in the field. While he may have been superficially acquainted with electrical theory in the 1730s and 1740s,[54] his teaching responsibilities at King's College prompted him to scrutinize the writings of J. T. Desaguliers and Benjamin Franklin. Both the student notes from his natural philosophy lectures and his own manuscripts on electricity dating from the mid-1750s exhibit an unresolved tension between pre-Franklinist theory derived primarily from Desaguliers and ideas taken from Franklin.[55] Thus he sometimes employed terminology that implied that electrical phenomena were explicable in terms of effluvia given off by bodies, while at other times he spoke the language of the Philadelphia system and invoked an electrical fluid consisting of subtle particles that were mutually repellent and attracted by ordinary matter.[56] And while he was cognizant of some of the problems facing Franklin's view, he did not attempt to reconcile the two explanatory schemes, preferring in his lectures to devote most of his classroom time to classifying natural substances into electrics and nonelectrics according to their capacity to "collect," "receive," or "imbibe" quantities of electricity (AUL MS 2131/6/V/11, fol. 2v; "Natural Philosophy, 1758," K. 160: 217, 219–20). A similar tension is to be found in his notes from the early 1760s on the anomalous electrical properties of the tourmaline crystal, which were first announced by F. U. T. Aepinus in 1756. Most electricians believed that friction was required to produce electricity, but Aepinus showed that tourmaline could be electrified by heating alone. Reid's notes indicate that he was familiar with both the Franklinists' explanation of the behavior of tourmaline and that of the followers of Jean Antoine Nollet, but there is no sign that he preferred one of the rival explanations over the other.[57]

Once Reid no longer had to lecture on electricity, his interest in the subject apparently waned. His Glasgow colleagues John Anderson and John Robison were both keen electricians, and in the late 1760s Robison performed a series of experiments, which showed that the force of electricity, like that of gravity, obeyed the inverse square law.[58] Robison's researches may have prompted Reid to read

Joseph Priestley's *History and Present State of Electricity* (1768) and the fourth edition of Franklin's *Experiments and Observations on Electricity* (1769) when they were published, but this can only be surmised.[59] In Reid's discourse "Of Muscular Motion in the human Body" he alludes to work carried out in the 1770s on the shock of the electric eel, but apart from this hint of an interest in animal electricity there is no evidence that he kept himself informed about the latest currents in electrical theory during the latter part of his career.[60] Thus even though the science of electricity was one of the most widely cultivated branches of natural philosophy in the eighteenth century, Reid's engagement with the subject was somewhat perfunctory and largely tied to his teaching at King's College. Nevertheless, his manuscripts on electricity reinforce the point made above that notwithstanding his frequent attacks on the use of hypotheses, he was willing to countenance theories that invoked unobservable entities such as electrical effluvia and fluids.[61]

III. THOMAS REID: NATURAL HISTORIAN

In the Enlightenment, the most popular field of scientific enquiry was natural history, which encompassed a wide range of subjects, from the classification of the mineral, vegetable, and animal kingdoms to the study of geology and the analysis of human nature. As I have shown elsewhere, Reid was a serious natural historian for much of his life.[62] We know that he was something of a botanist as well as a keen gardener while he was Minister at New Machar, and circumstantial evidence suggests that he was interested in the natural history of man in the 1740s if not before.[63] Consequently, he was well placed to lecture on natural history at King's College following the curriculum reforms of 1753, and in his classes he provided his students with classification systems for the three kingdoms of nature, along with detailed information regarding the chemical properties of the various constituents of these kingdoms. In addition, he detailed the anatomy and physiology of plants and animals, discussed their comparative anatomy, and briefly described the workings of the human body. Not surprisingly, he encouraged his pupils to study natural history because he maintained that the knowledge it generated could be used not only for practical, economic benefit but also for tracing out God's design in nature.[64]

During this period, Reid also engaged in a number of natural historical enquiries outside of the classroom. Evidence survives, for example, of his botanizing with David Skene in the Aberdeen area, and we know that in 1758 he was experimenting with the cultivation of potatoes, a plant which was only beginning to be widely grown in Scotland.[65] In the meetings of the Gordon's Mill Farming Club and the Aberdeen Philosophical Society, he addressed such questions as the use of lime as a fertilizer, the distillation of potatoes, and the nutrition of plants.[66] He collaborated with the Marischal Professor of Natural History, George Skene, in making chemical analyses of spa waters and a range of natural substances.[67] More importantly, at some point in the 1750s he began reading Buffon's *Histoire naturelle*.

Reid's extant reading notes from the *Histoire* show that four topics caught his attention: Buffon's attack on the use of systematic classification schemes in natural history, his controversial theory of the earth, his view of human nature, and his account of the generation of plants and animals.[68] Significantly, Reid disagreed with the great French naturalist on all of these subjects.[69] In his natural history lectures at King's, Reid emphasized the importance of order, method, and system when classifying the three kingdoms of nature, and he later defended the taxonomic enterprise by arguing that it was rooted in our common sense. Reid thus had little time for Buffon's critique of classification systems, preferring the systematic approach to natural history adopted by Linnaeus, among others.[70] He was equally unimpressed by Buffon's theory of the earth. He apparently understood on a first reading that Buffon assumed that the age of the earth was far greater than most eighteenth-century naturalists were prepared to contemplate, and quickly dismissed the cosmogony outlined in the first volume of the *Histoire* as a hypothesis which went far beyond the available evidence.[71] The question of Buffon's religious orthodoxy was also sharply posed by the portrait of human nature sketched in the *Histoire*. Reid was troubled by Buffon's Cartesian depiction of higher animals as mere machines because he believed that this view ultimately led to materialism, and his suspicion about Buffon's position was reinforced with the publication of Helvétius's *De l'esprit* in 1758. For like Buffon, Helvétius held that what differentiates humankind from the higher animals is our superior sense of touch, which Reid viewed as tantamount to materialism. In his Glasgow lectures, he therefore attacked the two *philosophes* for their heterodoxy, while conceding that Buffon was not, strictly speaking, a materialist because he apparently recognized that there is an immaterial sentient principle in human persons.

But Reid's suspicions about Buffon's orthodoxy were further aroused by the Frenchman's explanation of the reproduction of plants and animals. Reid had long been interested in the theory of generation when he first read the *Histoire naturelle*, and probably consulted the *Histoire* in the first instance to gather information about the different forms of reproduction to be found in the plant and animal kingdoms, as well as other topics covered in his natural history lectures. And whereas Buffon's extended discussion of generation was rich in empirical detail, the theory he advanced to explain the facts he catalogued must have struck Reid as deeply suspect, not least because Buffon's conception of a *"matière vivante"* smacked of materialism because it ascribed to matter the power of self-organization.[72] This was anathema to a good Newtonian like Reid, who denied that any such power could be intrinsic to matter, and he likewise took exception to both Buffon's explicit denial that God plays a role in reproduction and his dismissal of final causes.

Even when Reid no longer had to teach natural history in Glasgow, he deployed evidence drawn from the three kingdoms of nature and discussed the theory of generation as well as the subject of muscular motion at various points in his lectures.[73] He also took part in the consideration of natural historical topics in the Glasgow Literary Society, and in November 1795 delivered his discourse "Of Muscular Motion in the human Body."[74] In addition, he made the acquaintance of natural historians visiting from abroad, acquired books on natural history for his own library, and traded ideas with his correspondents, most notably David Skene and Lord Kames.[75] From Skene, Reid obtained information about the work of Linnaeus (with whom Skene corresponded), while Kames solicited Reid's opinion on topics covered in Kames's *The Gentleman Farmer*, first published in 1776. Apart from exchanging views on manures and the properties of clays, Kames and Reid debated the generation of plants and animals. Like Buffon, Kames suggested that matter has the power to organize itself into the structures of living beings, to which Reid retorted, "Would your Lordship allow that certain Letters might be endowed with the Power of forming themselves into an Iliad or Eneid, or even into a sensible discoarse [*sic*] in Prose?" (C: 77). Reid countered with his own "conjecture" that "both plants and Animals, are at first organized Atoms, having all the parts of the Animal or Plant; but so slender and folded up in such a Manner as to be reduced to an Atom far beyond the reach of our senses" (C: 76).[76] Although both Kames and the naturalist, the Rev. John Walker, were unimpressed with Reid's conjecture, he began to sketch out his theory of organized atoms in his Glasgow lectures on the culture of the mind.[77] But during the latter stages of his career he grew increasingly skeptical about our capacity to account for the generation of plants and animals. When he read the works of Charles Bonnet in the late 1770s or early 1780s, he found Bonnet's formulation of the theory of organized atoms highly problematic, and in a late discourse read to the Glasgow Literary Society he commented that the "ways by which animals and vegetables produce their kind are various and all equally mysterious & incomprehensible to human understanding" (PRLS: 225).[78] After roughly sixty years of enquiry dating back to the meetings of the Philosophical Society held at Marischal College in 1736, therefore, Reid had made little headway in solving the puzzle of the theory of generation. Nonetheless, by the time of his death he had amassed a considerable stock of empirical knowledge about the three kingdoms of nature, and had proven himself to be one of the more accomplished natural historians of the Scottish Enlightenment.

IV. CONCLUSION

In the 31st Query of the *Opticks*, Sir Isaac Newton observed that "if natural Philosophy in all its Parts, by pursuing this method shall at length be perfected the Bounds of Moral Philosophy will be also enlarged."[79] This passage inspired Reid and many other eighteenth-century moralists to apply Newton's method of analysis and synthesis to the study of human nature, and it also speaks to the ways in which Reid's life-long engagement with the natural sciences interacted with his philosophical endeavors. The influence of Bacon and Newton on Reid's methodological approach to the science of the mind was first emphasized by Dugald Stewart, and this theme has subsequently been taken up by L. L. Laudan and others, albeit with more attention given to Newton than to Bacon.[80] Combined with the teachings of his regent George Turnbull, Reid's early reading of the Newtonian corpus shaped his understanding of the inductive method and his critical attitude towards hypotheses. His critique of the theory of ideas and the use of hypotheses in his Aberdeen and Glasgow lectures, his philosophical orations, the *Inquiry*, and the *Essays on the Intellectual Powers* were rooted in the antihypotheticalism of Newton and the Newtonians, while Newton's deployment of an *experimentum crucis* in his first paper on light and colors informed Reid's attack on the "ideal system" in the *Inquiry*.[81] The extent to which his outlook was structured by the methodological lessons he derived from Newton can be measured by his comment that Newton's "*regulae philosophandi* are maxims of common sense" (IHM I. i: 12). However, we should not overlook the fact that Reid's activities as a natural historian also had an impact on the method he employed in the science of the mind, for in general terms he saw himself as compiling "the History of the Human Mind and its Operations & Powers," while his catalog of the various principles of human action in the *Essays on the Active Powers* reflects his penchant for natural historical classification.[82]

In addition, Reid's work in mathematics and the natural sciences left its mark on his epistemology, moral theory, and metaphysics. His essay on abstraction in the *Essays on the Intellectual Powers*, for instance, addressed not only the philosophical debate provoked by Locke's account of abstract ideas but also a disagreement among mathematicians regarding the origins of our mathematical concepts. Moreover, in this essay the chapter "Of general conceptions formed by combination" incorporates a defense of the use of systematic classification schemes in natural history which reads like a direct response to the argument of the "Premier Discours" of Buffon's *Histoire naturelle*.[83] Elsewhere in the *Essays*, Reid articulated his view that knowledge should be organized into deductive structures resting on the foundation of first principles and, as he indicates, the inspiration for this view came from Euclid's *Elements*, as well as Newton's *Principia* and *Opticks*.[84] His attempt to clarify Euclid's definitions and axioms recounted above can thus be seen as being part and parcel of his answer to Hume, insofar as he was trying to secure Euclidean geometry against the threat of Humean skepticism and thus to show that the *Elements* could legitimately serve as a model for human knowledge. But even before he grappled with Hume, his work on the foundations of mathematics in the 1730s was closely related to his philosophical concerns, for the analysis of proper and improper quantities which he eventually published in his "Essay on Quantity" was intended to discredit not only Leibniz's concept of *vis viva*, but also Francis Hutcheson's use of algebraic equations to calculate the quantity of virtue or vice in our actions.[85]

Writing to James Gregory in August 1790, Reid acknowledged that "there is some merit in what you are pleased to call *my Philosophy*; but I think it lies chiefly in having called in question the common theory of *Ideas*" (C: 210).[86] No better illustration of the melding of Reid's scientific and philosophical thought can be found than his attack on "the ideal system." Norman Daniels and Geoffrey Cantor have shown, for example, that Reid's lengthy treatment of the sense of sight in the *Inquiry* is grounded in the science of optics.[87] His knowledge of anatomy and physiology also framed his interpretation of the theory of ideas, for he believed that the ideal system rested on a set of anatomical and physiological hypotheses which purported to explain how images of external objects were transmitted to the brain and there perceived as ideas by the mind.[88] Last, as noted above, his assault on the theory of ideas drew on the methodological ideals he derived from Newton, although we should not forget that in the course of mounting his attack he in turn refined the reading of the first of Newton's *regulae philosophandi* that was later enshrined in the *Essays on the Intellectual Powers*.[89] If we accept Reid's assessment that his critique of the ideal system formed the core of his philosophy, then we must turn to his scientific pursuits in order to understand fully his philosophical achievements.

Another notable example of the interplay of Reid's scientific and philosophical inquiries is his account of causation. In a manuscript written four years after the publication of the *Essays on the Active Powers*, Reid restated his distinction between "natural" and "efficient" causes, and repeated his claim that "When we attend to objects without us we see innumerable changes or Events, some constantly conjoyned with a certain Effect which succeeds; but we perceive no real connexion between them" (AUL MS 2131/2/II/2: 4) He then remarked, "Mr Humes reasoning on this Subject In <his> Essay on Necessary Connexion would have convinced me if I have not been convinced before, by S. I Newton" (ibid.).[90] This striking observation reminds us that Reid was influenced not only by Newtonian science but also by Newtonian metaphysics, especially as formulated by Newton's closest disciple, Samuel Clarke. Newtonians such as Andrew Baxter and Colin Maclaurin debated the nature of causation in their writings, and Reid undoubtedly knew the details of this debate.[91] More importantly, in the 1720s and 1730s he absorbed the voluntarist theology and metaphysics espoused by both Newton and Clarke, and their ideas shaped the account of causation, active power, and human free will he later gave in the *Essays* of 1788.[92] Reid's indebtedness to Newton and his immediate disciples was thus more far-reaching than has hitherto been appreciated, for Reid's intellectual debt extended well beyond methodology to the domain of metaphysics.

In sum, when Reid's activities and interests as a man of science are taken into account, we see that there is a richer and more complex intellectual context for his published philosophical works than has previously been recognized. Conversely, we also need to see that his scientific inquiries were bound up with his epistemological, metaphysical, and moral concerns. Rather than rest content with the narrowly circumscribed portrait of Reid inherited from Dugald Stewart, therefore, we need to move beyond the dichotomy imposed by Stewart between Reid's science and his philosophy in order to make sense of the connections between all of his published and unpublished writings. To do so we must first recognize that Reid was as much a man of science as he was a moralist, for only then will we be in a position to grasp the totality of his thought as well as the interconnections between his natural and moral philosophy. This chapter represents an initial step towards that end.

Thanks go to Carol Gibson-Wood for her constructive comments on an earlier draft of this chapter.

NOTES

1. In Hutton 1795–96, 1: 558.
2. On Stewart's *Account*, see Wood 1985.
3. Wood 1985, 2000a, and 2001.
4. Wood 1984 is the first systematic study of Reid's mathematical and scientific papers. I subsequently elaborated on some of this work in PRLS. A selection of Reid's manuscripts on mathematics and natural philosophy edited by myself will appear as volume 9 of the Edinburgh Edition of Thomas Reid.
5. Stewart 1803: 12, 19, 170–3.

6. On Reid's mathematical work, see Wood 1984, Chap. 3, and especially Guicciardini 2001.

7. AUL MSS 2131/5/II/1 (dated 19 July 1729) and 2131/7/III/15 (dated 6 October 1729); Guicciardini 2001: 79.

8. AUL MSS 2131/5/I/20 and 5/I/22.

9. The major Scottish replies to Berkeley were Maclaurin 1742 and Stewart 1745. Reid's work on fluxions is surveyed in Guicciardini 2001: 75–8.

10. For a more detailed discussion of Reid on parallel lines, see Wood 1998.

11. THN 1.2.4; EIP VI.i: 419–20, VI.vi: 491–2; Wood 1998: 29.

12. "Observations on the Elements of Euclid," AUL MSS 2131/5/II/47 (dated June 1756) and 2131/3/I/13 (an undated set of reading notes from Simson).

13. Ulman 1990: 237; Reid to [William Ogilvie], [1763], and Reid to [Robert Simson], [1764] (C: 23–6, 32–4).

14. AUL MSS 2131/5/I/1, 5/II/47, and 3061/11. A copy of Reid's discourse was read by the Edinburgh Professor of Mathematics, John Playfair, who referred to Reid in his edition of the *Elements* first published in 1795.

15. Davie 1981, Chaps. 5–7; see also Olson 1975, Chap. 3. For a more detailed discussion of Reid's mathematical style, see Wood 1984, Chap. 3.

16. The phrase comes from Robison 1797, 17: 504.

17. Guicciardini 2001: 79–81.

18. Guicciardini 2001: 74. Guicciardini provides helpful references to the recent literature in the history of mathematics relevant to understanding Reid as a mathematician.

19. Reid to Kames, 1 October 1775 (C: 93); compare IHM VII: 211.

20. Maclaurin 1737–38: 191 for Maclaurin's reference to Stewart and his associates; AUL MS 2131/6/III/8, fol. 2r; Morton et al. 1748: 593. A loose sheet recording Reid's 1748 observations is inserted in AUL MS 2131/2/I/1.

21. See Reid's reading notes (dated November 1739) from the 1738 English translation of Maupertuis's work in AUL MS 2131/3/I/2, and Reid to John Stewart, [1739] (C: 4–5). He later took detailed notes from the original French text in January 1751; AUL MS 2131/3/I/7.

22. "Natural Philosophy, 1758," AUL MS K. 160: 145–84.

23. Reid reported on his observations in a paper read to the Wise Club on 14 July 1761; see AUL MS 2131/2/I/7. See also Reid's comments in IHM VI.xii: 131. The Wise Club discussed how best to observe the transit as early as 12 April 1758, when Robert Traill addressed the question "What are the proper Methods of determining the Suns Paralax by the Transit of Venus over his Disk in 1761?"; Ulman 1990: 189.

24. Wilson 1769.

25. AUL MSS 2131/3/I/6, 3/I/9 and 7/III/13. Herschel received an honorary degree from the University when he visited Glasgow in July 1792; Coutts 1909: 306.
26. Laudan 1968; Iltis 1973.
27. Reid's linguistic argument in favor of *mv* foreshadows the appeals to the structure of language he later made in his published philosophical works.
28. AUL MS 2131/7/II/12, fol. 1r-v. Reid was later highly dismissive of his treatment of the *vis viva* question; see the postscript to the manuscript version of the "Essay," AUL MS 3061/7: 13.
29. John Stewart was a subscriber to Robert Smith's *Compleat System of Optics*, published in 1738. The *System* covered geometrical and physical optics, as well as the theory of vision, and it is likely that Stewart and Reid shared a common interest in Smith's work. In the late 1720s the two of them also probably studied together Propositions XCIV–XCVIII in Book I of the *Principia* which related to the behavior of light. Reid later cited Proposition XCIV in his optics lectures; "Natural Philosophy, 1758," AUL MS K. 160: 262. For more details of Reid's optics lectures at King's, see Wood 1984: 73.
30. Melvill 1756. For later references by Reid to Boscovich's matter theory, see EIP II.xix: 220 and PRLS: 171–2, 197, 220.
31. IHM VI.i: 77; Reid to David Skene, 13 July 1765 (C: 40). Reid continued to be interested in achromatic telescopes, for his last extant manuscript on physical optics consists of notes taken in November 1792 on the work of the Edinburgh Professor of Practical Astronomy, Robert Blair, related to the improvement of achromatic lenses. See AUL MS 2131/3/I/3.
32. AUL MS 2131/7/II/5.
33. "Laws of the Literary Society in Glasgow College," Glasgow University Library, MS Murray 505: 36; Wilson 1782. Wilson also read a paper to the Glasgow Literary Society on the refraction and refrangibility of light in January 1777; "Laws of the Literary Society": 45–6.
34. AUL MSS 2131/2/I/3, 3/III/11, 5/II/55, 7/II/15, and 7/VIII/2.
35. Pederson 1980.
36. Reid to Robison, [1788–1790]. AUL MS 2131/3/III/11.
37. Cantor 1983, Chap. 2.
38. Wood 1984: 261; Cantor 1983, Chap. 3.
39. Reid was familiar with Boerhaave's theories of heat and fire, Stahl's theory of phlogiston, the concept of chemical affinities, and, just before moving to Glasgow, Joseph Black's theory of latent heat. See AUL MS 2131/7/II/4, fol. 2v; Reid to [William Ogilvie], [1763] (C: 26); IHM II.i: 25; III: 46; V.i: 55. His detailed empirical knowledge is best seen in "The Chemical History of Salts," AUL MS 2343, a manuscript related to his

natural history lectures. The chemical analysis of the three kingdoms of nature is emphasized in his "Scheme of a Course in Philosophy" from 1752, AUL MS 2131/8/V/1.

40. Wood 1984: 271.
41. The best guide to the achievements of Cullen and Black remains Donovan 1975.
42. Reid to David Skene, 13 July 1765. See also the letters from 20 December [1765] and 23 March 1766 (C: 39, 44, 48–50) that document Reid's attendance at Black's lectures.
43. Stewart 1803: 47, 49.
44. Reid to David Skene, 20 December [1765]. Reid's critical comments on Black's lectures indicate that he had more than a superficial knowledge of chemistry.
45. AUL MS 2131/7/III/6.
46. AUL MSS 2131/7/III/6: 8 and 7/III/11.
47. Crawford 1788: A3r, 6. On p. 1 Crawford quotes from Reid's *Inquiry* on the distinction between heat as a sensation and heat as a property of bodies.
48. AUL MS 2131/3/I/16, esp: 1, 3, 4, 13–18, 21-4. Dated 22 May 1789, the manuscript runs to 30 pages and contains the most detailed set of reading notes to be found amongst Reid's surviving papers.
49. AUL MS 2131/2/I/4.
50. For more detailed consideration of this issue, see Wood 1989.
51. AUL MS 2131/6/V/11, fol. 2v; Reid to Joseph Black, 17 January 1773 (C: 74–5). See also his reading notes from Cronstedt's *Mineralogy*, AUL MS 2131/3/I/14.
52. Robison lectured on chemistry at Glasgow from 1766 to 1770, while Cleghorn succeeded Hope in 1791. Cleghorn was a close associate of Reid's, and probably taught the new French chemistry; Thomson 1950: 166–7.
53. On these points, see Emerson and Wood 2002: 94, 103.
54. When Reid and John Stewart visited the Royal Society of London in 1736, he probably witnessed electrical experiments demonstrated by J. T. Desaguliers. See Royal Society of London, Journal Book (copy), xv (1735–6): 363–4 (unpublished).
55. Similarities in phraseology and theory indicate that Reid was heavily indebted to the dissertation on electricity published in Desagulier 1763 2: 316–36 (first published in 1744), a work he also used when teaching mechanics. Benjamin Franklin's *Experiments and Observations on Electricity* was first published in 1751 and appeared in a second edition in 1754.

56. AUL MSS 2131/6/V/11, 8/V/3, and "Natural Philosophy, 1758," K. 160: 217–20.

57. AUL MS 2131/6/V/20; Aepinus 1979: 92–5.

58. Muir 1950: 13, 33–6; Heilbron 1979: 465–8.

59. AUL MSS 2131/3/I/9 and 3/I/14, fols 1r-2v.

60. PRLS: 29, 119.

61. Compare his remarks on the action of subtle effluvia on our sense of smell in IHM II.i: 25–6.

62. PRLS: 3–20.

63. Stewart 1803: 18. For evidence of his interest in the natural history of man, see Reid to James Gregory, 26 August 1787 (C: 194), where he mentions that in the 1740s he read Charlevoix 1744.

64. PRLS: 4 and the references cited there.

65. AUL MSS 44 (entry dated 13 August 1764); 56 (entry dated 20 August with no year given), 482; 2131/5/II/2, fol. 1r; 2131/6/V/1 and 2131/6/V/11, fol. 2v. On the potato, see also IHM VII: 204.

66. "Minute Book of the Farming Club at Gordon's Mill, 1758," AUL MS 49, 38, 52; Ulman 1990: 92, 189.

67. George Skene served as the Marischal Professor of Natural Philosophy from 1760 until 1775, when he transferred to the chair of civil and natural history. For evidence of their collaboration, see Reid to Joseph Black, 17 January 1773 (C: 75), and "The Chemical History of Salts," AUL MS 2343.

68. PRLS: 83–92.

69. For a more detailed discussion of Reid's response to Buffon, see PRLS: 4–9 and Wood 1987: 171–80.

70. AUL MSS 2131/6/V/10a, fol. 1r and 6/IV/1.

71. PRLS: 6, 84.

72. PRLS: 87.

73. PRLS: 12, 26–7.

74. PRLS: 103–24. On natural history in the Glasgow Literary Society, see Emerson and Wood 2002: 103–4.

75. Reid to David Skene, 13 July 1765; Reid to William Creech, 19 May 1778; Reid to ?, 27 January 1789 (C: 39, 103, 203). Reid was also in contact with the printer and natural historian William Smellie; see Smellie 2001 2: 398.

76. Reid to Lord Kames, [November/December 1774].

77. PRLS: 14–15.

78. See, also, PRLS: 16–18, 93–8.

79. Newton 1952: 405.

80. Stewart 1803: 35–41, 56–66; Laudan 1970: 103–31.

81. IHM V.vii: 70; Wood 1989.

82. AUL MS 2131/8/V/1, fol. 2r; EAP III.i–iii. See also Wood 1994: 125–6.

83. EIP V.iv: 373–85; Reid to James Gregory, [spring 1786] (C: 182–3); Wood 1984: 200–12; Wood 1987: 171–3.

84. EIP VI.iv: 457.

85. EQ: 512–13.

86. Reid to James Gregory, 20 August 1790.

87. Daniels 1989; Cantor 1977.

88. IHM VI.xix: 161–6; EIP II.iii: 76–95.

89. EIP I.iii: 47–52.

90. "Of Power," dated 13, March 1792. Compare OP: 7.

91. On Maclaurin and Baxter in relation to Hume, see Russell 1997: 256–7.

92. The clearest statement of Newton's voluntarism is in the "General Scholium" of the *Principia*; Newton 1999: 939–44. Clarke's best known exposition of the metaphysical foundations of the Newtonian system is found in his exchanges with Leibniz; Clarke 1738, 4: 575–735. For Reid's detailed reading notes from Clarke, see AUL MSS 2131/3/II/7–8. Manuscripts dating from 1736 on active power and the will that are related to his notes from Clarke survive in AUL MSS 2131/6/I/34–5. For an exploration of the similarities (and differences) between the views of Clarke and Reid, see Rowe 1991.

3   Reid on Common Sense

Reid held that every sane human being who has emerged from infancy and is not severely impaired mentally shares in common with
all other such human beings certain "principles of common sense,"
as he called them. These principles, so he argued, lie at the foundation of our thought and practice.[1]

The claim proves interesting and challenging in its own right.
However, it seems unlikely that Reid would ever have developed his
doctrine of common sense had he not believed that these principles
play an important and indispensable role in the practice of philosophy. The doctrine of common sense has its home, in Reid's thought,
in his understanding of the limits of philosophical thought and in his
radical picture of the task of the philosopher which emerges from that
understanding.

The philosopher has no option but to join with the rest of humanity in conducting his thinking within the confines of common
sense. He cannot lift himself above the herd. Philosophy "has no
other root but the principles of common sense; it grows out of them,
and draws its nourishment from them; severed from this root, its
honours wither, its sap is dried up, it dies and rots" (IHM I.iv: 19).
Philosophers now and then profess to reject the "principles which
irresistibly govern the belief and conduct of all mankind in the common concerns of life" (IHM I.v: 21). But it turns out that to these
principles "the philosopher himself must yield, after he imagines he
hath confuted them" (ibid.). For "Such principles are older, and of
more authority, than philosophy: she rests upon them as her basis,
not they upon her. If she could overturn them, she must be buried
in their ruins; but all the engines of philosophical subtilty are too
weak for this purpose; and the attempt is no less ridiculous, than if a

mechanic should contrive an *axis in peritrochio* to remove the earth out of its place" (ibid.).

Alternatively, philosophers sometimes insist that it is the calling of the philosopher to *justify* the principles of common sense – not to reject them but to ground them. Close scrutiny shows that this too is a vain attempt; all justification takes for granted one or more of the principles. Philosophical thought, like all thought and practice, rests at bottom not on grounding but on trust.

Let us begin by considering what it is that Reid had in mind by what he called the principles of common sense, and then move on to consider the place in his thought generally of his doctrine of common sense.

I. PRELIMINARY COMMENTS ON COMMON SENSE

Discerning what Reid had in mind by the principles of common sense is no easy matter. In spite of the importance in his own thought of these principles, and the enormous influence of his doctrine of common sense on other thinkers, there is a good deal of wavering and ambiguity in Reid's text when he tells us how to identify the principles. In fact it's my judgment that his doctrine of common sense is the least carefully formulated part of his philosophy – though also one of the most interesting and creative parts.

Let's have some of the principles before us. Reid divides the principles into "first principles of contingent truths" and "first principles of necessary truths." For our purposes it will be sufficient to have before us examples of the former sort; none of the points I wish to make would be altered by bringing examples of the latter into consideration. Reid cites twelve first principles of contingent truths (in EIP VI.v), these twelve seen by him as a mere sampling from the totality of such principles.

1. First, then, I hold, as a first principle, the existence of every thing of which I am conscious.
2. Another first principle, I think, is, that the thoughts of which I am conscious are the thoughts of a being which I call myself, my mind, my person.
3. Another first principle I take to be, that those things did really happen which I distinctly remember.

4. Another first principle is our own personal identity and continued existence, as far back as we remember any thing distinctly.

5. Another first principle is, that those things do really exist
   which we distinctly perceive by our senses, and are what we
   perceive them to be.

6. Another first principle, I think, is, that we have some degree
   of power over our actions, and the determinations of our will.

7. Another first principle is, that the natural faculties, by which
   we distinguish truth from error, are not fallacious.

8. Another first principle relating to existence, is, that there
   is life and intelligence in our fellow men with whom we
   converse.

9. Another first principle I take to be, that certain features of
   the countenance, sounds of the voice, and gestures of the
   body, indicate certain thoughts and dispositions of mind.

10. Another first principle, appears to me to be, that there is a
    certain regard due to human testimony in matters of fact,
    and even to human authority in matters of opinion.

11. There are many events depending upon the will of man, in
    which there is a self-evident probability, greater or less, ac-
    cording to circumstances.

12. The last principle of contingent truths I mention, is, that, in
    the phenomena of nature, what is to be, will probably be like
    to what has been in similar circumstances.

A word about how we are to understand such principles as (1), (3),
and (5). It will seem to most of us that these are not contingently but
necessarily true. Necessarily it is the case that if one is conscious of
something, then it really exists, that if one remembers something,
then it did really happen, and that if one perceives something, then
it does really exist. You and I use "perceive" as a success term: One
perceives only if there does in fact exist an external object that one
perceives. One may *think* that one is perceiving when there exists
no external object that one is perceiving, it may *seem* to one that one
is doing so; but in fact one is not. And so too, *mutatis mutandis*, for
our use of "remember" and "is conscious of."

Clearly Reid is not using these terms that way here. If one perceives, then there is indeed *something* that one perceives. But in

Reid's usage, it may be that that which one perceives does not "really exist" – that is, does not exist as an external object.[2]

It would be fruitless to get into a discussion here as to whether Reid was abusing the language in speaking thus, or into a discussion as to whether it makes sense to think of a nonveridical perception, memory, or act of consciousness as having an object which may or may not "really exist."[3] (Notice that in speaking, quite naturally, of "a nonveridical perception, memory, or act of consciousness," I am not using the terms as success-terms. Perhaps there is more to be said for Reid's usage than initially appears!) More important is to discern what Reid was getting at; and that seems to me clear enough.

As Reid sees it, we human beings have a faculty of perception, a faculty of memory, and a faculty of consciousness. The heart of each of these faculties, on Reid's analysis, consists of a process for the formation of beliefs of a certain sort – beliefs about the external world, beliefs about events in one's own prior experience, beliefs about the contents of one's mental life. About each of these faculties we can raise the question whether it is a reliable source of belief-production. It's not impossible that they might not be reliable; there may be processes of belief-formation in us that produce a high proportion of false beliefs. The claim that that is in fact the case lies at the core of Marx's doctrine of ideology and of Freud's doctrine of rationalization. Reid's thought is that if perception, memory, and consciousness are reliable, that is a contingent fact about them.

Notice, next, that the belief-evoking experiences characteristic of each of these faculties may be distinct or indistinct, clear or hazy, and so forth. Reid, along with all the rest of us who are mentally competent adults, acknowledges that indistinct perceptual experience and hazy memorial experience are not reliable evokers of true beliefs.

Here then, so I suggest, is how the fifth in Reid's list of first principles is to be understood:

It's a first principle that distinct perceptual experience is a reliable producer of true beliefs about external objects.

And so too, *mutatis mutandis*, for the first principle, concerning consciousness, and the third, concerning memory.

But what is it that is being said, when it is claimed that these are principles of common sense? Reid observes that "in common language, sense always implies judgment. A man of sense is a man of judgment. Good sense is good judgment.... Common Sense is that degree of judgment which is common to men with whom we can converse and transact business" (EIP VI.ii: 424). In short, "sense, in its most common, and therefore its most proper meaning, signifies *judgment*, though philosophers often use it in another meaning. From this it is natural to think, that common sense should mean common judgment; and so it really does" (EIP VI.ii: 426–7).

The passage is instructive in one regard, somewhat misleading in a second, and ambiguous in a third. It's instructive in that Reid does not identify some special faculty as *the faculty of common sense* – i.e., the faculty that yields principles of common sense. Common sense for Reid is not some special sense.

What is somewhat misleading in the passage is that, after introducing the idea of *good sense*, and explaining that in terms of a person of *good judgment*, Reid proceeds to whittle away a good deal of what's included in our ordinary notion of a person of good judgment. One does not have to be a person of good judgment to conduct oneself in accord with the principles of common sense; foolish people do so as well. Common sense is shared by all those "with whom we can converse and transact business." As will become clear, Reid thinks we can converse and transact business, in the relevant way, with all who are not infants, deranged, or severely impaired mentally.

Last, the ambiguity. Common sense, for Reid, has to do with judgment. But our English word "judgment" is notoriously ambiguous as between *an act of judging* and *the content of an act of judging*. So does common sense have to do with acts of judging or with the propositional content of such acts? I could cite some passages in which Reid quite clearly has his eye on certain shared faculties of judgment-formation when speaking of principles of common sense.[4] However, if we take Reid's list of twelve first principles of contingent truths as strong evidence for what he had in mind by principles of common sense – as I think we should – then it's clear that the principles of common sense are not certain faculties of judgment-formation shared by all those "with whom we can converse and transact business" but certain propositions, or sorts of propositions, that all such people judge to be true, in what we shall see to be some rather wide sense of the word "judge." Naturally Reid might then be taking common sense itself, in distinction from its principles, as whatever it is in us that produces those principles.

So how do we go about identifying, from among the propositions or sorts of propositions that all sane and mentally adequate persons who have emerged from infancy judge to be true, those that are principles of common sense? My contention will be that two, quite different, lines of thought on this matter were in conflict in Reid's mind. Sometimes he thinks of the principles of common sense as *first principles of our reasoning*; at other times he thinks of them as *things taken for granted* in the living of our everyday lives. Let me articulate these two lines of thought, beginning with the former. That done, I will then consider whether there is any good reason for regarding one of these as more suitable for Reid's overall purposes than the other.

II. PRINCIPLES OF COMMON SENSE AS FIRST PRINCIPLES OF REASONING

A few pages after offering the rather loose definition of common sense that we just scrutinized, Reid offers a somewhat more articulate definition: "We ascribe to reason two offices, or two degrees. The first is to judge of things self-evident, the second to draw conclusions that are not self-evident from those that are. The first of these is the province, and the sole province of common sense; and therefore it coincides with reason in its [i.e., common sense's] whole extent, and is only another name for one branch or one degree of reason" (EIP VI.ii: 433).

I asserted above that Reid does not hold that there is some special faculty of belief – or judgment – formation which is the faculty of common sense. This passage appears to be a straightforward refutation of that claim: Reason, in its capacity of judging "of things self-evident," is said to be the "province of common sense." The passage is puzzling in an important way, however.

Two chapters later, in reflecting on the relation between judgment and evidence, Reid observes that judgment "is carried along necessarily by the evidence, real or seeming, which appears to us at the time" (EIP VI.iv: 452). He then observes that in some cases the proposition "has the light of truth in itself," whereas in other cases it has to borrow its evidence from another proposition. The former are of course the self-evident propositions. In fact, Reid proceeds immediately to formulate his concept of *the self-evident*. To all intents and purposes it's the traditional formulation. Self-evident propositions are "no sooner understood than they are believed. The judgment follows the apprehension of them necessarily . . . ; the proposition is not deduced or inferred from another; it has the light of truth in itself, and has no occasion to borrow it from another" (EIP VI.ii: 452).

Just a few chapters later Reid again distinguishes between the evidence which a proposition has in itself and the evidence which it borrows from another proposition. "It is demonstrable," he says,

and was long ago demonstrated by ARISTOTLE, that every proposition to which we give a rational assent, must either have its evidence in itself, or derive it from some antecedent proposition. And the same thing may be said of the antecedent proposition. As, therefore, we cannot go back to antecedent propositions without end, the evidence must at last rest upon propositions, one or more, which have their evidence in themselves, that is, upon first principles. (EIP VI.vii: 522)

What's puzzling is this: Unless we (not very plausibly) understand "having its evidence in itself" as a mere synonym of "not having its evidence in another proposition," the distinction that Reid here presents as exhaustive is shown by his own theories of perception, memory, and consciousness, not to be exhaustive. A proposition may have its evidence in something other than a proposition – in some experience, for example – hence neither in itself nor in another proposition. Suppose that, with all my faculties working properly in an appropriate environment, the perceptual belief is formed immediately (noninferentially) in me that there is something green before me. Believing the proposition is surely an example of "rational assent," to use Reid's phrase. But does it have its evidence in itself? It certainly does not satisfy the concept of a self-evident truth: a proposition that is "no sooner understood than believed." Its evidence consists of what Reid, in other places, calls "the evidence of sense." The evidence for it is neither the proposition itself nor some other proposition but the sensory experience one is having.

So I suggest a modification of Reid's way of identifying, in these passages, the principles of common sense. Principles of common sense are indeed to be found among those propositions that are believed immediately, i.e., not on the basis of inference; on this point, there is no ambiguity whatsoever. More particularly, principles of common sense are to be found among those that people believe immediately *for which they have adequate evidence* – evidence that makes their assent to them rational. That evidence may be evidence that the proposition has in itself, or nonpropositional evidence of some sort. In short, principles of common sense are to be found among beliefs held immediately and rationally – i.e., with good evidence.

Clearly something in addition must be said if we are to capture Reid's thought, however. I now believe, immediately and with good evidence, that my leg is bent at the knee. No one else believes this, though. Yet Reid's principles of common sense are *common*. So are the principles of common sense those propositions that we *all* believe immediately and with evidence? Or is it some more abstract form of commonality that Reid has in mind, so that that belief of mine about my leg, while not itself shared by anyone else, nonetheless possesses the requisite form of commonality? This is an issue that can best be discussed somewhat later.

We have focused thus far on what it is in our mental life that Reid wants to pick out as principles of common sense. In calling them "first" principles, Reid is alluding to their role, as he sees it, in our mental life. That role is well summarized in the following passages. Beliefs that are held immediately and with evidence,

> when they are used in matters of science, have commonly been called *axioms*; and on whatever occasion they are used, are called *first principles, principles of common sense, common notions, self-evident truths.* (EIP VI.iv: 452)

All knowledge got by reasoning must be built upon first principles.

> This is as certain as that every house must have a foundation.... When we examine ... the evidence of any proposition, either we find it self-evident, or it rests upon one or more propositions that support it. The same thing may be said of the propositions that support it; and of those that support them, as far back as we can go. But we cannot go back in this track to infinity. Where then must this analysis stop? It is evident that it must stop only when we come to propositions, which support all that are built upon them, but are themselves supported by none, that is, to self-evident propositions. (EIP VI.iv: 454–5)[5]

III. PRINCIPLES OF COMMON SENSE AS THINGS TAKEN FOR GRANTED

Now for the other line of thought, according to which the principles of common sense are those things that we all do and must take for granted in our lives in the everyday. In a passage in the *Inquiry* Reid says this:

> If there are certain principles, as I think there are, which the constitution of
> our nature leads us to believe, and which we are under a necessity to take for
> granted in the common concerns of life, without being able to give a reason
> for them; these are what we call the principles of common sense; and what
> is manifestly contrary to them, is what we call absurd. (IHM II.vi: 33)

On the things-taken-for-granted line of thought, the twelve principles of contingent truths that we quoted from Reid, along with the
principles of necessary truths, are to be interpreted as if they had
the preface, "We all do and must take for granted in our lives in the
everyday . . . ," with the "all" being understood, as usual for Reid, as
short for "all sane persons who have emerged from infancy and are
mentally adequate." For example, the third in Reid's listing is to be
interpreted as if it read, "We all do and must take for granted, in our
lives in the everyday, that those things did really happen which I distinctly remember." Quite obviously the statement of the principle,
if it's to be true, needs considerably more qualifiers than the "distinctly" that Reid attaches; most of us learn to distrust even distinct
memories of certain sorts. I judge that it would prove extremely difficult, if not impossible, to insert all the necessary qualifiers. Why
that is so, and why it is relatively unimportant for Reid's point, will
become clear shortly.

In addition to the basic theme of things taken "for granted in
the common concerns of life," four points are worth singling out
for attention in the above passage. One important feature of principles of common sense is that we are not "able to give a reason for"
these things.[6] What Reid emphasizes rather more often than that we
are incapable of giving reasons, is that we do not in fact hold them
for reasons. Thus what Reid offered as a *defining* characteristic of
principles of common sense, on the first-principles-of-reasoning interpretation, he here offers as an observation about the role in our
reasoning of things we take for granted in everyday life.

> Suppose a man's house to be broke open, his money and jewels taken away.
> Such things have happened times innumerable without any apparent cause;
> and were he only to reason from experience in such a case, how must he
> behave? He must put in one scale the instances wherein a cause was found
> of such an event, and in the other scale, the instances wherein no cause
> was found, and the preponderant scale must determine, whether it be most

probable that there was a cause of this event, or that there was none. Would any man of common understanding have recourse to such an experiment to direct his judgment?

Suppose a man to be found dead on the highway, his skull fractured, his body pierced with deadly wounds, his watch and money carried off. The coroner's jury sits upon the body, and the question is put, what was the cause of this man's death ... ? Let us suppose an adept in Mr. HUME's philosophy to make one of the jury, and that he insists upon the previous question, whether there was any cause of the event; or whether it happened without a cause?

Surely, upon Mr. HUME's principles, a great deal might be said upon this point.... But we may venture to say, that, if Mr. HUME had been of such a jury, he would have laid aside his philosophical principles, and acted according to the dictates of common prudence. (EIP VI.vi: 502)

A second feature of principles of common sense is that "what is manifestly contrary to them, is what we call absurd." What's contrary is indeed false, on Reid's view; but in calling them "absurd," we are saying something else than that they are false. Should a sane person single out one or another principle of common sense and profess to doubt it, then, realizing that reasoning will get us nowhere – his professed doubt will outweigh any contrary considerations we might adduce – we call what he says "absurd" and treat him with gentle ridicule:

opinions that contradict first principles are distinguished from other errors by this; ... they are not only false, but absurd: And, to discountenance absurdity, Nature hath given us a particular emotion, to wit, that of ridicule, which seems intended for this very purpose of putting out of countenance what is absurd, either in opinion or practice.

This weapon, when properly applied, cuts with as keen an edge as argument. Nature has furnished us with the first to expose absurdity; as with the last to refute error. (EIP VI.iv: 462)

And what if we come across a person whom we judge to be actually doubting certain principles of common sense – not just professing to doubt them but *actually* doubting them? All "men that have a common understanding ... consider [such] a man as lunatic, or destitute of common sense" (EIP I.ii: 39). We neither reason with such a person nor subject him to ridicule but get him treatment. If "any man were found of so strange a turn as not to believe his own eyes; to put no trust in his senses, nor have the least regard to their testimony; would any man think it worth while to reason gravely with such a person, and, by argument, to convince him of his error? Surely no wise man would" (ibid). He would instead be "clapped into a mad-house" (IHM VI.xx: 170).

The difference between professing to doubt certain principles of common sense and actually doubting them is obviously significant, as witnessed by our different treatment of the two cases: ridicule versus treatment. Nonetheless the similarity between professed lunacy and genuine lunacy is not to be overlooked. "When a man suffers himself to be reasoned out of the principles of common sense, by metaphysical arguments, we may call this *metaphysical lunacy* which differs from the other species of the distemper in this, that it is not continued, but intermittent: it is apt to seize the patient in solitary and speculative moments; but when he enters into society, Common Sense recovers her authority" (IHM VII: 215–16).

A third, related, feature of principles of common sense is that we "are under a necessity to take" these things for granted. In that way they are for us indubitable. We may think we doubt them, say we doubt them; but our behavior indicates otherwise. "[T]hose who reject [some principle of common sense] in speculation, find themselves under a necessity of being governed by it in their practice" (EIP VI.v: 480). A skeptic "may struggle hard to disbelieve the information of his senses, as a man does to swim against a torrent; but ah! it is in vain.... For after all, when his strength is spent in the fruitless attempt, he will be carried down the torrent with the common herd of believers" (IHM VI.xx: 169). A qualification must be understood. This is true for *normal* adults. As we have seen, persons suffering from some severe mental disorder do sometimes genuinely doubt some principle of common sense.

Before moving on to the last point to be singled out for attention in the passage quoted, let me cite a feature of common sense and its principles that Reid often discusses but happens not to mention in this particular passage. "In most men [common sense] produces its effect without ever being attended to, or made an object of thought" (EIP VI.v: 482). The principles have to be extracted from practice; and that's a fallible enterprise. For one thing, the "precise limits ... which divide common judgment from what is beyond it on the one hand, and from what falls short of it on the other, may be difficult to determine..." (EIP VI.ii: 427). More generally: "it is not impossible, that what is only a vulgar prejudice may be mistaken for a first principle. Nor is it impossible, that what is really a first principle may, by the enchantment of words, have such a mist thrown about it, as to hide its evidence, and to make a man of candour doubt of it" (EIP I.ii: 41). What Reid nowhere mentions is what seems to me the most important source of mistakes in identification of principles of common sense, understood as things taken for granted: The subtlety of our practices makes it extraordinarily difficult to identify and formulate with full accuracy what we all take for granted in our employment of those practices. Be that as it may, Reid offers a number of rules of thumb to help us in the difficult project of accurately identifying principles of common sense.[7]

The last point to be singled out for attention in the passage quoted is of a different order from the preceding ones. What we have noted thus far is the features that Reid ascribes to principles of common sense. This last point does not single out an additional such feature but expresses Reid's view as to why it is that we all take for granted, in our lives in the everyday, what we do there take for granted: The "constitution of our nature" leads us to do so.

IV. WHICH LINE OF THOUGHT IS TO BE PREFERRED?

There's no need to belabor the point that thinking of the principles of common sense as first principles in our reasoning, and thinking of them as things we all do and must take for granted in our everyday lives, are two very different ways of thinking of them. What is perhaps not obvious is that these two ways of thinking yield different sets of principles. If that were not the case, we could declare that these two ways of thinking highlight two quite different functions played in our lives by the same principles, and leave it there.

Presumably everything that a person believes immediately and with evidence is also taken for granted by her in the living of her life in the everyday: elementary propositions of logic and mathematics are examples. But the converse is definitely not true. We take for granted all sorts of things that we never bring to the point of being something that we believe; one does not have to believe something to take it for granted. Taking a proposition for granted is a different propositional attitude from believing it; one can do the former, with respect to a certain proposition, without doing the latter.

Second, if anybody did manage to extract one of these propositions taken for granted by her life in the everyday, and now, having extracted it, to believe it, surely she would not believe it immediately. Her belief would have emerged from a lengthy process of reflection and be based on a variety of considerations. And third, many of the things we take for granted do not function as beliefs on the basis of which we believe other things; they are not "principles, upon which I build all my reasoning" (IHM V.vii: 72). They are background and substratum for our beliefs, not basis.

In a passage that occurs in his discussion of his seventh principle of contingent truths, the one which says that "the natural faculties, by which we distinguish truth from error, are not fallacious," Reid himself takes note of the first of these points, and hints at the second:

We may here take notice of a property of the principle under consideration, that seems to be common to it with many other first principles, and which can hardly be found in any principle that is built solely upon reasoning; and that is, that in most men it produces its effect without ever being attended to, or made an object of thought. No man ever thinks of this principle, unless when he considers the grounds of skepticism; yet it invariably governs his opinions. When a man in the common course of life gives credit to the testimony of his senses, his memory, or his reason, he does not put the question to himself, whether these faculties may deceive him; yet the trust he reposes in them supposes an inward conviction, that, in that instance at least, they do not deceive him.

It is another property of this and of many first principles, that they force assent in particular instances, more powerfully than when they are turned into a general proposition.... Many have in general maintained that the senses are fallacious, yet there never was found a man so skeptical as not to trust his senses in particular instances when his safety required it; and it may be observed of those who have professed skepticism, that their skepticism lies in generals, while in particulars they are no less dogmatical than others. (EIP VI.v: 481–2)

Given that Reid thinks of the principles of common sense along these two very different lines, as propositions believed immediately and with adequate evidence that serve as first principles in our reasoning, and as things taken for granted in our everyday lives, and given, in addition, that not everything of the latter sort is also of the former sort, the interpreter of Reid is more or less forced to address two questions: Which of these two lines of thought should Reid have preferred, and why did he himself not take note of their difference?

The consideration most relevant to answering the former question is the use to which Reid proposed putting his doctrine of common sense. As I mentioned at the beginning, Reid's doctrine of common sense finds its home in his understanding of the limits of philosophical thought, and in the new and radical picture of the philosopher's task that he articulates in the light of that understanding. It's clear that, as Reid's philosophical career progressed, common sense became a matter of interest to him in its own right; that sort of thing happens often to philosophers. Nonetheless, I would say that even in his late work, *Essays on the Intellectual Powers*, it remains the case that what is for him most important about the doctrine is that it is an essential element in his picture of the philosopher's task.

We have not yet looked at what Reid says about the philosopher's task; so the answer I give here has to be proleptic. But I would say that when we look at Reid's doctrine of common sense from the angle of the use to which he puts it in his understanding of the philosopher's task, it becomes decisively clear that what he needs for that purpose is the things-taken-for-granted line of thought. The first-principles-in-our-reasoning line is a thoroughly traditional line of thought. Reid quotes Aristotle as one who had already claimed that every proposition to which we give "rational assent" either is itself believed immediately, or is believed ultimately on the basis of things believed immediately. Whether or not this foundationalist picture of things believed with evidence – "rational assent" – is correct, is an issue that has been much debated in recent years. What's not debatable is that it was in Reid's day already a very traditional picture. By contrast, the things-taken-for-granted line of thought was not at all traditional; Reid quotes no predecessors. It was this new line of thought that he needed for his purposes.

Of course there are similarities between these two ways of thinking of the principles of common sense. Nonetheless, the differences are striking. So why did Reid not sort out the differences between the two, as I have done – given that for his overall purposes the line of thought he needed was not the first-principles-in-our-reasoning line but the things-taken-for-granted line? Assuming that he was not just an incompetent blunderer, there must have been something in his thought that made it difficult for him to untangle the two lines and set the first-principles-in-our reasoning line off to the side as not relevant to his purposes. What might that have been?

My speculation is that the clue is there before us, in the passage I quoted for the things-taken-for-granted line of thought, in the clause, "which the constitution of our nature leads us to believe." Reid never so much as asked himself whether the things we all do and must take for granted are thereby *believed* by us; he simply assumed that they were. Given that assumption, his general doctrine of belief-formation then went to work. He had elaborately argued, in opposition to his predecessors, that perceptual and memorial beliefs are formed immediately, but that our assent to them is nonetheless "rational assent," assent with evidence. So where, then, are the things taken for granted to be found, in the set of propositions believed immediately but with evidence, or in the set of those believed on the evidence of other believed propositions? Obviously not in the latter set; hence, in the former. Things taken for granted are things believed immediately.

It is my own judgment that the only way out of this impasse is to conclude that taking for granted is a propositional attitude different from belief; in some cases one believes that which one takes for granted, in other cases, one does not. Accordingly, any views one may have about those faculties in our constitution which account for belief-formation simply do not account for how and why it is that we take such-and-such things for granted; they don't apply.[8] Unfortunately, I cannot here point to an articulate account of the propositional attitude of *taking for granted*; to the best of my knowledge, no one has ever developed such an account. It remains an item on the philosophical agenda.

V. AN AMBIGUITY IN REID'S STATEMENT OF THE PRINCIPLES

In a recent article, "Reid on the First Principles of Contingent Truths," James Van Cleve calls attention to an important ambiguity in Reid's formulation of his contingent principles of common sense.[9] Let me introduce the ambiguity by initially following Van Cleve in thinking and speaking of the principles as first principles in our reasoning,[10] rather than as things we take for granted, and by focusing on the epistemological principles (i.e., principles 1, 3, 5, 7, and

10 in Reid's listing). I will then consider whether the points made can be generalized from the epistemological to the ontological principles; and last, I will consider what emerges when we think of the principles as things we take for granted rather than as first principles in our reasoning.

Consider the first principle on Reid's list:

1. First, then, I hold, as a first principle, the existence of every thing of which I am conscious.

To get to his disambiguation, Van Cleve proposes that we shift from speaking of "things" to speaking of beliefs.[11] Then we get these two variants (my formulation is a bit different from Van Cleve's):

1.1. It is a first principle that, for every person, every belief evoked by and expressing what that person introspects as being the case, is true.

1.2. For every person, every belief evoked by and expressing what that person introspects as being the case, is a first principle for that person.

The first of these disambiguations – Van Cleve calls it the *generalist* interpretation – declares it to be a first principle that all the deliverances of introspection (consciousness) are true; the second, which he calls the *particularist* interpretation, declares all the deliverances of introspection to be first principles.

Which of these two interpretations is to be preferred? Van Cleve makes a firm choice for the latter interpretation, on the ground that what are there said to be first principles are indeed held immediately and with evidence, whereas that is not true for what the generalist interpretation says is a first principle. I think Van Cleve is right on both counts; but I am dubious that that is enough to make all the principles cited in 1.2 into first principles of *common sense* for Reid. To be a first principle of reasoning, it is sufficient that a proposition be believed immediately and with good evidence by someone or other; to be a first principle of *common sense*, it must be believed by all of us who are sane adults. What 1.2 cites as first principles, are thus not first principles of *common sense*. *My* faculty of consciousness produces in me, immediately and rationally, beliefs concerning what is going on in my mental life, *your* faculty produces in you, immediately and rationally, beliefs about what is going on in your consciousness, and so forth. What is common to us is not any of the believed propositions, but only the fact that each of us has a faculty of consciousness which produces in each of us immediate and rational beliefs that can function as first principles in the reasoning of each of us. But 1.2 does not declare that shared faculty to be a first principle, nor indeed does 1.1.

Moreover, 1.1 does not even qualify as a first principle, let alone as a principle of common sense. Very few people have ever believed what is expressed by this principle; a few philosophers, and that's about it. And they will not have come to believe it immediately but by thinking about it for a while, wondering whether there are counterexamples to it, and so forth. Add that if the phenomenon of consciousness offered us no other first principle than what is claimed to be such in 1.1, it would offer us far too few first principles to support our reasoning on associated matters. Exactly the same considerations apply to the other epistemological principles.

The second item on Reid's list of contingent principles is ontological:

2. It is a first principle that the thoughts of which I am conscious are the thoughts of a being which I call myself (my mind, my person).

Let us apply a Van Cleve style of disambiguation:

2.1. It is a first principle that, for every person and every thought, if that person is conscious of that thought, then that thought is a thought of the being which that person calls "me."
2.2. For every person and every thought, if that person is conscious of that thought, then it is a first principle that it is a thought of the being which that person calls "me."

The reasons we offered for concluding that what 1.1 claims to be a first principle of common sense is not even a first principle are reasons for drawing the same conclusion about 2.1. Relatively few people have ever believed what 2.1 says is a first principle; those who have will not have done so immediately; and if the phenomenon in question yielded only this one principle to function as a first principle in our reasoning, it would yield far too few first principles for our reasoning.

But what 2.2 declares to be first principles, are also not that, though for a somewhat different reason. Where 2.1 claims just one highly general proposition to be a first principle, 2.2 claims a host of particular principles to be first principles, such as the following:

This thought here, of which I am conscious, is a thought of the being that I call "me"; that thought there, of which Joe is conscious, is a thought of the being that Joe calls "me"; and so forth. But these, as they stand, are purely ontological propositions, not first principles. No proposition is ever a first principle as such; it is a first principle *for* one or more persons, and then only if they believe it immediately and with evidence.

Suppose, now, that instead of taking Reid's first and second principles as claims concerning first principles of our reasoning, we take them as claims concerning what we take for granted; let us then apply to them a Van Cleve style of disambiguation. From Reid's first epistemological principle we get these disambiguations:

1.3. We all take for granted that every object of a person's consciousness exists.

1.4. For every person and every object of that person's consciousness, that person takes for granted the existence of that object of consciousness.

No doubt Reid thought that the latter thesis is true. But the things that this thesis declares to be things taken for granted are definitely not things that we all do and must take for granted in the living of our lives in the everyday; the test of commonality is once again failed. By contrast, when we turn to the generalist disambiguation, thesis 1.3, we finally light upon something that fits what Reid says. Reid did think that we each take for granted that every object of a person's consciousness exists.

Let us apply the same treatment to the first of Reid's ontological principles. The disambiguation yields the following interpretations:

2.3. We all take for granted that, for every person and every thought, if that person is conscious of that thought, then it is a thought of the being which that person calls "me."

2.4. For every person and every thought, if that person is conscious of that thought, then he takes for granted that it is a thought of the being which he calls "me."

There can be no doubt, given Reid's analysis of how consciousness works as a belief-forming faculty, that he did hold 2.4. But since the things said to be taken for granted in 2.4 are not shared in common, 2.4, like all our other particularist disambiguations, does not give us principles of *common sense*. 2.3 does exactly that.

What emerges from these reflections on the disambiguation of the first two of Reid's contingent principles – the first, an epistemological principle, the second, an ontological – is that when we interpret those principles as specifying things taken for granted, the generalist disambiguation gives us something that fits what Reid requires of a principle of common sense, whereas when we interpret them as specifying first principles in our reasoning, neither disambiguation gives us something that fits. This is another reason for giving priority to the things-we-take-for-granted line in our interpretation of Reid on common sense.

VI. THE ROLE OF COMMON SENSE IN PHILOSOPHY

What remains to consider is the use to which Reid put his doctrine of common sense. European and American academics and intellectuals were abuzz with talk about common sense in the latter part of the eighteenth century. Manfred Kuehn's book, *Scottish Common Sense in Germany, 1768–1800*, shows decisively that, contrary to what has long been thought to be the case, Germany was no exception to this generalization.[12] Kuehn shows that Immanuel Kant was no exception, in spite of the well-known denigrating remarks about common sense that Kant makes at the beginning of the *Prolegomena*. What emerges from Kuehn's discussion is a sense not only of the extraordinary popularity of appeals to common sense, but of the very different ways in which different thinkers employed that appeal. My concern here will be exclusively with Reid.

To understand the use Reid made of his doctrine of common sense, one must attend, first, to his attack on the skeptic.[13] Skepticism comes in many forms; whenever we come upon a defense of skepticism or an attack thereon, we must ask what the writer understands by a skeptic. Reid's skeptic has in mind a certain understanding of the philosopher's role in culture – of the philosopher's high calling. Reid describes that high calling thus: "That our thoughts, our sensations, and every thing else of which we are conscious, hath a real existence, is admitted in this system [of skepticism] as a first principle; but every thing else must be made evident by the light of reason. Reason must rear the whole fabric of knowledge upon this single principle of consciousness" (IHM VII: 210). Given this understanding, the skeptic issues to the philosopher such injunctions as the one that comes to expression in the following passage. The skeptic asks of the philosopher, "Why do you believe in the existence of the external object which you perceive?" And then he adds: "There is nothing so shameful in a philosopher as to be deceived and deluded; and therefore you ought to resolve firmly to withhold assent, and to throw off all this belief of external objects, which may be all delusion" (IHM VI.xx: 168–9).

Those who have followed, even at a distance, discussions in epistemology of the past thirty years or so, will recognize, at a glance, that Reid's skeptic is a person who holds that philosophers should so organize their doxastic life (doxa=belief, in Greek) as to bring it about that it satisfies the demands of what has come to be called "classically modern foundationalism." It is the philosopher's high calling to empty his head of all beliefs except those immediate beliefs that are the deliverances of reason or of consciousness, and those mediate beliefs that are securely grounded in those deliverances.[14]

Reid's rejection of the skeptic's injunction to the philosopher is discussed in other essays in this collection.[15] What is important for us to note is the use he makes of his doctrine of common sense in his new understanding of the philosopher's task. Philosophers are related to the principles of common sense in the same way everybody else is – and in the same way that he, the philosopher, is related when not engaged in philosophy. The philosopher does and must take these principles for granted – in his posing questions to his fellow philosophers, in his raising doubts, in his offering reasons, in his putting pen to paper. Common sense is and must be the background of all his activity – not, for the most part, the premises from which he draws his conclusions, but the ever-present substratum of his philosophizing. One could put it like this: "though common sense and my external senses demand my assent to their dictates upon their own authority, ... philosophy is not entitled to this privilege" (EIP II.xiv 179). Or to quote again one of the passages with which I began: Philosophy is like all other human endeavors in that it "has no other root but the principles of common sense; it grows out of them, and draws its nourishment from them: severed from this root, its honours wither, its sap is dried up, it dies and rots" (IHM I.iv: 19).

Did Reid think it was possible that something we do and must take for granted might nonetheless be false? To the best of my knowledge, he nowhere addresses that question head on. I think it's clear how his answer would go, however. Over and over he emphasized that the actual workings of our belief-forming faculties are a matter of pure contingency, in the sense that our essential nature remaining what it is, those faculties might have worked differently. The same experiences might have triggered different beliefs, the same beliefs might have been triggered by different experiences. Hence there is nothing in our nature which guarantees that our faculties are reliable. When we bring God into the picture, however, something additional must be said. Though God could have brought it about that our faculties worked differently from how they do in fact work, our nature remaining the same, God's trustworthiness implies that, however they work, overall they are reliable.

This does not imply that we never fall into error; obviously we do – though Reid is always quick to observe that whenever we conclude that we were in error, we are perforce taking for granted the reliability of certain of our faculties. So might it be that a philosopher would succeed in showing that some component in what we do and must take for granted is in fact false? Reid was certainly not of the view that we should simply avert our gaze from any philosopher who argues against some component of common sense; he speaks often of how much he has learned from Hume. The question is whether there is any chance that what we might learn is that some component of what we do and must take for granted is in fact false.

Confronted with any such piece of reasoning, Reid is strongly inclined to conclude that we were mistaken in thinking that the items in question were things we do and must take for granted, rather than that, though they are things we do and must take for granted, they are false. But there is at least one passage in which he appears to countenance the more radical possibility. After remarking that deep grammar is sometimes a clue to what we do and must take for granted, he says this:

A Philosopher is, no doubt, entitled to examine even those distinctions that are to be found in the structure of all languages; and, if he is able to shew that there is no foundation for them in the nature of the things distinguished; if he can point out some prejudice common to mankind which has led them to distinguish things that are not really different; in that case, such a distinction may be imputed to a vulgar error, which ought to be corrected in philosophy. But when, in his first setting out, he takes it for granted, without proof, that distinctions found in the structure of all languages, have no foundation in nature; this surely is too fastidious a way of treating the common sense of mankind. When we come to be instructed by Philosophers, we must bring the old light of common sense along with us, and by it judge of the new light which the Philosopher communicates to us.... There may be distinctions that have a real foundation, and which may be necessary in philosophy, which are not made in the common language, because not necessary in the common business of life. But, I believe, no instance will be found of a distinction made in all languages, which has not a just foundation in nature. (EIP I.i: 26–7)

I take Reid to be saying that though he himself is of the view that whatever we take for granted in accord with the deep structure of our language is true, nonetheless he is open to the possibility of some philosopher showing that here or there it is false or confused. If that is in fact what he is saying, then the way to think of his understanding of the role of common sense within philosophy is that it is a doctrine concerning *burden of proof* in philosophy.

I judge that philosophers do in fact regard the burden of proof in philosophical discourse as resting exactly where Reid's view implies that it rests. The burden of proof rests upon the person who wants to oppose some element of common sense – for example, on the philosopher who holds that there are no external objects, not on the one who holds that there are. The burden of proof can in principle be borne in a particular case; but if so, the philosopher, in bearing the burden, will tacitly be accepting other components of common sense. Seen in this light, Reid's disagreement with his fellow philosophers lies in his judgment that they have not borne the burden of proof when they think they have.

Genuinely to doubt the principles of common sense is to be mad, insane. Much of philosophy wears the *semblance* of madness. The ordinary person, hearing the opinions of certain philosophers, "can conceive no otherwise of [such opinions], than as a kind of metaphysical lunacy; and concludes, that too much learning is apt to make men mad; and that the man who seriously entertains [these beliefs], though in other respects he may be a very good man, as a man may be who believes that he is made of glass; yet surely he hath a soft place in his understanding, and hath been hurt by much thinking" (IHM V.vii: 68).

But it's only pretence. Philosophers are not really mad. In "all the history of philosophy, we never read of any skeptic that ever stepped into fire or water because he did not believe his senses ..." (EIP II.v: 99). So the appropriate response to the philosopher is the same as the appropriate response to any sane person who professes to doubt fundamental components of common sense: not argument but gentle ridicule.

Let not the philosopher who is the subject of such ridicule mistake the point thereof. In the course of his discussion of Hume, Reid says, "I beg therefore ... that no offence may be taken at charging this or other metaphysical notions with absurdity, or with being contrary to the common sense of mankind. No disparagement is meant to the understandings of the authors or maintainers of such opinions.... [T]he reasoning that leads to them, often gives new light to the subject, and shows real genius and deep penetration in the author, and the premises do more than atone for the conclusion" (IHM II.vi: 33).

NOTES

1. I discussed Reid's doctrine of common sense in Chapter IX of Wolterstorff 2001. A few passages in what follows have been lifted almost verbatim from that earlier discussion. On some points of detail my discussion here diverges from, and is (in my judgment) an improvement on, that in the book. In addition, I explore some issues here that I ignored in the book.

2. The passage is not idiosyncratic with respect to this way of using the terms; Reid speaks thus in a good many other places as well. See my discussion in Wolterstorff 2001: 124ff.

3. I do discuss the latter of these issues in the passage cited in the preceding footnote.

4. Or certain shared faculties of *belief*-formation. Though Reid speaks, in general, much more of belief than of judgment, he tends to use the words "belief" and "judgment" interchangeably.

5. On the interpretation offered above, Reid should have said "to propositions believed immediately and rationally" instead of "to self-evident propositions."

6. Sometimes Reid speaks more cautiously and says that they "do not admit of *direct* proof" (EIP I. ii: 39, my italics).

7. See especially EIP VI.iv: 461ff.

8. Though Wittgenstein in *On Certainty* regularly speaks of things taken for granted as *beliefs*, he nonetheless thinks that it's not the indigenous belief-forming faculties of our constitution that account for our holding these beliefs. No doubt what contributes to this view is his reluctance

ever to appeal to our constitution. In Chapter IX of Wolterstorff 2001 I discuss, at some length, the striking similarities between Reid's and Wittgenstein's discussion of what we all do and must take for granted. What Reid calls "the principles of common sense," on the things-taken-for-granted line of thought, Wittgenstein calls "our shared world picture."

9. Van Cleve 1999.
10. Which is how Reid himself speaks of them when he lists the principles in EIP VI.v.
11. Reid's own thought on this matter is that consciousness, like the other faculties of immediate-belief formation, is a faculty whose activation consists in awareness of (acquaintance with) some entity and the formation of a belief whose content is a *de re* proposition about that entity. Reid's formulation of the first principle emphasizes the former side of the activation, Van Cleve's reformulation the latter side.
12. Kuehn 1987.
13. I give a much fuller account of Reid's attack on the skeptic in Chapter VIII of Wolterstorff 2001.
14. It's clear from Kuehn's discussion that a great many German philosophers of the latter part of the eighteenth century accepted this understanding of the calling of the philosopher. After professing to embrace common sense, they go on to say that it is the duty of the philosopher to *justify* the common sense of the multitude. Close scrutiny of the justifications they attempt to give makes it clear that justification, as they understand it, must make do with nothing more than the deliverances of reason and consciousness. Kant is a good example of the point.
15. See the essays by Greco, Van Cleve, and Falkenstein.

4   Reid's Theory of Perception

Perception bulks large in Reid's published writings. Nearly all of the *Inquiry into the Human Mind* is devoted to it, with chapters allotted to each of the senses of Smelling, Hearing, Tasting, Touch, and Seeing. And in the *Essays on the Intellectual Powers of Man*, by far the longest essay is Essay II, "Of the Powers we Have by Means of our External Senses." The main theme of this chapter is Reid's attack on the reigning "way of ideas" and his attempt to put in its place a direct realist theory of perception. Also covered are Reid's distinction between sensation and perception, his views on primary and secondary qualities, his nativism about our conceptions of hardness and extension, and his treatment of the phenomenon of acquired perception.

I. CRITIQUE OF THE THEORY OF IDEAS

Almost alone among the great modern philosophers, Reid sought to uphold a direct realist theory of perception. He repudiated the theory of ideas, the central tenet of which is that the object immediately present to the mind is never an external thing, but only an internal image, sense datum, representation, or (to use the most common eighteenth-century term) idea. Ideas were conceived of as mental entities that existed only as long as there was awareness of them. Some proponents of the theory of ideas (such as Descartes and Locke) were realists, conceiving of physical objects as things distinct from ideas that cause ideas of them to arise in our minds. Others (such as Berkeley) were idealists, repudiating the existence of a world outside the mind and believing that the things we call physical objects are simply bundles of ideas. In either case, the theory of ideas cuts us off from direct perception of the external world – either because there is no external world to be perceived, or because our "perception" of it is not strictly perception at all, according to Reid, but inference based on what we do perceive, namely, ideas.

Reid makes at least three important points against the theory of ideas. First, the arguments in favor of the theory are weak and without cogency. Second, the theory does nothing to explain how perception is possible. Third, the theory stands in the way of our knowing or even being able to conceive of the physical world.

In the fourteenth chapter of book two of the *Intellectual Powers*, "Reflections on the Common Theory of Ideas," Reid criticizes several arguments for the existence of ideas. One such argument is the "no action at a distance" argument, which may be put as follows:

1. Nothing can act or be acted upon where it is not.
2. When we perceive objects, we act upon them or they upon us.
3. Therefore, we perceive only those objects that are right where we are, smack up against our minds – in other words, ideas.

Reid's response to this argument is somewhat surprising by present-day lights. He challenges its second premise, denying that in perception there need be any "acting" of perceiver on percipient or vice versa, which puts him at odds with contemporary causal theories of perception and intentionality more generally. But another response to the argument would have been available to Reid. Even for its proponents, the first premise is plausible only if understood as saying that nothing can act *immediately* (that is, without mediation) where it is not. The lighting of a fuse here can cause the explosion of a keg way over there, provided there is an intervening series of contiguous causal links. With the first premise restated in this way, the second premise must also be restated in order for the conclusion to follow: When we perceive objects, we act upon them or they upon us *immediately*. Reid could have rejected the revised version of the second premise without denying the need for a causal connection between perceiver and percipient altogether. Indeed, in other places he makes it clear that he does believe that perception involves such a connection, provided the causation is thought of as lawful succession rather than "agent causation," which he sometimes says is the only true causation.[1]

Another argument for ideas Reid criticizes is a version of the argument from perceptual relativity. Hume had claimed that the "universal and primary opinion of all men" that they perceive external objects directly is "destroyed by the slightest philosophy." He offered the following argument as a specimen: "The table, which we see, seems to diminish as we remove further from it; but the real table, which exists independent of us, suffers no alteration. It was therefore nothing but its image which was present to the mind."[2] Recast somewhat, Hume's slight bit of philosophy takes the form of the following syllogism:

1. What I see diminishes in magnitude as I retreat from it.
2. The table itself does not diminish in magnitude as I retreat from it.
3. Therefore, what I see is not the table itself (but only an image or idea).

Reid contends that Hume's premises are true only if we restate them as follows:[3]

1. What I see diminishes in *apparent* magnitude as I retreat from it.
2. The table itself does not diminish in *real* magnitude as I retreat from it.
3. Therefore, what I see is not the table (but only an image or idea).

Here Reid is appropriating for his own purposes Berkeley's distinction between tangible and visible magnitude or, as Reid also styles it, real and apparent magnitude. As Reid develops the distinction, the real magnitude of an object (e.g., the edge of a table) is an intrinsic property of it, measured in inches or feet, whereas the apparent magnitude of an object is a relation between the object and a perceiver, measured by the angle the object subtends at the eye. It is easy to see that apparent magnitude varies with the distance between object and perceiver (objects subtending smaller angles when further away) while real magnitude does not. Once we record these facts correctly as in Reid's version of the syllogism, we see that the argument commits the fallacy of two middle terms.[4]

Reid's second point against the theory of ideas is that "ideas do not make any of the operations of the mind to be better understood"

(EIP II.xiv: 184). They are supposed to explain how we perceive or apprehend what is distant, what is past, and what does not exist at all, but in fact they are no help in this regard. Ideas are of no use in explaining the intentionality or aboutness of mental operations because such explanations inevitably presuppose intentionality. In the first place, ideas can represent objects for us only if the ideas are interpreted (like the symbols in a book) as standing for the objects, but that presupposes precisely the ability of the interpreter to have the object in mind.[5] In the second place, ideas themselves must be made objects of perception or some kind of awareness, but that again presupposes intentionality:

It is as difficult to conceive how the mind perceives images in the brain, as, how it perceives things more distant. If any man will shew how the mind may perceive images in the brain, I will undertake to shew how it may perceive the most distant objects: for if we give eyes to the mind, to perceive what is transacted at home in its dark chamber, why may we not make these eyes a little longer-sighted? (IHM VI.xii: 121)

Reid's third point against the theory of ideas is that it has led philosophers into conclusions shockingly at odds with common sense.[6] If we do not simply *see* external objects, it becomes necessary to prove their existence by arguments, but the arguments philosophers have offered to this end are all problematic.[7] Thus if we start down the way of ideas, we are in danger of losing the material world. Hume developed the consequences of the theory of ideas even further, showing that the mind itself must be reduced to a series of ideas. Reid tells us that although he once subscribed to the theory himself, Hume's philosophy convinced him (by making its inevitable consequences manifest) that it must be rejected.

II. SENSATION VERSUS PERCEPTION

To Reid we owe the now familiar distinction between sensation and perception.[8] These operations of the mind are often conflated, but are distinguishable if we pay attention:

Thus, *I feel a pain; I see a tree*: the first denoteth a sensation, the last a perception. The grammatical analysis of both expressions is the same: for both consist of an active verb and an object. But, if we attend to the things signified by these expressions, we shall find, that in the first, the distinction between the act and the object is not real but grammatical; in the second, the distinction is not only grammatical, but real.

The form of the expression, *I feel pain*, might seem to imply, that the feeling is something distinct from the pain felt; yet, in reality, there is no distinction. As *thinking a thought* is an expression which could signify no more than *thinking*, so *feeling a pain* signifies no more than *being pained*. What we have said of pain is applicable to every other mere sensation. (IHM VI.xx: 167–8)

When I see a tree, there is an object (the tree itself) apart from my act of seeing, but when I have a sensation, there is no object apart from the act of sensing. As he says elsewhere, "Sensation is a name given by Philosophers to an act of mind, which may be distinguished from all others by this, that it hath no object distinct from the act itself" (EIP I.i: 36). Is that because an act of sensing has *itself* for its object, or because it has no object at all? Although Reid's language sometimes suggests the former option, his proposal that *being pained* is the model for all sensation suggests the latter.

If we take Reid in the latter way to hold that sensation is objectless, he is a precursor of "adverbial" theories of sensation: To have a sensation of red is not to be the subject of an act directed upon a red item as its object, but is simply to sense in a certain way, "redly" as the adverbial theory styles it.[9] It is not to sense some*thing*, but to sense some*how*. If sensing required its own special objects, the argument from perceptual relativity for the theory of ideas could be reinstated. The mountain that looks blue from a distance and green from close up would do so by generating first blue and then green sensory objects in my mind, and these special objects would displace the mountain itself (which "suffers no alteration") as my immediate objects.

Although sensations do not *have* objects, they can *become* objects for us, in the sense that we can know through proper attention what sorts of sensations we are having. Reid's views about our epistemic relation to our sensations involve a delicate balancing act. If we attend carefully to our sensations, we can know perfectly what they are like; yet they commonly pass unnoticed, serving as mere cues or signs from which our minds leap instantly to other things that they signify. Our apprehension of that which sensations signify is perception, to which we now turn.

III. REID'S THREEFOLD ACCOUNT OF PERCEPTION

Reid's official characterization of perception involves three elements – conception, belief, and immediacy:

> If, therefore, we attend to that act of our mind which we call the perception of an external object of sense, we shall find in it these three things. *First,* Some conception or notion of the object perceived. *Secondly,* A strong and irresistible conviction of its present existence. And, *thirdly,* That this conviction and belief are immediate, and not the effect of reasoning. (EIP II. v: 96)

These three elements are already singled out by Reid in the *Inquiry,* and he mentions them repeatedly in the *Intellectual Powers.*[10]

Note that this account makes no mention of sensation. Although Reid says that sensation generally serves as the trigger for the conception and belief involved in perception, he does not usually list it as an *ingredient* in perception.[11] Why not? It is probably because Reid thinks it possible that there should be beings in whom perception occurs in the absence of sensation.[12] Moreover, he holds that there is one variety of human perception that actually does occur without any characteristic sensation – namely, the perception of visible form.[13]

Is the threefold account in terms of conception, belief, and immediacy meant to be a *definition* of perception? Probably not, for two reasons. In the first place, Reid sometimes cites two further conditions that are necessary for perception. One is that the object of perception must be an external object that really exists and is contemporaneous with the act of perceiving it.[14] Another is that there must be a causal process starting with the object and culminating with our conception of the object and belief in it.[15] In the second place, it may be that some of the conditions on Reid's list (e.g., belief) are included not because they are analytical ingredients in perception, but because they are inevitable effects of it. Reid does not generally attach much importance to this distinction.[16]

IV. WHAT REID MEANS BY "CONCEPTION"

What is the nature of the "conception" that Reid lists as one of the ingredients in perception? Contemporary readers are likely to think of Kant when they encounter that term. They are likely to connect "conception" with *concepts*, and to think that when Reid talks of conception, he is talking about subsuming something under a concept – classifying an object in some way or thinking of it as being of a certain sort. If so, the conception involved in perception would already be implicit in the belief component; it would simply be a matter of possessing and deploying the concepts that enter into the belief. Forming a conception of an object would be entertaining some proposition about it, and the belief component of perception would consist in affirming that proposition. Reid's account of perception would make perception simply a matter of forming noninferential beliefs about objects, as in the contemporary accounts advanced by Pitcher and Armstrong.[17]

It would be overly hasty, however, to conclude that Reid holds a pure belief theory of perception along such lines, or even a theory of perception as noninferential belief accompanied by sensation. As Alston and Wolterstorff have forcefully pointed out, if we are to understand Reid, we must set aside our Kantian lenses.[18] We must pay full heed to Reid's own official explanation of what he means by "conception."[19] There we learn that conception is the most basic operation of the mind, presupposed in all others. It is "that operation of the understanding, which the Logicians call *simple apprehension*," and which they define as "the bare conception of a thing, without any judgment or belief about it" (EIP IV.i: 295). Reid goes on to characterize judgment (or belief – he tends to use the terms interchangeably) as involving assent or denial. Given just this much, it could be that simple apprehension is always an act with propositional content, but an act in which the propositional content is simply entertained without being affirmed or denied. His further discussion makes clear, however, that simple apprehension may have nonpropositional as well as propositional objects: "Judgment can be expressed by a proposition only, and a proposition is a complete sentence; but simple apprehension may be expressed by a word or words, which make no complete sentence" (EIP VI.i: 408).[20] He also tells us that the objects of simple apprehension expressed by words or subsentential phrases may be either individuals or universals.[21]

Reid mentions two ways in which we may obtain conceptions of individuals.[22] If I have never seen Westminster Bridge, I may conceive of it by means of a description it satisfies, e.g., *a bridge from*

Westminster over the Thames. This mode of conception is similar to what Russell calls knowledge by description, and it does involve Kantian concepts. But if an object is present to my senses, I need no such description in order to conceive of it; I need only mentally point it out. This mode of conception is similar to what Russell called knowledge by acquaintance, and it is more akin to Kantian intuition than to Kantian conceptualization.[23]

Reid's taxonomy of the operations of the mind leaves room, then, for acts of apprehension or acquaintance whereby an object is presented to the mind without any conceptualization. Should we so understand the conception that is an ingredient in perception? I believe the answer is yes, for two reasons.

First, Reid tells us in a number of places that perception is a *ground of belief*. He seems to mean this in both a genetic and a normative sense: If I see a tree, that induces me to believe in the tree and gives me evidence for my belief. Both of these claims seem to presuppose that seeing a tree is something distinct from the belief I form about it. If the real core of perception is conception and conception is a nondoxastic act, we have something distinct from belief that can serve as a ground of it in both senses.

Second, Reid tells us that the conception involved in perception can be *more or less distinct*. We see an object more distinctly at a small than a great distance, and more distinctly on a clear than a foggy day.[24] Can the merely conceptual apprehension of an object be subject to this sort of variation? One conceptual apprehension can involve descriptions or concepts that are more determinate than those involved in another (the bird-like thing over there versus the seagull over there ...). But I do not think that greater distinctness of conception is to be *analyzed* as greater conceptual determinacy. Rather, it is the former that makes the latter possible.[25]

I shall assume, then, that the conception involved in Reidian perception is some sort of apprehension or acquaintance that is not constituted by conceptualization or judgment. I offer further confirmation for this assumption in Sections IX and XII below.

V. REID'S NATIVISM

Reid believes that we have a number of important conceptions – including those of external extended objects – that are not abstracted from sensation. This makes him a *nativist* in one sense of that term.[26] Negatively, his doctrine is that a being endowed with sensations and rational powers alone would never be able to arrive at any conception of extension. There is no "internal" connection between any sensation and anything extended – no resemblance between them nor any connection discernible by reason. Reid supports this contention with a thought experiment he calls his *experimentum crucis*.[27] He asks us to imagine a person furnished with a progressively richer array of sensations, beginning with the prick of a pin, advancing to more complex sensations such as the pressure of a blunt object against his body, and culminating with the sensations accompanying the motion of his limbs. He asks at each step in the series whether those sensory materials would suffice to give anyone a conception of extension, and his answer is no. Positively, Reid's doctrine is that the conception of extension is innate, not in the sense that we have it from birth, but in the sense that it is triggered in us by certain sensations from which it could never have been abstracted. We are enabled to form the conception of extended things only because we are innately programmed to do so. "That our sensations of touch indicate something external, extended, figured, hard or soft, is not a deduction of reason, but a natural principle" (IHM V.vi: 72). The natural principle is entirely contingent: We might have been so constituted as to have the same conceptions on the occasion of qualitatively different sensations, or different conceptions on the occasion of qualitatively the same sensations.

When Reid's nativism about the conception of extension and other spatial attributes is combined with the view that the conception involved in Reidian perception is akin to Kantian intuition, there emerges a striking similarity between Reid and Kant. To put the point in Kantian language, our notion of space is an *a priori* intuition.[28]

VI. PRIMARY AND SECONDARY QUALITIES

Reid endorses a version of Locke's distinction between primary and secondary qualities. He thinks that some of Locke's teachings on this topic are wrong – in particular, he thinks there is no resemblance between any primary quality and any idea or sensation in our minds. If there were such a resemblance, we could obtain our notion of extension by excogitation from our sensations, which is precisely what we cannot do according to the *experimentum crucis* described in the previous section. But Reid thinks there is something to Locke's distinction nonetheless:

[T]here appears to me to be a real foundation for the distinction; and it is this: That our senses give us a direct and a distinct notion of the primary qualities, and inform us what they are in themselves: But of the secondary qualities, our senses give us only a relative and obscure notion. They inform us only, that they are qualities that affect us in a certain manner, that is, produce in us a certain sensation; but as to what they are in themselves, our senses leave us in the dark. (EIP II.xvii: 201)

Our conception of the squareness of a body is direct: In knowing that a body is square, we know something about how it is intrinsically. By contrast, our conception of the redness of a body is not direct, but relative: In knowing a body to be red, we know only that it is so constituted as to produce a certain kind of sensation in us, not how the body is intrinsically or in itself.

Does Reid take secondary qualities to be mere dispositions to produce certain sorts of sensations in us, or does he take them to be the physical properties underlying such dispositions as their categorical bases? In the former case, secondary qualities would differ in their nature from primary qualities, the secondaries being dispositional and relational while the primaries are categorical and intrinsic. In the latter case, the secondaries would be as categorical as the primary, differing just in the sort of cognitive access we have to them.

On a purely dispositional account, redness would be given a definition along the following lines:

x is red = df if a normal human observer were to view x, the observer would be affected with red* sensations.

Here "red*" designates a type of sensation known to us by introspection, and we define redness as the property of producing in us sensations of this type. On a purely physicalistic account, by contrast, we would take whatever physical property is the basis for the disposition just defined (e.g., the molecular constitution responsible for its reflecting light of a certain sort) and identify redness with that physical property. Which account (if either) would Reid prefer?

In favor of the purely dispositional account is the fact that Reid says the sensations associated with a secondary quality "bear a capital part in the notion we form of it. We conceive it only as that which

occasions such a sensation, and therefore cannot reflect upon it without thinking of the sensation which it occasions" (EIP II.xvii: 204).[29]
This is clearly true given the dispositional definition, which refers
to red* sensations in its definiens, but less clearly true if secondary
qualities are physical bases.

In favor of the physicalist account is the fact that Reid often says of
the secondary qualities that we are ignorant of their natures.[30] This
is true if secondary qualities are physical bases, but not if they are dispositions, for we do know perfectly well what the dispositions are.[31]

Can we fashion a compromise between the dispositional and physicalist accounts of secondary qualities, according to which (1) knowing what redness is requires knowing what red* sensations are like,
and yet (2) redness supervenes on intrinsic physical properties, in the
sense that anything just like a given red thing in all intrinsic physical respects would have to be red, regardless of its sensory effects on
human observers? I believe the answer is yes, provided we make use
of two devices of contemporary philosophical logic: quantifying over
properties and indexing to the actual world. For then we can frame
the following definition:

> x is red in w = df x has in w some physical property P such
> that the following is a law of nature in @, the actual world:
> Things with P produce red* sensations in normal human
> observers.

Here, as in the dispositional definition above, we mention red* sensations in the definiens, so thesis (1) is presumably true. Thesis (2)
is also upheld, because a thing in a world w just like a red thing in @
in its intrinsic physical properties would have whatever property P
produces red* sensations in @. That would qualify it as red even if P
does not produce red* sensations in w.

VII. THREE FORMS OF DIRECT REALISM

Reid is clearly a realist, i.e., one who holds that there are physical
things existing outside the mind. As I understand him, he is also
a *direct* realist in each of three senses to be explained below: He
is an epistemological direct realist, a perceptual direct realist, and
a presentational direct realist. These three claims are progressively
more controversial.

The first form of direct realism is *epistemological direct realism*, according to which some beliefs about physical things are epistemically basic. The warrant they have for a subject does not derive from the warrant of any other propositions that subject believes; they are justified apart from any reasons the subject has for believing them. It is amply clear that Reid is a direct realist in this sense. Here is just one of many passages one could cite:

> If the word axiom be put to signify every truth which is known immediately, without being deduced from any antecedent truth, then the existence of the objects of sense may be called an axiom. (EIP II.xx: 231)[32]

The second form of direct realism is *perceptual direct realism*, according to which physical things are perceived directly, in a sense to be spelled out further below. It amounts roughly to this: Physical things are perceived without any perceived intermediaries. I believe it is clear that Reid is a perceptual direct realist, or at least that he intends to be one. Here is one of many passages one could quote on this score:

> When we see the sun or moon, we have no doubt that the very objects which we immediately see are very far distant from us, and from one another. . . . But how are we astonished when the Philosopher informs us, that we are mistaken in all this . . . because the objects we perceive are only ideas in our own minds. . . . (EIP II.xiv: 172)

Our first two forms of direct realism are arguably independent of one another. It would be possible to hold that although we perceive physical objects directly, beliefs about them are not epistemically basic, but need to be supported by background information, e.g., about the proper functioning of one's senses. Conversely, it would also be possible to hold that beliefs about physical objects are basic despite the fact that we do *not* perceive them directly.[33] But in Reid's mind, the two forms of direct realism are closely linked. He observes, "It was this theory of ideas [the paradigm of an indirect theory of perception] that led Des Cartes, and those that followed him, to think it necessary to prove, by philosophical arguments, the existence of material objects" (EIP II.xiv: 186). In other words, if you are not a perceptual direct realist, you cannot be an epistemological direct realist. He also makes the converse claim: That if a philosopher holds that the existence of external objects requires proof, it must be because he is of the opinion that we do not perceive external objects, but only ideas of them.³⁴ In other words, if you are not an epistemological direct realist, that shows you are not a perceptual direct realist.³⁵

The third form of direct realism is *presentational direct realism*: Not only are physical things perceived directly, but our perception of them is a matter of their being presented to us, or of our being acquainted with them in a Russellian sense. As Alston further describes this view:

> In perception an external object is directly 'presented' to our awareness; it is 'given' to consciousness. We are immediately aware of it, as contrasted with just thinking about it, forming a concept of it, or believing something about it.... This is 'knowledge by acquaintance' rather than 'knowledge by description.'³⁶

It is possible to be a perceptual direct realist without being a presentational direct realist. Armstrong and Chisholm are both perceptual direct realists, because both hold that we perceive physical things without perceiving sense data or suchlike intermediaries, but neither is a presentational direct realist, because neither thinks any such relation as acquaintance enters into perception at all. Armstrong analyzes perception as a kind of noninferential belief,³⁷ Chisholm analyzes it as a kind of appropriately caused sensation,³⁸ and neither countenances such a relation as acquaintance – an irreducible cognitive relation with nonpropositional objects. Reid does countenance such a relation (as argued above in section IV), but it has been questioned whether he thinks we stand in this relation to external things. Thus it is controversial whether he is a presentational direct realist.

The first question to ask, however, is whether he is a perceptual direct realist, and to answer that, we need the promised further elucidation of "direct perception." I shall use the following definition proposed by George Pappas as a point of departure:

> A person S directly perceives an object O at a time t = df (1) S perceives O at t, and (2) it is false that: S would perceive O at t only if S were to perceive R at t, where R ≠ O, and where R is not a part of O.³⁹

Pappas says that clause (2) is supposed to capture the idea of "nondependence on perceived intermediaries": I do not perceive something directly if I perceive it only by perceiving something distinct from it. More accurately (as the further proviso brings out), I do not perceive something directly if I perceive it only by perceiving something else that is not a *part* of it. If I perceive an elephant by perceiving a side of it, I still perceive the elephant directly. But if I perceive Hume's table only by perceiving an image or idea of it (which is not part of it, but something existing only in my mind), I do not perceive the table directly. Indeed, Reid would say that in that case I do not perceive the table at all.

VIII. DO SENSATIONS OBSTRUCT DIRECT PERCEPTION?

It is abundantly clear that Reid has banished *one* type of objectionable intermediary in perception, namely, ideas. But many of his readers, from Sir William Hamilton to the present day, have thought that sensations play a role in Reid's philosophy analogous to ideas, and that in the end Reid fails to be a perceptual direct realist despite his best intentions.[40] I consider here several reasons for thinking that sensations do or do not make trouble for direct perception.

John Immerwahr has proposed that there is a significant difference in Reid's views about the relation of sensation to perception as we move from the *Inquiry* to the *Intellectual Powers*.[41] In the *Inquiry*, Reid holds that in the causal chain leading from objects to perceptions, sensations serve as links between physical impressions (e.g., retinal imprints) and perceptions:

External Object →Impression → Sensation → Conception & Belief (Perception)

In the *Intellectual Powers*, by contrast, the picture according to Immerwahr is this:

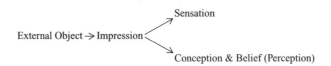

Here sensations are effects produced in parallel with perceptions rather than serving as intervening links. Immerwahr thinks that this difference makes Reid an indirect realist in the *Inquiry*, but a direct realist in the *Intellectual Powers*.

Immerwahr's view is subject to two criticisms. First, as he himself notes, the difference he alleges between the *Inquiry* and the

Intellectual Powers does not amount to a clean break. There are a good many passages in the *Intellectual Powers* that reaffirm the *Inquiry*'s model of the relation between sensation and perception.[42] Second, the fact that sensations come between impressions and perceptions in the first of the causal chains depicted above would not jeopardize direct perception if sensations (like impressions) were merely *causal* intermediaries in the perceptual process. The crucial question, if we operate with the Pappas definition above, is whether sensations are *perceived* intermediaries.

In this connection, some may think it relevant that according to Reid, we seldom attend to our sensations. They pass largely unnoticed. Here are several representative passages:

> But it is one thing to have the sensation and another thing to attend to it, and make it a distinct object of reflection. The first is very easy; the last, in most cases, extremely difficult. We are so accustomed to use the sensation as a sign, and to pass immediately to the hardness signified, that, as far as appears, it was never made an object of thought, either by the vulgar or by philosophers; nor has it a name in any language. (IHM V.ii: 56)

> When a primary quality is perceived, the sensation immediately leads our thought to the quality signified by it, and is itself forgot. We have no occasion afterwards to reflect upon it; and so we come to be as little acquainted with it as if we had never felt it. (EIP II.xvii: 204)

> There are many phenomena of a similar nature [to seeing double], which shew, that the mind may not attend to, and thereby, in some sort, not perceive objects that strike the senses. (IHM VI.xiii: 135)

Reid says similar things about visible figure – the shape a body actually presents to the eye at a given perspective. It requires the skill of a painter to discern the shapes that are really before the mind, our attention normally being focused instead on the features of the external scene that the presented features signify.[43]

Could our normal inattention to our sensations be what keeps everyday perception direct? The idea would be that if we do not notice our sensations – if "in some sort" we do not perceive them – then it cannot be that we perceive external things by perceiving sensations.

It seems to me, however, that what we do or do not pay attention to can hardly be the key to direct perception. Suppose I spend the morning painting a landscape and the afternoon playing tennis. Do

I perceive things indirectly in the morning when I am carefully attending to the way things look and directly in the afternoon when I am preoccupied with whacking the ball? That seems an unlikely shift. Let us inquire, therefore, whether there is a sense in which we perceive physical things directly even on occasions when we are attending to the accompanying sensations.

For one such sense, we may turn to an example discussed by Pappas. Suppose that on a certain occasion I have sensations that induce in me conception of and immediate belief in a chair. On Reid's standard threefold account, this means that I have a perception of the chair occasioned by the sensation. Suppose that on this occasion I do attend to the sensation, leading me to conceive of and believe in *it* as well. Applying Reid's threefold account again, I therefore have a perception of the sensation.[44] Pappas distinguishes two ways of understanding the situation as so far described. First, there is the *double-tier* account, which we may diagram as follows, using arrows to indicate causation and boxes to indicate the ingredients that together constitute perception:

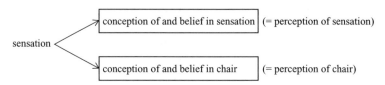

The other way of understanding the situation is provided by the *single-tier* account, which we may diagram as follows:

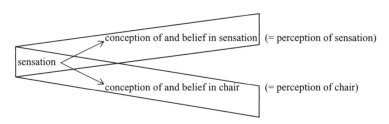

The difference is that on the double-tier view, the sensation is regarded as the common *cause* of two perceptions, whereas on the single-tier view, it is regarded as a common *constituent* of the two perceptions. In Pappas's view, this makes a difference as to whether perception of the chair is direct. He thinks that on the double-tier view, the subjunctive conditional *I would perceive the chair only if*

I perceived the sensation is true. There is thus dependence on perceiving the sensation and no direct perception. But on the single-tier view, there is no reason to affirm such dependence.

I have two reservations about Pappas's approach.[45] First, why should we think that the crucial conditional *I would perceive the chair only if I perceived the sensation* is *true* according to the double-tier view? Consider another case of two effects with a common cause: The firing of a pistol results both in a loud report and in the disintegration of a can. We cannot infer that the can would have disintegrated only if the noise had occurred, since the pistol might have been fired with a silencer.[46] Second, why should we think that the same conditional is *false* according to the single-tier view? Here is an argument for thinking it true: The perception of the chair would have occurred only if the sensation occurred (since the sensation is a constituent of it); the sensation would have occurred only if the perception of it occurred (since it caused the remaining elements needed to constitute, along with itself, perception of a sensation); therefore, the perception of the chair would have occurred only if the perception of the sensation had occurred.[47]

My own view is that even if perception of the chair does depend on perception (or some sort of awareness) of the sensation, perception of the chair may still be direct. That requires me to modify Pappas's definition of direct perception.

Pappas's definition, reworded somewhat, runs as follows:

> S directly perceives O at t = df (1) S perceives O at t, and (2) it is false that: S would perceive O only if there were an object R distinct from O such that (a) R is not part of O and (b) S perceives R.[48]

There are two difficulties with this definition as it stands: In one way it is too strict, in another way too lax.

To see that the definition is too strict, suppose two objects A and B are inseparably connected in such a way that one never enters my field of view unless the other does. Then I would never perceive one without perceiving the other, but it seems that I might still perceive each of them directly. Or suppose I can never perceive an object without perceiving a bit of background (though no particular bit); then my perception of the object will depend on there being something else that I perceive, yet it seems I might still perceive both background and object directly.[49]

Perhaps we can avoid this first difficulty if we turn to a definition of direct perception offered by Frank Jackson. Jackson's definition is similar in spirit to Pappas's, but importantly different in one way:

> S directly perceives x at t = df (1) S perceives x at t, and (2) there is no object y distinct from x such that S perceives x *in virtue of* perceiving y.[50]

Here the "in virtue of" notion replaces the notion of dependence that Pappas tries to capture with subjunctive conditionals. This definition arguably avoids the "too strict" difficulty raised above. Even if I never see A without seeing its inseparable companion B (or a bit of background), it seems wrong to say that I see A *in virtue of* seeing B.[51]

Unfortunately, the second difficulty – that the definition is too lax – affects Jackson's definition as well as Pappas's. They both characterize direct perception as perception that does not depend on (or occur in virtue of) *perceived* intermediaries. Well, consider the following view: "When we perceive any object, the object causes certain ideas or sense data to arise in our minds; our awareness of these sense data then leads us to infer the existence of the object." That is a textbook case of indirect perception, if it is perception at all. Yet the proponent of the view could insist that such perception is not indirect by Pappas's or Jackson's definition. We do not *perceive* sense data, since for one thing they do not cause any further sense data to arise in us. Our cognitive relation to sense data is not perceiving, but something else.

It seems to me that the view just sketched is an indirect view of perception nonetheless. The sense data it posits are objectionable intermediaries precisely because they are *objects* to which we stand in some sort of *cognitive* relation – apprehension, awareness, acquaintance, or what have you. So it seems to me that in Pappas's or Jackson's definition, we should replace the final occurrence of "perceive" in the definiens by some more general cognitive verb, such as "is acquainted with."[52] If we do this in Jackson's definition, we arrive at the following:

> S directly perceives x at t = df (1) S perceives x at t, and (2) there is no object y distinct from x such that S perceives x in virtue of being acquainted with y.

Let us now return to the question of whether sensations obstruct direct perception.

It seems clear to me that the answer is no, for at least one and possibly two reasons. In the first place, sensations are not *objects* at all. Though they may be "objects of awareness," they are not objects ontologically speaking. They are not individual things, but states of a subject – manners in which a subject is affected.[53] So when Reid speaks of awareness of sensations, the awareness in question is really the apprehension of a fact about oneself – that one is sensing in a certain way – rather than acquaintance with any object. Perception is not rendered indirect just because it involves apprehension of some fact about oneself. Otherwise, no philosopher who believes that perception necessarily involves apperception – that you cannot perceive O without being aware that you perceive O – could be an upholder of direct perception.

A second reason for holding that sensations do not compromise direct perception would be this: One does not perceive physical objects *in virtue of* being acquainted with one's sensations. I hesitate to put much weight on this consideration, however, lest a sense datum theorist maintain that one does not perceive physical objects (solely) in virtue of being acquainted with sense data.[54]

IX. IS REID A PRESENTATIONAL DIRECT REALIST?

I have argued that Reid's theory of sensations does not stand in the way of his being a perceptual direct realist. I turn now to the question of whether he is a presentational direct realist. Recall that a presentational direct realist holds not only that we perceive physical objects directly, but also that our perception of them is a matter of their being presented to us or, equivalently, our being acquainted with them.

Although Alston and Wolterstorff have brought it to our attention that Reid's scheme of things includes a relation of acquaintance, both of them have denied that it is Reid's view that we stand in this relation to external things in cases of perception. Here is Alston's argument on this score:

Most crucially, if the conception involved in perception is the direct awareness of [i.e., acquaintance with] an external object, how is that object presented to that awareness? There would seem to be no alternative to holding that it is presented as exhibiting 'sensible' or 'phenomenal' qualities – colors, shapes, heat and cold ... and so on. ... But this construal is not open to Reid. For, as noted earlier, he places all the qualitative distinctness of perceptual consciousness (except for visual extension) in the sensations, which he takes to involve no awareness of any object other than itself. What it is natural to refer to as an awareness of colors, warmth, and odours (or of objects as colored, warm, and odorous) Reid construes as *modes* of feeling (awareness), as ways of being aware, directed on to no object beyond themselves.[55]

If I understand this difficult argument correctly, it may be compressed into two premises and a conclusion as follows:

1. If the conception involved in perception is direct awareness of (acquaintance with) an external object, it is an awareness in which the object is presented as having some color or shape or other sensible quality – an awareness in which these very qualities are presented to us.
2. For Reid, all the sensible qualities of objects are "drained away" into sensations – they are modes of sensing rather than qualities objects are presented as having. Thus in Reid's view, the consequent of 1 is false.
3. Therefore, the conception involved in Reidian perception is not acquaintance with external objects.

My reply to this argument is that the second premise is false. Alston has forgotten all about the primary qualities. Even if he were right in saying that Reid drains colors and odors away from objects,[56] he is wrong in claiming that seen shapes or felt hardnesses are drained away. These are by no means modes of sensing, but are qualities of external objects of which we have a clear conception that owes nothing to sensation. So there is nothing in Reid's view to prohibit him from saying that (in the case of the primary qualities, at least) our perception is a form of acquaintance.

Another argument against interpreting Reid as a presentational direct realist has been presented by Wolterstorff. It runs thus:

On this view [that there is acquaintance with external objects or qualities], there would, in fact, be a superfluity of information. ... [I]f awareness of primary qualities involved acquaintance with those qualities, there would be too much information. My acquaintance with the primary quality yields me information about it; but the sensory experience [i.e., sensation] is also supposed to function as a source of information about the primary quality. Something seems definitely wrong here. Given acquaintance with primary qualities, the sensory experience seems otiose; given the sensory experience, acquaintance with primary qualities seems otiose. . . . I submit that if perception consisted in acquaintance with the object perceived, there would also be "no necessity, no use" for [a sensation serving as] a *sign* of the object.[57]

This argument deserves extended scrutiny, which I have given it elsewhere.[58] Here I shall simply note that there must be *something* wrong with it, as shown by the following parody: "There can be no such thing as grasping the thought expressed by the words of another. If there were, there would be *two* sources of information about any such thought: Grasping the thought itself and hearing the words expressing it. Given the grasp, the words would be otiose, and given the words, the grasp would be otiose." Here, of course, one wants to object that the words could be necessary for evoking a grasp of the thought without there being any objectionable doubling of information.

X. DO VISIBLE FIGURES OBSTRUCT DIRECT PERCEPTION?

Reid distinguishes real from visible figure. He holds that real figure is ascertained originally only through touch, but that with experience a given visible figure comes to be a sign of a certain real figure, the mind passing automatically from the sign to the real figure associated with it. On these points he was deeply influenced by Berkeley. Unlike Berkeley, however, he believes that "the visible figure of objects is a real and external object to the eye" (IHM VI.viii: 98) and that visible figures are a fit subject matter for geometry. In fact, they obey a geometry of their own, distinct from the Euclidean geometry that governs tangible figures.

What is visible figure? "As the real figure of a body consists in [i.e., is determined by] the position of its several parts with regard to one another," Reid tells us, "so its visible figure consists in the position of its several parts with regard to the eye" (IHM VI.vii: 96). He explains further that two points have the same position with regard to the eye if and only if they lie on the same straight line extending out from the center of the eye, regardless of their distance from it.

This definition reflects his agreement with Berkeley that the eye alone is incapable of making any discriminations of depth: In the visual field there are seen differences of left, right, up, and down, but not of near and far. It follows that a plane triangle and its projection on a sphere centered on the eye have the same visible figure, despite the fact that one is flat and the other curved. (The two triangles differ in real figure, but that difference is ascertainable only by touch.) We may also say that a round plate seen obliquely has the same visible figure as an elliptical plate seen head on.[59]

As noted, Reid believes that visible figures have a geometry of their own, distinct from the Euclidean geometry that governs tangible figures:

When the geometrician draws a diagram with the most perfect accuracy – when he keeps his eye fixed upon it, while he goes through a long process of reasoning, and demonstrates the relations of the several parts of his figure – he does not consider that the visible figure presented to his eye, is only the representative of a tangible figure, upon which all his attention is fixed; he does not consider that these two figures have really different properties; and that, what he demonstrates to be true of the one, is not true of the other. (IHM VI.viii: 102–3)

He goes on to provide a list of theorems that he takes to govern visible figures. For example, any two straight lines in my visual field eventually intersect (so there are no parallels), and the sum of the angles of a visible triangle always exceeds 180 degrees.[60] These are theorems belonging to what we would nowadays classify as Riemannian geometry, but Reid advanced them almost a century before Riemann.

For exploration of why Reid thought the geometry of visible figures is non-Euclidean, I refer the reader to what I have said elsewhere.[61] Here I wish to raise a different question: Are visible figures an impediment to direct perception? There is prima facie reason to think that the answer is yes. Although visible figures may themselves be objects of direct perception – Reid calls them "the immediate objects of sight" (IHM VI.viii: 102 and VI.ix: 105) – they threaten to make our perception by sight of other physical things indirect. When I look at a triangular tabletop, the visible figure presented to my eye (according to Reid) is a triangle with an angle sum exceeding 180 degrees, even if only by a slight amount. But the tabletop

itself has an angle sum of exactly 180 degrees, since its real figure
(according to Reid) is Euclidean. It follows that my immediate object
of sight is not the tabletop. With experience, it comes to be a sign
of the real figure associated with it, and I pass automatically from
an awareness of the sign to a conception of the Euclidean tabletop
that it signifies. But what all this seems to add up to is the following: I perceive the table only by being aware of something else that
is distinct from it and not even a part of it. So I do not perceive the
tabletop directly.[62]

Why should we think that visible figures make trouble for direct
perception if we do not find any trouble with sensations? After all,
sensations are used as signs in perception just as much as visible figures are. Wherein lies the difference? The answer is that sensations
do not get in the way of direct perception because being aware of a
sensation is not being aware of any object – it is only being aware of
the fact that you are modified in a certain way. By contrast, being
aware of a visible figure is definitely being aware of an object – an
object that is extended in length and breadth.[63] It is an external object rather than an idea, but it is no less an obstacle to direct visual
perception of tables and trees for all that.

XI. ALL PERCEPTION IS DIRECT

I have been working so far with the following rough notion of the distinction between direct and indirect perception: You perceive something indirectly when you perceive it by perceiving (or otherwise apprehending) something else. You perceive something directly when
you perceive it, but *not* by apprehending anything else. We should,
however, pause to ask: Could there really be such a thing as indirect perception? I am not asking whether the theory-of-ideas assay
of the perceptual situation could be correct. I am asking the following question instead: *Assuming* that assay is correct, is our cognitive
relation to external things properly classified as perception? In other
words, is what you do when you "perceive one thing by apprehending another" really *perceiving*? Could *both* clauses in the definition
of indirect perception ever be satisfied?

I believe Reid's answer is no. When you move a stone by moving a
stick that touches the stone, you really do move the stone. But when

you perceive a table by perceiving or apprehending something else that is not even a part of it, you are not really perceiving the table at all:

A body in motion may move another that was at rest, by the medium of a third body that is interposed. This is easily understood; but ... to think of any object by a medium, seems to be words without a meaning. (EIP II.ix: 134)

A little later on the same page he concludes:

I apprehend, therefore, that if Philosophers will maintain that ideas in the mind are the only *immediate* objects of thought, they will be forced to grant that they are the *sole* objects of thought. (EIP II.ix: 134, emphasis added)

Since Reid takes "thinking" to be "a very general word, which includes all the operations of our minds" (EIP I.i: 22), what he says here implies that there is no such thing as a mediate object of perception.

Reid has another point to make against the propriety of the phrase "mediate object of perception." He asks,

Whether, according to the opinion of Philosophers [who embrace the theory of ideas], we perceive the images or ideas only, and infer the existence and qualities of the external object from what we perceive in the image? Or, whether we really perceive the external object as well as its image? (EIP II.vii: 105)

And he answers,

If the last be their meaning, it would follow, that, in every instance of perception, there is a double object perceived: That I perceive, for instance, one sun in the heavens, and another in my own mind. But I do not find that they affirm this; and, as it contradicts the experience of all mankind, I will not impute it to them. (EIP II.vii: 106)

Reid's view, then, is that "indirect perception" is an oxymoron – if we perceive something at all, we perceive it directly.[64]

The preceding reflections suggest to me that we should change our tack in discussing such questions as whether sensations and visible figures "get in the way" of direct perception. We have been asking: Is our cognitive relation to various intermediaries such as to preclude direct perception? Is it a matter of being acquainted with some object that serves as a sign of the thing to be perceived? We have been assuming that an answer of yes would imply that our perception of the thing signified is indirect. But this now seems wrongheaded. We should ask instead: Are we acquainted with the thing signified? If we are *not*, then no acquaintance with anything else can count as perceiving the thing signified, however indirectly. If we *are*, then no acquaintance with anything else can stand in the way of our perceiving the thing signified as directly as you like. In short, what is important in securing direct perception is not downgrading our relation to the sign, but upgrading our relation to the thing signified.

Acquaintance with a sign would exclude acquaintance with the thing signified only through a "no double object" argument. But double objects may be admissible in certain cases, as Reid tells us:

The sign, by custom, or compact, or perhaps by nature, introduces the thought of the thing signified. But here the thing signified, when it is introduced to the thought, is an object of thought no less immediate than the sign was before: And there are here two objects of thought, one succeeding another, which we have shown is not the case with respect to an idea, and the object it represents. (EIP II.ix: 134)

Unfortunately, Reid gives no example of the sort of case he has in mind, and he does not make it clear whether he would extend what he says here to perception in particular. But I propose a possible perceptual example at the end of the next section.

XII. ACQUIRED PERCEPTION

"Our perceptions are of two kinds," Reid tells us. "[S]ome are natural and original, others acquired, and the fruit of experience" (IHM VI.xx: 171).[65]

Reid's favorite examples of acquired perceptions are the perceptions of distance and three-dimensionality that we have by sight. As noted above, he agrees with Berkeley that the original deliverances of sight include extension in two dimensions only: Depth (or distance out from my eye) and three-dimensional figure are not presented to me originally in vision, but are known only through touch. With the passage of experience, however, I come to know that certain sensations associated with adjusting the "trim" of the eye and certain patterns of light and shade are signs of the presence of three-dimensional objects as known through touch. I can infer the presence of a three-dimensional globe from the way in which light and shade are distributed across a two-dimensional visual disk. Eventually the transition from sign to thing signified becomes so automatic that it is no longer a matter of inference or reasoning: When the sign is presented, I spontaneously conceive of and believe in the thing signified. When the transition has thus become a matter of habit or custom, I am said to have *acquired perception* of the thing signified. As Reid sums it up:

It is experience that teaches me that the variation of colour is an effect of spherical convexity.... But so rapid is the progress of the thought, from the effect to the cause, that we attend only to the last, and can hardly be persuaded that we do not immediately see the three dimensions of the sphere. (EIP II.xxi: 236)

We can have acquired perceptions through one sense of things originally perceived only through another. I can now see wetness (a tactile quality) on the pavement ahead where I originally saw only a patch darker in color than its surroundings. "I can say, without impropriety ... I hear a great bell, or I hear a small bell; though it is certain that the figure or size of the sounding body is not originally an object of hearing" (EIP II.xiv: 182). A butcher can perceive by sight the weight of a sheep, and a sailor the capacity and build of a distant ship.[66] As these examples illustrate, the signs in acquired perception may be either sensations or things perceived by original perception.[67]

Acquired perception is undoubtedly a powerful means of gaining information through the senses, but is it really *perception*? Berkeley's answer is no: "In short, those things alone are actually and strictly perceived by any sense, which would have been perceived, in case that same sense had then been first conferred on us."[68] Reid's answer is more equivocal. In the remark about the globe quoted above, he insinuates that our acquired perception of three dimensions is not immediate perception, which would imply for him that it is not perception at all. In another passage, he says that although we are authorized by language to classify acquired perceptions as perceptions, they are not properly the testimony of our senses, and that errors in acquired perception should not be accounted errors of the senses.[69] In yet other places, he says the question whether to classify acquired perception as perception or judgment is verbal.[70]

Despite Reid's wavering on the question, acquired perception seems to qualify as perception according to his threefold account: It involves conception of and belief in the object perceived, and once the transition from sign to thing signified has become automatic, the belief is as immediate as any.[71] It can also meet the further conditions requiring the present existence of the object and its causal connection to our experience. Yet there are cases of acquired perception that no one would regard as genuine perception. I return home and see my wife's car keys on the counter (or hear my son say "Mom's home"), whereupon I automatically conceive of her and believe that she is home. Since she is upstairs, I do not perceive her, but it seems that I fulfill all the conditions for Reidian perception. So is there something missing in Reid's account of perception? If so, what is it?

Shall we say that I do not perceive my wife because appropriate sensations are lacking, and that the threefold account is to be faulted for not including sensation? But what is meant by "appropriate" sensations? If sensations are appropriate to X just in case they are highly correlated with X, then the sensations involved in seeing the keys or hearing my son's testimony may qualify as appropriate.

Shall we say that an experience E does not qualify as perceiving X unless there is some sort of internal connection between E and X, making it necessary that anyone who had an experience that was the same in its sensory aspects as E would conceive of X? But then not even original perception would count as perception, for as Reid insists, the connection between our conception of hardness and the sensations that trigger it is entirely contingent.

Shall we say that an experience E does not qualify as perceiving X unless the experience by itself, in the absence of any collateral information about how it is correlated with X, would justify belief in X? Even if otherwise acceptable, this could not be a final answer, in view of the supervenient character of justification. If a certain experience justifies a certain belief, there must be some feature of the experience, describable in nonepistemic terms, in virtue of which it justifies the belief. Why is it that certain experiences and not others are eligible as justifiers of a given belief?

I propose the following answer to the conundrum of the car keys: An experience does not qualify as perception unless it involves *conception of the acquaintance variety*. That is why I do not perceive my wife on the occasion of seeing her keys: Though I may conceive of her in the sense of thinking of her, I am not acquainted with her. She does not appear to me in any way, shape, or form. By contrast, in original perception (as I have argued above), my conception *is* of the acquaintance variety. Most cases of acquired perception probably do not count as perception by this standard. But *if* there are cases of acquired perception in which my perceiving one thing leads me not merely to think of another but to be acquainted with it, they are cases of genuine perception.

Perhaps our perception by sight of three-dimensional objects is a case in point. When I see the visible figure consisting of the various polygons in a cube that is presented to my eye, it is not implausible to hold that I am led to genuine acquaintance with a three-dimensional cube. If this is what happens, it may be possible to square Reid's geometry of visibles with perceptual and presentational direct realism after all.[72]

NOTES

1. Reid held that causation in the strictest sense of the term is exercised only by intelligent agents and that what is ordinarily referred to as causation in nature, such as the causation of smoke by fire, is really just a case of succession in accordance with law. But he often enough calls such succession causation and plainly thinks it is part of the perceptual process. On the latter point, see IHM VI.xxi: esp. 174 and EIP II.ii: 76.
2. EHU XII: 201.
3. See EIP II.xiv: 180–2.
4. It is crucial here that Reid refuses to analyze the dyadic relation "Object O appears large (small) to observer S" into the triadic relation "O presents to S a sense datum D that is large (small)." Otherwise, an additional criticism of Hume's argument he makes would be inadequate. In this criticism, Reid notes that by the laws of geometry, it is necessary that the real table must diminish in apparent magnitude as we move away from it. "How then can this apparent diminution be an argument that it is not the real table? When that which must happen to the real table, as we remove farther from it, does actually happen to the table we see, it is absurd to conclude from this, that it is not the real table we see" (EIP II.xiv: 182). If the table's appearing smaller as we retreat from it were a matter of its presenting successively smaller sense data to us, however, we *would* have to conclude that it is not the real table we see. So it is not enough for Reid's purposes to observe that the apparent diminution of the table is just what we should expect; it is essential as

well that he insist on a dyadic rather than a triadic analysis of apparent magnitude. For more on this point, see Broad 1959: 234–6.

5. This point is developed by Lehrer 1989: 13–14. In Reid's own writings it is perhaps most explicit in PO: 62. The point also occurs in one of Reid's Aberdeen Philosophical Society manuscripts, reproduced in IHM: 297.

6. See EIP II.xiv: 185–7.

7. For more on this issue, see Greco's essay in this volume.

8. Reid is credited with this distinction by Price 1932: 22 and by Gibson 1966, 1: 319.

9. See Chisholm 1957, Chap. 8 and 1966: 94–6.

10. See, for example, IHM VI.xx: 168, EIP II.xvi: 199, II.xvii: 210, II.xviii: 211, II.xx: 226. The first of the EIP passages mentions conception and immediate belief; the last three mention conception and belief.

11. See IHM VI.xx: 168. There are exceptions. For example, Reid says that sensation is an ingredient in the perception of external objects at EIP II.xvi: 197. But he more often says that perceptions are *accompanied by* sensations or that they have sensations *corresponding to* them. See, for example, EIP I.i: 37 and II.xvi: 194.

12. See IHM VI.xxi: 174–6 and EIP II.xx: 227.

13. See IHM VI.viii: 99–101 and VI.xxi: 176.

14. See EIP I.i: 22–3, II.xx: 232, IV.i: 311. He is actually vexingly inconsistent on this point, sometimes insisting that perception must concern an existing object (as at EIP IV.i: 310–1), but occasionally admitting cases of hallucinatory perception in which there is no existing object (e.g., perception of pain in an amputated limb at EIP II.xviii: 214).

15. See IHM VI.xxi: esp. 174 and EIP II.ii: 76.

16. For example, he says in one place that belief is part of the "meaning" of seeing a chair (EIP II.xx: 232), but in another place says that every man feels that belief is an "immediate consequence" of perception (EIP II.xv: 193). And at EIP VI.i: 409 he says this: "The man who perceives an object, believes that it exists ... nor is it in his power to avoid such judgment.... Whether judgment ought to be called a necessary concomitant of these operations, or rather a part or ingredient of them, I do not dispute."

17. Armstrong 1968 and Pitcher 1971.

18. Alston 1989: 35–47 and Wolterstorff 2001: 9–12.

19. See EIP IV.i.

20. See also IHM VI.xxi: esp. 174 and EIP II.ii: 76.

21. See EIP IV.i: 302 and 305.

22. See EIP IV.i: 303.

23. For more on this, see the discussion of conceptual apprehension and apprehension by acquaintance in Wolterstorff 2001, Chap. 1.

24. See EIP II.v: 96–7.

25. I would say that Reidian conception carries information in analog form, whereas conceptualization, judgment, and belief carry information in digital form. See Dretske 1981: 135–53.

26. See the chapter by Falkenstein in this volume for more on the senses in which Reid is and is not a nativist.

27. See IHM V.vi-vii: 65–72.

28. See Kant's "Metaphysical Exposition" of the representation of space, running from A23/B38 to A26/B40 of the *Critique of Pure Reason*. One may ask whether the ascription of nativism to Reid is compatible with his allowance that if we had never felt anything hard or figured, we would never have had a conception of extension (IHM V.v: 62). The answer is given in Kant's well-known remark: "But though all our knowledge commences **with** experience, yet it does not on that account all arise **from** experience. For it could well be that even our experiential cognition is a composite of that which we receive through impressions and that which our own cognitive faculty (merely prompted by sensible impressions) provides out of itself . . ." (Kant 1998: 136).

29. As Lehrer puts it, "Our conception of secondary qualities incorporates the sensation as a semantic constituent" (Lehrer 1989: 47).

30. See, for example, IHM V.i: 54 and EIP II.xvii: 202.

31. As pointed out by Wolterstorff 2001: 110–15.

32. Reid's usual term for "direct" is "immediate." I shall use the two terms interchangeably. I have made the case for Reid's being an epistemological direct realist in greater detail in Van Cleve 1999: 3–30.

33. This is advocated as a possibility in Greco 1995: 279–96.

34. See EIP II.vii: 106.

35. It is possible, however, that Reid is not here advancing the conditional ~EDR → ~PDR, but is instead advancing an abductive argument using the converse conditional ~PDR → ~EDR. That idea-theorists hold the antecedent would explain their holding the consequent.

36. Alston 1989: 36.

37. Armstrong 1968, Chap. 10.

38. Chisholm 1957, Chap. 10: esp. 148–9.

39. Pappas 1989: 155–67, at 156. To simplify exposition, I have omitted a further condition that Pappas includes in clause (2): "nor is O [a part] of R." I surmise that Pappas includes this to deal with the "background" problem that is discussed below. I have also omitted one further clause that is not germane to present purposes.

40. According to Galen Strawson, "the question of whether [Reid] is really a 'direct realist' about perception, or whether he is really some kind of indirect realist, has been seen as the central question of Reid scholarship ever since Hamilton" (Strawson 1990: 15). For Hamilton's suggestion

that Reid's sensations play a role analogous to the indirect realist's ideas, see Supplementary Dissertation C, "On the Various Theories of External Perception," in W: 816–24. For a contemporary version of this suggestion, see Chappell 1989: 49–64.

41. Immerwahr 1978: 245–56.

42. Immerwahr cites EIP II.xvi: 312, II.xvii, II.xix, II.xxi, and VI.v.

43. See IHM VI.iii: 82–3.

44. Whether these conditions are sufficient for saying we perceive sensations has been challenged by Cummins 1990: 755–62. Pappas replies in Pappas 1990: 763–6.

45. Setting the following difficulty aside: Can a difference in how we draw the boxes in the diagrams really make the difference between direct and indirect perception?

46. For further discussion, see the Cummins–Pappas exchange cited above in n. 44.

47. I advance this inference as plausible in the present instance, even though the rule of Hypothetical Syllogism is not generally valid for subjunctive conditionals.

48. I have resolved an ambiguity about where the quantifier governing "R" in clause (2) should be placed by putting it inside the consequent of the subjunctive conditional.

49. The trouble here is that the extraneous item I perceive is not an item of the sort to which a direct realist would object – it is not an image, sense datum, or the like. One might think to avoid the difficulty, then, simply by modifying Pappas's second clause to read thus: It is false that S would perceive O only if there were a *mental* item R that S perceived. That would allow direct perception to depend on the perception of physical background. Unfortunately, however, it would also allow one to perceive the President directly by perceiving his physical image on a TV screen – no doubt an unwanted consequence.

50. Jackson 1977, Chap. 1: esp. 19–20. Jackson's word for "direct" is "immediate."

51. But why exactly is it wrong? Is it because one perceives A in virtue of perceiving B only if *necessarily*, any case of perceiving B would be a case of perceiving A? If so, not even a paradigm case of indirect perception, such as perceiving a physical object by perceiving a sense datum, would count as indirect, since perceiving a sense datum is not enough by itself to constitute perceiving a physical object.

52. I am assuming here that acquaintance is a genus of which perception is a species, even though (as we saw above) some philosophers do not take perception to be a variety of acquaintance at all.

53. See, for example, EIP II.xvi: 199.

54. Nor do I altogether dismiss this consideration, since it may be necessary to remove another obstacle to direct perception. Consider the view that one never perceives an external object without being acquainted with oneself. (Reid does not hold this view, for he thinks that we have only a relative and not a direct notion of the self – in effect, that knowledge of the self is knowledge by description rather than knowledge by acquaintance. See IHM II.vii and I.ii: 42–3.) Even if we add that a self is an object, such a view does not seem to compromise direct perception. Why not? A possible answer is that one does not perceive physical objects in virtue of being acquainted with oneself.

55. Alston 1989: 44–5.

56. Reid insists that there is a clear sense in which the color and fragrance of the rose are in it – they are in the rose as properties causing certain sensations in us. But colors and fragrances in this sense probably do not count as sensible objects of acquaintance, so they do not constitute an exception to Alston's claim that the consequent of premise 1 is false.

57. Wolterstorff 2001: 148–9.

58. Van Cleve forthcoming a.

59. Note that having corresponding parts that occupy the same position with regard to the eye is sufficient, but not necessary, for having the same visible figure: The two plates just mentioned may have the same visible figure even when seen side by side.

60. See IHM VI.ix: 105.

61. Van Cleve forthcoming b.

62. It is true that Reid says we scarcely ever attend to visible figure, but (as I have suggested above) it does not seem plausible that mere inattention to things that pass before the mind can turn us into direct perceivers.

63. "Figure" can be either an object word, as in "he drew a figure on the blackboard," or a property word, as in "these two objects have the same figure." Reid uses it both ways, but more often in the former way, and visible figures in the object sense are what he generally means by "visibles."

64. Elsewhere, commenting on Locke's doctrine that ideas are the only immediate objects of thought, he says this: "Every object of thought, therefore, is an immediate object of thought, and the word *immediate*, joined to objects of thought, seems to be a mere expletive" (EIP VI.iii: 437).

65. For more on this important distinction, the reader should consult IHM VI.xx–xxiv and EIP II.xxi–xxii.

66. See IHM VI.xx: 172.

67. See IHM II.xxiv: 191 and EIP II.xxi: 237.

68. Berkeley 1979: 40.

69. See EIP II.xxii: 247–8.

70. See EIP II.xiv: 182.
71. For confirmation of the point that acquired perception is psychologically immediate, involving no reasoning, see IHM VI.xxi: 178.
72. For advice on earlier drafts, I wish to thank Panayot Butchvarov, Terence Cuneo, Baron Reed, Ernest Sosa, Dale Tuggy, and participants in the 2002 meetings of the Reid Society.

5   Reid's Reply to the Skeptic

Reid tells us that his rejection of "the common theory of ideas" is the centerpiece of his reply to skepticism. He often writes, in fact, as if rejecting that theory is *by itself* sufficient to answer the skeptical arguments of Berkeley, Hume, and others. In this essay I will argue that Reid's reply to skepticism is more complex than Reid himself portrays it. While Reid's rejection of the theory of ideas clearly plays a central role in his reply to skepticism, it seems to me that this is only one important element of his reply, and not one that is sufficient to do the job all by itself. On the contrary, Reid's reply to the skeptic depends also on (a) Reid's own theory of perception, (b) his theory of evidence, and (c) an important aspect of Reid's methodology. In the sections that follow, I will discuss each of these elements of Reid's philosophy in turn. In addition to explicating Reid, I will also be defending him. That is, I will argue that, taken together, these four elements of Reid's philosophy constitute a successful reply to the skeptic.

I. REID'S REJECTION OF THE THEORY OF IDEAS

According to Reid, the theory of ideas is both necessary and sufficient for generating sweeping skeptical results. This means that any successful reply to skepticism requires rejecting the theory of ideas. In this section of the essay, I consider what Reid means by "the common theory of ideas," and why he thinks the theory is so closely connected with skepticism. I also review some of Reid's reasons for rejecting the theory.

A. Why the Theory of Ideas Entails Skepticism

The "common theory of ideas," as Reid understands it, is that the immediate object of thought is always some idea in the mind. In particular, we do not perceive external objects immediately. Rather, the immediate object of perception is always some idea (or image, or sensation) in the mind. This theory is "common," Reid thinks, in the sense that it is accepted almost universally by philosophers.

Modern philosophers, as well as the Peripatetics and Epicureans of old, have conceived, that external objects cannot be the immediate objects of our thought; that there must be some image of them in the mind itself, in which, as in a mirror, they are seen. And the name *idea*, in the philosophical sense of it, is given to those internal and immediate objects of our thoughts. The external thing is the remote or mediate object; but the idea, or image of that object in the mind, is the immediate object, without which we could have no perception, no remembrance, no conception of the mediate object. (EIP I.i: 31)

These shadows or images, which we immediately perceive, were by the ancients called *species, forms, phantasms*. Since the time of DES CARTES, they have commonly been called *ideas*, and by Mr HUME *impressions*. But all philosophers, from PLATO to Mr HUME, agree in this, That we do not perceive external objects immediately, and that the immediate object of perception must be some image present to the mind. So far there appears an unanimity, rarely to be found among Philosophers on such abstruse points. (EIP II.vii: 105)

Nevertheless, this common theory leads inevitably to skeptical results.

[We have] reason to apprehend that Des Cartes' system of the human understanding, which I shall beg leave to call *the ideal system*, and which, with some improvements made by later writers, is now generally received, hath some original defect; that this scepticism is inlaid in it, and reared along with it. ... (IHM I.vii: 23)

We ought, however, to do this justice to the Bishop of Cloyne and to the author of the *Treatise of human nature*, to acknowledge, that their conclusions are justly drawn from the doctrine of ideas, which has been so universally received. ... The theory of ideas, like the Trojan horse, had a specious appearance both of innocence and beauty ... but carried in its belly death and destruction to all science and common sense. ... (IHM V.viii: 75)

How so? According to Reid, the theory of ideas leads to skepticism via various arguments due to its modern proponents, Berkeley and Hume. The genius of those men, Reid thinks, consists in their seeing clearly the skeptical consequences of this seemingly innocent doctrine. Here is one argument that Reid sees in Berkeley.

Bishop Berkeley gave new light to this subject, by showing, that the qualities of an inanimate thing, such as matter is conceived to be, cannot resemble any sensation; that it is impossible to conceive anything like the sensations of our minds, but the sensations of other minds.... But let us observe what use the Bishop makes of this important discovery. Why, he concludes, that we can have no conception of an inanimate substance, such as matter is conceived to be, or of any of its qualities; and that there is the strongest ground to believe that there is no existence in nature but minds, sensations, and ideas: If there is any other kind of existence, it must be what we neither have nor can have any conception of. But how does this follow? Why, thus: We can have no conception of anything but what resembles some sensation or idea in our minds; but the sensations and ideas in our minds can resemble nothing but the sensations and ideas in other minds; therefore, the conclusion is evident. (IHM V.viii: 74–5)

Berkeley's argument can be reconstructed as follows. We may label it the "No Possible Conception" argument.
(NPC)

1. We can have no conception of anything but what resembles some sensation or idea in our minds.
2. But the sensations and ideas in our minds can resemble nothing but sensations and ideas. In particular, sensations and ideas cannot resemble inanimate substances.

Therefore,

3. We can have no conception of inanimate substances. (1,2)
4. Our having evidence or knowledge of a thing requires our being able to conceive of it. (implicit assumption)

Therefore,

5. We can have neither evidence nor knowledge of inanimate substances. (3,4)

Reid's analysis of this argument is straightforward:

This argument, we see, leans upon two premises. The last of them [premise 2] the ingenious author hath, indeed, made evident to all that understand his reasoning, and can attend to their own sensations: but the first proposition [premise 1] he never attempts to prove; it is taken from the doctrine of ideas, which hath been so universally received by philosophers, that it was thought to need no proof. (IHM V.viii: 75)

The conclusion is entailed by the premises, and there are no questionable premises other than premise 1, which is implied by the theory of ideas. Hence the theory of ideas is sufficient to generate the skeptical conclusion.

There is another aspect of the theory of ideas that, according to Reid, generates skeptical results even more straightforwardly. Specifically, Reid considers Locke's claim that "the mind, in all its thoughts and reasonings, hath no other immediate object but its own ideas...."[1] Here is what he says.

[Locke] has never attempted to show how there can be objects of thought which are not immediate objects; and, indeed, this seems impossible. For, whatever the object be, the man either thinks of it, or he does not. There is no medium between these. If he thinks of it, it is an immediate object of thought while he thinks of it. If he does not think of it, it is no object of thought at all. Every object of thought, therefore, is an immediate object of thought, and the word *immediate*, joined to objects of thought, seems to be a mere expletive. (EIP VI.iii: 437)[2]

From Locke's position, Reid thinks, it follows easily that there can be no knowledge of external objects. We may call this the "No Mediate Object" argument.
(NMO)

1. We can have no immediate object of thought but our own ideas.
2. All objects of thought are immediate objects of thought.

Therefore,

3. We can have no object of thought but our own ideas. (1,2)
4. We can have knowledge only of what is an object of thought.
5. External objects are, by definition, not ideas.

Therefore,

    6. We can have no knowledge of external objects. (3,4,5)

Again, premise 1 of the argument is a central thesis of the theory of ideas. Premises 2, 4, and 5 are also independent premises of (NMO), but Reid considers each of them to be unquestionable. Therefore, again, the theory of ideas is sufficient to generate a sweeping skeptical result.

B. Reid's Arguments Against the Theory of Ideas

If the theory of ideas is sufficient for generating skeptical results, then skepticism can be avoided only by rejecting that theory. Reid gives several reasons for doing just that. Here I will focus on just two of those, both of which Reid relates to Newton's criteria for explaining natural phenomena:

The first rule of philosophising laid down by the great NEWTON, is this: *Causas rerum naturalium, non plures admitti debere, quam quae et verae sint, et earum phaenomenis explicandis sufficiant.* "No more causes, nor any other causes of natural effects, ought to be admitted, but such as are both true, and are sufficient for explaining their appearances." ... If a Philosopher, therefore, pretends to show us the cause of any natural effect, whether relating to matter or to mind, let us first consider whether there is sufficient evidence that the cause he assigns does really exist.... If the cause assigned really exists, consider, in the next place, whether the effect it is brought to explain necessarily follows from it. Unless it has these two conditions, it is good for nothing. (EIP I.iii: 51)

According to Reid, the theory of ideas fails both tests. There is no evidence to show that ideas (as the theory of ideas conceives them to be) actually exist. And even if such ideas did exist, they would not explain the phenomena that they are supposed to explain.

    It seems odd, at first, to say that there is no evidence that ideas exist. But Reid clarifies:

To prevent mistakes, the reader must again be reminded, that if by ideas are meant only the acts or operations of our minds in perceiving, remembering, or imagining objects, I am far from calling in question the existence of those acts; we are conscious of them every day and every hour of our life.... The ideas, of whose existence I require the proof, are not the operations of any mind, but the supposed objects of those operations. They are not perception, remembrance, or conception, but things that are said to be perceived, or remembered, or imagined. (EIP II.xiv: 171)

In other words, Reid sees no evidence for ideas considered as distinct from the acts (or operations) of the mind, but which are rather the immediate objects of the mind's acts, whenever we perceive, remember, imagine, etc. Reflection does not reveal any such objects, for reflection tells us that the immediate object of perception is the *external* object perceived, not an idea of the external object. Likewise, reflection tells us that the immediate objects of memory and imagination are the objects remembered and imagined, not our ideas of such objects, which somehow stand in for or represent them.

When we see the sun or moon, we have no doubt that the very objects which we immediately see are very far distinct from us, and from one another.... (EIP II.xiv: 172)

I see the sun when she shines; I remember the battle of Culloden; and neither of these objects is an image or perception. (EIP II.xiv: 179)

Such comments might seem too quick, and to therefore beg the relevant questions at issue. After all, the skeptic will claim that Reid has identified the *mediate* objects of our thought in these examples, not the immediate objects, which are our ideas. But elsewhere Reid relies on careful analysis to make the point. Consider the following passage, where Reid argues that (a) the immediate objects of thought in tactile perception are the real qualities of the body touched, and (b) our sensations are not an object of thought at all in typical cases of perception. It is worth quoting Reid at length here, since much of his case against the theory of ideas rests on such analysis.

When the parts of a body adhere so firmly that it cannot easily be made to change its figure, we call it *hard*; when its parts are easily displaced, we call it *soft*. This is the notion which all mankind have of hardness and softness: they are neither sensations, nor like any sensation; they were real qualities before they were perceived by touch, and continue to be so when they are not perceived....

There is, no doubt, a sensation by which we perceive a body to be hard or soft. This sensation of hardness may easily be had, by pressing one's hand against the table, and attending to the feeling that ensues, setting aside, as much a possible, all thought of the table and its qualities, or of any external thing. But it is one thing to have the sensation and another thing to attend to it, and make it a distinct object of reflection. The first is very easy; the last, in most cases, extremely difficult.

We are so accustomed to use the sensation as a sign, and to pass immediately to the hardness signified, that, as far as appears, it was never made an object of thought, either by the vulgar or by philosophers; nor has it a name in any language. There is no sensation more distinct, or more frequent; yet it is never attended to, but passes through the mind instantaneously, and serves only to introduce that quality in bodies, which, by a law of our constitution, it suggests. (IHM V.ii: 55–6)

Again, the question in dispute is not whether ideas, images or sensations exist. If by these we mean acts or operations of the mind – acts of sensing, of perceiving, of imagining, of thinking – then clearly such things exist. The question is whether there exist ideas *as the theory of ideas conceives them to be*; that is, as distinct from acts of sensing, perceiving, imagining, etc., and as the immediate objects of thought whenever we sense, perceive, imagine, etc. It is the existence of ideas in this sense that Reid denies. On the contrary, Reid argues, ideas (or sensations, or images) are almost never objects of thought *at all*, much less the *immediate* objects of thought, *whenever* we perceive, imagine, etc.

Or at least reflection (or introspection) does not reveal this to be so. On the contrary, reflection counts squarely against the theory of ideas on this point. Are there any good arguments for positing the existence of ideas, conceived as the immediate objects of our thought? In other words, do philosophers give us any good reasons for positing their existence, even if their existence is not revealed by introspection? Such arguments are rarely offered, Reid observes: "the doctrine of ideas ... hath been so universally received by philosophers, that it was thought to need no proof" (IHM V.viii: 75). But those arguments that are given Reid finds wanting. After reviewing the few he has discovered in Hume and others, he concludes: "I cannot help thinking, that the whole history of philosophy has never furnished an instance of an opinion so unanimously entertained by Philosophers upon so slight grounds" (EIP II.xiv: 183–4).[3]

Suppose that Reid is correct – that reflection does not reveal the existence of ideas (as the theory of ideas conceives them to be), and that we have no good arguments for their existence either. Reid's second objection is that, even if such ideas did exist, they would not explain what they are supposed to explain. That is, they would do nothing to show how perception, imagination, memory, and other mental phenomena are possible.

Reid's thinking is as follows. The theory of ideas tries to explain various mental phenomena by reducing them to one – to the immediate perception of ideas in the mind. Thus in imagination we perceive an image that is constructed out of previous sensations, and that might have no corresponding existence in external reality. In memory we perceive an image that was caused by an earlier sensation, and that is now recalled for another viewing. In perception proper, we immediately perceive a sensation that is caused by some external object that resembles it. Now suppose that such ideas do indeed exist and that they are involved in memory, imagination and perception in just the ways that have been suggested. This would explain nothing, Reid insists, for we are at a loss to understand how the immediate perception of ideas is possible.

But, this feeling, or immediate perception, is as difficult to be comprehended as the things which we pretend to explain by it. Two things may be in contact without any feeling or perception; there must therefore be in the percipient a power to feel or perceive. How this power is produced, and how it operates, is quite beyond the reach of our knowledge.... This power of perceiving ideas is as inexplicable as any of the powers explained by it. (EIP II.xiv: 185)

Reid concludes as follows:

The dark cave and shadows of PLATO, the species of ARISTOTLE, the films of EPICURUS, and the ideas and impressions of modern Philosophers, are the productions of human fancy, successively invented to satisfy the eager desire of knowing how we perceive external objects; but they are all deficient in the two essential characters of a true and philosophical account of the phaenomenon: For we neither have any evidence of their existence, nor, if they did exist, can it be shewn how they would produce perception. (EIP II.xx: 226)

II. REID'S THEORY OF PERCEPTION

The two skeptical arguments above show that the theory of ideas is sufficient to generate broad skeptical results. That is why Reid thinks that any successful reply to skepticism must reject the theory of ideas. But Reid also claims that the theory of ideas is necessary for generating skeptical results:

> For my own satisfaction, I entered into a serious examination of the principles upon which this sceptical system is built; and was not a little surprised to find, that it leans with its whole weight upon a hypothesis, which is ancient indeed, and hath been very generally received by philosophers, but of which I could find no solid proof. The hypothesis I mean, is, That nothing is perceived but what is in the mind which perceives it: That we do not really perceive things that are external, but only certain images and pictures of them imprinted upon the mind, which are called *impressions and ideas*. (IHM Dedication: 4)

> All the arguments urged by BERKELEY and HUME against the existence of a material world, are grounded on this principle, That we do not perceive external objects themselves, but certain images or ideas in our own minds. (EIP VI.v: 478)

This claim seems wrong, however, and that is why an adequate reply to the skeptic must do more than reject the theory of ideas.

The claim is wrong because there are arguments for skepticism that do not invoke the theory of ideas at all. For example, consider the following remarks from Reid himself:

> Ideas are said to be things internal and present, which have no existence but during the moment they are in the mind. The objects of sense are things external, which have a continued existence. When it is maintained, that all we immediately perceive is only ideas or phantasms, how can we, from the existence of those phantasms, conclude the existence of an external world corresponding to them?
>
> This difficult question seemed not to have occurred to the Peripatetics. DES CARTES saw the difficulty, and endeavoured to find out arguments by which, from the existence of our phantasms or ideas, we might infer the existence of external objects. The same course was followed by MALEBRANCHE, ARNAULD, and LOCKE; but BERKELEY and HUME easily refuted all their arguments, and demonstrated that there is no strength in them. (EIP III.vii: 289–90)

Here the problem is not that it is impossible to conceive inanimate substances and their qualities, nor is it that we can have no object of thought beyond our immediate thought of ideas. Rather, it is that our sensations cannot give us adequate *evidence* for our beliefs about external objects. Put differently, there is no way to *infer* external

objects from our sensations of them. Let us call this the "No Good Inference" argument. It may be reconstructed as follows.
(NGI)

1. All knowledge is either immediate (not inferred from evidence) or mediate (inferred from immediate knowledge that serves as its evidence).
2. All immediate knowledge is about our ideas or sensations.

Therefore,

3. If we are to have knowledge of external objects, it must be by means of an adequate inference from knowledge of our ideas and sensations. (1,2)
4. But there is no adequate inference from knowledge of our ideas and sensations to our beliefs about external objects.

Therefore,

5. We can have no knowledge of external objects. (3,4)

Notice that (NGI) does not invoke the theory of ideas at all. On the contrary, we could understand "ideas" and "sensations" in the argument in various ways, including the way that Reid would understand them; i.e., as *acts* of the mind. On that reading, premises 2 and 4 would remain plausible. In fact, Reid agrees that Berkeley and Hume have established premise 4, as the last sentences of the passage just quoted testify.

Here is another way to see that (NGI) raises a problem different from either the "No Possible Conception" argument or the "No Mediate Object" argument. Whereas all three arguments employ a distinction between what is and is not "immediate," (NPC) and (NMO) talk about immediate and mediate *objects of thought*. (NGI), on the other hand, talks about immediate and mediate *knowledge*. We might call the first kind of immediacy "conceptual immediacy." Here the idea is that we can conceive ideas directly, so to speak, whereas we can conceive other things, such as external objects, only indirectly, by means of ideas that represent them. Problems then arise when we consider how it is possible to conceive external objects accurately on this model, or how it is possible to conceive them at all. That is not the problem raised by (NGI), however. Rather, (NGI) grants that we can conceive and make judgments about external objects. But the argument asks how we can know that such judgments are true. Here the distinction is between immediate knowledge (or knowledge not inferred from further evidence), and mediate knowledge (or knowledge that is inferred from what is known immediately). This issue concerns what we might call "epistemic immediacy." Assuming that our knowledge of external objects is not epistemically immediate, the question becomes how we can *infer* that our judgments about external objects are true. Put another way, the question concerns what evidence is available to ground such inferences.

The present point is that this question makes sense independent of the theory of ideas. For no matter how we conceive sensations, it would seem that sensations are the evidence for our perceptual judgments about external objects. And no matter how we conceive sensations, there seems to be no good inference from that kind of evidence to that kind of judgment. Reid needs a reply to this line of reasoning. But since this reasoning does not depend on the theory of ideas, his reply must go beyond rejecting that theory.

At least part of Reid's reply, I suggest, is to be found in his theory of perception. In a nutshell, perception is not an inferential process at all, according to Reid, and therefore perceptual knowledge does not require an adequate inference from sensations to judgments about external objects. Let us take a look at some things that Reid says about the perception of external objects. That will put us in a position to make some general points about Reid's theory of perception, and to apply those points to the "No Good Inference" argument and to the other skeptical arguments above.

In the passages that follow, Reid is talking about tactile perception, or perception by touch.

When I grasp a ball in my hand, I perceive it at once hard, figured, and extended. The feeling is very simple, and hath not the least resemblance to any quality of body. Yet it suggests to us three primary qualities perfectly distinct from one another, as well as from the sensation which indicates them. When I move my hand along the table, the feeling is so simple that I find it difficult to distinguish it into things of different natures; yet, it immediately suggests hardness, smoothness, extension, and motion, things of very different natures, and all of them as distinctly understood as the feeling which suggests them.... It is true we have feelings of touch, which every moment present extension to the mind; but how they come to do so, is the question; for those feelings do no more resemble extension, than they resemble justice or courage: nor can the existence of extended things be inferred from those feelings by any rules of reasoning. (IHM V.v: 63)

Let a man press his hand against the table: *he feels it hard*. But what is the meaning of this? The meaning undoubtedly is, that he hath a certain feeling of touch, from which he concludes, without any reasoning, or comparing of ideas, that there is something external really existing, whose parts stick so firmly together, that they cannot be displaced without considerable force.... And as the feeling has no similitude to hardness, so neither can our reasoning perceive the least tie or connection between them; nor will the logician ever be able to show a reason why we should conclude hardness from this feeling, rather than softness, or any other quality whatsoever. But in reality all mankind are led by their constitution to conclude hardness from this feeling. (IHM V.v: 64)

How a sensation should instantly make us conceive and believe the existence of an external thing altogether unlike it, I do not pretend to know; and when I say that the one suggests the other, I mean not to explain the manner of their connection, but to express a fact, which every one may be conscious of; namely, that, by a law of our nature, such a conception and belief constantly and immediately follow the sensation. (IHM V. viii: 74)

For our purposes, we may highlight three points in the passages above. In cases of perception:

a. there is no resemblance between the sensation (in this case, the way the object *feels* to the touch) and the external property that the object is perceived to have;

b. it is not by reasoning, nor any sort of inference, that one moves from the sensation to the belief that the perceived object has the relevant external property;

c. although not by inference, the relevant perceptual belief nevertheless follows upon the sensation "by a law of our nature," in virtue of our natural "constitution."

To these points we may add another that was emphasized earlier:

d. in typical cases, we do not think of the sensation at all, but only about the object perceived. "We are so accustomed to use the sensation as a sign, and to pass immediately to the hardness signified, that, as far as appears, it was never made an object of thought, either by the vulgar or by philosophers; nor has it a name in any language" (IHM V.ii: 56).

Reid makes all of these points about other modes of perception as well.

> The sensations of touch, of seeing, and hearing are all in the mind, and can have no existence but when they are perceived. How do they all constantly and invariably suggest the conception and belief of external objects, which exist whether they are perceived or not? ... Not by custom surely; not by reasoning, or comparing ideas, but by the constitution of our nature. (IHM VI.xii: 124–5)

> When a primary quality is perceived, the sensation immediately leads our thought to the quality signified by it, and is itself forgot. We have no occasion afterwards to reflect upon it; and so we come to be as little acquainted with it, as if we had never felt it. (EIP II.xvii: 204)

The passages above stress that perception does not involve reasoning (point (b)) and that perceptual beliefs are due to natural laws governing our cognitive character (point (c)). Neither of these points, however, implies that perception is not learned or acquired. Most perception, Reid thinks, is acquired perception.

> In all our senses, the acquired perceptions are many more than the original.... Not only men, but children, idiots and brutes, acquire by habit many perceptions which they had not originally.... The farmer perceives by his eye, very nearly, the quantity of hay in a rick, or of corn in a heap. The sailor sees the burthen, the built, and the distance of a ship at sea, while she is a great way off. (IHM VI.xx: 171–2)

But even acquired perception is devoid of reasoning or inference, according to Reid.

> This power which we acquire of perceiving things by our senses, which originally we should not have perceived, is not the effect of any reasoning on our part: It is the result of our constitution, and of the situations in which we happen to be placed. (EIP II.xxi: 238)

> Perception, whether original or acquired, implies no exercise of reason; and is common to men, children, idiots, and brutes. (IHM VI.xx: 173)

Reid's general model of perception, therefore, is as follows: An external object causes some physical change in some organ of sense, which, by the laws of nature, causes some sensation in the mind. This sensation, again by the laws of nature, gives rise to a conception of and belief about the external object.[4] In original perception the process is "hardwired," so to speak. In acquired perception the process is shaped by previous experience. But neither original nor acquired perception involves reasoning or inference, and neither need involve thinking about the relevant sensations at all.

The question we need to address now is this: How is Reid's theory of perception antiskeptical? Certainly, the theory provides no guarantee that our perceptual beliefs are true. There is no guarantee, that is, that the beliefs that result from perception accurately represent the objects that cause those beliefs. In fact, Reid concedes that perception is fallible, and so it is part of this theory that perceptual beliefs are sometimes *not* true. So again, even if Reid is correct about points (a) through (d) above, how does any of that help to answer the skeptic, or to provide any resources against skepticism at all? The answer is that Reid's theory of perception grounds replies to each of the skeptical arguments that we have seen above. In other words, the theory explains why at least one premise in each argument is false. First consider the "No Good Inference" argument. Premise (2) of (NGI) claims that all immediate knowledge is about our ideas or sensations. In other words, it claims that all noninferential knowledge is of ideas or sensations. On the basis of this premise, the argument concludes that knowledge of external objects must be inferred from knowledge of our sensations. Reid's theory of perception, however, denies premise (2) and hence blocks the inference. Specifically, point (b) tells us that it is not by reasoning, or any sort of inference, that we go from sensation to belief in perception. To require an adequate inference from sensation, therefore, is to misunderstand the nature of perception.

Reid's theory also explains missteps in the "No Possible Conception" argument and the "No Mediate Object" argument. It answers the "No Possible Conception" argument by denying premise (1) of (NPC): That we can have no conception of anything but what resembles some sensation or idea in our minds. Point (a) tells us that there is no resemblance between our sensations and the properties that objects are perceived to have. But since perception involves conception, we do conceive such properties, and so premise (1) of (NPC) must be false. Reid makes this point explicit in the following passage.

Upon the whole, it appears, that our philosophers have imposed upon themselves, and upon us, in pretending to deduce from sensation the first origin of our notions of external existences, of space, motion, and extension, and all the primary qualities of body.... They have no resemblance to any sensation, or to any operation of our minds; and, therefore, they cannot be ideas either of sensation or of reflection. The very conception of them is irreconcilable to the principles of all our philosophic systems of the understanding. The belief of them is no less so. (IHM V.vi: 67)

Finally, consider the "No Mediate Object" argument. Premise (1) of (NMO) claims that we can have no immediate object of thought but our own ideas. This premise is contradicted by point (d) of Reid's theory: In cases of perception, the *only* object of thought is the object perceived. In the typical case, we do not think of our sensations at all, but rather the external objects that our sensations signify.

Hence Reid's theory of perception gives him resources for answering each of the skeptical arguments that we have seen above. Of course none of this shows that perception *does* give rise to knowledge. It is one thing to show that there are no good arguments for skepticism – it is another to show that skepticism is false. This is why an adequate reply to the skeptic requires more than just a critique of skeptical arguments. Specifically, it requires a theory of evidence that explains *why* our faculties of perception give rise to knowledge.

III. REID'S THEORY OF EVIDENCE

Reid's theory of evidence may be described as a moderate and broad foundationalism. The theory is "moderate" in the sense that Reid does not require infallibility for knowledge. Neither does he require indefeasibility or irrevisability, or some other high-powered epistemic property. It is "broad" in the sense that Reid allows a wide variety of sources of both foundational and nonfoundational knowledge. For Reid, introspective consciousness, perception, memory, testimony, deductive reasoning, and inductive reasoning are all sources of evidence and knowledge.

For present purposes, we may focus on two points that Reid stresses about these various sources. The first is that none of these sources is reducible to the other.

The evidence of sense, the evidence of memory, and the evidence of the necessary relations of things, are all distinct and original kinds of evidence, equally grounded on our constitution: none of them depends upon, or can be resolved into another. (IHM II.v: 32)

One aspect of this independence is that perception does not need the vindication of reason. In other words, perception does not get its status as a source of knowledge because reason shows it to be such: "perception commands our belief upon its own authority, and disdains to rest its authority upon any reasoning whatsoever" (EIP II.v: 99).

The second point that Reid stresses is that all the sources of evidence are of equal authority. "The first principles of every kind of reasoning are given us by Nature, and are of equal authority with the faculty of reason itself, which is also the gift of Nature" (IHM VI.xx: 172). In particular, "the evidence of sense [is] no less reasonable than that of demonstration" (EIP II.xx: 230). In other words, the evidence of demonstration (or reason) should not be privileged over the evidence of perception. Here Reid finds the skeptic about perception to be inconsistent.

Reason, says the sceptic, is the only judge of truth, and you ought to throw off every opinion and every belief that is not grounded on reason. Why, Sir, should I believe the faculty of reason more than that of perception; they came both out of the same shop, and were made by the same artist; and if he puts one piece of false ware into my hands, what should hinder him from putting another? (IHM VI.xx: 169)

In fact, Reid observes, reason and perception are on the same footing with respect to their trustworthiness.

The imagination, the memory, the judging and reasoning powers, are all liable to be hurt, or even destroyed, by disorders of the body, as well as our powers of perception; but we do not on this account call them fallacious. (EIP II.xxii: 244–5)

They are all limited and imperfect. . . . We are liable to error and wrong judgment in the use of them all; but as little in the informations of sense as in the deductions of reasoning. (EIP II.xxii: 252)

So far, we have that perception is an independent source of knowledge. In other words, our perceptual faculties can give rise to knowledge all by themselves, without the benefit of some prior vindication from reason. But we would like to know *why* this is so: What is it about perception that *makes* it a source of knowledge?

In some places, Reid writes as if he has no answer to that question. For example,

Philosophers have endeavored, by analysing the different sorts of evidence, to find out some common nature by which they all agree, and thereby to reduce them all to one. . . . I confess that, although I have, as I think, a distinct notion of the different kinds of evidence above mentioned . . . yet I am not able to find any common nature to which they all may be reduced. (EIP II.xx: 229)

Here Reid seems to be saying that he can find nothing in common among the various sources of evidence and knowledge – that he can find nothing in their common nature that makes them fit to be such sources. However, Reid's next sentence rehearses a common theme in his writing, and one that points to an implicit theory about the nature of evidence.

They seem to me to agree only in this, that they are all fitted by Nature to produce belief in the human mind, some of them in the highest degree, which we call certainty, others in various degrees according to circumstances. (EIP II.xx: 229)

Here Reid comes back to a theme we have seen before (in point (c) above): That all the sources of knowledge, including perception, are "fitted by Nature" to operate in us as they do, that they are "given us by Nature" and "the result of our constitution." We may add to this that the various sources of knowledge are equally trustworthy in their normal and healthy state. "We are liable to error and wrong judgment in the use of them all; but as little in the informations of sense as in the deductions of reasoning" (EIP II.xxii: 252). These points taken together imply a kind of "proper function" faculty reliabilism. According to Reid, our cognitive faculties give us knowledge so long as they are part of our natural constitution and "not fallacious." Put another way, knowledge arises from the proper functioning of our natural, nonfallacious (i.e., reliable) cognitive faculties.[5]

And now we have the explanation of perceptual knowledge that we were looking for. According to Reid, perception is a source of knowledge because it is a natural and nonfallacious cognitive faculty. As such, it is of equal authority with reason, and with all other natural, nonfallacious cognitive faculties.

I have been arguing that Reid's theory of evidence is an important part of his reply to the skeptic. This claim contradicts Reid's official view, which is that a rejection of the common theory of ideas is sufficient to refute skepticism. But Reid himself, at least unofficially, recognizes that skepticism trades on a bad theory of evidence as well as a bad theory of ideas. Thus Reid attributes the theory of ideas to ancient philosophers, but notes that their positions were not skeptical. This is because the ancients, like Reid, accepted a broad range of first principles.

The old system admitted all the principles of common sense as first principles, without requiring any proof of them; and, therefore, though its reasoning was commonly vague, analogical, and dark, yet it was built upon a broad foundation, and had no tendency to scepticism. (IHM VII: 210)

The same is not true of the modern philosophers, however.

The new system admits only one of the principles of common sense as a first principle; and pretends, by strict argumentation, to deduce all the rest from it. That our thoughts, our sensations, and every thing of which we are conscious, hath a real existence, is admitted in this system as a first principle; but everything else must be made evident by the light of reason. Reason must rear the whole fabric of knowledge upon this single principle of consciousness. (IHM VII: 210)

And this is at least one reason that modern philosophy falls into skepticism.

We do not find that any Peripatetic thought it incumbent upon him to prove the existence of a material world; but every writer upon the Cartesian system attempted this, until Berkeley clearly demonstrated the futility of their arguments; and thence concluded that there was no such thing as a material world; and that the belief of it ought to be rejected as a vulgar error. (IHM VII: 210)

In short, an adequate reply to the skeptic requires a substantive theory of evidence. In other words, it needs a theory that explains why perception is itself a source of knowledge, contra the modern view.

IV. REID'S METHODOLOGY

At this point one might think that Reid has reached an impasse with the skeptic: Reid endorses a broad and moderate foundationalism, admitting a variety of sources of knowledge, including perception. The skeptic endorses a more strict view, allowing only consciousness and reason as sources of knowledge. Clearly, Reid's antiskeptical conclusions follow from his theory of evidence, but so do the skeptic's conclusions follow from his. Which theory of evidence is correct, and who is to say? To understand how Reid breaks this impasse we must consider one more aspect of his reply to the skeptic. Namely, we must consider Reid's methodology for investigating which theory of evidence is correct.

First, note that there are three options available when undertaking an investigation into our cognitive faculties: (a) we may begin by trusting none of our faculties until we have reason for believing them trustworthy, (b) we may begin by trusting some of our faculties but not others, or (c) we may begin by trusting all of our faculties until we have reason for believing them untrustworthy. Reid argues that the first option is a nonstarter and that the second is inconsistent. Hence we are left with the third option: to begin by trusting all of our faculties until we have reason not to. But if we adopt this third methodology, Reid argues, we will find no reason to think that our cognitive faculties are not trustworthy. In other words, the only viable methodology leads us to Reid's broad foundationalism.

Again, consider the various options that are available when undertaking an investigation into our cognitive faculties. The first option is to trust no cognitive faculty until its trustworthiness has been vindicated. This might seem like a viable methodology at first, and Descartes seems to have adopted it. But it is easy to see, Reid argues, that this methodology goes nowhere.

If a Sceptic should build his scepticism upon this foundation, that all our reasoning and judging powers are fallacious in their nature, or should resolve at least to withhold assent until it be proved that they are not; it would be impossible by argument to beat him out of his strong hold, and he must even be left to enjoy his scepticism.... For if our faculties be fallacious; why may they not deceive us in this reasoning as well as in others? (EIP VI.v: 480–1)

Reid's point is that we must use our cognitive faculties to investigate the reliability of those faculties. This is not an unfortunate aspect of the human condition – it is a simple matter of logic. That is, investigating and reasoning are a kind of cognition, and we have no choice but to cognize by means of our powers of cognizing. But then any sort of reasoning about our cognitive faculties will employ those very faculties, and so it will be impossible to vindicate them *before* we trust them.

Every kind of reasoning for the veracity of our faculties, amounts to no more than taking their own testimony for their veracity; and this we must do implicitly, until God gives us new faculties to sit in judgment upon the old.... (EIP VI.v: 481)

At which point, of course, we would remain in the same predicament with respect to these new faculties.

To begin by distrusting all of our cognitive faculties is therefore a nonstarter. If we were to adopt this methodology, our investigation could not get off the ground. But neither should we begin by trusting some of our faculties and not others. This is the method of the skeptic,[6] but this method is inconsistent.

Thus the faculties of consciousness, of memory, of external sense, and of reason, are all equally the gifts of Nature. No good reason can be assigned for receiving the testimony of one of them, which is not of equal force with regard to the others. The greatest sceptics admit the testimony of consciousness, and allow that what it testifies is to be held as a first principle. If therefore they reject the immediate testimony of sense or of memory, they are guilty of an inconsistency. (EIP VI.iv: 463)

The point here is that even the skeptic (Hume, for example) trusts some of his faculties. We saw that the skeptic trusts the deliverances of consciousness, and demands that all else "must be made evident by the light of reason." But why trust consciousness and reason, but not perception and memory? Again, "they came ... out of the same shop, and were made by the same artist; and if he puts one piece of false ware into my hands, what should hinder him from putting another?" Such a skeptic, Reid thinks, is being inconsistent – he is demanding the vindication of some faculties but not others, and for no good reason.

To begin by trusting none of our faculties is pointless. To begin by trusting some but not others is inconsistent. The remaining alternative is to begin by trusting all of our faculties until we find some reason not to trust them. If we adopt this methodology, Reid argues, we will continue to trust consciousness and reason, for we will find no reason to think them unreliable. But neither will we find perception (or others of our natural faculties) to be unreliable:

There is no more reason to account our senses fallacious, than our reason, our memory, or any other faculty of judging which nature hath given us. They are all limited and imperfect.... We are liable to error and wrong judgment in the use of them all; but as little in the informations of sense as in the deductions of reasoning. (EIP II.xxii: 251–2)

Again, the present methodology drives us to a broad foundationalism: There are many natural, nonfallacious, original sources of belief. There are also many natural, nonfallacious ways to reason from belief. Moreover, these original sources of belief (because they are natural and nonfallacious) are also sources of knowledge. And these powers of reasoning (because they are natural and nonfallacious) are powers for extending our knowledge. This is not to say that our cognitive faculties are infallible – Reid's foundationalism is moderate as well as broad. Neither is it to say that our faculties do not develop – Reid is clear that both our original sources of belief and our reasoning powers develop and fine-tune over time. Nevertheless, our sources of knowledge are many, and are of equal authority with consciousness and reason, the preferred faculties of skeptics.

Notice that Reid's methodology effectively blocks some other familiar routes to skepticism. For example, the skeptic commonly complains that one cannot prove that external things exist. The appropriate reply to this complaint is that it is true but irrelevant. It is true that one cannot prove that external things exist – at least one cannot prove it from premises that the skeptic will allow. But it does not follow from this that we do not know that external things exist. That is because, put simply, we do not know such a thing by proving it. Again, there are many sources of knowledge, including perception, and there is no problem accounting for knowledge of external things if we recognize all of those sources.[7]

Another common complaint from the skeptic is that "we cannot get outside the circle of belief." Put another way, we cannot judge belief except by means of further belief, which in turn is in need of judgment. But this is just another way of raising the point that judging is a kind of cognition, and cognition requires cognizing. Reid's reply is evident: *Of course* we can only judge by judging, but the proper methodology of epistemology reveals that we have many nonfallacious sources of judgment.

In conclusion, we have reviewed four major elements of Reid's reply to the skeptic: one critical, two substantive, and one methodological. It seems to me that Reid is right about which methodology we should adopt, and for just the reasons he gives. I suggest that if we join this methodology with the other elements of Reid's philosophy reviewed above, then Reid's reply to the skeptic is unanswerable.[8,9]

NOTES

1. Quoted by Reid at EIP VI.iii: 436. The passage is from E IV.i.1.
2. See also EIP II.ix: 134.
3. For a discussion of these arguments and Reid's analysis, see the essay by Van Cleve, this volume.
4. The exception to this general model is the perception of visible figure, where Reid thinks that no independent sensations are involved at all. For a discussion of Reid's account of the perception of visible figure, see the essay by Van Cleve, this volume.
5. See Plantinga 1993: esp. 50.
6. IHM V.vii: 71–2.
7. See Greco 2002.
8. I defend Reid's reply to the skeptic, including methodological aspects of that reply, in Greco 2000 and Greco 2002. For further discussion of Reid's reply to the skeptic, see DeRose 1989; Lehrer 1989; Greco 1995; and Wolterstorff 2001.
9. I would like to thank Terence Cuneo and Lorne Falkenstein for comments on an earlier draft of this essay.

6 Nativism and the Nature of Thought in Reid's Account of Our Knowledge of the External World

In a strictly literal sense, to say that a thought is "innate" is to claim that we are born with it. Reid was not concerned to claim that we have such thoughts. When discussing Locke's views on our knowledge of first principles he wrote:

[Locke] endeavours to show, that axioms or intuitive truths are not innate. To this I agree. I maintain only, that when the understanding is ripe, and when we distinctly apprehend such truths, we immediately assent to them. (EIP VI.vii: 520)

This statement might seem to qualify Locke's rejection of innate principles, but it does not. Since a truth that is immediately assented to as soon as it is distinctly apprehended just is an intuitively evident truth,[1] the statement claims no more than that there are intuitively evident truths, while allowing that our intuitions of these truths may not be "innate" in the sense of being inborn. Locke would not have disagreed with either point.

Yet there was a dispute between Locke and Reid, not made explicit in this passage. Locke thought that we intuit by inspecting ideas previously obtained from sensation or reflection and simply seeing that they stand in certain relations to one another. Reid was willing to countenance intuitions that are obtained in other ways than by discerning relations between "ideas" obtained from sensation or reflection. He was also willing to countenance types of thought that may not have fit comfortably under Locke's notions of an idea of sensation or an idea of reflection. In so doing, Reid countenanced beliefs and thoughts that are innate in something other than the crude sense of having been inborn.

Reid's nativism has consequences for his rejection of the way of ideas and of skepticism about our knowledge of an external world. But drawing these consequences out requires considering Reid's position on the nature of thought as well as his position on its "innate" origin. I therefore devote some attention to the former topic and specify the role played by each of these importantly distinct sets of commitments in establishing Reid's results.

I. VARIETIES OF NATIVISM

In addition to being used to refer to thoughts that are inborn, the term "innate" has been used to refer to thoughts that are original, a priori, or unlearned.

Whereas an inborn thought is one that is present at birth (or so shortly thereafter that experience cannot be supposed to have any role in its development) an original thought need not be. An original thought is one that has been produced by the mind rather than received or copied from some external source. This is the sense of "innate" that Descartes had in mind when he claimed that all our ideas are innate.[2] Descartes justified this claim by asserting that nothing reaches our minds from external objects except certain motions of animal spirits that bear no resemblance to the ideas the mind goes on to form when these motions occur. The ideas must therefore be originally produced by the mind. Even our sensations are innate in this sense.

Original thoughts may be considered to be of two types: those that, despite being originally produced by the mind, can only first be produced by it on the occasion of sensory stimulation, and those that the mind is able to produce prior to or independent of having specific sense organs stimulated in specific ways. Thoughts of the latter type can be described as "a priori." If we accept that no one who has not had the appropriate sense organ stimulated in the appropriate way can conceive what it is like to have a sensation (that the blind can form no adequate concepts of color, for example), then those sensations are not a priori, even though they are original. His attacks on *inborn* ideas notwithstanding, when Locke set out to deny that we have "innate" ideas, he was principally concerned to reject a priori ideas.

The terms "native" and "innate" are employed in yet another sense to refer to what is immediately perceived, as opposed to learned from past experience. If we follow Locke in maintaining that nothing more is needed to conceive of solidity than to grasp a flint or a football between one's hands,[3] then our conception of solidity is innate in this sense, even though it is neither inborn nor a priori. If we follow Berkeley in supposing that the distance of the objects of vision is only perceived through learning that particular visible appearances have in the past been associated with particular tangible distances, then our perceptions of visual distance are not innate in this sense.

II. NATIVISM IN REID'S ACCOUNTS OF CONCEPTION, SENSATION, AND PERCEPTION

Reid maintained that the term "idea" had been used by philosophers to refer to things that do not exist. It is therefore best not to ask whether he accepted that we have innate "ideas." However, he did accept that we experience sensations, that we perceive, remember, and judge, that we are self-conscious, and that we conceive of objects; and we can ask whether he considered anything we encounter through these operations to be innate, and if so in what sense.

A. Conception

For Reid perception and memory involve the conception of something, but they also involve a belief in this thing's present or past existence. "Bare conception," in contrast, is the "simple apprehension" of something, that is, an apprehension without an attendant belief.[4] Reid denied that we can form a bare conception of anything that has not previously been encountered by way of sensation, perception, or some other act of the mind, or that has not at least been constructed from the components of such experiences.

[W]hen we barely conceive any object, the ingredients of that conception must either be things with which we were before acquainted by some other original power of the mind, or they must be parts or attributes of such things. Thus a man cannot conceive colours, if he never saw, nor sounds, if he never heard. If a man had not a conscience, he could not conceive what is meant by moral obligation, or by right and wrong in conduct. (EIP IV.i: 308–9)[5]

The question of whether we have innate conceptions therefore reduces to the question of whether there is anything in sensation, perception, consciousness, or judgment that is innate.

B. Sensation

Reid identified sensations as the states of feeling that we enjoy when we smell, taste, hear, feel hot or cold, view a colored object, or are pressed upon by an object. As states of feeling had by a sentient creature, they bear no resemblance to any quality of the inanimate objects that act on our sense organs or any of the physical effects these objects have on us. However, they are immediately enjoyed upon the occasion of sensory stimulation, with no further cognitive operation (other than a degree of attention) being required for us to apprehend them. They are therefore both original and unlearned. But Reid maintained that they also only first arise in us as a consequence of objects acting on our sense organs;[6] and that none can be known in advance of that experience.[7] Subsequent to experience the "feel" of the sensation may be simply conceived or the sensation itself remembered. But this can only happen subsequently.[8] Sensations are therefore neither inborn nor a priori. In sum, they are innate in the second and fourth of the senses identified earlier, but not in the first or the third.

C. Perception

Reid maintained that we have two types of perceptions, "original" and "acquired." Since the term, "original" has already been given a special meaning, I will refer to what Reid called "original perceptions" as "primitive perceptions." Our acquired perceptions are of (i) the distance, figure, magnitude, and color of the objects of vision, and (ii) the objects we have learned are the causes of our sensations of smell, taste, sound, heat and cold, and color. The former are acquired by learning to associate primitive "visible appearances" with tangible distance, figure, and magnitude, and by learning to take such factors as illumination and distance into account in estimating color.

Included among our primitive perceptions are the perceptions we receive through the sense of touch of the primary qualities of bodies – of their hardness, softness, roughness, smoothness, figure, motion, and extension – as well as our perceptions of certain visible features of bodies – the position of bodies with regard to the eye, the figure that is projected from the positions that their parts have with regard to the eye, and the distance between these positions.

On Reid's account, these qualities are not "in" us in the way our sensations are in us. They are not states of feeling enjoyed by a mind. They are rather qualities of external objects.[9] When we perceive these qualities, we perform a particular act, the act of perception. This act exists in us. But it is nothing like any of the qualities that are perceived by means of it. The perception is not extended or figured, or hard or soft. It is an act that involves two components: a conception of something with these qualities, and a belief that this thing currently exists. As thus understood, the relation between perception and object is something like the relation between a proposition that describes an object and the object it describes. I can say *about* a concrete cube *that* it is angular and hard, but the proposition that expresses this fact is not angular or hard. Similarly, when I perceive a concrete cube what I am really doing is "conceiving *about* a concrete cube *that* it is angular and hard" and believing there to be a currently existing object that satisfies this description. It is the object that has the qualities, rather than the perception. The perception merely refers to them in the way that the proposition does.

Exactly the same things can be said about the innateness of our primitive perceptions that were said about the innateness of our sensations: They are original and unlearned, but neither inborn nor a priori.

1. ORIGINALITY AND TACTILE PERCEPTION. Reid believed that tactile perceptions involve generally accurate, even if not completely adequate conceptions of the primary qualities possessed by external objects. But he also doubted that the effects that these objects have on our sense of touch or our brains bear any resemblance to these objects or to the perceptions we have of them.[10] Objects doubtless have some effect on the brain, and this effect doubtless plays some role in causing our perceptions, but it is not itself perceived. The primary qualities of the object that caused it are perceived. Paraphrasing Descartes, we can say that for Reid nothing reaches our minds through the senses except certain effects that bear no resemblance to the objects that the mind goes on to conceive of on the

occasion of attending to those effects. The conceptions that we form of the primary qualities of objects are therefore original productions of the mind, albeit ones of the qualities of the objects that affected the sense organ. They are innate in the second sense.

2. LEARNING AND TACTILE PERCEPTION. Reid maintained that when bodies press upon us we enjoy certain tactile sensations. These "pressure sensations"[11] are not the primary qualities we perceive by touch. They are feelings in us rather than qualities of external objects. No association of these feelings in us, nor any operation of comparing them and discerning relations between them, is adequate to produce a conception of any primary quality. The sensations we enjoy when we feel a hard body, for example, are nothing like the hardness of that body. Hardness is the quality of having parts that resist relative motion. The sensations we enjoy are feelings, akin to pain, and no combination of pain-like feelings, association of pain-like feelings, or relation that we can discover between pain-like feelings resembles the quality of hardness.

Though pressure sensations neither constitute the primary qualities of bodies nor permit us to infer the existence of the primary qualities by any process of reasoning or association, they do signify the primary qualities of bodies and as a consequence "suggest" perceptions of those qualities, just as the words of a language signify their referents. Importantly, these sensations are "natural" as opposed to "acquired" signs. The perceptions they suggest are not learned from past experience, the testimony of others, or reasoning from anything that we can discern in our pressure sensations, but arise immediately upon the first encounter. As Reid at one point put it, the sensation "[conjectures the perception of the signified quality] up, as it were, by a natural kind of magic" (IHM V.iii: 60).

3. LEARNING, VISUAL PERCEPTION, AND REID'S REALISM. Reid believed that we are naturally so constituted as to enjoy sensations of color on the occasions when light affects our eyes. However, in contrast to what he believed concerning the sensations of pressure, he did not think that our sensations of color suggest perceptions of extension, figure, or position to us. These perceptions are instead "suggested" by the impression made by light on the eye (he called this the "material impression").[12]

Reid also maintained that our primitive visual perceptions are not as adequate as our tactile perceptions. Our tactile perceptions are not perfectly adequate, either. They tell us what relations the parts of objects have to one another, but the only parts they tell us about are the ones on the surfaces of objects, not the ones beneath those surfaces. They are further limited insofar as they only tell us about those parts that touch us, not about anything set at a distance. Our primitive visual perceptions do tell us about objects set at a distance, but this advantage is mitigated by the fact that they do not tell us how great this distance is. A firefly and a star are both at a distance from me. But vision tells me so little about the existence of the immense distance between them that I can confuse the one with the other. Vision does tell me, however, about the compass direction and the angle of inclination from the horizon at which these objects are positioned relative to my eye. Since, unlike stars and fireflies, most objects exhibit many parts to the eye, and vision tells me only about the compass direction and the vertical angle of inclination of these parts, but not their distances outward, objects will appear to the eye to have a shape and size that are a two-dimensional projection of their actual shape and size, produced by straight lines that originate at the center of the eye and pass through the parts of objects to points on the inner surface of a sphere set indeterminately far out from the eye and centered on it, like the sphere of the heavens. Reid referred to this projection of the actual shape and size as visible figure and magnitude, and to the position that objects are perceived to have with regard to the eye as visible position.[13]

That we should perceive visible figure, position, and magnitude was a natural supposition for Reid to make given his belief that visual perceptions are "suggested" by material impressions on the retina. Since the material impression on the retina is not affected by the distance of an object, but only by its compass direction and its angle of inclination from the horizon, relative to the position of the eye, it was hard for Reid to see how the material impression could suggest anything about distance. Indeed, Reid went so far as to claim that "such as the picture on the retina is, such is the appearance of the object, in colour and figure, distinctness or indistinctness, brightness or faintness" (IHM VI.xii: 120).

This is not what we tend to think that we perceive by vision. We think we see objects to be at a distance and to have the same figure and magnitude that touch reveals them to have. Reid maintained that, since infancy, we have learned to associate particular features of the objects we immediately perceive by vision, or "visible appearances," as he called them,[14] with the distance, figure, and magnitude that objects are discovered to have by touch. The visible appearances have thus acquired the status of signs, and their signification is so readily grasped that they pass unnoticed and only painters, whose job it is to attend carefully to the actual character of what it is that they really see, have recovered any awareness of them. This was Berkeley's view as well, and Reid was happy to endorse it.[15]

However, unlike Berkeley, Reid maintained that visible appearances are immediately perceived to have position and figure.[16] In taking this view, he resisted the Berkeleyan program of attempting to explain our visual perception of all spatial features as consequences of the association of more primitive, completely aspatial visual and tactile sensations. As Reid saw it, when Berkeley claimed that "distance" is not immediately perceived, he traded on the ambiguity of that term. "Distance" can refer to separation in any direction whatsoever. However, Reid pointed out, Berkeley only argued that the distance of objects outward from the eye is not immediately perceived. We can grant that distances outward are not immediately perceived, but this does not mean that distances from left to right or top to bottom are not immediately perceived.[17] In opposition to Berkeley, Reid maintained that our perceptions of visible position, figure, and magnitude are not the product of association or reasoning.[18] They arise, as Reid at one place put it, "by a kind of inspiration" (IHM VI.vii: 97) on the occasion of the imprinting of particular parts of the eye by light.

Reid also differed from Berkeley in maintaining that we see the same objects that we touch. Even though the objects that we see and the objects that we touch may have quite different figures and magnitudes, these figures and magnitudes are not incompatible. We need to consider that when we perceive visible figure we are not perceiving "figure" understood as the product of the positions of the parts of an object with regard to one another. We are rather perceiving the positions of its parts with regard to the eye, which is an equally real feature of those parts, even if it produces a different figure.[19] Visible magnitude is not the magnitude of the object, but another, equally real feature: the magnitude of the angle that light from the extremities of that object subtends at the eye.[20] Consequently, there is no incompatibility between the objects of vision and the objects of touch. Indeed, both refer to positions in a common, external space, though in the case of vision, these positions are not as completely specified. When I grasp a globe between my hands, the pressure sensations I receive from touch suggest the perception of a sphere located between my hands, or, more precisely, of two, oppositely positioned convex surfaces. When I look at it, the material impression on my retina "suggests" the perception of a circular array of parts, positioned indeterminately far out from me, but in the same compass direction and at the same elevation as the parts I feel between my hands. This allowed Reid to deny Berkeley's view that the objects of vision and the objects of touch exist only in the mind as two heterogeneous sets of sensations that we must learn to associate with one another. It allowed him to maintain instead that the objects of vision are located outside of us in the same space as the objects of touch.[21] Indeed, it allowed him to explain the association of visual and tangible phenomena as the consequence of a mathematical law describing how objects set at a distance from us are projected onto the inner surface of a sphere, rather than treat it as a merely arbitrary correlation.

The rules [geometers] have demonstrated about the various projections of the sphere, about the appearances of the planets in their progressions, stations, and retrogradations, and all the rules of perspective, are built on the supposition that the objects of sight are external.... add to this, that, upon the contrary hypothesis – to wit, that the objects of sight are internal – no account can be given of any one of those appearances, nor any physical cause assigned why a visible object should, in any one case, have one apparent figure and magnitude rather than another. (EIP II.xiv: 183)

In this passage Reid observed that the realist postulate, that we see objects that are set at a distance outward from us in an external space, allows us to formulate a law, the law relating solid objects to the projections of their parts cast onto the inner surface of a sphere centered on the eye, that permits us to calculate, in advance of actually seeing it, how any given object of touch would look from any of the infinitely many different positions from which it might be viewed. The Berkeleyan hypothesis that the objects of vision are heterogeneous from the objects of touch, in contrast, treats the various visual appearances associated with the different perspectives from which an object might be viewed as arbitrarily instituted by God, and discoverable only by experience. Insofar as it fails to reduce the various phenomena of vision to a single law relating visual and tangible phenomena, the Berkeleyan account fails to provide us with as adequate a science of vision as the realist account. Reciprocally, our explanations of why objects have the visible appearances that they do (notably, of why the actual course of the planets has the visible appearance that it has) presuppose the existence of an external space containing objects set at a distance from us. Berkeley wanted to claim that his idealism is compatible with an acceptance of such scientific truths as that concerning the motion of the Earth.[22] Reid showed that insofar as this truth depends on an inference from the visible appearance of astronomical phenomena, it presupposes the existence of an external space, through which the actual positions of objects set at a distance are projected towards the position of perceivers on the Earth. In doing so he mounted, with exemplary simplicity and clarity, what is in effect a transcendental argument in refutation of Berkeley's idealism – an argument that Kant only managed to hint at.[23]

4. ORIGINALITY AND VISIBLE APPEARANCES. Even though the figures and positions that we perceive by sight resemble the material impressions on the back of the eye, Reid denied that this is because those impressions migrate from our eyes into our minds.[24] He supposed (wrongly as it turns out) that it is unlikely that the impressions on the retina bear any resemblance to their effects on the brain,[25] and he maintained that they certainly do not bear any resemblance to our perceptions. As noted earlier, for Reid perceptions are mental acts of conception and belief. Unlike the pattern of excitation on the retina, these acts do not consist of parts that are relatively disposed in space, though through them we conceive of figures that are disposed indeterminately far out from the eye in particular compass directions and at particular elevations. Since our perceptions of visible position, figure, and magnitude do not copy or resemble anything transmitted from the sense organs to the brain, they must be recognized to be original products of the mind, albeit products that involve a conception

of the actual positions of distant objects relative to the eye (abstracting from their distance outwards), and the actual figures and magnitudes that their parts exhibit when projected towards the eye.

5. PRIORITY, GENETIC INNATENESS, AND TACTILE AND VISUAL PERCEPTIONS. But while these features of Reid's account mean that he treated the conceptual content of our primitive visual and tangible perceptions as original and unlearned, he did not consider this content to be a priori or inborn. For Reid our conceptions of the primary qualities of bodies and of visible figure and position do not arise independently of sensory experience. Someone who has never touched an object can have no conception of hardness, for example.[26] In this sense, our perceptions of the primary qualities are as empirical as any of our sensations.

The same holds for our conceptions of visible figure and position. Admittedly, Reid maintained that an astute blind person, such as the mathematician Saunderson, who had a good enough knowledge of tangible spatial concepts to do geometry, could conceive of visible figure and position independent of having had any visual experience whatsoever.[27] But Reid also maintained that Saunderson's knowledge of visible figure and position would have to arise from reasoning based on the reports of the sighted and employing spatial concepts originally learned from touch.[28] Saunderson did not gain a new set of concepts independent of sensory experience. His concepts of extension and figure were first suggested to him through his enjoyment of the sense of touch, and he simply modified those concepts in light of what he was told about the nature of visible space. His knowledge was based on reasoning from testimony and from tactile experience of a richer, three-dimensional manifold, and so was not even original or unlearned, let alone a priori or inborn.

CONCLUSIONS. Among the important questions that can be asked about a thought there is one that concerns its origin and another that concerns its nature. There is no difference between Reid's sensations and Reid's primitive perceptions as concerns their origin. Both are original products of the mind that are immediately or intuitively formed on the occasion of sensory stimulation and that cannot be apprehended prior to having experienced the appropriate stimulus. Neither resemble the stimuli that occasion them. That either should occur on the occasion of sensory stimulation is something that cannot be further explained, other than by saying that we are originally constituted to enjoy such sensations or conceive and believe in such qualities upon such occasions.

However, there is a very notable difference in the nature of sensation and perception. Sensations are acts of feeling, perceptions acts of thinking something about an object. Sensations are not "about" anything other than themselves. Perceptions involve an act of reference to something other than themselves. This distinction has profound consequences that will be examined in Part V, after making some points concerning how Reid's views relate to those of Kant and Hume.

III. REID AND KANT

Kant believed that immediate sensory experience has two components: (i) a material component, which corresponds to "sensation," understood as "whatever it is in the effect of an object on our representative capacity that arises due to the fact that it is that object that is affecting us," and (ii) a formal component, which ensures that the parts of a sensible object will be disposed in a certain order. He identified sensation or the material component as the properly empirical or a posteriori aspect of sensory experience, but held that the formal component is not due to the objects that affect us; it is rather grounded in those features of the subject's constitution that give it the capacity to be affected by objects. As long as the subject's affective capacity does not change, this formal component can be anticipated in advance to be exhibited in all sensory experience. It is therefore "a priori" in the sense in which that term has been employed in this paper, since it can be known independent of having any specific sense organ affected in any specific way, even if it cannot be known in advance of all sensory experience whatsoever. For Kant, this a priori, formal component is responsible for the spatiotemporal order in which sensations are disposed. Since our representations of space are thus a priori, the principles of geometry, which are just descriptions of the structure of space, are similarly a priori.

Reid could not agree. For Reid neither our perceptions of visible position and figure nor our perceptions of the primary qualities of bodies are a priori. We acquire specific concepts of specific shapes, angles, and distances from specific experiences. We can analyze the objects of such concepts into their simplest component parts (point, straight line, etc.). We can then combine these elements into "various, accurate, and elegant forms, which the senses never did nor can exhibit" (EIP VI.i: 419). The principles of geometry are still necessarily true, but this is because they follow from analysis of the definitions of these stipulatively constructed figures,[29] not because (as for Kant) they describe a form of intuition that accompanies all of our immediate sensory experiences, but that may not be shared by other living things.

Reid's position on geometry is complicated by the fact that even though he took Euclidean axioms to be necessary truths, he did not take the figures and positions that we originally perceive through vision to conform to Euclidean axioms. As a consequence, while he identified the axioms of mathematics and the conclusions drawn from them as necessary truths,[30] he denied that immediately visible triangles have internal angles that sum to 180 degrees, except in limit cases,[31] and while he criticized Hume for denying that we can be certain that parallel lines do not intersect,[32] he maintained that creatures who could see but lacked a sense of touch would deny the Euclidean parallel postulate.[33] Reid resolved these tensions by observing that visible figures have the same geometrical properties as figures drawn on the inner surface of a sphere in Euclidean three-dimensional space that has the eye at its center. But since vision tells us nothing about distance outward from the eye, it cannot lead us to think that the parts of visible figures are all equidistant from us, and so are confined to the surface of a sphere that curves toward us (or to any other sort of surface, for that matter). So in vision we see figures that have the same geometrical properties as projections made on the inner surface of a surrounding sphere without perceiving them as concave figures. This means that, rather than being an incompatible alternative to Euclidean geometry, visible geometry is simply an impoverished version of it. It is the geometry of Euclidean two-dimensional figures on a curved surface, done without knowing that the figures are contained on such a surface. The result is not incompatible with Euclidean geometry, much less false; it is simply not completely informed. For all we know, Reid observed, our tactile perceptions of the world may be correspondingly inadequate, and other beings may have a yet more complete understanding of geometry (as opposed to an alternative geometry).[34]

Reid's and Kant's different accounts of geometry have implications for our understanding of the objects of knowledge. Kant's position implies that the objects that we come to know as occupying space and time cannot be considered to be things as they are in themselves, but must instead be regarded as being these things as they appear under our forms of intuition. Reid's account carries no such implication. Indeed, because Reid was committed to the tenet that we perceive objects as they are, his account carries the contrary implication. To this extent, it entails a more robust epistemological realism than any that could be countenanced by Kant. Reid's realism is the product of both his commitment to the view that we are innately so constituted as to perceive objects as they are, and his *rejection* of a type of "nativism": the view that we possess a priori concepts of spatial form.

IV. REID AND HUME

Writing to Hugh Blair on 4 July, 1762 concerning an early draft of part of the *Inquiry* that he had read, Hume remarked, "If I comprehend the Author's [viz., Reid's] Doctrine, which, I own, I can hitherto do but imperfectly, it leads us back to innate Ideas."[35] Elsewhere, Hume was explicit about what it means to "lead us back to innate ideas."

It is probable, that no more was meant by those who denied innate ideas, than that all ideas were copies of our impressions....
    ... admitting these terms, *impressions* and *ideas*, in the sense above explained, and understanding by *innate*, what is original or copied from no precedent perception, then may we assert, that all our impressions are innate, and our ideas not innate.[36]

It is hard to see how Reid could have "led us back to innate ideas" in this sense, if for no other reason than because it is expressed in terms that Reid rejected. Reid remarked that he could understand what it means for there to be an impression upon wax or upon some part of the body firm but pliable enough to receive it, but that he could make no sense of what it might mean for there to literally be an impression on or in the mind.[37] And he had no sympathy for

Hume's claim that what distinguishes ideas from impressions is that they are less vivacious.

It is also hard to effect any translation between Hume's idiom and Reid's that would make sense of Hume's charge that Reid led us back to innate ideas:

(1) Since Hume thought that bare ideas do not inspire belief, whereas impressions do, we might seek to bridge the differences between Reid and Hume by taking Hume's "ideas" to correspond to Reid's "bare conceptions" and Hume's "impressions" to correspond to the things conceived through those acts of the mind that Reid recognized as involving belief (perception, memory, consciousness). But then we must recognize that just as Hume said that there are no ideas that have not been copied from impressions, so Reid said that there are no bare conceptions that were not first given through some other act of the mind.

(2) If we remark that Reid maintained that our perceptions of the primary qualities are not copied from any of our sensations, then we need to consider that Hume would have agreed that none of the things that Reid called "perceptions of the primary qualities" are copied from any of the things that Reid called "sensations." For Reid, the term "sensation" applies just to smells, tastes, sounds, feelings of heat and cold, and feelings of pressure,[38] and Hume no more thought that our ideas of the primary qualities are copied from these things than did Reid.

(3) Admittedly, Hume thought that we have "impressions" and not just "ideas" of the primary qualities. But, as has already been noted, it is difficult to translate the notion of having an "impression" as distinct from an "idea" into Reid's idiom, since Reid thought that both terms, particularly as employed by Hume, give a seriously distorted picture of what is going on in the mind when we sense, perceive, and conceive.

If saying that we have "impressions" and not just "ideas" of the primary qualities can be made to mean anything that Reid could be persuaded to understand, it may just be that our conceptions of the primary qualities belong in the same category as the other things Hume called "impressions": our sensations of smell, taste, sound, etc. Hume and Reid did disagree about this.

But this disagreement concerns the nature of these thoughts, not their origin. As regards their origin, Reid maintained that sensations and perceptions stand on the same footing: Both are original products of the mind that can only first be produced by it on the occasion of having particular sense organs stimulated in particular ways, and that are produced as immediate consequences of such stimulation. Hume maintained that they originate on the same footing as well: as "original and copied from no precedent perception."

As regards the nature of these thoughts, however, there was no affinity between Hume and Reid. Reid insisted that a "sensation" of smell or taste is a phenomenon very different from a "perception" of hardness or extension. He also insisted that if the ambiguous words, "smell" and "taste," are used to refer to the object that causes our sensations of smell or taste, then these objects are not sensed but perceived, and a smell or taste *sensation* is a very different phenomenon from a *perception* of the objects we also call "a smell" or "a taste" just as the sensation of pressure is a very different phenomenon from the perception of hardness.[39]

More radically, Reid wanted to reject the very terms in which Hume distinguished between impressions (sensations) and ideas (conceptions). In Reid's view, the theory that these representations are distinguished only by their degree of "vivacity" is patently false. Sensations are states of feeling rather than more vivacious perceptions, "perception" refers to acts of conception and belief, rather than serving as a blanket term for all mental phenomena, and conceptions are acts whereby the mind thinks of an object rather than less vivacious sensations.

The most important consequence of this different account of the nature of our thoughts concerns the concept of mind. Reid was a dualist who insisted that no state that involves extension can be literally attributed to the mind.[40] His account of sensation and perception allowed him to sustain that commitment. It allowed him to say that the mind can have states of feeling (sensations) attributed to it. It can also have acts of conceiving and believing (perceptions) attributed to it. But it cannot be said to *be* round or square or hard or soft. Its cognition of these properties could not possibly occur by its literally being "impressed" with an image, but must instead take the form of an act whereby it thinks *of* or makes reference to spatial properties.

On Hume's radically different account, our representations of the primary qualities differ from our representations of sensible qualities such as color or heat only in composition and not in kind. Hume supposed that we have compound impressions that consist of a number of simultaneously present, minimally perceptible sensations of pressure or color that are disposed alongside one another in space, so that it is possible for a pain, say, to occur to the left of a tickle, or for a sensation of color to be round or square, large or small. Impressions of extension and figure are the product of the aggregation of these minimally perceptible sensations in a compound, and so are literally extended and figured.[41] Consequently, whether we have original "impressions" of the primary qualities, or ideas that copy them, Hume's claim is that those impressions or ideas depict the primary qualities by having those qualities, in the same way that a bust of Socrates depicts the face of Socrates by having the facial features of Socrates. For Hume, if extended impressions and ideas are not the sort of things that can reasonably be attributed to an immaterial mind, then so much the worse for the hypothesis of an immaterial mind.[42]

There is a further important consequence of Reid's different account of the nature of thought: It avoids Hume's skepticism about our knowledge of an external world. I consider this point below.

V. REID'S REPLY TO THE SKEPTIC

Reid's account of sensation and perception involves various nativist commitments. He supposed that we are innately so constituted as to enjoy particular sensations and to perceive particular visible appearances upon the occasion of having specific sense organs stimulated in specific ways (that is, that these sensations and perceptions are unlearned). He supposed that our tactile sensations of pressure are "natural signs" of the primary qualities of bodies, that is, that we are innately so constituted as to perceive particular shapes at particular positions and in particular states of motion upon the occasion of enjoying particular sensations, prior to any reasoning or association (hence, that these perceptions are unlearned as well). He also had two other important nativist commitments that have so far only been alluded to: He supposed (i) that we are innately so constituted as to form visual and tangible perceptions of the very properties possessed by the objects that affect our sense organs, touch telling us about the relations that the parts of bodies actually have to one another, and vision about the compass direction and the degree of elevation that their parts actually have with reference to the eye. And he supposed (ii) that our visual and tangible perceptions provide us with an irresistible belief in the existence of the objects of these conceptions. Consequently, Reid maintained we are innately so constituted as to directly perceive objects as they are.

If this appeal to our innate constitution were all that there is to Reid's argument for direct perceptual knowledge of external objects, then he would have deserved Kant's indictment of him as someone who called upon common sense as an oracle whenever he found himself unable to give a rational or empirical justification for his biases.[43] Skepticism about our knowledge of the external world is based on the charge (underwritten by appeals to perceptual relativity and perceptual error) that all that we are actually aware of are effects that objects bring about in us when they stimulate our sense organs, not the objects themselves. To answer this argument by saying that we are innately so constituted as to perceive the things as they are ignores the skeptic's reasons for saying that we instead perceive their effects on us and the skeptic's more general challenge to explain why we should suppose that the objects of our perceptions are anything like external objects.

To appreciate the force of Reid's answer to these worries we need to consider his views on the special nature of perception in tandem with his nativist commitments. In Reid's own estimation, were it not for these views, skeptical arguments would be invincible. Indeed, they would not just establish the negative thesis that our knowledge of external objects is uncertain, but the positive thesis that we could not possibly have any such knowledge. Reid credited Berkeley with having established this point. Proceeding from the skeptical premise that we only directly perceive the effects that objects have on our minds, Berkeley had argued that these effects must be feelings or sensations of some sort. Since the mind is not extended or solid, these states or sensations could not be extended or solid. So they could not be anything like material things. As Berkeley put it, nothing could be like an idea (or mental state) but another idea. But if all our knowledge is obtained from sensations or from contemplating relations among sensations, then no conception of material things and certainly no knowledge of them could possibly be obtained.[44]

Reid's answer to Berkeley was to deny that the only conceivable effect that an object could have on a mind is to cause it to enjoy a different sensation or feeling.[45] Sensory stimulation also leads us to form conceptions, and what is of the utmost importance is that these conceptions are about something else. To have a conception is not to be conscious of some state of being in which I currently exist; it is rather to be in a state that consists of having an awareness of something else, entirely different from the state itself. If we grant this, then we can say that affection by objects leads us to perform acts of conceiving, but that these acts of conceiving are ones that refer to objects. Berkeley's charge that it is impossible to conceive of anything but a state of mind is scuttled.

Much the same point can be made about the argument for direct perception of external objects that Reid drew from his theory of vision (Part II.C.3 above). As noted, that argument is based on the claim that the objects of vision are perceived to be located in the same space as the objects of touch, rather than belonging to a completely distinct and heterogeneous class of visual sensations, as Berkeley had claimed. When making this point, Reid maintained that we are innately so constituted as to perceive an object to be located somewhere indeterminately far out in a certain compass direction and at a certain elevation, depending on what part of the retina it impresses. We perceive this object to be "out" in the same space that contains the objects that we touch. But this only makes sense in the context of Reid's account of perception. Reid agreed with Berkeley that our tactile sensations of things like pain, heat, or pressure are not located in space at all, let alone in a common space. His attack on Berkeley proceeded on the assumption that we do not just enjoy sensations of color or pressure, but have perceptions that are of or about objects – visible figures, located at particular positions with regard to the eye, and solid objects, set at particular positions relative to one another. It is the objects of these perceptions that are conceived to be located in a common space, not our visible and tactile sensations.

It remains a question why we should accept that our perceptions are of the objects that affect our senses, especially if there are times (occasions of perceptual error or illusion) when they are admittedly not of these objects or at least not accurately so. But this question is now of a different sort. If what happens when we perceive is not that we conceive of effects that objects have on our sense organs, but that the stimulation of our sense organs by objects has the effect of leading us to conceive of something, then the question is not why the effects that objects have on us should be supposed to resemble those objects. It is taken for granted that the effects objects have on us do not resemble those objects in the least. They are perceptions, which are acts of a thinking creature involving conception and belief, and such acts are nothing like the objects that affect us. The question is rather why these effects should be acts of conceiving of and believing in the present existence of the very object that affected us.

The answer to this modified question is that it is reasonable to suppose that something that was designed to perform a task will perform that task under normal conditions, as long as it was designed well. So as long as we have reason to suppose that our senses were designed to give us knowledge of the external world and that they were designed well, we should accept that they will generally give us conceptions of the very objects that affect us. Perceptual errors will still occur as a result of damage to the system, the performance of tasks that exceed design specifications, or the "bugs" that normally arise when a system that is designed to perform efficiently in the generally arising case is used in abnormal circumstances. But we should expect that the system will usually yield reliable outcomes. This is particularly incumbent on those who accept that the system was designed well in other respects. Those who trust our reasoning powers or our consciousness of our sensations ought, by parity of example, to trust our powers of perception.

A more fundamental question ought to be considered: Why should we accept Reid's account of perception in preference to the theory that we perceive "impressions," "ideas," or "appearances"? Reid had a number of points to make in reply to this question. I will mention just two of the most compelling. He observed that the theory that we perceive the effects that objects have on us explains nothing. Even if we grant that objects have some effect on us, the production of an alteration in one thing by another does not by itself account for the second thing's awareness of that alteration. If a seal causes an imprint in wax or a clapper causes a bell to vibrate, we do not think that the wax or the bell perceives anything. Similarly, if objects cause "impressions" or motions in us, the bare existence of these effects is not perception. Some act of consciousness, involving a conception of these effects, is required. This act is utterly mysterious. No one understands how it is produced or can say what conditions govern its operation. Since we must nevertheless accept that it occurs, we might as well allow that we are so constituted as to conceive external objects, rather than brain impressions. After all, the former is no more mysterious an operation than the latter, it provides us with a more direct and simple account of the cognitive achievement we are seeking to explain, and it conforms better with the introspective evidence (we seem to perceive objects outside of us in space, not impressions in our brains).[46]

Reid also remarked that to suppose that all that we perceive is the effects that objects have on us is tantamount to supposing that all that we are conscious of is our own sensations. But in that case our possession of concepts of extension, figure, and hardness is unaccountable. Reid was willing to rest his whole case on this claim.

This I would therefore humbly propose as an *experimentum crucis*, by which the ideal system must stand or fall; and it brings the matter to a short issue: Extension, figure, motion, may, any one, or all of them, be taken for the subject of this experiment. Either they are ideas of sensation, or they are not. If any one of them can be shown to be an idea of sensation, or to have the least resemblance to any sensation, I lay my hand upon my mouth, and ... must suffer the ideal [theory] to triumph. (IHM V.vii: 70)

This passage claims that our conceptions of the primary qualities of matter are not "ideas of sensation" but are formed by some other power of the mind. But the point about the origin of these conceptions is made in the service of a more important point concerning their nature. Reid took introspection to be the principal source of information for investigations in the science of the mind,[47] and he asked us to introspect upon the nature of our sensations. He was confident that we would find, upon doing so, that our sensations are all feelings and that while these feelings have quality and intensity and duration, they cannot have shape or size or location. Accordingly, he declared, we must admit that our conceptions of shape, size, and location cannot be sensations and cannot arise from anything we can learn by reflecting upon or associating our sensations. They must arise from a power of the mind different from the power to feel: a power to form conceptions that refer to something other than themselves, where conception is understood as involving an act of thinking *about* an object, rather an act of turning into a copy of it. This does not mean that the power to form conceptions is any more "innate" or "natural" than the power to enjoy sensations. As the passage also makes clear, all simple notions (sensations as well as conceptions) are equally the work of nature and the result of our constitution. The point is that they are different in kind, and attributing their origin to a distinct power is a way of getting that point across.[48]

SOURCES CITED

Abbreviations
　　　　Ak - Kant 1910–
　　　　AT - Descartes 1971–75
　　Principles - Berkeley 1710

NOTES

1. Locke E IV.ii.1.
2. AT VIIIB: 358–9.
3. E II.iv.6.
4. EIP IV.i: 295.
5. Reid was not speaking in his own voice in this passage, but reporting on an observation made by "many authors." However, that he meant to endorse the observation is clear from the paragraphs that follow. Note particularly EIP IV.i: 310: "Though our conceptions must be confined to the ingredients mentioned in the last article. . . ." See also EIP II.xx: 226–7.
6. IHM II.i: 25/21–29; III: 46/9–10; IV.i: 49/15–25; V.i: 54/21–33 and 55/1–8; V.ii: 55/37–56/2; VI.i: 77/32–36. In these passages Reid often remarked that the sensation is quite unlike the effect that objects have on the organ or the features of objects that produce these effects, and that it merely arises on the occasion of affection. He also remarked that the occasional cause of our sensations is not known to common sense but is rather a matter for scientific investigation. But he had no hesitation about declaring that each of our sensations is "occasioned" by something in objects that acts in a specific way on a specific sense organ. See further EIP II.xvi: 195/11 and EIP II.xvii: 204, where Reid described objects or their secondary qualities as occasioning sensations in us.
7. IHM II.x: 44/4–7. As this chapter makes clear, affection is a necessary but likely not ever (or only rarely) a sufficient condition of sensation. Some act of attention is also required. But Reid evidenced no inclination to say that the mind might be altogether active in the production of sensations.

8. "[S]ensation must go before memory and imagination" (IHM II.iv: 29).
9. This holds of the visible as well as the tangible qualities. See EIP II.xix: 223; II.xiv: 180–4, and Weldon 1982.
10. IHM VI.xii: 121 and EIP II.iv: 94.
11. Reid maintained that our tactile sensations have no name in any language (IHM V.ii: 56–7). Calling them "pressure sensations" reflects his description in IHM V.ii: 56 and flags the point that the sensation is something entirely different from the quality it suggests, an important point that might be submerged were the sensation not described in any way.
12. IHM VI.viii: 101/14–17, but compare 99/23–27. Giovanni Grandi, in a doctoral dissertation in progress, argues that the latter passage is a remnant of an earlier view that Reid neglected to excise from the mature text of IHM.
13. IHM VI.vii: 96.
14. Note that, the term "appearance" notwithstanding, Reid's visible appearances are not ideas or images in the mind of the perceiver but real properties of the objects of perception. This is discussed more fully below.
15. IHM VI.ii: 82/3–8; VI.xi: 117; VI.xxii–xxiii.
16. Berkeley occasionally acknowledged that we perceive "apparent" magnitude but also occasionally attempted to claim that the only immediate objects of vision are light and colors. For more on the tensions in Berkeley's thought that led him to this conflict and his difficulty resolving them, see Falkenstein 1994.
17. EIP II.x: 139–40.
18. IHM VI.viii: 100/14–29.
19. "[T]he visible figure of bodies is a real and external object to the eye, as their tangible figure is to the touch ..." (IHM VI.viii: 101).
20. IHM VI.vii: 96/19–34.
21. See Falkenstein 2000a for a fuller explanation of this argument.
22. *Principles* 58–9.
23. *Prolegomena* Ak IV: 374–5.
24. IHM VI.xii: 120–1 and EIP II.iv: 93–5.
25. In fact, patterns of excitation of neurons on the back of the retina produce topologically similar patterns of excitation of neurons, first in the lateral geniculate nucleus and then in both the striate and extrastriate visual cortex. Relative locations of neural activation and hence the basic topological features of the retinal impression are preserved, though with some distortion (e.g., shrinking or twisting) of the metrical and affine features, and with mirror-image reflection. Pioneering research on this topic was done by Roger Tootell and his collaborators (classically,

Tootell, et al. 1982), though the results are now referred to in most textbooks and popular accounts of vision. See, for instance, Palmer 1999: 155–6.

26. "I take it for granted, that the notion of hardness, and the belief of it, is first got by means of that particular sensation, which, as far back as we can remember, does invariably suggest it; and if we had never had such a feeling, we should never have had any notion of hardness" (IHM V.iii: 61).

27. IHM VI.ii: 79 and VI.vii: 95–6.

28. IHM VI.vii: 97–8.

29. EIP IV.i: 303–4; V.iv: 373; VI.i: 419–20; VI.vi: 491–2; VI.vii: 523/15–17; VII.i: 545–6.

30. EIP VI.5: 469/34.

31. IHM VI.ix: 104–6.

32. EIP VI.i: 419 and VI.vi: 491.

33. IHM VI.ix: 105/3–7 and 16–19.

34. See EIP II.xix: 224–5 and Weldon 1978.

35. As cited in IHM: 256/37–38.

36. EHU II n.1.

37. IHM VI.vii: 101.

38. More precisely, our sensation terminology is ambiguous, and sometimes applies to the feelings we enjoy when our senses of smell, taste, hearing, and touch are affected, but more commonly is applied to name "some power, quality, or virtue, in the [object that causes the feelings we enjoy] . . . which hath a permanent existence, independent of the mind, and which, by the constitution of nature, produces the [feeling] in us" (IHM II.x: 43).

39. IHM II.x: 42–3 and VI.vi: 90–1.

40. IHM VII: 208–9, 217/19–23. EIP II.x: 89/1–2. See also Reid's lectures on the nature and duration of the soul as reprinted in EIP: 617–18.

41. THN 1.4.5.15. For a fuller account, see Falkenstein 1997.

42. THN 1.4.5.16 and 33. Compare IHM VII: 217/3–26. For a fuller treatment of these points, see Falkenstein 1995.

43. Kant, *Prolegomena* Ak IV: 258–9.

44. IHM V.viii: 74–5. See also IHM VII: 209–10.

45. IHM V.viii: 75.

46. IHM VI.xii: 121; EIP II.xiv: 184–5.

47. IHM I.ii: 13/8–13.

48. I would like to thank Terence Cuneo, John Greco, John Nicholas, and René van Woudenberg for helpful criticisms and advice.

7 Reid and the Social Operations of Mind

I. INTRODUCTION

Thomas Reid is justly famous for his critique of the metaphysics, epistemology, and psychology of his influential predecessors and overlapping contemporaries. Debate continues about the success of his critique, but the philosophical intelligence displayed in his dissection of the faults in "the way of ideas" common to such otherwise disparate thinkers as Descartes, Locke, and Hume is beyond doubt. Indeed, Reid's critique is an exemplary piece of philosophical art in that it aims to detect a central flaw in the underpinnings of a great enterprise. It exhibits the "subtle but well balanced intellect" that was later praised by C. S. Peirce.[1] But this very achievement has tended to obscure some of Reid's more positive contributions to philosophy. Of course, his defense of common sense and his elaboration of what it means have been subject to plenty of critical attention, but there are many other areas in which Reid developed creative and original positions that have been relatively neglected in the literature. In what follows, I shall expound and discuss one that has been largely ignored both in its general form and in its particular applications.

The idea in question is that of "the social operations of mind." Reid develops this idea both in his *Inquiry* and in the *Essays* and deploys it in his discussion of a number of important topics, most notably those of promising and testimony.

II. HUME, REID, AND PROMISING

I will begin the exploration of this concept of social operations with a dispute between David Hume and Thomas Reid over promising, contracting, and justice. Their disagreement is in any case interesting in its own right and displays some of Reid's characteristic modes of thought. Hume professes to find a sort of paradox or contradiction in a promise, and this is connected with his analysis of justice as an "artificial virtue." Although Hume rejects the social contract tradition in his famous essay "Of the Original Contract" and elsewhere, his analysis of justice has distinct affinities with it. He makes, for instance, considerable use of the device of a state of nature to explain the origin of justice, though he thinks it a useful "philosophical fiction" rather than an ancient state of affairs.

Similarly, although Hume is a critic of the outlook of psychological egoism, and raises objections to the idea that human motives are always egoistic, he founds his account of justice upon an essentially self-interested basis, in the sense that repaying debts, keeping promises, and acting fairly are justified by the interest each of us is said to have in the existence of the sort of social order where people generally conform to these norms. Justice is conventional in so far as we have contrived an order that promotes a public interest through the expectation each has that his or her private interest will generally be furthered by conforming to its demands. Our natural affections and passions would not drive us to just conduct, because, at their best, they are too limited; but our interest in maintaining the convention helps us develop an artificial sentiment for justice that underpins our honesty. For Hume, justice is primarily concerned with the regulation of property relations, though it spills over into other matters. It is an underlying premise of his "construction" of justice that it is a virtue necessitated by scarcity of goods, limited benevolence, and rough equality of power between people.

Hume's theory is developed with considerable sophistication, but it is exposed to the same problem that bedeviled Hobbes before him. It is the problem posed by the free (or "foul") rider whom Hobbes calls "the fool" in deference to the Biblical characterization of the atheist ("the fool has said in his heart, there is no God"). The parties to the justice convention have a lot at stake in the convention's being maintained and this should make them very cautious about defecting. But surely a cunning rogue can exploit circumstances in which his injustice is virtually undetectable, and, even if it is detected, the convention will stand and he may have ways of avoiding the bad consequences for himself. On the other side, there may, as

Hume admits, be circumstances in which particular adherence to justice hardly seems to serve either the public interest or an individual's private interest: You have borrowed a small sum of money from an immensely wealthy person and can only repay it at considerable inconvenience, but justice requires that you do so even though the original lender has no serious need of the money and may even have forgotten the loan entirely.[2]

Hume faces this predicament partly because he has a particular sort of moral psychology – it is an axiom of his theorizing about morals that the motives for a moral action must always be themselves independent of morality. Hence in the case where there is no "natural" motive for some category of moral behavior, its motivation must be sought in the desire to conform to convention and this desire in turn must be founded on the natural motive supporting the convention. With justice (and the contracting and promising that fall under it) this natural motive is ultimately self-interest or self-love. Justice is an artificial or contrived virtue that serves our self-interest by its promotion of the sort of stability and benefit that we could not have in a state of nature. By contrast, generosity is a natural virtue in that we are moved to it by certain natural motives, such as sympathy. Of course, there are various obscurities around the word "natural" as Hume himself realized (see below) and Hume wants to insist that justice may be called natural in the sense that using reason to arrive at a convention to promote advantage is a natural thing to do. Nonetheless, justice does not rest directly on natural impulse as generosity does.

Similar reasoning applies to the obligations involved in promising. Indeed, viewed as a natural phenomenon, promising itself becomes something mysterious and even contradictory. As Hume puts it: "A promise therefore is *naturally* something altogether unintelligible, nor is there any act of the mind belonging to it."[3] What Hume seems to mean, here, is that the obligation to perform that is inherent in promising cannot arise from merely saying that you will perform, from simply uttering the words. The obligation must arise from some natural motive associated with promising, but what could this be? It cannot be the "act of mind" of intending to perform, because you are obliged whether you intend to perform or not. The obligation involved in promising must therefore be the creation of artifice, and since contracting is simply a form of promising in which several people commit themselves to act on the condition that others act in specified ways, the same is true of it.

And, again, the fundamental backing for the obligation of promising is that of a contrivance to promote and protect self-interest. This is a fundamental philosophical reason, quite apart from sociological or historical objections, why Hume must oppose one central element in the social contract tradition: That tradition appears to establish social morality and justice on the prior "natural" obligation to keep promises whereas Hume regards this obligation as conventionally established. To quote Hume again: "But as there is naturally no inclination to observe promises, distinct from a sense of their obligation; it follows that fidelity is no natural virtue, and that promises have no force, antecedent to human conventions."[4] And again, "interest is the *first* obligation to the performance of promises. Afterwards a sentiment of morals concurs with interest, and becomes a new obligation on mankind. This sentiment of morality, the performance of promises, arises from the same principles as that in the abstinence from the property of others."[5]

I shall not pursue the question whether, in dealing with "the fool," Hume's conventional theory of justice built upon a subjectivist theory of morality fares any better than Hobbes's social contract theory built upon a narrow version of natural law. What I will pursue is a response that Thomas Reid makes to Hume's moral psychology and, in particular, to his claim that there is no act of mind that naturally belongs to promising. Here Reid has direct recourse to his distinction between the solitary and social acts of mind, thereby challenging Hume's thinking not merely by objecting to his theory's inability to account for the moral realities (though Reid does that too) but by exposing something deeply wrong with its underpinnings. Indeed, Reid thinks that not only Hume, but many philosophers writing on social and political theory have failed to distinguish between the solitary and social operations of mind. They have treated the social operations as if they are merely versions of the solitary or reducible to them without loss.

III. EXPLAINING THE SOCIAL OPERATIONS

What is Reid's purpose in distinguishing between solitary and social operations of the mind? His idea is that there is a fundamental difference between the operations of the mind that require no reference to other intelligent beings and those that do. The social operations or acts of mind are essentially geared to "intercourse with some other intelligent beings" (EAP V.vi: 664a), whereas the solitary operations are not. Solitary operations are seeing, hearing, remembering, judging and reasoning, forming purposes and executing them. None of these require "the intervention of any other intelligent being" (ibid.). By contrast, asking questions, testifying, commanding, making a promise, or entering into a contract are social acts that "can have no existence without the intervention of some other intelligent being, who acts a part in them" (ibid.). Reid adds that the social operations are essentially geared to expression whereas the solitary operations are not. Reid thinks of expression as intrinsically oriented toward communication and as requiring symbolic form. It is at least conceivable that a person without some form of language might think, reason, deliberate and will, have desires and aversions, experience joy and sorrow, but it would be impossible for such a being to "put a question, or give a command, to ask a favour, or testify a fact, to make a promise or a bargain" (ibid.). Nonetheless, as we shall see, Reid does not think that "artificial" languages, including those often called natural languages to distinguish them from formal symbolic systems, are the only form that language can take.

The powers upon which the social operations rest may well be innate. Reid sometimes appears to leave this an open question, though many of his comments make it seem that the powers are part of our constitution. In any case they are clearly universally present in human beings, though their operation is weaker in infancy. Reid thinks that the social operations initially rest upon what he calls a "natural language" of signs, such as looks, gestures, and modulations of the voice, without which artificial languages would be impossible. These signs make for a communicative and receptive orientation among people that underpins the obligations, duties, and moral expectations involved in promising and other social operations.[6] Contrary to Hume, promising – like entreating, questioning, and commanding – is therefore a perfectly natural phenomenon and there is no need to seek its morality in some contrivance or convention designed to promote public and private interest. It is clearly Reid's view that promising, though no doubt of a very simple kind, may be expressed in the natural language, just as much as entreaties and warnings.

Reid's emphasis on the social operations has understandably been compared by some commentators to J. L. Austin's discovery of "performative utterances" and the subsequent development of speech act theory.[7] One point of similarity is Reid's insistence that the social operations are precisely social and actions. Another is the idea that an act of promising, for example, is constituted by a certain sort of expression, namely, one uttered with an understanding and "a will to engage" (EAP V.vi: 670a). There is a third resemblance in that Reid seems to recognize the need for some condition of "uptake" (as Austin called it) if a social operation is to be adequately performed ("felicitous" in Austin's terminology). This is a condition on the audience, though it implies a responsibility in the speaker, that, minimally, the utterance be understood for what it is. In the case of promising, moreover, the act is not adequately performed unless the one to whom the promise is offered accepts it. The flavor of Reid's account and parallels with Austin can be glimpsed in such remarks as the following: "such is the nature of all social acts of the mind, that, as they cannot be, without being expressed, so they cannot be expressed knowingly and willingly, but they must be" (ibid.). And again: "What makes a promise is, that it be expressed to the other party with understanding, and with an intention to become bound, and that it be accepted by him" (EAP V.vii: 669b).

Yet another parallel with Austin's work can be seen in Reid's interest in the degree to which an account of these neglected social operations is ill-served by the (then) standard logicians' treatment of discourse as the expression of propositions assessable straightforwardly as true or false. Beginning with those performatives that are not plainly assessable as true or false (e.g., commands or questions) Austin, in his early treatment of performative utterances, was inclined to make much of performatives not being "descriptive" and therefore not in the business of being true or false, though later he realized that the story was more complex. Reid also seems drawn to this temptation and, although he resists its full force, he is led partly by it to some strange comments, especially about testimony, which he thinks cannot erroneously express judgment, though it can be deceitful. As I have argued elsewhere and will emphasize in the discussion of testimony to follow below, this halfway house is unsatisfactory, but Reid reaches this pass because of his view that the social operations do not express "judgments." Again, we shall examine this further when we discuss testimony since the view raises more obvious problems with such social operations as testimony and warning than with promising or commanding. For now, it is sufficient to note that Reid is here pioneering an approach to speech act theory that would become more judicious and sophisticated later, even though much still remains unsettled on these topics.[8]

Reid, like Austin after him, is anxious that the social operations not be misconstrued as created by private (solitary) mental acts.[9] But he is also clear that they are themselves mental in a broader way, which is why he distinguishes the solitary from the social operations of mind. Consistent with this, Reid castigates Hume both for denying that there is any act of mind constitutively belonging to promising and for constantly construing the mental element in promising as the intention (or purpose) of performing what one has said one would. Hume generates his supposed contradiction partly by insisting that no mere intention could have the force that promising clearly does, and by insisting at the same time that the intention to perform as indicated is crucial. But, as Reid points out, this intention may or may not be present; the crucial, constitutive mental element is not the solitary act of intending to perform, but the social mental act of intentionally *binding* oneself to perform.[10]

IV. SOME CONSEQUENCES OF REID'S POSITION

Reid's perspective on justice, promising, and contract allows us to afford appropriate respect to contractual and other justice-related notions by situating them within an understanding of human life and interaction which takes our life in community as fundamental, but is not foolishly sentimental about it. Reid holds that the treatment of justice (and promising) as artificial, in Hume's sense, flies in the face of elementary moral experience. He sees our natural tendency to fidelity in declarations and promises and its counterpart in the widespread trust and reliance upon them as fundamental to our life as social beings.[11]

There is a discussion of Hume's that illustrates nicely, I think, the advantages of Reid's approach. In *An Enquiry concerning the Principles of Morals*, Hume has a revealing account of what our obligations would be to a class of people who lived among us but who were so weak as to constitute no threat to us were we to treat them in ways they resented. Here is what he says:

Were there a species of creatures, intermingled with men, which, though rational, were possessed of such inferior strength, both of body and mind, that they were incapable of all resistance, and could never, upon the highest provocation, make us feel the effects of their resentment; the necessary consequence, I think, is that we should be bound, by the laws of humanity, to give gentle usage to these creatures, but should not, properly speaking, lie under any restraint of justice with regard to them, nor could they possess any right or property, exclusive of such arbitrary lords. Our intercourse with them could not be called society, which supposes a degree of equality; but absolute command on the one side, and servile obedience on the other. Whatever we covet, they must instantly resign: Our permission is the only tenure, by which they hold their possessions: Our compassion and kindness the only check, by which they curb our lawless will: And as no inconvenience ever results from the exercise of a power, so firmly established in nature, the restraints of justice and property, being totally *useless*, would never have place in so unequal a confederacy.[12]

Some may be tempted to think that this accurately describes the position of women in a male-dominated society, and Hume indeed shows the courage of his convictions by going some way towards drawing this conclusion. In the next paragraph, he tests the idea on animals, Indians, and women, claiming that it is "plainly" the situation with regard to animals (supposing them to have some degree of reason) and that "civilized" Europeans have been tempted to see themselves in the same relation to "barbarous" Indians and so thrown off all restraints of justice and even humanity in regard to them. As for women, let me quote Hume in full:

In many nations, the female sex are reduced to like slavery, and are rendered incapable of all property, in opposition to their lordly masters. But though the males, when united, have, in all countries, bodily force sufficient to maintain this severe tyranny, yet such are the insinuation, address, and charms of their fair companions, that women are commonly able to break the confederacy, and share with the other sex in all the rights and privileges of society.[13]

The full import of this passage is not altogether clear, but it seems that if women are spared the fate of animals and admitted to the confederacy of justice, it is only because of their insinuating charm.

It would not be surprising for feminists to jib at this remarkable conclusion. And not only modern feminists. As Reid remarks, "If Mr Hume had not owned this sentiment as a consequence of his Theory of Morals, I should have thought it very uncharitable to impute it to him" (EAP V.v: 66ob). By contrast, Reid grounds justice and its offspring (the obligations of promising and contracting) in those social operations that are based upon a fundamental mutuality of kind rather than equality of power.[14]

Reid's theory certainly avoids such counterintuitive (and offensive) conclusions, since the subjects to whom the rights and duties of justice are relevant are not determined by exigencies of power, scarcity, and so forth, but by profound relations of sociality that are "natural." Of course, it may be objected that not a great deal is achieved by calling something "natural" and contrasting it with "artificial." Hume himself was conscious of much that is problematic about the distinction, and went to some lengths to distance himself from any connotations of "conventional" or "artificial" that suggested something unimportant or simply arbitrary about the emergence of justice as a virtue or institution. In the *Treatise*, he says: "Tho' the rules of justice be *artificial*, they are not *arbitrary*."[15] And in *An Enquiry concerning the Principles of Morals*, he comments: "The word *natural* is commonly taken in so many senses and is of so loose a signification, that it seems vain to dispute whether justice be natural or not. If self-love, if benevolence, be natural to man; if reason and forethought be also natural; then may the same epithet be applied to justice, order, fidelity, property, society."[16]

There are indeed many obscurities about contrasts between the natural and the conventional or artificial, whether the distinction is deployed in connection with rights or virtues, tendencies or abilities. It is also clear that Hume does not want to underplay the importance of justice as a virtue and a phenomenon. But the basic contrast that Hume needs is contained in his quoted response, and it still puts him at odds with Reid, and with others, like Aristotle and many contemporary feminists and communitarians, who want to see human beings as essentially social. For them, justice does not arise from mutual reasoning about what is advantageous to self-interest and promotional of social utility; it is inherent in the interactive social realities of human nature.

V. THE ROLES OF THE SOCIAL AFFECTIONS

The social operations to which Reid is attentive are allied to what he calls "social affections" and should remind us that there are certain fundamental human reactions intimately connected with the idea of justice that pre-date (so to speak) the prospect of any contrivance of the kind Hume imagines as establishing the virtue. Such reactions were emphasized by P. F. Strawson years ago in his important paper, "Freedom and Resentment"[17] but were also stressed by Reid in the context of his disagreement with Hume. (They have also been reconsidered by Joan McGregor, who cites Strawson's account in a good discussion of some aspects of Reid's views on justice as a natural virtue.)[18] As Reid puts it: "man is evidently made for living in society. His social affections show this as evidently, as that the eye was made for seeing. His social operations, particularly those of testifying and promising, make it no less evident" (EAP V.vi: 666a). And again: "Every man thinks himself injured and ill used, and feels resentment, when he is imposed upon by it....I know of no evidence that has been given of any nation so rude, as not to have these sentiments" (EAP V.vi: 666b).

These "reactive attitudes," as Strawson calls them, such attitudes as resentment, indignation, and gratitude, are basic to reflective humans and already embody a moral perspective. They require some development of the reasoning faculty, though there are premonitions of them in animals and very young children.[19] As Reid puts it, "I take it for granted that gratitude and resentment are no less natural to the human mind than hunger and thirst; and that those affections are no less naturally excited by their proper objects and occasions than these appetites" (EAP V.v: 654b). The proper object of resentment is an injury, and not merely a hurt, and this involves the idea of justice directly; the object of gratitude is a favor done and this involves the idea of justice indirectly in so far as one must go benevolently beyond the demands of justice in order to do someone a favor. Nor should we think that resentment, at any rate, must be an attitude to an injury done to oneself; we can resent wrongs inflicted on others, especially if the wrongs are great and we can readily have fellow-feeling for those others. A mother can resent the treatment of her child, and I can resent the wrongs inflicted on others by those who purport to act in my name. There seems no incoherence in my saying sincerely, "I deeply resent the Australian government's appalling treatment of refugee boat people landing on our shores." Similarly a parent can be grateful for favors bestowed on his child, though gratitude does not seem to extend coherently to favors bestowed on those not intimately connected to oneself. In any case, the picture Reid presents of the connection between human nature and justice is far removed from the self-interest model. As he says himself, he rejects the various attempts "to reduce all our social affections to certain modifications of self-love" (EIP I.viii: 69).

VI. PROBLEMS FOR THE SOCIAL OPERATIONS OF MIND

None of this is intended to suggest that Reid's ingenious idea of the social operations of mind is without problems. One question that needs addressing is this: In what sense are the social operations "mental"? If we are in the grip of a Cartesian picture of the mind, we will find it strange to speak of such overt public acts as promising or testifying as acts of mind at all. Even adherents of certain popular forms of materialism who treat the mind as a particular physical rather than nonphysical thing, to wit, the brain, will have similar qualms since the interactions involved in testifying or promising seem far from the merely neural. Indeed, there are certain respects in which theories such as central-state materialism simply take over the Cartesian picture of the mind but hold that the stuff of the substantial mind is physical rather than spiritual – thereby propounding what the philosopher William Ginnane once aptly called "one-legged dualism." Of course, the social operations involve the mind (and/or brain) in so far as agents need to be mindful to perform them, but Reid seems to mean something richer than this.

If so, he doesn't really elaborate on what it is. As we saw earlier, he thinks the social operations are essentially oriented to "intercourse with other intelligent beings" whereas the solitary operations such as seeing, hearing, remembering, and reasoning are not. These latter do not require "the intervention of any other intelligent being." By contrast, asking questions, testifying, commanding, making a promise, and entering into a contract are social acts that "can have no existence without the intervention of some other intelligent being, who acts a part in them" (EAP V.vi: 664a). They are also essentially geared to communicative expression whereas the solitary operations are not.

These comments suggest that we should think of the mind in such a way that there are certain mental states (those involving social operations) that cannot exist without the existence and reciprocal orientation of other intelligent beings. This goes against the picture, associated with Descartes, that a person (or a soul) could have exactly the mental states she now has whether or not any other being (except possibly God) existed at all. Reid does not mount a direct attack upon this picture, and in many respects he accepts a good deal of Descartes' thought about the mind. On the other hand, his rejection of the way of ideas and his attempts to analyze perception in a fashion that is object-involving but also respects the role of sensation both suggest an approach to the mind that is initially not as introverted as that of Descartes.

I think it is not implausible to see Reid as foreshadowing some developments in recent philosophy of mind and semantics that pose a challenge to the Cartesian picture. This challenge is sometimes put in terms of the idea of wide mental content. The thesis of wide content argues that at least some mental states are necessarily connected with certain nonmental realities that they represent. Hence, were it not for the existence of that reality, they couldn't be the states they are. The reality may be either physical or social.

A simple example concerns proper names. On accounts of the semantics of proper names influenced by the work of Kripke on rigid designation, the meaning of a sentence such as "Cathy Freeman is in excellent form" involves essential reference to that actual athlete. Someone who has the thought involved in that sentence is, as it were, connected to Freeman by that very thought. This is not a connection that is fully mediated by any private descriptions of Freeman that the thinker has. There is already a sort of externality built into the mental state. More broadly, it has been argued that much of what makes particular thoughts and other psychological states what they are is contributed by the conceptual and linguistic expertise of others. Hilary Putnam has spoken of a "linguistic division of labor" whereby any individual's grasp of what an expression like "elm" or "neutron" means, for example, is partly a gift of others in the community more expert on these matters. Considerations like these lead Putnam to announce triumphantly that meanings "ain't in the head."[20] The picture of the mind as having a wholly individualistic grasp of the world from "within" is threatened by these considerations.

The theories of wide content have many ambiguities and complexities, and although very influential, have not been without their critics.[21] Nonetheless, this more expansive attitude to what counts as mental may make us more sympathetic to the way Reid seems to think of some of the workings of the mind as essentially social. But, of course, there are various differences between the contemporary perspectives and that adopted by Reid in speaking of the social operations of mind. For one thing, in the Cathy Freeman example, the "externality" involved is different in that the Australian athletic champion need know nothing of her involvement in my thought that she is in good form and so the "externality" is not social in the way Reid is concerned with sociality: It is not interactive. But in testifying and promising, it is not that (or only that) the mind reaches out to external objects in being dependent upon them for the identity of its thoughts; the mind involves certain types of those objects, namely, persons, in a mutual transaction requiring at least "uptake." Minimally, as mentioned earlier, this will mean an understanding of what is on offer, though it may require more in some cases. Promising, for instance, may need a certain sort of acceptance (as contracting clearly does). In other words, the kind of mutuality of mind involved will vary from category to category with the social operations.

Another complexity about the social operations is that Reid's presentation of them and their associated social affections may suggest that they are an unqualified boon. But Reid is well aware that the social operations are not uniformly benign, although this recognition tends to be relegated to the background of his discussion. Our sociality yields the flowers of promises and fidelity, but it also gives us the thorns of threats and collusion; it makes justice natural, but it also underpins corruption and conspiracy. Trust itself can degenerate into degrading dependence and gullibility; it can also provide the cement of evil enterprises (as Annette Baier acknowledges). Even the mother/child relationship may involve its own excesses, as a good deal of contemporary humor highlights.

Reid himself acknowledges the distorting power of our moral impulses in his account of resentment where he treats resentment under the heading of "the malevolent affections" and judges that its proper operation in connection with justice may easily sweep on to dangerous exaggerations of grievance and vengefulness. And much the same is true of the other malevolent emotion he discusses, namely, "emulation," which is his term for what we might call competitiveness. Of these, Reid writes: "But, as their excess or abuse, to which human nature is very prone, is the source and spring of all the malevolence that is to be found amongst men, it is on that account that I call them malevolent" (EAP III.ii.v: 566b). This tendency to excess or abuse is what the institutions of justice, such as courts, police, enacted laws, and regulations, are required to restrain and here there is plenty of room for artifice and contrivance. Justice may be natural to our kind, but the forms and institutions that it requires may need the constructions of reason built partly upon fear and partly on consent. These constructions need to acknowledge both our powerful natural tendencies to social virtue, preeminently justice and fidelity, and our very strong tendencies to selfishness and partiality (upon which both Hobbes and Hume place such emphasis.)

VII. THE CASE OF TESTIMONY

We must turn now to another significant philosophical example of the social operations, this time in the area of epistemology, namely, the giving and receiving of testimony. Reid's placing of testimony within the social operations is part of his antireductionist attitude to the reliability and value of testimony. He sees the futility of attempting to justify the widespread and crucial dependence upon what others report by consulting only solitary intellectual resources. This resort to self-reliance is, Reid believes, as doomed as the parallel resort to self-love in the case of promising. Both ignore the primitive nature of our intellectual and practical involvement with others. Trust in the information given by others cannot sensibly be viewed merely as a useful strategy that an individual knower could and should develop on grounds of self-interest and with the aid of the self-reliant equipment of sense, memory, and inference. The quest for knowledge begins with dependence upon the word of others rather than validating that dependence some way down the path as a secondary supplement to individual knowledge. This "beginning" is historical and also epistemically normative.

Reid points out that a child's development is in fact dependent upon a primary attitude of trust, and, in these very early stages, the trust is virtually total. Were the child's attitude to the reliability of testimony one of indifference, or *"in equilibrio"* as Reid has it, then "no proposition that is uttered in discourse would be believed, until it was examined and tried by reason; and most men would be unable to find reasons for believing the thousandth part of what is told them" (IHM VI.xxiv: 194). Hence, the child's "credulity" seems no accident. Indeed, on the "in equilibrio" supposition, a child would (says Reid) be absolutely incapable of instruction. Here Reid seems to be supporting his view that reliance on testimony stems from a principle of human nature rather than from experience. Indeed he thinks that there are twin principles that act as "counterparts" – the principle of veracity and the principle of credulity. Reid characterizes the former as "a propensity to speak truth, and to use the signs of language so as to convey our real sentiments," and claims that: "Truth is always uppermost, and is the natural issue of the mind. It requires no art or training, no inducement or temptation, but only that we yield to a natural impulse" (IHM VI.xxiv: 193). The latter principle – the principle of credulity – is a disposition to, as Reid puts it, "confide in the veracity of others, and to believe what they tell us" (IHM VI.xxiv: 194). And this too Reid takes to be a natural disposition: "It is evident that, in the matter of testimony, the balance of human judgment is by nature inclined to the side of belief; and turns to that side of itself, when there is nothing put into the opposite scale" (ibid.).

Reid's argument from the child's development is then partly an elaboration of the force of the twin principles, but it also has something in common with arguments of a transcendental form. There are certain things we know and do that we couldn't know or do if reliance on testimony were justified by reasoning from experience. Yet, in what follows the comment on the child, he seems to allow that *some* people might come to accept the reliability of testimony by reasoning from experience. So he says, commenting on the "in equilibrio" supposition:

Children, on this supposition, would be absolutely incredulous; and therefore absolutely incapable of instruction: those who had little knowledge of human life, and of the manners and characters of men, would be in the next degree incredulous: and the most credulous men would be those of greatest experience, and of the deepest penetration; because, in many cases, they would be able to find good reasons for believing the testimony, which the weak and ignorant could not discover. (IHM VI.xxiv: 194–5)

This *may* be indicative of a certain tension in Reid's thought on the matter, though it is clear from what follows later that he does not envisage the operations of reason and experience entirely eliminating our reliance upon testimony. Shortly after the comments above, when discussing the way that mature reason can set bounds to the authority of testimony to which "she was at first entirely subject," Reid says: "But still, to the end of life, she finds a necessity of borrowing light from testimony, where she has none within herself, and of leaning in some degree upon the reason of others, where she is conscious of her own imbecility" (IHM VI.xxiv: 195).

So it seems that Reid holds that reliance on testimony is weaker in the mature than in young children, but nonetheless remains significant. Hence, we should probably treat the argument about the greater credulity of those with "deepest penetration" as a kind of *reductio*. Reid is supposing *per impossibile* a world in which people have no innate tendency to believe testimony and merely believe what they are told when they can somehow test it for themselves, and then deducing from this scenario the contrary to fact conclusion that mature, highly experienced and intelligent people would be most accepting of testimony and young children the most skeptical.

In the real world, of course, the child's unquestioned trust becomes modified by the experience of betrayal, exploitation, and the mistakes of witnesses, though much of this useful experience is itself second-hand or otherwise mediated by the experience of others. The testimony-saturated nature of much that individuals treat as part of their own experiential knowledge is a striking fact that Reid could have made use of in his analysis, but somewhat surprisingly neglects. The growing awareness an individual has that witnesses betray, exploit, and mistake is founded to a considerable degree on the reliable reports of those other than the betrayers, exploiters, and mistaken. Some purely personal checking and criticism certainly goes on, but much of the critical posture toward particular testimony that maturity rightly brings arises from an amalgam of individual experience, reasoning, reliance upon witnesses, and respect for intellectual authority. Reid was certainly conscious of the mutuality of support that existed between testimony and what he calls "Reason" but he does not sufficiently realize the complexity of this support, nor the degree to which "Reason" itself has a social, testimonial dimension. He shows how reasoning about the context of particular reports can strengthen testimony that might otherwise be quite weak. This happens through reflection on the "character, the number, and the disinterestedness of witnesses, the impossibility of collusion, and the incredibility of their concurring in their testimony without collusion" (IHM VI.xxiv: 195). But knowledge of such things as character and disinterestedness, even impossibility of collusion, will often be available only through some reliance upon other witnesses. These will often be untested (by you) in this context.

These considerations reinforce Reid's rejection of the idea that testimony begins as a fundamental source of knowledge but is quite supplanted in later life. The capacity to use an instrument can become more sophisticated and refined by experience and one can come to appreciate its defects and limitations without ceasing to rely upon its special advantages. Reid directly compares testimony with perception, and I, and others, have followed him, though there is also a significant similarity with memory. There are analogies (and, of course, disanalogies) of varying degrees and types between testimony and each of the traditional senses with respect to epistemic role. In the *Inquiry into the Human Mind*, Reid's comparison occurs in the section on sight, but a comparison with hearing can also bring out some of the significance of the way our trust in testimony changes with experience and development. (Reid does not use hearing in this connection; indeed, his treatment of hearing is the most perfunctory of his accounts of the different senses.)

As children grow and develop and interact with the environment, they learn that their hearing can "play tricks" upon them. In certain circumstances, things can sound to be coming from one direction when they are coming from another; too many sounds can distort what they think they hear; they are very good at hearing and identifying some sounds and not so good at others. Furthermore, they are good listeners in certain contexts and not in others; they realize from hearing interactions with others that, with very advanced age, for instance, hearing becomes impaired in various ways, and so on. All of this tempers the epistemic reliance they put upon hearing, but none of it means that hearing is no longer a fundamental way of relating to the world around them. Indeed, many of these hearing defects, they correct by hearing itself, just as they correct some of the judgments of the other senses by the verdict of hearing ("it looks very like a blue wren, but it doesn't sound like one").

It is similar in the case of testimony. The general point is that developed understanding of the limitations of an informational modality does nothing to undermine the primitive aspects of its operation. Just as our developed understanding of the frailties inherent in memory and the various perceptual modalities does not show that we cannot have immediate (noninferential) knowledge through perception or memory, so too an increased awareness of the fallibility of testimony need not count against testimony as a frequent provider of immediate knowledge. This at least suggests strongly that, like our reliance upon perception, our basic trust in testimony needs no further justification in terms of some other source of knowledge.[22]

VIII. JUDGMENT, TESTIMONY, AND THE SOCIAL OPERATIONS

In his discussions of both testimony and promising, and indeed of the other "social operations," Reid displays a robust sense of pluralism that is characteristic of much of his philosophical outlook. But although this pluralism is a strength of his outlook, it sometimes leads him astray, or at least involves him in obscurity. His comments on the relations between judgment and testimony seem to fall into this category.

The basic problem is that Reid's contrasting of the solitary and the social operations draws him unwittingly into an equally sharp contrast between things that in reality overlap. In complaining of the widespread philosophical neglect of the social operations, Reid associates this with the futile attempts "to reduce all our social affections to certain modifications of self-love"; and he also notes that where there have been "voluminous tracts" devoted to the analysis of propositions as the expressions of judgment there has been a neglect of any comparable analysis of questions, commands, and promises. This neglect extends even to the fact that what these acts express has not even been given "a name different from the operations which they express" (EIP I.viii: 70).

The neglect has been remedied in later twentieth-century philosophical discussions of what is known as speech act theory. One thing, however, that close attention to these matters has revealed is that some of the social operations may well express something like propositions, even though others are better understood as expressing different contents or orientations of the mind. J. L. Austin distinguished between locutionary and illocutionary acts, that is, (roughly) between saying something and further doing something communicative *in* saying it. Like Reid, Austin had initially been inclined to link saying and expressing propositions ("constatives") and contrast these with verbal doings ("performatives") and he also campaigned against the traditional obsession with the constatives, but he came to see that the matter was more complex. Adapting Austin, P. F. Strawson later argued that there are certain basic categories of "sayings" that enter into a variety of illocutionary acts. There are at least two such categories: propositions, having the form that S is P, and imperatives, having the form that someone Z is to do some act Y. Strawson allows that there may be more, as, for example, if the range of speech acts associated with questioning could not be accommodated under the heading of imperatives but needed a separate category of interrogatives.

There is more to be said about these issues in the philosophy of language, but, for our present purposes, the interesting point is that the contrast between these basic categories of saying does not match exactly Reid's contrast between the solitary and social operations of mind. The crucial problem for Reid is that many of the social operations clearly require the pronouncement of propositions, and so, on Reid's own account, belong with the solitary operations, since this pronouncement is an affirmation or denial expressing judgment. This seems to land Reid in contradiction. His awkward position results from not noticing, or refusing to admit, that making a judgment can serve a solitary or a social purpose. A person can be interested in just determining the truth of some matter for herself and, in thinking the matter through, come to the judgment that p. But the same person, having done so, may be interested in warning someone else that p, or testifying to someone else that p. Reid correctly sees that solitary judgment is different from warning or testifying and locates the difference in that between judgment as such and the social operations. But the fact seems rather to be that judgment may operate in a solitary or in a social way, since such social operations as warning or testifying clearly involve a form of judgment. My private judgment that the ice is thin becomes a component in the social act of warning that the ice is thin. Certainly, some of the social operations (such as warning that the ice is thin) involve the expression of propositions that are either true or false.

Reid's confusion here surfaces in some of his comments on testimony. He contrasts testimony and judgment in the following way:

A judge asks of a witness what he knows of such a matter to which he was an eye or ear witness. He answers, by denying or affirming something. But his answer does not express his judgment; it is his testimony. Again, I ask a man his opinion in a matter of science or of criticism. His answer is not testimony; it is the expression of his judgment. (EIP VI.i: 406–7)

There are two contrasts between testimony and judgment here. The first is an example of palpable testimony that is not the expression of judgment and the second, conversely, is an example of expressed judgment that is said not to be testimony. Let us begin with the first. On any account, what the witness says is either true or false – it is propositional in form. This might predispose us to think of it as expressing the witness's judgment that things are so and so. Indeed, unless a witness so judged (on the basis of seeing or hearing) he or she would not be entitled to offer the testimony, though of course the testimony might still be given as what we sometimes call false witness. Perhaps it is this idea of false witness that leads Reid to support his claim that testimony is not judgment with the comment: "In testimony a man pledges his veracity for what he affirms; so that a false testimony is a lie: But a wrong judgment is not a lie; it is only an error" (EIP VI.i: 407). But this clearly won't do. Testimony is often false because deceitful, but it is also sometimes false because erroneous. A witness can be mislead by her perceptions, mistaken in her judgment, led astray by her memory. So Reid's first contrast is unpersuasive. His second would take us too far afield into the theory of testimony to be fully treated here. It turns on whether there can be testimony to matters of expertise, and I have argued elsewhere that there can.[23] Reid is right that there are some sorts of theorizing, some matters of opinion and judgment, that are unsuited for a testimonial role, but he is wrong to rule out all results of expertise, theorizing, and judgment as so suitable. The courts, I would argue, are a good guide here in allowing expert testimony in certain circumstances, and our ordinary epistemic practices increasingly reflect this sort of dependence on the authority of experts.

We must conclude, then, that Reid's sharp contrast of judgment and testimony is flawed. Can we say more about the source of his confusion? In discussing the solitary operations, Reid is impressed by the fact that some mental act of judgment may express a truth without that act having any intrinsic reference to intercourse with other thinking beings. But it does not follow that judgment is not involved when our minds are employed in the social operations that do so refer. Reid may have thought otherwise because, first, some of the social operations do not in themselves involve judging that something is true or false – commands, questions, even promises are geared toward bringing it about that the world conforms to our desires and thoughts, whereas warnings and testimony are oriented, at least in part, towards our beliefs conforming to the world. For the former group we are primarily interested in satisfaction conditions, for the latter in truth conditions. This is of course rough, but it is roughly right.

Second, in the *Inquiry*, Reid introduces the idea of judgment with the caution that it is part of a traditional classificatory system for the intellectual powers of the mind that he does not find satisfactory. Part of this dissatisfaction is that the classification ignores the social operations, but Reid is also suspicious of other elements in the divisions of simple apprehension, judgment, and reasoning. He says, for instance, "The powers of the mind are so many, so various, and so connected and complicated in most of its operations, that there has never been any division of them proposed which is not liable to considerable objections" (EIP I.vii: 64). So it may be that the stark opposition of testimony and judgment that Reid commits himself to inherits some of the defects of the divisions about which he has already expressed skepticism. In the *Essays on the Intellectual Powers*, where Reid makes the comments complained of earlier, he seems less skeptical about the divisions, yet admits that both judgment and testimony involve affirmation and denial. Had he restricted himself to the idea that judgment (as he points out) may be private, involving no public affirmation or denial, whereas testimony must be expressed in a public language, he would have been on safer ground. But he immediately goes on to make the contrasts complained of above. He compares the act of judgment with the verdict of a judge in a "tribunal of justice" and speculates that the word may have been "borrowed" from the practice of tribunals. But this suggests not only that there is an intimate relation between public and private judgments, and that judgments of both kinds may be based on testimony, but also that a judge who reports his verdict to a fellow judge is thereby passing on a judgment with his testimony.

Part of the trouble here may reside in the language of acts. If we are thinking of relatively discrete acts, then we may be inclined to say that when Jones testifies that p, he is not then judging that p, since he will already have judged that p. Perhaps so, but this does not license us to say that his testimony cannot express his judgment, in the sense of carrying his commitment to the proposition he judged to be true. And this would leave us free to hold rightly that testimony can be erroneous. Reid seems to have been guilty in this aspect of his thought of neglecting the very thing he warned about, namely, the variety, connection, and complication of the powers of the mind and its operations.

IX. CONCLUSION

But if Reid's rich discussion of the concept of the social operations is indeed flawed in certain ways, the imperfections are the almost inevitable accompaniments of a pioneering investigation. His fashioning of the concept of the social operations and his deployment of it in relation to deep philosophical puzzles concerning promising and testimony constitute ground-breaking theoretical achievements of a very high order. They exhibit the subtlety and balance praised by Peirce, and they also show that flash of originality that has helped make Reid an increasingly interesting and influential figure in contemporary philosophy.

NOTES

1. Peirce 1934: 296–7.
2. The example is not Hume's, but it is consonant with his discussion of the problem in THN 3.2.2: 319–20.
3. THN 3.2.5: 332.
4. Ibid.: 333.

5. Ibid.: 335.
6. See EAP V.vi: 664–5.
7. The similarity is briefly noted in Lehrer 1989: 93 and 253 and is discussed in some detail in Coady 1992: 54–62. In that discussion I am principally concerned with epistemology, and I discuss Reid's treatment of the social operations in his *Essays on the Intellectual Powers of Man*, especially in EIP I.viii and VI.i. This treatment is consistent with the treatment in the *Essays on the Active Powers*, but the emphasis is different and supplementary. Reid's anticipation of modern speech act theory is thoroughly discussed by Schuhmann and Smith 1990: 47–62. I thank the editors of the present volume for acquainting me with this excellent article.
8. For more discussion of Reid's views in connection with testimony, see Coady 1992: esp. 54–62.
9. See Austin 1961: 223.
10. See EAP V.vi: 669.
11. EAP V.vi: 669.
12. EPM 3.1: 88.
13. Ibid.: 89.
14. For a more sympathetic interpretation of Hume's thought in these passages, see Kuflik 1998: 53–70. Kuflik's interesting essay argues that rough equality of power should not be treated as one of the "circumstances of justice" but he admits that these passages remain "difficult and puzzling" (66).
15. THN 3.2.1: 311.
16. EPM App. 3: 173.
17. Strawson 1968.
18. McGregor 1987: 483–95.
19. In Essay III, Chap. V of *Essays on the Active Powers of Man*, Reid in fact distinguishes two senses of resentment, sudden and deliberate, corresponding on the one hand to the instinctive hostility to any hurting and, on the other, to the more focused reaction of hostility to deliberately inflicted injuries. See EAP III.ii.v: 568–70.
20. See Putnam 1975: 215–71 (esp. 227) and also Burge 1979: 73–121.
21. See, for instance, Bach 1987 and Loar 1988.
22. In this elucidation of the implications of the two principles of nature and of the way in which Reid views testimony as a fundamental source of knowledge, I have avoided a direct discussion of the exact epistemic status of the principles and of their connection with Reid's theory of common sense as expounded more fully in the *Essays*. There, he lists various "first principles" including one concerning testimony. Like the philosophy of common sense more generally, they raise complex issues

of interpretation, such as what precisely in them is to be taken as "self-evident," whether they are to be understood as principles of truth or evidence, or whether they are principles of reliability open to indirect justifications. It would require too great a detour to canvass these matters here, but there is a good analysis of some of the central issues in Van Cleve 1999. Van Cleve also refers to a good deal of the important secondary literature around this topic.

23. See Coady 1992: esp. 57–62.

8 Reid on Memory and the Identity of Persons

This essay is a discussion of Reid's views on memory and the identity of persons through time. These topics are closely related, although there has been, and still is, a serious controversy about the exact nature of the relation. John Locke, on the one hand, made the case for what has come to be called the "Memory Theory of Personal Identity," according to which the identity of persons through time is *constituted* by the memory that a person has of his or her past actions, experiences, and so forth. Thomas Reid, on the other hand, thought this was absurd, and argued for the thesis that the relation between memory and identity is simply of an *evidential* nature: Memory gives a person evidence that he or she is the same person as the person who did, or experienced some thing at some previous time.

The first section is a discussion of Reid's views regarding memory as a source of knowledge, while the second considers his views on personal identity through time. In both sections, I will pay special attention to two features of Reid's thought. The first feature is that there are, as Reid says, things that are "obvious and certain" with respect to memory and personal identity. Unlike Descartes, Reid doesn't start by methodically doubting everything that seems obvious and certain. Rather, he endorses the principle that what seems obvious and certain is innocent until proven guilty. That is, what seems obvious and certain may legitimately be accepted as a starting point for philosophical reflection until it is shown that such acceptance is irrational, unjustified, or unwarranted. This endorsement is at least part of what makes Reid a common sense philosopher.

The second feature I will pay attention to is that Reid holds that there are certain things with respect to memory and personal identity that are "unaccountable." Reid firmly rejected skepticism with respect to a variety of topics; nonetheless, he was convinced that there are a great many things that we cannot explain, many things that are unaccountable. Instead of filling these gaps in our knowledge with bold conjectures or unproved hypotheses, Reid preferred to acknowledge ignorance in these cases.

I. MEMORY AS A SOURCE OF KNOWLEDGE

One of the things that Reid holds is obvious and certain with regard to memory is that "by memory we have an immediate knowledge of things past" (EIP III.i: 253). At least two remarks should be made about this statement. First, Reid says here that memory is a source of *knowledge*; elsewhere, though, he says that memory occasions *belief*.[1] However, this should not be taken to indicate an inconsistency, for unlike Descartes, Locke, and Hume, Reid held that knowledge is a species of, and is not to be contrasted with, belief.[2]

Second, Reid says that memory is a source of *immediate*, or as he says elsewhere, "intuitive" knowledge (EIP III.iii: 258). Although the expression "immediate knowledge" can mean various things, Reid uses it primarily to denote *knowledge that does not result from reasoning*. So, my (distinctly) remembering that I had a grapefruit for breakfast this morning yields what Reid calls "immediate knowledge" of this fact. This remembering yields immediate knowledge only in the sense that my current knowledge of this fact isn't the result of reasoning.

Another thing that Reid holds is obvious and certain is that memory has an object: "The object of memory, or thing remembered, must be something that is past" (EIP III.i: 254). This implies that memory, like perception, but unlike sensation, requires an act/object analysis. In every case of remembering, there is an object that is remembered and an act of remembering that object.[3] Moreover, Reid contends that the object of memory must be "something that is past." Now understood strictly and literally, what Reid says here is not true. You may remember something that is the case *now* (e.g., your present telephone number) or even something *yet to come* (e.g., that the concert will begin tomorrow at 8:15 p.m.). But this need not refute Reid's claim. For, as Reid says when speaking more carefully, to remember these things you must have learned about them at some previous time.[4] When interpreted in a charitable fashion, then, we can understand Reid's claim that memory is of things past to say that the objects of memory are past, present, or future things about which we have learned in the past.

Reid, we've seen, holds that memory has objects. It is worth emphasizing that there are two quite different ways to think about the objects of memory. Consider the memory reports included in lists A and B respectively:

> *List A*
> Jack remembers himself climbing Mt. Everest.
> Mary remembers her former telephone number being 63.89.30.
> The Queen remembers the fall of Byzantium.
>
> *List B*
> Jack remembers that he climbed Mt. Everest.
> Mary remembers that her telephone number is 63.89.30.
> The Queen remembers that Byzantium fell.

The objects on list A are of a varied nature – they are experiences, states of affairs and events. What Jack, on list A, is reported to remember is having undergone a certain experience, the experience of climbing Mt. Everest. The objects of memory on list B, by contrast, are propositions. What Jack is reported to remember on list B is *that he climbed Mt. Everest.* For convenience's sake, we may refer to the types of report included in list A as *objectual memory reports*, and those included in list B *propositional memory reports.* Of note for our purposes is the way in which objectual and propositional memory reports can diverge. It is possible, for example, that Jack remembers that he climbed Mt. Everest without being able to remember himself climbing Mt. Everest. In order for us accurately to ascribe to Jack the memory of climbing Mt. Everest, it must be the case that he remembers what the experience of climbing that mountain was like. But this is not required for us accurately to ascribe to Jack the memory that he climbed Mt. Everest.[5]

What did Reid take to be the objects of memory? In order to find out, let us consider a memory report of his own, as well as his own comments on it:

I remember the transit of Venus over the sun in the year 1769. I must therefore have perceived it at the time it happened, otherwise I could not now remember it. Our first acquaintance with any object of thought cannot be by remembrance. Memory can only produce a continuance or renewal of a former acquaintance with the thing remembered. (EIP III.i: 254–5)

Reid describes the object of his own act of remembering with the words "the transit of Venus over the sun in the year 1796." On the face of it, this is not a propositional memory report; Reid doesn't report that he remembers *that Venus made a transition over the sun in 1769*. Rather, he reports that he remembers *Venus's transit over the sun in 1769*. The object of what Reid says he remembers, then, is an event. It should be added that this is not an idiosyncratic example of a memory report on Reid's part; by far and away, Reid's usual manner of stating memory reports is objectual in character. And this, I suggest, gives us reason to believe that Reid thinks of memory as being objectual in nature.

In order to understand Reid's thought more fully on this matter, we need to consider something else that Reid holds is obvious and certain, namely, that "[m]emory is always accompanied with the belief of that which we remember": "in mature years, and in a sound state of mind," Reid says, "every man feels that he must believe what he distinctly remembers, though he can give no other reason of his belief, but that he remembers the thing distinctly" (EIP III.ii: 254).

What is particularly interesting about this passage is that Reid doesn't identify the act of remembering something with the act of believing something; *remembering* is a phenomenon distinct from *believing something on the basis of remembering* (or, for short, *having a memory belief*). Moreover, Reid says that memories come in different degrees of vivacity. These two points suggest that it is possible, in Reid's view, to remember something without a memory belief following in its wake. Suppose – to borrow an example from Carl Ginet[6] – you are asked what your telephone number was twenty years ago and, although you are very uncertain of it, give the correct number, say, 63.89.30. Then we would not want to say that you have the memory belief that your former telephone number is 63.89.30, although we would want to say that you remembered your former telephone number. The reason the memory belief didn't form in this case is that the remembering wasn't distinct enough.

When we put these points together, the following picture of Reid's thought emerges. Memory has objects. These include events such as the transit of Venus over the sun in 1769, states of affairs such as your former telephone number's being 63.89.30, and past actions and experiences such as your climbing Mt. Everest. The memory of these objects can be more or less distinct. When the memory of these objects is above a certain threshold of distinctness (and the agent remembering is of sound mind), beliefs are elicited. For example, since Reid's remembering the transit of Venus over the sun in 1769 is above this threshold, he believes that Venus made a transit over the sun in 1769. So, given that Reid distinguishes *remembering* from *believing something on the basis of remembering*, and also holds that believing is a propositional attitude, we should say that for Reid the objects of remembering are not propositions, but objects such as events, states of affairs and experiences; the objects of beliefs formed on the basis of rememberings, by contrast, are propositions. Otherwise put, what Reid calls memories are those types of item picked out by style A reports, while beliefs formed on the basis of memory are those types of item picked out by style B reports.

Let me now point to a final feature of the quotation from Reid that we have been exploring. What this quotation indicates is that Reid not only subscribes to the thesis that distinct memory is always accompanied by belief, but also subscribes to the stronger thesis that to remember distinctly a past or currently existing object entails that that object exists or existed at some time. Reid's example of the transit of Venus testifies to this: He says that he could not have remembered the transit of Venus had he not actually perceived the transit of Venus. Generalizing over this case, we can say that Reid endorsed the following principle:

(A) S's distinctly remembering p entails p's existence

– where S is a person of sound mind, and p is a variable for objects such as events, states of affairs, etc., that exist or existed at some time.

From this it follows that Reid is committed to the thesis that it is self-contradictory to speak of incorrect memories.[7] However, this is a strong claim that is likely to provoke two objections.

The first objection has its roots in ordinary language: "It is not unusual," it might be said, "for people to say such things as 'I remember there were four people in the room,' when in fact there were five, and 'I remember visiting Salt Lake City over the weekend,' when the visit took place only during the middle of the week. These are cases of incorrect memory, and what we call in ordinary language 'incorrect memories.' Hence, Reid is wrong to claim that there are no incorrect memories, and (A) is false."

Reid doesn't explicitly address the issue of incorrect memories, but we can identify in his work two strategies of reply. One strategy of reply can be discerned in his discussion of the problem of the so-called "fallacies of the senses" – a discussion that immediately precedes his treatment of memory.[8] In this discussion, Reid says that to understand so-called misperceptions, we must distinguish *what is seen* from *what is believed on the basis of what is seen*. A large array of so-called perceptual errors, suggests Reid, are not errors with respect to what is seen, but errors with respect to what is believed on the basis of what is seen. In such cases, these beliefs are rashly formed, or suffer from other deficiencies such as being outweighed by counterevidence. Likewise, we have seen that Reid distinguishes *what is remembered* from *what is believed on the basis of remembering*. This suggests that some so-called incorrect memories can be thought of as beliefs formed too hastily on the basis of what is remembered or formed in the teeth of excellent countervailing evidence. What we have in this type of case is not an incorrect memory, but a deficient belief formed on the basis of remembering.

Another strategy of reply that can be gleaned from Reid's analysis of the fallacies of the senses involves distinguishing *seeming perceptions* from *genuine perceptions*.[9] In Reid's view, some cases of perceptual misrepresentation are not a matter of forming deficient beliefs on the basis of perception, but of being subject to what we might call "perceptual mimics." Likewise, we can distinguish *seeming memories* from *genuine memories*. Some cases of inaccurate memory are not beliefs formed in an inappropriate way on the basis of remembering, but are "memory mimics." Reid's position can thus allow that not all seeming memories – even particularly vivid ones – are genuine memories. Granted, having this distinction in hand may be of little help when trying to determine in one's day-to-day experience whether some mental episode is a genuine case of memory. Nevertheless, the success of the second strategy (along with the first) leaves (A) untouched.

The second objection to (A) is broadly Humean in character, and runs as follows: "Granted, distinct memory is always accompanied by a memory belief. But Reid gives us no account of why or how this happens. And in the absence of such an account, we have no reason to regard memory as reliably giving rise to true memory beliefs."

Reid's response to this skeptical charge can be gathered from the following quotations:

Why sensation should compel our belief of the present existence of a thing, memory a belief of its past existence, and imagination no belief at all, I believe no philosopher can give a shadow of reason, but that such is the nature of these operations; they are all simple and original, and therefore inexplicable acts of the mind. (IHM II.iv: 28)

And

I think it appears, that memory is an original faculty, given us by the Author of our being, of which we can give no account, but that we are so made.

The knowledge which I have of things past by my memory, seems to me as unaccountable as an immediate knowledge would be of things to come; and I can give no reason why I should have the one and not the other, but that such is the will of my Maker. I find in my mind a distinct conception, and a firm belief of a series of past events; but how this is produced, I know not. I call it memory, but this is only giving a name to it; it is not an account of its cause. I believe most firmly what I distinctly remember; but I can give no reason of this belief. It is the inspiration of the Almighty that gives me this understanding.

When I believe the truth of a mathematical axiom, or of a mathematical proposition, I see that it must be so: Every man who has the same conception of it sees the same. There is an evident and necessary connection between the subject and the predicate of the proposition; and I have all the evidence to support my belief which I can possibly conceive.

When I believe that I washed my hands and face this morning, there appears no necessity in the truth of this proposition. It might be, or it might be not. A man may distinctly conceive it without believing it at all. How then do I come to believe it? I remember it distinctly. This is all I can say. This remembrance is an act of my mind. Is it possible that this act should be, if the event had not happened? I confess I do not see any necessary connection between the one and the other. If any man can shew such a necessary connection, then I think that belief which we have of what we remember will be fairly accounted for; but if this cannot be done, that belief is unaccountable, and we can say no more but that it is the result of our constitution. (EIP III.i: 255–6)

Reid affirms in these passages that memory is "unaccountable," by which he means three things: First, that we don't know why distinct memory, in contrast with, e.g., imagination, is always accompanied by belief; second, that we don't know why it tends to give rise to *true* beliefs; and, third, that we cannot establish that memory beliefs are true.

Not all beliefs, it should be noted, are, in Reid's view, unaccountable; nor are all questions as to how or why true beliefs arise without answer. Belief in necessary truths such as mathematical truths is Reid's example to illustrate this. Someone may believe that 2 + 2 = 4 because he *sees that it must be so.* In (some) mathematical propositions, says Reid, there is a necessary and evident connection between the subject and the predicate of the sentence expressing the proposition, a connection that can be "seen." This "seeing" is the evidence that supports one's belief in the mathematical proposition and, hence, (when all goes well) accounts for the formation of it.

Memory belief, by contrast, stands without the evidential support of such "seeing" and is therefore *un*accountable in at least two senses. We cannot discern any necessary connection between (i) a memory belief and a remembering and (ii) a memory belief and the object remembered. When someone remembers that he washed his hands and face this morning he sees no necessary connection between (i) this memory and the belief that he washed his hands and (ii) the belief that he washed his hands and the event that consisted in his doing so. Because we cannot discern a necessary connection between these things, there is, suggests Reid, no account (save the will of God) of the formation of this belief.[10]

But it hardly follows from this, says Reid, that we should be skeptical about whether memory is reliable. Contrary to what Hume suggests in numerous places,[11] our not being able to explain why or how a putative faculty works in a certain way has no bearing on whether we have such a faculty or whether it is reliable. The knowledge we have of things by way of memory, Reid says, is the "result of our constitution" – a constitution that Reid repeatedly emphasizes is the product of a benevolent Maker and, thus, fundamentally reliable.

Nevertheless, it is tempting to object that, in this case, Reid is calling certain things unaccountable when they are really not. Reid might be correct to say that we have no account of why certain mental episodes are accompanied by memory beliefs or why these beliefs are generally true. But, in this passage, Reid has offered no reason for thinking that we cannot justify the reliability of memory. So, it might be said: "There are various types of evidential bases for a belief. There is the type that Reid has identified – that of *seeing that the proposition under consideration must be true.* Reid has shown that a memory belief doesn't rest on *that* evidential basis. He's also shown we cannot discern a necessary connection between the object remembered and the memory belief formed. But there may be alternative types of evidential basis on which a memory belief rests. If so, there is a sense in which memory beliefs *can* be given an account of."

Reid anticipates this objection. In one passage he describes (and rejects) such an alternative:

Perhaps it may be said, that the experience we have had of the fidelity of memory is a good reason for relying upon its testimony. I deny not that this may be a reason to those who have had this experience, and who reflect upon it. But I believe there are few who ever thought of this reason, or who found any need of it. It must be some rare occasion that leads a man to have recourse to it; and in those who have done so, the testimony of memory was believed before the experience of its fidelity, and that belief could not be caused by the experience which came after it. (Ibid.)

The alternative evidential basis for memory belief that Reid considers here is a favorable track record. The idea is that we have a reason to believe that our memory beliefs are mostly true because we have inductive evidence that distinct memories typically yield true memory beliefs.

Reid doesn't spell out this line of reasoning in any detail. Still, he makes a brief remark on the inductive track record procedure that is of utmost philosophical significance. This procedure, Reid indicates, can only be successful if the reliability of memory can be established by a line of reasoning that nowhere involves or presupposes the reliability of memory.[12] But this is impossible, suggests Reid, because it cannot be shown that memory is reliable without presupposing the reliability of memory. It is possible for B to check the reliability of A's memory. And it is possible for C to check B's memory. But this process cannot go on indefinitely. At some point, some agent in this chain of verification must presuppose the reliability of *his own* memory, if only while running a credit check on someone else's memory. As Reid says: "The operations of reason, whether in action or in speculation, are made up of successive parts. The antecedent are the foundation of the consequent, and without the conviction that the antecedent have been seen or done by me, I could have no reason to proceed to the consequent, in any speculation, or in any active project whatever" (EIP III.iv: 262). If that's right, there is a kind of circularity involved in any attempt to run a credit check on memory. Although the circularity is not the most direct kind of logical circularity – the track record argument doesn't have among its premises the proposition that memory is reliable – the reliability of memory is assumed in both generating and assessing the evidential force of the premises of the argument.[13]

I have claimed that it is Reid's view that we cannot offer a noncircular justification for the reliability of memory. I have also claimed that it is Reid's view that we cannot discern how or why memory works as it does. It is this latter claim in particular that distinguishes Reid's views from those of Locke and Hume. What Locke claims is that remembering something is a matter of "ideas" being before our mind and furthermore that "our ideas [are] nothing, but actual Perceptions in the Mind, which cease to be anything when there is no perception of them...."[14] Spelled out a little more, Locke's account of the workings of memory comes to this: Memory is "the Power to revive again in our Minds those Ideas which, after imprinting, have disappeared, or have been, as it were, laid out of Sight ... and this is Memory, which is as it were, the storehouse of our *Ideas*."[15] This Lockean account, Reid points out, is unacceptable as it implies two incompatible claims: (i) to remember is to revive in our minds certain ideas, and (ii) ideas cease to exist when they are not perceived. Reid says in reply that "[i]t seems to me as difficult to revive things that have ceased to be anything, as to lay them up in a repository, or to bring them out of it. When a thing is once annihilated, the same thing cannot be produced" (EIP III.vii: 284). Moreover, Locke's account is too broad insofar as it fits certain mental goings on that definitely are not cases of remembering: "I see before me the picture of a friend. I shut my eyes ... and the picture disappears.... I have the power to turn my eyes again towards the picture, and immediately the perception is revived. But is this memory? No surely; yet it answers the definition as well as memory itself can do" (EIP III.vii: 285).

Hume's account of the workings of memory fares no better. Among other things, the thesis that the only items we are directly acquainted with are ideas in our minds gives rise to skepticism: "since ideas are things present, how can we, from our having a certain idea presently in our mind, conclude that an event really happened ten or twenty years ago, corresponding to it?" (EIP III.vi: 290).[16] Hume's answer is that this cannot be done. His theory of ideas, then, leads to scepticism about memory beliefs. Reid regards this result as a *reductio* of the Humean theory. Better than having an obviously wrong account of memory is to acknowledge that one doesn't know why or how memory works the way it does.

II. THE IDENTITY OF PERSONS THROUGH TIME

I now turn to the topic of personal identity. One way to enter Reid's thought on this matter is to review his criticism of how Locke construed the relation between memory and personal identity. As mentioned at the outset of this essay, Locke endorsed a version of what is often called the "Memory Theory of Personal Identity," according to which, in Reid's summary of it,

personal identity, that is, the sameness of a rational being, consists in consciousness alone, and, as far as this consciousness can be extended backwards to any past action or thought, so far reaches the identity of that person. So that, whatever hath the consciousness of present and past actions, is the same person to whom they belong. (EIP III.vi: 275–6)[17]

To properly understand what is said here, three clarifications are in order. In the first place, Locke's expression "consciousness of past actions" must be taken to mean "memory of past actions." Moreover, to say that personal identity "consists in consciousness" is to claim that *what makes it the case* that a person at time t2 is identical with, say, the person who climbed Mt. Everest at an earlier time t1 is that person's remembering at t2 that he climbed Everest at t1, when in fact he did climb Everest. Finally, in this context, "remembering" something admits of two interpretations. It can mean *occurrently* remembering or *being able* to remember some thing. Locke, suggests Reid, can be read as espousing either view.

Against the second interpretation of Locke, Reid offers two sorts of counterexample. The first counterexample shows that what we can call the "potential memory" interpretation of Locke has "strange consequences" (EIP III.vi: 276). Says Reid, "if the intelligent being may lose the consciousness of the actions done by him, which is surely possible, then he is not the person that did those actions" (ibid.). So, according to Locke's theory, were Gerald Ford such that he could not remember that he was Nixon's vice-president, then he would not be the same person as the man who was Nixon's vice-president. This implication of the theory is absurd, and indicates that an agent's identity isn't, as Locke suggests, constituted by his ability to remember certain things:

> It is . . . true, that my remembrance that I did such a thing is the evidence I have that I am the identical person who did it. . . . But to say that my remembrance that I did such a thing . . . makes me the person who did it, is, in my apprehension, an absurdity too gross to be entertained. . . . For it is to attribute to memory . . . a strange magical power of producing its object . . . [and this] appears to me as great an absurdity as it would be to say, that my belief that the world was created, made it to be created. (EIP III.vi: 277 and III.iv: 265)

Another, related, absurd consequence of the theory is that a person may at the same time be and not be the person that did a certain deed. Reid illustrates the point by means of the well-known Brave Officer Paradox:

> Suppose a brave officer to have been flogged when a boy at school, for robbing an orchard, to have taken a standard from the enemy in his first campaign, and to have been made a general in advanced life: Suppose also, which must be admitted to be possible, that when he took the standard, he was conscious of his having been flogged at school, and that when he was made a general he was conscious of his taking the standard, but had absolutely lost the consciousness of his flogging.
>
> These things being supposed, it follows, from Mr LOCKE's doctrine, that he who was flogged at school is the same person who took the standard, and that he who took the standard is the same person as he who was made a general. Whence it follows, if there be any truth in logic, that the general is the same person with him who was flogged at school. But the general's consciousness does not reach so far back as his flogging, therefore, according to Mr LOCKE's doctrine, he is not the person who was flogged. Therefore the general is, and at the same time is not the same person with him who was flogged at school. (EIP III.vi: 276)

Reid's point is that identity is transitive, and that Locke's theory, absurdly, implies the denial of this.

Reid's final objection to Locke's view is best understood as having the occurrent memory interpretation of Locke's theory as its target. The objection hinges on a principle that Reid says he takes for granted.

I take it for granted that all the thoughts I am conscious of, or remember, are the thoughts of one and the same thinking principle, which I call *myself*, or my *mind*. Every man has an immediate and irresistible conviction, not only of his present existence, but of his continued existence and identity, as far back as he can remember. (EIP I.ii: 42)

Two thoughts are present here. Reid contends that thoughts and remembrances do not exist all by themselves but require a "bearer," which he calls a "self," or, as I will call it, a *person*. This contention puts Reid in opposition to Hume, who held instead that persons are "bundles" of thoughts ("a succession of ideas and impressions without any subject" (IHM II. vi: 32)). To be sure, Reid is aware of the fact that he gives no argument for this thesis. Reid held, however, that this thesis is so obvious that it *cannot* be argued for. In his own words: "if any man should demand a proof, that sensations cannot be without a mind, or sentient being, I confess I can give none; and that to pretend to prove it, seems to me almost as absurd as to deny it" (IHM II.vi: 32).

Second, Reid maintains that we irresistibly believe that we have "continued existence and identity," where "uninterrupted existence is . . . necessarily implied in identity" (EIP III.iv: 262, 263). Reid, then, means to endorse the following principle:

(P1) Object O at t2 is identical with an object at t1, only if O has uninterruptedly existed during the time interval between t1 and t2.

Reid endorses (P1) but again acknowledges that it cannot be proved that persons have uninterrupted existence:

If any man . . . should demand a proof that he is the same person to-day as he was yesterday, or a year ago, I know no proof can be given him: He must be left to himself, either as a man that is lunatic, or as one who denies first principles, and is not to be reasoned with.

Every man of sound mind, finds himself under the necessity of believing his own identity, and continued existence. The conviction of this is immediate and irresistible; and if he should lose this conviction, it would be a certain proof of insanity, which is not to be remedied by reasoning. (EIP I.ii: 42–3)

Given his endorsement of (P1), Reid is committed to the claim that the pain I now feel in my left arm is not identical with the pain I felt there yesterday. For, between now and yesterday, there has been a time interval during which I was without that pain in my left arm. The two pains are, although sortally the same, numerically diverse. But the person who has the pain now, is the same person as the one who had the pain yesterday, for he uninterruptedly existed during that time interval. Reid endorses (P1) because he deems its denial to have deeply counterintuitive consequences: "That which hath ceased to exist, cannot be the same with that which afterwards begins to exist; for this would be to suppose a being to exist after it ceased to exist, and to have had existence before it was produced, which are manifest contradictions" (EIP III.iv: 263).[18]

According to Reid, Locke endorses (P1).[19] But the application of (P1) to the occurrent memory interpretation of Locke's theory reveals a problem: "Identity can only be affirmed of things which have a continued existence. Consciousness, and every kind of thought [memory included], is transient and momentary, and has no continued existence; and therefore, if personal identity consisted in consciousness, it would certainly follow that no man is the same person any two moments of his life" (EIP III.vi: 278).

Reid's polemic against the Memory Theory of Personal Identity sets the stage for a more general argument for the claim that persons are not identical with (or constituted by) their bodies. This more general argument rests on three claims that Reid holds are obvious and certain:

(P2) An object O has strict identity through time if it doesn't gain or lose parts.

(P3) Persons have no parts.

(P4) Persons have perfect identity through time.

(P2) rests on the distinction – defended by Joseph Butler before and Roderick Chisholm after him – between perfect and imperfect identity through time.[20] For something to have perfect identity over time, according to Reid, it cannot change parts. Whenever a thing changes parts, e.g., when a ship "has successively changed her anchors, her tackle, her sails, her masts, her planks, and her timbers" it may have "something which, for the conveniency of speech, we call identity" (EIP III.v: 266) – or imperfect identity. One good answer, then, to the question "Is this the ship that Stilpo built?" is "Yes, more or less." The ship that Stilpo built may thus be imperfectly identical with a particular ship that has over time successively changed her anchors, masts, planks, etc. But the right answer to the question "Is this man named Demjanjuk the same person as Ivan the Terrible?" is either "Yes" or "No," not "More or less." The man named Demjanjuk either is or is not the same person as Ivan the Terrible, for persons, Reid contends, do not gain or lose parts. The reason for this is that persons *have* no parts. They are metaphysical simples: "all mankind place their personality in something that cannot be divided, or consists of parts. A part of a person is a manifest absurdity" since a person "is something indivisible and is what LEIBNITZ calls a *monad*" (EIP III.iv: 263–4). Consequently, Reid says, "identity, when applied to persons, has no ambiguity, and admits not of degrees, or of more and less" (EIP III.v: 267).

Reid offers no direct argument for (P3) or the claim that persons have no parts, but he points out the implausibility of its denial:

When a man loses his estate, his health, his strength, he is still the same person, and has lost nothing of his personality. If he has a leg or an arm cut off, he is the same person he was before. The amputated member is no part of his person, otherwise it would have a right to a part of his estate, and be liable for a part of his estate, and be liable for a part of his engagements; it would be entitled to a share of his merit and demerit – which is manifestly absurd. (EIP III.iv: 264)[21]

In any case, when we combine these principles together with other plausible propositions, we have the ingredients for two closely related arguments for the claim that persons are not identical with their bodies. The first argument hinges on (P3), and says:

(1) Bodies have parts.
(P3) Persons have no parts.
(2) If object A has parts and object B does not, then objects A and B cannot be identical. (From Leibniz's Law)
(C) Therefore, persons are not identical with their bodies.

The second argument rests on (P4), and goes as such:

(3) If persons are bodies, then persons do not have perfect identity through time.
(P4) Persons have perfect identity through time.
(C) Therefore, persons are not identical with their bodies.

It goes without saying that, in the light of so-called "brain transplant" thought experiments in which part of a person's brain is removed and transferred to a different body, many contemporary philosophers would not find (P3) and (P4) obvious and certain. The seeds of a Reidian reply to such cases can be found in Reid's critique of Locke, although I cannot enter that discussion here.[22] Instead, I shall close by indicating that Reid took it to be clear that (P3) and (P4) commit us to a form of dualism.[23] It is often said these days that dualism is the upshot of a theistic world view. This would be an accurate assessment of its place in Reid's thought. In Reid's view, God is a nonmaterial person in possession of active power for whose existence we have good evidence.[24] Accordingly, there was a precedent in Reid's view for the claim that at least one person is immaterial. And it was, to some degree, natural for a theist such as Reid to think that human persons are also immaterial. It is, however, especially important to note that Reid's dualism is not simply, or even primarily, driven by his theism. Reid held that the position that persons are not identical with their bodies is dictated by the best science of his day.[25] The best science of his day was Newtonian science, and Newton, as well as his followers, held that matter is inert or does not act. But, as Reid argued in the *Essays on the Active Powers*, persons *do* act – they have, as he says, active power. They are able to act because they are endowed with intelligence and freedom. Matter, by contrast, is without intelligence or freedom and, hence, cannot act. These ideas together suggest a third argument for (C):

(4) Human bodies are material objects.
(5) Matter has no active power (it is "essentially inert").
(6) Persons have active power.
(C) Therefore, persons are not identical with their bodies.

In conclusion, Reid's dualism is the vector resultant of various pressures – his claim that principles such as (P2)–(P4) are obvious and certain, his acceptance of theism, and his high regard for science.[26]

NOTES

1. See EIP III.i: 254.
2. Reid nowhere gives an explicit analysis of the concept of knowledge, but his view is plausibly thought of as being broadly reliabilist in character. See de Bary 2001.
3. Reid believed that no such analysis can be given of sensation. We cannot distinguish between, say, feeling pain in one's tooth and the object of

that act, namely, the pain in one's tooth. For, as Reid says, sensations consist in being felt. See IHM XI.xx.

4. See EIP III.ii: 254.
5. The difference I have in mind has an analogue in reports of perceptions. Jack may be said to see a cat on the mat, but he may also be said to see that the cat is on the mat. And it is possible to report the former truthfully but the latter falsely.
6. Ginet 1975: 147.
7. Malcolm 1963: 188 also notes that "remembering incorrectly" is self-contradictory.
8. EIP II.xxii.
9. See EIP II.xvii: 320.
10. Appealing simply to the will of God, however, doesn't amount to an "account" of memory as Reid thinks of an account. See Wolterstorff 2001: 49.
11. See especially EHU VII.
12. See Reid's remarks at EIP VI.v: 481ff.
13. Alston 1993 calls this kind of circularity "epistemic circularity."
14. E II.xx.2: 150.
15. Ibid.: 149–50.
16. This is a type of argument that John Greco calls a "No Good Inference" argument in his essay in this volume.
17. This is Reid's summary of E II.xxvii.9: 335.
18. Baruch Brody thinks that Reid's argument for P1 is a bad one. His summary of Reid's view is that "no object can have two beginnings of existence" and it is bad for the following reason: "If by 'beginning of existence' one means 'first moment of existence,' then an object with interrupted existence has only one beginning. If, however, one means 'first moment of existence after a period of nonexistence,' then objects with interrupted existence have two beginnings of existence, but there is nothing incoherent with that" (Brody 1980: 80). A Reidian reply to this would be that Brody's argument is, at best, directed against (P1) understood as a principle about imperfect identity.
19. EIP III.vi: 275.
20. See especially Butler 1975 and Chisholm 1976, Chap. 3.
21. A recent exposition of this thesis is Chisholm 1991.
22. EIP III.vi: 276.
23. Reid was convinced that the relation between body and person is clouded in mystery: "There appears to be a vast interval between body and mind; and whether there be any intermediate nature that connects them together, we know not" (EIP Preface: 11).
24. See LNT as well as EIP VI.vi.

25. See PRLS: 21, 48, 201–7.

26. For comments on an early draft of this essay, I thank John Greco, Joe Houston, Peter Schouls, and members of the Vrije Universiteit research group "Foundationalism and the Sources of Knowledge." For comments and advice on subsequent drafts, I am especially indebted to Terence Cuneo.

9   Thomas Reid's Theory of Freedom and Responsibility

It is fitting that one of the last pieces of philosophical writing to come from Reid's hand should bear the title "Of Power."[1] For the concept "power" lies at the foundation of Reid's account of agent-causation, which in turn is the central idea in his account of human freedom and responsibility. In this final piece of philosophizing on this subject, Reid begins by pointing out that: "Every voluntary exertion to produce an event implies a conception of the event, and some belief or hope that the exertion will be followed by it" (OP: 3). Accordingly, our willing (deciding) to take a walk in the woods implies our having a conception of our taking a walk in the woods and some belief or hope that an exertion of ours intended to bring that about will be followed by our taking a walk in the woods. Reid takes this claim of his to imply that a conception of power is antecedent to every deliberate act.

Does he think that the earliest exertions by an infant involve a conception of power? No. Reid thinks that our earliest exertions are instinctive, unaccompanied by a conception of some goal to be accomplished. It is only when experience teaches us that certain exertions are followed by certain events that we learn to make these exertions voluntarily and deliberately in order to produce such an event. And once we believe that the event depends upon our exertion, we then have "the conception of power in ourselves to produce the event" (ibid.). Reid therefore concludes that our conception of power "is the fruit of experience and not innate" (ibid.).

Reid proceeds to distinguish an exertion of power from the volition (act of will) to produce an event. If I will to rise immediately from my chair, the willing and the exertion involved in rising from my chair may occur together, and may be difficult to distinguish. But if I will to rise from my chair in five minutes, the willing precedes the exertion of rising from my chair. Moreover, he points out that although volition does not vary in degrees and is incapable of more or less, exertion can be great or small. And he concludes from this that exertions themselves, unattended by volition, may give us the conception of power "... and teach us that the events known to be consequent upon such exertions are in our power" (OP: 5).

The passages we've quoted appear to leave open the possibility that although an exertion of active power may be required to bring about what the agent wills to do – rising from his chair, for example – no exertion of active power is required for an agent *to will* to rise from his chair. But this is not Reid's view. Reid's view is that any change in an agent that is not caused by something external to the agent either is caused by some event internal to the agent or is directly caused by the agent. (Indeed, toward the end of this final discussion "Of Power" he reiterates his view "that every event and every thing that has a beginning must have a cause" (OP: 8)). And whenever an agent wills to do something, that act of willing is just as much an event, a change, as is a change involving a movement of the agent's body, such as the agent rising from his chair. So acts of will, no less than changes involving one's body, require a cause.

I. REID'S ACCOUNT OF HUMAN FREEDOM

In his earlier, major work in which he discusses freedom and morality, *Essays on the Active Powers of Man*, Reid notes Locke's account of power and carefully distinguishes it from his own. Locke drew a distinction between active and passive power, a distinction we may characterize as follows:

S has an *active power* provided it is in S's power to cause a change in itself or in some other thing.

S has a *passive power* provided S has the capacity to undergo a change as a result of the causal activity of some agent.

This is the distinction Locke had in mind when he said: "Fire has the power to melt gold ... and gold has a power to be melted."[2] "Power thus considered is two-fold, viz., as able to make or able to receive any change. The one may be called *active*, and the other *passive* power."[3] The sea has the active power to crush a submarine that goes too deep, just as fire has the active power to melt gold. Of course, the submarine must go down too deep to withstand the pressure of the sea (the gold must be placed sufficiently close to the fire) in order for the sea (the fire) to actually cause the change in the submarine (the gold). Nevertheless, Locke's distinction between something's having the power to cause a change and something's having the capacity to undergo a change seems to be applicable in a large range of examples of entities causing a change and entities undergoing a change.

Locke makes use of his concept of (active) power when he tells us that an agent is free with respect to performing an action A just in case the agent has both the power to do A if she so wills and the power to refrain from doing A if she so wills.[4] Thus, for Locke, an agent's being free with respect to some action A requires a two-way power: the power to do A if the agent wills to do A, and the power to refrain from doing A if the agent wills to refrain from doing A. Perhaps the best way to approach Reid's understanding of power and freedom is to see in what ways it differs from Locke's understanding of these two concepts.

Reid makes two major alterations in Locke's account of power. First, he rejects the notion of "passive power." Noting that Locke means by it nothing more than "the possibility of being changed," he says: "To call this *power*, seems to be a misapplication of the word" (EAP I.iii: 519a). Second, he makes a very important addition to Locke's account of active power. In Locke's view, when an agent exercises active power to bring about some event, the exercise of power must originate within that agent. (If one billiard ball strikes another, setting it in motion, Locke would not attribute active power to the ball that strikes another if it too had been set in motion by a third ball.) But Locke does not rule out factors within the agent *causing* the agent to exercise his active power to bring about an event. He holds, for example, that once a prisoner's chains are knocked off and the prison door set open to him, he is "perfectly at liberty, because he may either go or stay as he best likes."[5] And this perfect liberty, Locke contends, is in no way abridged by the fact that the prisoner's fear of the darkness of the night *makes* him stay in prison. The difficulty with Locke's view is that it allows that the prisoner lacks power to refrain from willing to stay. For given his fear of the darkness of the night, he simply is unable not to will to stay in prison. Reid rejects such a view, contending that active power to cause (a volition) *implies* a power not to cause (that volition). And the power not to cause is, for Reid, simply inconsistent with the exercise of power to cause being the necessary causal product of one's desires, fears, or other involuntary states of the mind or body. In short, an agent's exercise of power to cause (active power) precludes his exercise of power being causally determined by prior causes within the agent.[6] So active power for Reid is such that an agent's exercise of it simply cannot itself be caused to occur. And our acts of will are free only in so far as they are agent-caused by us. Reid means to preclude prior sufficient causes of an agent's exercise of active power when he says: "power to produce any effect, implies power not to produce it ..." (EAP I.v: 523a).

Another striking difference between Locke and Reid centers on the issue of what it is for an agent to be *free* in performing an action. Locke tells us that an agent is free with respect to performing an action A just in case the agent has both the power to do A if she so wills and the power to refrain from doing A if she so wills.[7] Reid is generally understood to say that in addition the agent must have *the power to will* to do A and *the power to will not* to do A. Thus Reid is viewed as taking over Locke's account, but adding to it the condition that the agent has power over the determinations of her will.[8] This is the standard account of Reid's view of freedom. But here is what Reid actually says in the well-known passage about freedom (liberty).

> By the *Liberty of a Moral Agent*, I understand, *a power over the determination of his own Will.*
>
> If, in any action, he had power to will what he did, or not to will it, in that action he is free. (EAP I.iv: 599a–b)

A careful look at the passage just quoted suggests that the standard account may be wrong in two ways. First, the standard account has Reid attributing to the agent a power to will to do A and a power to will not to do A. But in the passage Reid does not attribute a power to *will not to do A*, he attributes to the agent only the power *not to will to do A*. Power over one's will requires, for Reid, the power not to will what one did will. It does not require the power to will the opposite of what one willed. (While this distinction may seem insignificant, as we shall later see it is quite important.) Second, the standard account may be wrong in attributing to Reid Locke's condition that the agent must have had the power to do otherwise had he willed to do otherwise. All that Reid really says in this famous passage is that an action the agent performs as a result of willing it is a free action (i.e., the agent is free in that action) provided the agent had the power not to will what he did. Reid says nothing about the agent also having it within his power *to do otherwise* had he willed to do otherwise. If I am right in thinking that Reid's view does not include this condition, there will be actions that are free on Reid's account that are not free on Locke's account, and, of course, actions that are free on Locke's account that are not free on Reid's account. An example of the latter would be the following. Suppose I hook up a machine to your brain so that by activating the machine I cause your decision to remain sitting and thus *deprive* you of the power to will to do otherwise. It still may be true that you had the power to get up and walk *if* you had willed to do so. So Locke's account is satisfied but Reid's is not. For you here lack power over the determination of your will. An example of the former would be the one Locke provides in distinguishing a voluntary action from a free action. Locke considers the case of a man who wills to stay in a room, not knowing it to be locked. This person acts voluntarily, not freely (that is, with Lockean freedom) in staying in the room. For it was not in his power to leave the room had he willed to leave. As I've suggested, however, there is nothing in Reid's account that implies that the agent must have had the power *to do otherwise* had he so willed. What Reid says is that if a person wills to perform some action and does so, then he performs that action freely provided he had the power to will or not will what he did. The person in Locke's example acts freely in staying (on Reid's account) because it was in his power not to will to stay in the room.

The importance of Reid's condition that the agent have power over the determinations of the will is that it precludes a voluntary action from being free when the act of will is causally necessitated by some involuntary state of the agent's mind or by anything external to the agent. For then the agent lacks power over the determination of his will. Indeed, in the very next sentence to the one I quoted earlier he says this:

But if, in every voluntary action, the determination of his will be the necessary consequence of something involuntary in the state of his mind, or of something in his external circumstances, he is not free; he has not what I call the Liberty of a Moral Agent, but is subject to necessity. (EAP I.iv: 599b)

Having quoted Reid's account of human freedom and having pointed out first that it most certainly differs from Locke's in insisting on the agent having power over the determinations of the will, and second that it may well also differ in not insisting that the agent have the power to act otherwise should he so will, I turn now to Reid's view of agent-causation. For, as we shall see, what it means for an agent to have power to will or not will some action is for that agent to have the *power to cause or not cause* that act of will.

II. REID ON THE AGENT AS CAUSE

On Reid's view of agent-causation the following three conditions are necessary and sufficient for X to be an agent-cause of some event e.

1. X is a substance that had power to bring about e.
2. X exerted its power to bring about e.
3. X had the power to refrain from bringing about e.

Our first point establishes that an agent-cause of an event e is always a substance. Actually, Reid's view is that only intelligent substances possessing will and active power (i.e., agents) can be causes.[9] Inanimate substances, events, motives, laws of nature, etc., therefore, cannot be agent-causes for the simple reason that they are not intelligent beings with will and active power. To forestall misunderstanding, however, we must note that Reid thought that the words "cause," "power," and "agent" are ambiguous, used both in the sense we are engaged in explicating, the "original, strict and proper" sense (as he called it), and in what he calls the "lax and popular" sense.[10] In the lax and popular sense of "cause," "power," and "agent," substances lacking intelligence, events, laws of nature, and even motives may be causes.

We can say that the fire has the power to melt gold. We might also say that when this happens the fire exercises that power. Indeed, as we've noted, Locke would say that the fire exerts its active power in melting the gold, and the gold has the passive power to be melted by the fire. Reid, however, must deny that in the strict sense the fire has active power to melt the gold. For the fire has no power to refrain from melting the gold when the gold is sufficiently near the fire. Our third condition is not satisfied. So the fire is not the agent-cause of the gold's being melted, it is not a cause in Reid's "strict and proper" sense, although it is a cause in the "lax and popular" sense.

Suppose I invite you to write down the word "cause." Let's suppose that you have the power to do so and that you exert that power with the result that a change in the world occurs, the word "cause" is written on a piece of paper. Here, when we look at Reid's third condition, we believe that it does obtain. We believe that you had the power to refrain from initiating your action of writing down the word "cause." The fire had no such power of refraining from melting the gold when the gold was sufficiently near the fire, but you had the power not to bring about your action of writing down the word "cause." If these things are so, then in this instance you are a true agent-cause of a certain change in the world, for you had the power to bring about that change, you exerted that power by acting, and finally, you had the power not to bring about that change.

Reid used the expression "efficient cause" for a cause that satisfies our three conditions. He used the expression "physical cause" mainly for events (or things) that are connected to their effects by a law of nature. (To simplify matters, I will take Reid's physical causes to be events connected to their effects by a law of nature.) From his remarks it is clear that Reid believes that efficient causes and physical causes are not two species of a common genus. An efficient cause is a substance that exercises its power to produce an effect, having the power not to produce that effect. A physical cause is an event whose effect follows by virtue of a law of nature. In deference to contemporary usage, I will henceforth use the expression "agent-cause" for any cause that satisfies Reid's three conditions, and will use "event-cause" for (our simplification of) Reid's physical causes. An agent-cause is a cause in what Reid calls the "strict and proper" sense; an event-cause is a cause in what Reid calls the "lax and popular" sense.

Suppose that a person wills to do a certain action and does it as a result of willing to do it. What is it for the agent to be *free* in that action? Reid expresses his answer in terms of power over the determination of the will that resulted in that action. Here is Reid's succinct answer to the question: What is it for the agent to be free in that action?

If the person was the cause of that determination of his own will, he was free in that action, and it is justly imputed to him, whether it be good or bad. (EAP IV.ii: 602a–b)

There is something wonderfully simple, some would say naïve, in this account of a free action. For the entire matter is made to rest on the answer to one simple question: Who or what caused the act of will (the volition) to perform the action? This question implies that an act of will (a determination of the will) is an event occurring in the agent and, as such, requires a cause. (As we've seen, Reid holds that every event must have a cause.) And Reid's point is that the action is free just in case the person whose action it is was the agent-cause of the volition resulting in the action. So, for example, if a person performs the action of shooting his neighbor as a result of agent-causing his volition (decision) to shoot his neighbor, then that person was free in that action and the shooting of his neighbor is justly imputed to him.

There is, however, a complexity in Reid's description of an agent's accountability for shooting his neighbor. For in the strict sense all that the agent directly causes is his *volition* to shoot his neighbor. What follows from his directly causing his volition to shoot his neighbor is, strictly speaking, not up to the agent. The connections between his volition and his finger pulling the trigger are not willed by the agent, nor are they within his direct control. And unless those connections exist, and many other connections as well, the event of the bullet entering the body of his neighbor won't occur. But this doesn't preclude Reid from asserting the moral accountability of the agent for his neighbor's death. In a revealing passage Reid notes that much of the causal chain between the agent's volition to kill his neighbor and his neighbor's death by being shot is not directly up to the agent. He says in fact that between the volition to shoot his neighbor and his neighbor's death "there may be agents or instruments of which we are ignorant." In light of this he remarks:

This may leave some doubt, whether we be, in the strictest sense, the efficient cause of the voluntary motions of our body. But it can produce no doubt with regard to the moral estimation of our actions.

The man who knows that such an event depends upon his will, and who deliberately wills to produce it, is, in the strictest moral sense, the cause of the event; and it is justly imputed to him, whatever physical causes may have concurred in its production.

Thus, he who maliciously intends to shoot his neighbor dead, and voluntarily does it, is undoubtedly the cause of his death, though he did no more to occasion it than draw the trigger of the gun. He neither gave to the ball its velocity, nor to the powder its expansive force, nor to the flint and steel the power to strike fire; but he knew that what he did must be followed by the man's death, and did it with that intention; and therefore he is justly chargeable with the murder. (EAP I.viii: 528b)

In light of these remarks we need to see that Reid's simple account of our responsibility for our actions ("If the person was the cause of that determination of his own will, he was free in that action, and it is justly imputed to him, whether it be good or bad" (EAP IV.ii: 602a–b)) is indeed somewhat simple. For we have to enlarge it by noting both that (a) his volition to shoot his neighbor initiates a causal chain of event-causes that culminates in the right way with the death of his neighbor, and that (b) our agent intended that his pulling the trigger should result in his neighbor's death.[11]

Now that we have linked freedom to agent-causation, I want to consider several objections that come to mind when one reflects on this agent-causation account of what it is for an agent to be free in performing an action and, therefore, responsible for that action.

Objection I

According to Reid the agent may agent-cause her decision (volition) to perform some action. But surely the agent must have *decided* to cause that volition rather than some other. So our agent's action of causing her volition (volition$_1$, let's say) must result from a prior volition (volition$_2$) to cause volition$_1$. But what of volition$_2$? It too must have been caused by the agent. But then there must have been an even earlier volition$_3$ to cause volition$_2$. And so we are off to the races. An agent-causing of a volition presupposes an earlier volition to agent-cause it, ad infinitum.

The mistake in this objection, as Reid himself was aware, is its assumption that one can agent-cause an action only if one first *wills* to agent-cause that action. An agent-causing of a voluntary action is the exercise of active power to produce a volition and the action that flows from it. The exercise of that power does not require a prior act of will to *bring about* that exercise of power.[12]

Objection II

In response to the first objection, we've noted that an agent may cause his act of will without first deciding or willing to cause that volition. But what if some event other than the agent's volition, an event over which that agent has no control, event-causes him to agent-cause that act of will?[13] That is, what if the person agent-causes her volition but her doing so is *causally necessitated* by some event or circumstances over which she has no control? Clearly, if this were so the agent would not enjoy power over her will and we should not, on Reid's own theory, regard the action resulting from that act of will as a *free action*. So, contrary to Reid, it seems that the fact that the person agent-causes the act of will is insufficient to ensure that her action is free.[14]

The answer to this objection is that what it asks about is impossible. We sometimes speak of causing someone to cause something else. But if we fully understand the notion of agent-causation, we can see, I think, that no event or agent can cause someone to *agent-cause* some change. (Here is something even God cannot do.) And this is because of Reid's third condition of agent-causation, the condition that requires that you have the power to refrain from bringing about the change.[15] Since having the power not to cause a change is required for you to be the agent-cause of some change, and since being caused to cause some change implies that you cannot refrain from causing that change, it follows that no one can be caused to agent-cause a change. If you are the agent-cause of some change, you were not caused to agent-cause that change.

Objection III

Our third objection follows on the heels of the previous two. Suppose we grant that an agent-causing of one's volition to do something is neither the causal product of an earlier act of will nor the causal product of the agent's desires or any other earlier state of his body or mind. Won't then an agent-causing of a volition to perform a certain action be simply something that happens to the agent out of the blue, unrelated to any earlier state of his body or mind? And if the answer is "Yes," then that alone should lead us to reject Reid's account of free human action. Here Reid would entirely agree with the critic. If denying that any state of the agent's body or mind can causally necessitate an agent-causing of a volition by that agent implies that any agent-causing by that agent happens out of the blue, then Reid would concede that his theory of agent-causation is a rope of sand.

We may, perhaps, be able to conceive a being endowed with power over the determinations of his will, without any light in his mind to direct that power to some end. But such power would be given in vain. No exercise of it could be either blamed or approved. As nature gives no power in vain, I see no ground to ascribe a power over the determinations of the will to any being who has no judgment to apply it to the direction of his conduct, no discernment of what he ought or ought not to do. (EAP IV.i: 600a)

Reid distinguishes reasons from desires. The latter directly prompt the will and, when strong enough, may causally necessitate the agent's volition and subsequent action. The former come to us more like advice, pointing out what is in our best interest in the long run or what is our moral duty. Sometimes the passions may press so strongly that the agent lacks any power to resist the impulse to act in accordance with the passions. In such cases the agent is not morally responsible for his action, although he may be morally responsible for placing himself in a situation he had reason to believe would render him powerless to act against his passions. Sometimes, however, an agent is free to act *solely* in terms of the judgments of reason. As Reid puts it:

Sometimes, however, there is a calm in the mind from the gales of passion or appetite, and the man is left to work his way, in the voyage of life, without those impulses which they give. Then he calmly weighs the goods and evils, which are at too great a distance to excite any passion. He judges what is best upon the whole, without feeling any bias drawing him to one side. He judges for himself as he would do for another in his situation; and the determination is wholly imputable to the man, and not in any degree to his passion. (EAP II.ii: 534a)

We have then three cases. In the first, the force of the passions upon the will is irresistible and the agent has no power to prevent their bringing about his volition and action. In the second, the passions incline the will but it is within the power of the agent to successfully resist their influence. In the third, the passions provide virtually no impulse to the will and the agent is free calmly to determine the matter in terms of the best judgments of reason. Since reason does not act directly on the will, when the passions provide little or no impulse to the will and the agent acts in the light of the judgments of reason, the action is imputed solely to the agent. In the first case, when the passions are irresistible the action is imputed solely to them and the agent is not the agent-cause of her volition, she is not accountable for what she has done. But in the second case, when the passions "incline but do not necessitate" (to use Leibniz's phrase), it is not an all or nothing matter. The action is imputed partly to the passions and partly to the agent. What we need to do is give some account of this in terms of Reid's agency theory of causation.

If the force of the passions is strong and the agent yields with the result that he willingly performs the action in question, what causal role does the agent play? We here suppose that it is in the agent's power to successfully resist the force of his passions but he does not exercise that power. In this case we may say that his not exercising that power completes a sufficient causal condition of his act of will and subsequent action. Thus his not doing what it is in his power to do *causally contributes* to his volition and action.[16] Perhaps, however, the passions, in the absence of the agent's resisting their influence, are still causally insufficient to produce the volition and action. Perhaps, that is, the volition will occur only if the agent exercises his power to cause it in cooperation with the influence of his passions. Here the causal responsibility of the agent for his volition and action is greater than the case in which his passions are of sufficient force to cause the volition and action provided the agent does not exercise his power to resist their influence. But in each subcase the agent bears some causal responsibility for his volition and action and the action may be imputed in part to the agent and in part to his passions.

Objection IV

When we compared Reidian freedom with Lockean freedom we noted that in Reid's account there is no mention at all of a power to do or will otherwise. That is, Reid insists only that when he causes his volition, the agent had the power *not* to cause *that* volition. He does not require in addition that the agent had the power to cause some other volition or action instead. In view of this, suppose we conjure up a Frankfurt-type example[17] wherein a mad scientist has gained access to your volitional capacity and not only can tell what act of will you are about to bring about but, worse yet, can send electrical currents into your brain that will cause a particular act of will to occur even though it is not the act of will that you would have brought about if left to your own devices. We will suppose that you are deliberating on a matter of great concern: killing Jones. Our mad scientist happens to be interested in Jones's going on to his reward, but he wants Jones to die by your hand. And rather than activate the machine to cause your act of will to kill Jones, he would prefer that you bring about that act of will and the subsequent action of killing Jones. As it turns out, you do conclude your deliberations by agent-causing your act of will to kill Jones. The mad scientist could and would have caused that act of will in you had you been about to will not to kill Jones. But no such action was necessary on his part. There is a process in place (the mad scientist's machine, etc.) that assures that you shall will to kill Jones.[18] But the process is activated *if but only if* you are not going to cause your volition to kill Jones. Given the machine, your willing to kill Jones was inevitable; it was not in your power to avoid willing to kill Jones. Are we to say in such circumstances that your action of killing Jones is *free*? And if Reid's account of free action requires such a conclusion, shouldn't we reject it?

In answering this objection, the first point to note is that Reid's account does imply that in these circumstances you acted freely in killing Jones. Initially, just the opposite point of view would recommend itself. For in his first and frequently quoted statement of what it is for an action to be free he says: "If, in any action, he had power to will what he did, or not to will it, in that action he is free" (EAP IV.i: 599b). And in our mad scientist case it is clear that you do not have the power *not* to will to kill Jones. (Should you be about to will to do something else or to refrain from willing to kill Jones, the machine is programmed to cause in you the volition to kill Jones.) So initially the mad scientist case seems to be one in which you do not have power over the volition to kill Jones.

But I think the concept of agent-causation requires a different answer. For there is nothing in our mad scientist case that conflicts with the view that you are the agent-cause of the act of will to kill Jones. Indeed, you are the cause; the scientist's machine monitors your brain but does nothing in the way of causing your volition. What this means is that we must distinguish between

    1. It was in your power *not to will* to kill Jones;

and

    2. It was in your power *not to cause* your volition to kill Jones.

In our mad scientist case, (1) is false. But (2) is not false. You do have the power not to cause your volition to kill Jones. The mad scientist has so arranged matters that the machine automatically causes the volition to kill Jones in you if, but only if, you are about to not will to kill Jones. This being so, (1) is clearly false. You cannot prevent your willing to kill Jones; for if you do not cause your willing to kill Jones the machine will cause it. But (2) is not false. You do have the power not to cause your volition to kill Jones. The mad scientist has so arranged matters that the machine automatically causes that volition in you if, but only if, you are about to not will to kill Jones. But it still may be up to you whether *you* shall be the cause of your volition to kill Jones. This power, Reid would argue, depends on a number of factors: the will of God, the continued existence of the agent, the absence of prior internal events and circumstances determining the occurrence of the volition to kill Jones, etc. It also depends on the mad scientist's decision to activate the machine *only if* you are about to not will to kill Jones. The scientist can cause you to will to kill Jones. He does this by causing that act of will in you.[19] But if he does so, you do not agent-cause your volition to kill Jones. The real agent-cause is the scientist. So if you have the power to cause your volition to kill Jones, you also have the power *not to cause* that volition. It is impossible to have the one power without having the other.

In saying that Reid's account of a free action requires that you act freely in the mad scientist case I'm interpreting Reid's "power to will or not will" as the power to cause or not cause the act of will. Under this interpretation, as I've argued, you do have power over your will in the mad scientist case. Since this is all Reid requires for your act to be free, it seems that his view requires that you kill Jones freely in the mad scientist case. My own intuitions suggest that you do act freely in this case and are prima facie responsible for what you have done. So my answer to the objection is (1) that Reid's theory does imply that you kill Jones freely (in the mad scientist case) and (2) that this conclusion is no reason to reject his theory.

Objection V

This objection follows on the solution I've just suggested to the objection that the counterfactual intervener precludes your *freely* willing to kill Jones. At the heart of the solution I gave was Reid's view that your act of will is *free* provided you are the agent-cause of it. But we should also note that Reid appears to hold that being the agent-cause of your act of will is sufficient for your being prima facie responsible for that act of will and the action you perform as a result of willing it. For after saying that if the person was the cause of that determination of his will he was free in that action, Reid adds "and it is justly imputed to him, whether it be good or bad." I take Reid to mean here that the agent is responsible, both causally and morally, for the act of will and the action resulting from it, provided the action is one that is subject to moral appraisal. And our present objection, developed by John Fischer in *The Metaphysics of Freedom*,[20] is that the degree of freedom allotted to the agent in the counterfactual intervener case is simply not "robust enough" to ground moral responsibility.

Before examining Fischer's objection, let's create an example that will help us understand it, as well as my reply. Suppose Jones desires to keep for himself a significant sum of money he finds on the pavement. He knows the money was lost by a poor woman who had withdrawn her life savings to provide an operation to restore her son's vision. He knows that keeping the money is morally wrong. And this troubles him. But, after some soul searching, he yields to greed, tells himself that God will surely look after the poor woman and her son, and decides to keep the money for himself. Is he responsible for his decision and subsequent act of keeping the money? Let's consider three distinct cases.

Case 1: It was in his power to agent-cause his decision to keep the money and, of course, in his power not to cause that decision. In addition, it was also in his power to translate his decision into the overt action of keeping the money. Finally, even though he decides to keep the money, it was also in his power to cause the contrary decision to return the money and to translate that decision into the overt action of returning the money. Here, we shall say, there was a *big alternative* open to him: deciding to return the money and returning it as a result of so deciding.

Case 2: As he was contemplating what to do with the money, someone overpowered him and gave him a drug and instructions that actually caused him to decide to keep the money. Hardly knowing what he was doing, he found himself deciding to keep the money and so doing. He did not agent-cause his decision to keep the money. Nor, given the drug and hypnotic instructions was it in his power to choose or do anything else. Unlike case 1, our agent has *no alternative* to what he does. He wills and acts of necessity in keeping the money, having no power not to will and act as he did.

Case 3: No outside influence or internal desire or want caused him to decide to keep the money. He was free to cause and free not to cause his decision to keep the money. As it happened, he followed his selfish desire, rather than the advice of his conscience, and caused his decision to keep the money, having it within his power, nevertheless, not to have caused that decision. However, had he been about to agent-cause the decision to return the money, the devil, let us suppose, would have directly caused in him the decision to keep the money, effectively preventing any decision or action on his part to return the money. Here we have a *little alternative* open to him: *not* causing his decision to keep the money. He is not free, however, to decide to return the money. For had he not caused his decision to keep it, the devil would have caused him to decide to keep it. In a way, given the steady resolve of the devil, it is up to our agent whether he himself *or* the devil will be responsible for his decision to keep the money. By exercising his power to cause his decision to keep the money, he makes himself responsible for that decision. Had he not caused that decision, the devil, and not he, would have been responsible for his decision to keep the money. Here, at long last, we would have a case in which someone might *truthfully* say: "The devil made me do it."

Case 3 is the case at issue. Fischer allows that the decision to keep the money is caused (in the actual sequence) by the agent himself. He also allows that the agent had the power not to cause that decision. What the agent lacked, however, was the power to prevent his decision to keep the money. For we suppose that somehow the devil would have caused the agent to decide to keep the money, had the agent not caused that decision himself.[21]

Fischer is right to note that in this case the agent has a very *little alternative* in terms of what he could will and do. There is no alternative volition or action he can bring about. Given the power and resolve of the devil, all that is open to the agent – apart from his actually causing his decision and act of keeping the money – is to not cause that decision. And Fischer's point is that *if* moral responsibility requires genuine alternative possibilities for the agent, it requires something more significant than what this case provides. For this case provides no alternative act of will or action to the agent. It provides only a minute "flicker of freedom," the agent's causing his decision to keep the money while having the power not to himself cause his decision to keep the money. And that, Fischer claims, is insufficient, not robust enough, to ground the agent's moral responsibility for deciding and acting to keep the money.

I agree with Fischer that in our third case there is no alternative action or volition open to the agent. But I think he is mistaken to conclude from this that the alternative open to the agent is not robust enough to ground his moral responsibility for his actual decision to keep the money. In the actual sequence the agent uses his own causal power, in accordance with the thrust of his selfish desires, to will to keep the money for himself, having the power not to cause that act of will and its resulting action. In the alternative sequence the agent does not use his own causal power to will and act in accordance with his selfish desires. Sure enough, because of the intervention of the devil, the agent is unable to prevent his decision to keep the money. But in the alternative sequence that decision is the responsibility of the devil, and not our agent. My own intuitions tell me that the fact that the agent had the power *not* to determine his will and action in accordance with his selfish desires is itself sufficient to ground his moral responsibility for using his causal power (in the actual sequence) to will and act in accordance with those desires.

Objection VI

Let's return now to the critical question of what is required to ground the responsibility of the agent for her volition and action. To get at this problem, it is helpful to review what Reid thinks is required if the agent is to be genuinely *responsible* for her voluntary action. As we noted earlier, Reid holds that it is not sufficient for such responsibility that the agent had it in her power to perform (or not perform) the action she willed. She must also have had the power to cause or not cause her volition to do that action, and she must have exerted that power. For if something outside her caused her to will as she did, she would not be responsible for that voluntary action. So, her being responsible for her voluntary action requires, on Reid's view, that she had the power to cause that act of will and the power not to cause it, and that she exerted her power to cause it. Suppose we assume that he is right about that. What then of her exertion of active power in producing that act of will? For the question may well be raised: How can she be responsible for her act of will if she is not responsible for her exertion of active power in bringing about that act of will? And if we say that she was responsible for her exertion of active power in producing her volition, the question will then be raised as to what grounds or explains her responsibility for her exercise of active power in producing that volition. And again, it seems we are off to the races. Where does the buck of responsibility finally stop?

My proposal is that the buck of responsibility stops with *the agent's exertion of active power in producing her volition.* Unlike the agent's willing to perform some action, something which could be caused by some being other than the agent – in which case the agent herself would not be responsible for her act of will – the agent's exertion of active power in producing her volition is intrinsically such that nothing could be an efficient cause of it. For suppose something could be. Suppose, applying Reid's remark about volitions to exertions of active power,[22] I say: "I consider the exertion of active power as an effect." If so, then like my volition that could be produced in me by God or some other efficient cause, my exertion of active power in bringing about something could be caused by God, me, or some other efficient cause. But it is a *conceptual impossibility* within Reid's theory for God or any other efficient cause to produce in me an exertion of active power. For my exertion of active power in producing something is identical with my agent-causing that thing. And it is impossible that I should be caused to agent-cause anything. If x causes y to cause z, then, given x's activity, y does not have the power *not* to cause z. But an agent has power to cause only if he has power not to cause. For Reid that is a conceptual truth. "Power to produce any effect, implies power not to produce it" (EAP I.v: 523a).

Still, even granted that Reid's theory blocks an agent-causing of a volition from being caused by any other agent or by the agent himself, are we thereby entitled to conclude that when an agent exerts his active power in producing a volition he is thereby *responsible* for that exertion of active power? Suppose his exerting active power just happens "out of the blue," without any cause at all. Suppose the agent, as it were, simply finds himself agent-causing a volition to do x. Could my agent-causing my volition to do x be something that just happens to me in such a way that I am not responsible for it, and do not control its occurrence? The answer, I believe, is no.

Although I do not have it in my power to cause *my agent-causing my volition*, it is in my power to make it true that a certain event, *my agent-causing my volition*, occurs. For by exercising my active power to cause my volition, I thereby make it true that *my agent-causing my volition* occurs. But it is also in my power to prevent that event from occurring. For it is in my power not to cause my volition. (Power to cause implies power not to cause.) And if I do not cause that volition, the event which is *my agent-causing my volition* simply does not occur. What this means is that it is in my power so to act that the event, *my agent-causing my volition*, occurs; and it is also in my power to prevent *my agent-causing my volition* from occurring. This being so, we are justified, I believe, in saying that the agent is in control of the occurrence of that event and is prima facie responsible for it. And this is true even though the agent does not agent-cause *that* event. So, I think we may legitimately hold the agent responsible for the occurrence (nonoccurrence) of the event which is his agent-causing some volition. Moreover, the issue of whether that event occurs may well be in his control. And that is where the buck of responsibility and control stops.

III. CONCLUSION

In this paper, I have tried to set forth Reid's libertarian theory of freedom and responsibility, being careful to distinguish my account of it from what I have called the "standard account" of his theory. But a libertarian theory of freedom and responsibility is worthless unless it has the resources to respond to a variety of challenges. So I have also tried to show that Reid's theory has the resources to respond to several important objections that can be leveled against his agent-causation account in particular or libertarian theories generally. Of course, even if these responses to important objections should be successful, there remains the very important question: Can we prove that Reid's agent-causation theory of freedom and responsibility is true? And to this question I confess to being a skeptic. What I believe can be shown is that something like an agent-causation theory of freedom and responsibility is presupposed by us in our practical affairs. Indeed, we may even succeed in showing that along with other beliefs of common sense, the belief that we are free agents in many of our actions is such that it is reasonable to take it to be true unless we have convincing arguments for its falsity.

NOTES

1. "Of Power" was written in Reid's eighty-first year. Several sections of what follows are taken from Rowe 2000.
2. E II.xxi.1: 233.
3. E II.xxi.2: 234.
4. See E II.xxi.21.
5. E II.xxi.33.
6. Locke is a compatibilist about free will. Provided the determining causes of your volition are your desires, apprehensions, and so forth, your volition and subsequent action are free. Reid is a libertarian about free will. Your volition and subsequent action are free only if you exercise your power to cause that volition, having at the time the power not to cause that volition.
7. See E II.xxi.21.
8. See Duggan 1976 and Weinstock 1975: 335.
9. "I am not able to form a conception how power, in the strict sense, can be exerted without will; nor can there be will without some degree of understanding. Therefore, nothing can be an efficient cause, in the proper sense, but an intelligent being" (C: 174–5).
10. See his letters to Dr. James Gregory, September 23, 1785 (C: 178–9), July 30, 1789 (C: 205–8), and spring 1786 (C: 181–6).
11. I am indebted to Dale Tuggy for helpful suggestions on understanding Reid's account of the agent's moral accountability for events that the agent does not agent-cause. See Tuggy 2000: 18–19.
12. Reid considers and replies to a version of this objection, which he traces to Hobbes. See EAP IV.ii: 601a–b.
13. Another supposition might be that some person has agent-caused our agent's causing of that act of will.
14. This point is nicely put by Hamilton as a critical note to the very sentence in Reid that we are discussing. "Only if he were not determined to that determination. But is the person an *original undetermined cause* of the determination of his will? If he be not, then is he not a *free* agent, and the scheme of Necessity is admitted" (W: 602).

15. Put somewhat differently, it is because the concept of active power requires that you as agent have the power *to cause or not to cause* that change.

16. In order to say that the *agent* causally contributes to his volition by not exercising his power to resist his passions we may need to add that his not exercising that power is a deliberate omission on the agent's part.

17. A Frankfurt-type example is one in which an agent wills and acts all on his own but would have been prevented from acting differently had he been about to will to act differently. The classic essay is Frankfurt 1969.

18. I will ignore here the issue of what *grounds* the intervener's assurance that you shall will to kill Jones. If it is some event (your blushing, say) that is causally sufficient in the circumstances for your willing to kill Jones, then we have a case of overdetermination, as opposed to failsafe causation, of the volition. If what grounds the assurance is something less than a causally sufficient condition, it is not clear that the agent lacks the power not to perform the act of will in question. (I owe this observation to David Widerker.)

19. I take Reid to hold (rightly) that to cause a volition to do A in an agent is to cause *the agent's willing to do A*. Thus when an agent wills to do A we can raise the question of whether the cause of his so willing is the agent himself or something else.

20. Fischer 1994: 134–47.

21. The question can well be raised how the agent can cause and be responsible for his decision to keep the money when it was not in his power to prevent that decision. For more on this matter see Rowe 1989: 153–9.

22. "I consider the determination of the will as an effect" (EAP: IV.ii: 602a).

10   Reid's Moral Philosophy

The organizing theme of Reid's *Essays on the Active Powers* concerns the nature of human agency – whether human agents are endowed with an active power, what constitutes its exercise, and so forth. There is, however, an important subtheme woven through the text, one that concerns the objectivity of morality, or what we nowadays call "moral realism." My purpose in this essay is to examine several strands of Reid's version of moral realism. In particular, I want to consider four constituents of Reid's broadly realist view: Reid's moral ontology, his account of moral thought and discourse, his account of moral motivation, and his account of moral knowledge. Since each of these topics is of interest to contemporary philosophers, I shall also be concerned to relate Reid's thought on these matters with what recent Anglo-American moral philosophers have said about them.

I. MORAL ONTOLOGY

Sometimes what is deepest in a philosopher's thought is not what receives the most attention from that philosopher. This is the case, I submit, with respect to Reid's views concerning the moral realm. Although issues of moral ontology do not receive much explicit attention in Reid's work, they are what lie deepest in his moral philosophy. It is Reid's views on the nature of moral reality that ultimately shape his views on the nature of moral discourse, moral motivation, and moral epistemology. I propose, then, to start with Reid on moral ontology.

Let me begin by making two distinctions between different kinds of moral fact that should help us better to understand Reid's view. (I use the term "moral fact" to denote those features of the world that make our moral judgments true.) The first distinction is that between general and particular moral facts. *That murder is wrong* and *that wicked deeds ought to be despised* are good examples of general moral facts. They are facts that have the logical form: If x is a token of some intention, action, etc., type y (e.g., murder), then x has some moral property p. Reid calls the propositions that correspond to a certain subset of such facts "axioms" (EIP VI.iv: 452). By contrast, *that this murder is wrong* and *that Jones is wicked* are good examples of particular moral facts. They are facts that consist in some particular's having some moral property at a time. The propositions that denote facts of this kind are what Reid calls moral propositions proper.[1]

The second distinction is between deontic and evaluative moral facts. *That one ought not to murder* is a good example of a deontic moral fact; it is a directive of a certain kind. *That this murder is wicked*, however, is an evaluative moral fact; it is a fact that merits a response of a certain kind, but is not itself a directive.

With these distinctions in hand, we can state Reid's views about moral facts. It is Reid's conviction that general deontic facts or norms are necessary facts; they exist in all possible situations.[2] More precisely, they are necessary facts whose constituents are person-types that bear a certain type of relation to act-types of certain kinds:

When we say a man ought to do such a thing, the *ought*, which expresses the moral obligation, has a respect, on the one hand, to the person who ought, and, on the other, to the action which he ought to do. Those two correlates are essential to every moral obligation....So that, if we seek the place of moral obligation among the categories, it belongs to the category of *relation*. (EAP III.iii.v: 589a)

Particular moral facts, by contrast, are contingent facts. They are what, in contemporary jargon, are called "supervenient" facts – facts that are determined by, or result from, nonmoral facts.[3] Reid's view appears to be that the reason particular nonmoral facts determine particular moral facts is that they are subsumed under general moral facts.[4] For example, the reason this instance of lying is wrong, according to Reid, is that there is a necessary general moral fact that tells us that lying in such and such circumstances is wrong, and that this is an instance of lying in those circumstances.

Now let me try to bring out why Reid's account of moral facts is best viewed as a paradigmatic species of moral realism. What the realist about moral facts believes is that moral facts of certain kinds have a particular type of existential independence from our mental states. Roughly, the idea is that (in the ordinary case) things have moral features of certain kinds independent of human persons having (or being disposed to have) attitudes of various sorts toward those things. In this respect, moral features are different from properties such as *being a dollar bill* or, according to some views, *being red*. These properties are plausibly viewed as being imparted to entities by virtue of our cognitive activity. Moral features, according to the realist view, are not.

Moral realism of this sort came under challenge from two sources in Reid's day. On the one hand, "contractarians" such as Hobbes (as he was usually understood) and Hume claimed that moral facts of certain kinds are the product of convention. On the other, "sentimentalists" such as Hutcheson (and Hume on some interpretations) maintained that moral facts are constituted by the way in which certain nonmoral features of the world elicit feelings of certain kinds in human persons. Reid proffers arguments against both types of view.

Reid's response to contractarian views is intricate and fascinating. His chief target is Hume's view that the very notion of a moral obligation depends on conventions having already been "enter'd into."[5] Here I shall highlight one argument that Reid himself develops at some length.

In Book III of the *Treatise*, Hume provides an account of how we arrived at our idea of justice. Hume's story tells us that we cannot have the notion of justice until we have the concept of our own good because it is from a concern to secure our own good that we create the rules of justice by convention.[6] Reid points out two things in response. First, the concepts of *being a favor* and *being an injury* are as "early in the mind of man as any rational notion whatever" (EAP V.v: 654b). And, second, Hume would seem to be committed to as much. For Hume, the sentiments of gratitude and resentment are "natural," and the objects of these sentiments are favors and injuries. Reid believes that both points tell against Hume's story. For it is plausible to believe, says Reid, that the concept of a person's good must be understood in terms of the concepts of *being a favor* and *being an injury*. However, a person cannot have the concepts of *being a favor* and *being an injury* unless that person has the concept of *being just*. This is because to understand that an act is a favor or an injury (as opposed to merely being harmful) is to understand that the performance of that act is not required or forbidden. In the first case, the performance of the act is not required because it goes beyond what is owed; in the second case, it is not required because it falls below what is owed. So the acquisition of the concept of *being just* is not posterior to that of a person's good or "society's interest." It follows that Hume's conceptual priority claim is false. We do not acquire the notion of justice from having engaged in a contract of any sort. Rather, we have the concept as soon as we have a conception of our own good.

Reid's attack on sentimentalist views is different yet. Refined a bit, his argument is as follows:[7] Suppose we let "x" range over tokens of certain intention, belief, act, etc., types. If sentimentalism is true, then, necessarily, for any x, x has some moral property simply because human agents are so constituted that they have (or are disposed to have) attitudes of a certain kind toward x. However, it's possible that, had we been constituted differently, we would have had different attitudes toward x. So, for example, according to the sentimentalist view, it's possible that we might be so constituted that we would approve of random killings of human persons. But if we had different attitudes toward x, then x would have different moral properties. And, thus, according to the sentimentalist view, it would follow that, if human persons were so constituted as to approve of random killings, then random killings would be morally admirable. Some x's, however, are such that they necessarily exemplify moral properties of certain kinds. Random killing of human persons, for example, is such that it is necessarily wrong. So sentimentalism is false.

Reid does little more than appeal to intuition in support of the premise that some entities necessarily exemplify moral properties of certain kinds. But it is a plausible premise that even contemporary moral antirealists have tried to accommodate.[8]

It is within this broadly realist framework that I have sketched that Reid develops a practical or normative moral theory that concerns the way we ought to govern our conduct. Reid's view on this score is broadly deontological. And by a "deontological" theory I mean the view that (i) moral norms or rules are explanatorily the most fundamental type of moral entity; and (ii) that these norms are not justified by appeal to the good consequences of obeying them. Reid's allegiance to (i) is indicated by the fact that he defines other moral concepts in terms of moral norms. So, for example, moral virtues are defined as "fixed purposes of acting according to a certain rule" (EAP II.iii: 540a),[9] morally good actions are those that an agent "ought to do" (EAP V.iv: 649a), and moral rights are said to be the mere correlates of obligation.[10] In maintaining that moral norms are explanatorily most basic, Reid's view stands firmly in the deontological tradition of Clarke, Balguy, and Price, and at odds with the virtue-based theories of Shaftesbury, Hutcheson, and Hume.

Reid's allegiance to (ii) is expressed in his critique of the Humean view that the rules of justice are justified because of their utility. In Reid's view, when agents exercise their moral faculty, "they perceive a turpitude in injustice . . . and consequently an obligation to justice, abstracting from the consideration of its utility" (EAP V.v: 653a). Reid goes so far as to claim that utility lacks any intrinsic connection with morality.[11] However, as we shall see in a moment, Reid does not believe that the consequences of our actions are irrelevant to morality.

The development of Reid's deontological theory is not as systematic, or as elegant, as Kant's or Aquinas's. Nor does it purport to be. He says that a system of morals

is not like a system of geometry, where the subsequent parts derive their evidence from the preceding. . . . It resembles more a system of botany, or mineralogy, where the subsequent parts depend not for their evidence upon the preceding, and the arrangement is made to facilitate apprehension and memory, and not to give evidence. (EAP V.ii: 642b)

What Reid offers us is a somewhat motley list of moral "principles" that he divides into the general and the particular.[12] Reid's general principles tell us that what is done from necessity cannot be the object of blame or approbation, that persons may be highly culpable in omitting what they ought to have done (as well as in doing what they ought not), that we ought to use the best means we can to be informed of our duty, and so forth. The particular principles fall into two groups. The first group divides neatly under the traditional three heads of duties to self, others, and God.[13] The first two of these principles concern duties to self. The first says that a person ought to prefer his greater good to a less. The second (tacitly borrowed from Butler) says that a person ought to comply with "the intention of nature" as it is manifest in his constitution (EAP V.i: 638b). The next two principles concern duties to others. The third principle makes the anti-Hobbesian point that persons are intended to live in society, and that a person ought to benefit the society of which he is a part. The fourth is a formulation of the Golden Rule. Finally, the fifth, a duty to God, enjoins those who believe in God to venerate God. Having articulated this group of principles, Reid offers us a second group of particular principles that provide us with general guidelines for how we ought to act when our duties seem to conflict. No lover of moral quandaries, Reid is exceedingly brief here, and indicates that the ranking of the different rules is self-evident.

These, I suggest, are the broad outlines of Reid's moral ontology and normative moral theory. Let me close this section by considering several ways in which Reid's position intersects with three prominent debates among moral philosophers of his day.

Central to seventeenth- and eighteenth-century British moral philosophy was a concern to reconcile the claims of morality with those of self-interest. Reid shares this concern and defends a view squarely in the tradition of Shaftesbury, Hutcheson, and Butler.[14] As Reid sees things, there are at least two ways in which one's "good upon the whole" and one's moral duty or virtue are intertwined. First, Reid says that all the moral virtues can be derived from considering how to secure one's good upon the whole.[15] Second, Reid holds that one's good on the whole and one's duty cannot conflict and, indeed, are extensionally equivalent.[16] Why so?

In short, because of God's providential design. What the extensional equivalence between self-interest and morality shows, says Reid, is "the strong connection between morality and the principles of natural religion; as the last only can secure a man from the possibility of an apprehension, that he may play the fool by doing his duty" (EAP III.iii.viii: 598a). However, Reid does not leave this claim as a bare assertion on his part. He offers a broadly Butlerian argument for thinking that a person's violation of her duty threatens her good upon the whole.[17] Reid puts it thus: "Every vicious action shows an excess, or defect, or wrong direction of some natural spring of action, and therefore may, very justly, be said to be unnatural. Every virtuous action agrees with the uncorrupted principles of human nature" (EAP V.i: 638b). The idea is that God has created us in such a way that it is our nature to act in accordance with the principles of virtue. A person's acting viciously does violence to her nature, and thereby directly undermines her happiness. We might say that Reid's second "particular" principle of morality provides a reason for adhering to the first.

But how exactly does a person's acting viciously do violence to his nature? Reid says that immoral conduct puts a person "at variance with himself" by inducing a sense of "dread" and "worthlessness." And "no man can bear the thought of being absolutely destitute of all worth" (EAP III.iii.vi: 594a). Moreover, immoral conduct ruptures the bonds of affection that "next to a good conscience ... make the capital part of human happiness" (EAP III.ii.iii: 559b). By contrast, a person's conforming to duty, "cannot fail a present reward" by giving "strength of heart" and making "his countenance to shine" in the "joy of good conscience" (EAP III.iii.vi 594b). Nowhere does Reid claim that this constitutes a sufficient defense of the thesis that virtue is coextensive with happiness. And I think it should be admitted that it does not. Rather, Reid indicates that on this issue, as on so many other issues, it is trust that is ultimately called for.[18]

The second debate I wish to consider is connected with the last. Contemporary moral philosophy (as well as that of late modernity) has tended to disconnect the realms of the ethical and the aesthetic. Nothing could seem more alien to the dominant tradition among eighteenth-century British moral philosophers, however. And in this respect, Reid is a typical philosopher of his day. In addition to the moral philosopher's standard division of moral predicates into "thin" (e.g., good, right, etc.) and "thick" (e.g., cowardly, kind, conscientious, etc.), Reid adds a third category of aesthetic predicates such as "lovely," "disgusting," "deformed," and "beautiful" that, when applied to a person, indicate a moral assessment of that person by ascribing an aesthetic property to her.[19] Unlike Shaftesbury, Reid doesn't attempt to derive moral qualities from aesthetic ones. Indeed, he turns Shaftesbury's approach on its head; according to Reid's view, "it is in the moral and intellectual perfections of mind ... that beauty originally dwells; and ... from this as the fountain, all the beauty which we perceive in the world is derived" (EIP VIII.iv: 602).[20] So, aesthetic properties, according to Reid's position, supervene on moral ones. This connection between the beautiful and the virtuous has two theoretical payoffs for Reid. First, it provides an additional reason to be moral. To the question, "why be moral?" Reid's answer is that it is beautiful. It follows that the answer to the question, "why be moral?" is doubly overdetermined in Reid's thought; it is both in our self-interest and beautiful to be moral. The second theoretical payoff is that, because acting virtuously is beautiful, it is a motivational incentive to resist temptation for the sake of virtue.[21]

The final point I should like to make concerns the manner in which Reid's thought on moral ontology resists two powerful trends among his predecessors and contemporaries. Stephen Darwall has helpfully pointed out that fundamental to seventeenth and eighteenth-century British moral philosophy is the commitment to what he terms "existence internalism."[22] Existence internalism is (roughly) the view that what makes it the case that a given moral norm holds is that a suitable agent would be motivated in one way or another. For instance, an existence internalist such as Richard Cumberland holds that being obligated to x just consists in "having motives raised through the use of theoretical reason."[23] It is telling that one finds no trace of this position in Reid. In Reid's view, there is a sharp distinction between obligation and motivation.[24] Motivation to be moral is typically the upshot of a *response* to moral reality; obligation is not constituted by our motivations. Reid, then, denies that moral obligations properly understood have a "to-be-pursuedness" built into them in the sense that the existence internalist believes they do and would thus deny that moral realism is suspect because it cannot account for this apparent feature of moral obligation.[25] The second trend that Reid's position resists is the Hobbesian and Lockean view that sanctions of some sort are necessary in order for morality to be genuinely rationally binding. In contrast to such a view, Reid champions a species of rationalism; moral features themselves give us decisive reasons to act.[26] Thus, there is no worried search on Reid's part to provide morality with some additional heft that is supposed to render it rationally compelling.

II. MORAL THOUGHT AND DISCOURSE

The type of moral ontology that Reid develops does not by itself en-
tail any view concerning the nature of moral thought and discourse.
Nevertheless, this type of view fits most comfortably with a broadly
cognitivist approach to moral thought and discourse. It is this type
of view that Reid defends.

Suppose we use the term "moral sentiment" to stand for whatever state of mind is expressed by the sincere uttering of a moral
sentence. And suppose we understand a "moral sentence" to be any
sentence that has the logical form of predicating a moral property of
a thing.[27] Reid's view is that the content of a moral sentiment is a
moral proposition. In Reid's view, then, moral sentiments are moral
judgments – where a judgment is a cognitive act or state in which one
thing is affirmed or denied of another.[28] Reid conjoins this account
of moral sentiments with a cognitivist theory of moral discourse.
The cognitivist holds that moral discourse (i.e., roughly, discourse
that consists in the use of moral sentences) is assertoric in purport;
its function is to express moral propositions. For ease of reference,
let's call the combination of these two views "moral cognitivism."

Reid dedicates the final chapter of the *Active Powers* to defending
this view against Hume's attacks. Hume, on Reid's interpretation,
rejects cognitivism in favor of a noncognitivist approach to moral
thought and discourse. In contrast to the cognitivist, the noncognitivist denies that the content of a moral sentiment is a moral proposition. Rather, moral sentiments are pro or con attitudes directed
toward nonmoral entities of various sorts. A person's being in the
mental state of "having a moral sentiment" is, according to the
noncognitivist view, for that person to be in a state in which he expresses some attitude of approval or disapproval toward a nonmoral
object or state of affairs such as a killing.[29] To this the noncognitivist
adds the further claim that moral discourse expresses moral sentiments thus understood. So, even though the surface form of moral
discourse makes it *appear* as if moral discourse expresses moral
propositions, it does not really do so. Rather, moral discourse primarily expresses the pro or con attitudes of the speaker. Let's call
the combination of these two claims concerning moral thought and
discourse "moral noncognitivism."

Rationalists such as Price attacked Hume's noncognitivism on the ground that it relies on an implausibly restrictive empiricist epistemology.[30] Reid's attack is interestingly different; it makes an extensive appeal to the nature of language.[31]

We can identify at least three arguments that Reid marshals against moral noncognitivism. The first argument proceeds from what we can call the "same meaning" test.[32] In barest form, the strategy runs as follows.[33] Suppose a person S sincerely utters the sentence

(1) "X acted wrongly."

Reid claims that, if noncognitivism is true, then, in uttering (1), S merely reports something about how he feels, viz.,

(2) "Disagreeable feelings are aroused in me by X's conduct."

But if noncognitivism is right, then (2) ought to mean the same thing as (1). However, this is implausible. (1) is about X, but "says nothing of the speaker" (EAP V.vii: 673b). (2), by contrast, is about S's feelings. In addition, (2) cannot be contradicted without implying that S is misreporting his feelings; but this is not true of (1). So, noncognitivism is false.

The argument does not hit its mark. The fundamental problem is that Reid conflates a noncognitivist view of moral discourse with what we can call a "subjective naturalist" account of moral discourse. The subjective naturalist holds that utterances of moral sentences express *reports about* the speaker's feelings. The noncognitivist, by contrast, does not. She claims that utterances of moral sentences express the speaker's attitudes without reporting them. Although Reid's argument is a powerful objection to subjective naturalism, it fails to touch noncognitivism.[34]

Reid's other two arguments fare somewhat better. The second argument Reid develops is one from introspection.[35] In brief, it says that a person's judging, say, *that pain is to be avoided* has a very different qualitative feel from a person's feeling pain. In the first case, this person feels *that* something is the case; in the second, she has an unpleasant sensation of burning, itching, or whatever. We can, however, tell by introspection that moral sentiments are not mere pro or con attitudes, but include moral judgments. The phenomenology of moral judgment is one in which a person feels *that* something or other has a moral property. But if that's right, then noncognitivism implies that we are badly confused about the nature of our own thoughts. And any view that implies this is suspect.

Hume has an answer to this complaint. In Hume's view, although "[m]orality ... is more properly felt than judg'd of ... this feeling or sentiment is commonly so soft and gentle, that we are apt to confound it with an idea, according to our common custom of taking all things for the same, which have any near resemblance to each other."[36] Reid does not explicitly consider Hume's response. But it's not difficult to guess what it would be. In Reid's view, Hume has overestimated the phenomenological similarity between judging that something is the case and having a pro-attitude toward something. The difference is not one of phenomenological intensity but of *kinds* of qualitative feel.[37]

Reid's final argument is perhaps the best and anticipates some of the prominent contemporary criticisms of noncognitivism:

That every form of speech, which language affords to express our judgments, should, in all ages, and in all languages, be used to express what is no judgment; and that feelings, which are easily expressed in proper language, should as universally be expressed by language altogether improper and absurd, I cannot believe; and therefore must conclude, that if language be the expression of thought, [then] men *judge* of ... virtue and vice ... by the moral faculty. (EAP V.vii: 674a)

At the heart of Reid's argument is what we might call "the linguistic transparency thesis," which tells us that language is "the express image and picture of human thoughts" (EIP VI.iv: 466) and that, all other things being equal, "the analysis of the one must correspond to that of the other" (W: 692a).[38] The transparency thesis is a principle of common sense for Reid. And while it is a thesis that Hume, and later, Wittgenstein, would deny, there is much to be said in favor of something akin to it. After all, we take the principle (or something like it) for granted when we interpret many domains of discourse other than moral discourse. For instance, we ordinarily assume that if discourse about the external world has the form of being assertoric, then it *is* assertoric.

Nevertheless, there is a worry that Reid's argument does not address. The worry is rooted in the widely accepted claim that moral sentiments have a tight connection with moral motivation. If noncognitivism is true, we have an explanation of this tight connection: Moral sentiments just are states of being motivated. But it is not all evident that cognitivism can explain this connection. Accordingly, one might be concerned that, even if the transparency principle is true, cognitivism about moral thought and discourse cannot be correct because it does not account for the intimate connection between moral thought and moral motivation. This is a worry of which Reid was aware. Let's now turn to what he says about it.

III. MORAL MOTIVATION

It is well known that Reid had nothing but contempt for philosophical theories that are empirically inadequate because of their undue emphasis on theoretical simplicity. Perhaps nowhere else does Reid's contempt for theoretical simplicity shine through more clearly than in his treatment of "the principles of action," or motives, in the second and third essays of the *Active Powers*.[39] Like Shaftesbury, Hutcheson, and Butler before him, Reid is insistent that there are multiple springs of action, and that many of our actions are motivationally overdetermined.

The account of the various springs of action that Reid offers us is extraordinarily detailed and subtle. Reid divides the principles of action into three: "mechanical principles" such as blind instincts, "animal principles" such as benevolence, and "rational principles" such as a consideration for one's good on the whole and moral duty. I won't try to reproduce Reid's detailed taxonomy of motives here. Instead, let me attempt to highlight how Reid's account of moral motivation allows him to respond to the worry broached at the end of the last section, viz., that moral cognitivism cannot explain the intimate connection between moral thought and motivation.

This worry surfaced in eighteenth-century ethics with the sentimentalist complaint that rationalists such as Clarke had no intelligible explanation of how our apprehension of putative moral facts could motivate us to action. In Hume's hands (as commonly interpreted), this latter objection takes something like the following form:[40]

> (1) Moral sentiments are intrinsically motivating: It is (conceptually or metaphysically) necessary that, if a person is in the state called "having a moral sentiment," then that person is motivated to act as that sentiment directs.

(2) It is (conceptually or metaphysically) possible that an agent
    judges that she ought to x, but is not motivated to x.
(3) So, moral sentiments are not moral judgments.

Let's call the view expressed in the first premise "motivational internalism" and its denial "motivational externalism." Rationalists
such as Price are motivational internalists; they reject the second
premise of the argument while accepting the first. Their claim is
that it is a brute feature of reality that moral judgments are intrinsically motivating.[41] Reid, I shall suggest, embraces a line of response
different from that of Price.

Perhaps the best manner of viewing Reid's response is to place his
account of moral motivation before us. Reid's account starts from
the conviction that there is a complex mental state that he calls
"moral approbation." Moral approbation includes "not only a moral
judgment of ... [an] action, but some affection, favourable ... toward
the agent, and some feeling in ourselves" (EAP III.iii.vii: 592a). The
idea is that, for a person S to morally approve of an act-token A is (i)
for S to judge that A has one or another (positive) moral feature; and
(ii) to have some affection toward the agent who does A, or toward
his A-ing, which is itself accompanied by a positive feeling tone of
some sort.

The question I should like to pursue on this occasion is whether
Reid believes that the connection between (i) and (ii) is conceptually
or metaphysically necessary. That is, I wish to ascertain whether
Reid is a motivational internalist or externalist. Although Reid's
thought on the matter is not entirely clear, I shall contend that he
rejects premise (2) of the Humean argument we're considering and,
thus, that his considered view is motivational externalism.

It is evident that Reid himself felt pulled in two directions on the
issue of whether the tie between normative judgment and motivation is necessary or contingent. For instance, in his "Essay on Taste,"
Reid broaches the question of whether the connection between aesthetic judgments and consequent aesthetic feelings is necessary or
"conjoined ... by the good pleasure only of our Maker" (EIP VIII.iv:
592). Reid is coy in his answer, and simply refers the reader to what
Price says on the subject as meriting consideration.[42] In other places,
however, Reid seems sympathetic with motivational internalism.
When discussing the notion of our good on the whole, Reid writes "I
am very apt to think, with Dr. Price, that, in intelligent beings ... it

is a contradiction to suppose such a being to have the notion of good without the desire of it" (EAP III.iii.ii: 581a). And later he says "our moral judgments are not, like those we form in speculative matters, dry and unaffecting, but from their nature, are necessarily accompanied with affections and feelings" (EAP III.iii.vii: 592a).

But there are three reasons for thinking that motivational internalism is not Reid's considered view. First, Reid says that judgments about what ought to be done "convince, but they do not impel, unless, as *may* often happen, they excite some passion . . ." (EAP IV.iv: 611b, my emphasis). Second, Reid repeatedly insists that it is by the "constitution of our nature" that affections of various sorts follow upon normative judgments.[43] And as Reid makes eminently clear in the *Inquiry* and elsewhere, that which is due to the constitution of our nature is contingent and dependent on the will of God. Third, Reid tells us that the connection between moral judgment and affection is a causal one.[44] But Reid is a Humean about (non-agent) causation; the connection between cause and effect is a contingent one. Consequently, it is difficult to avoid the conclusion that for Reid there is an intimate but ultimately contingent relationship between moral judgment and motivation. We are so constituted that, when all goes well, a person's judging that she ought to x is accompanied by the appropriate motivational state. In Reid's view, we should be no more astonished at this than at our having been designed in such a way that sensations of various sorts give rise to conception and belief.

In sum, then, Reid's position is what we might call a "proper function" account of moral motivation: When an agent's cognitive and affective faculties are working well in an appropriate environment, moral judgment yields the motivational state he calls moral approbation. The qualification "when all goes well" is not idle; it highlights the fact that, for Reid, the intimate connection between moral judgment and motivation is *normative* in character.

IV. MORAL EPISTEMOLOGY

If what I have claimed thus far is correct, Reid's views are a blend of insights borrowed from both the rationalist and sentimentalist traditions. On issues of moral ontology, Reid's thought is indebted to rationalists such as Price and Clarke. On the topic of the connection between virtue and happiness, by contrast, Reid's views more nearly mirror those of Hutcheson and Hume. It is with respect to issues of moral knowledge, however, that Reid's synthetic tendencies are in full bloom.[45]

Central to the views of Reid's predecessors and contemporaries was a commitment to a broadly Lockean faculty psychology, which divided the mind into the two faculties of sense and reason. Impressed by the intimate connection between moral judgment and motivation, sentimentalists such as Hutcheson found themselves defending the view that the objects of moral judgments are particular qualities of agents, and not abstract relations (the latter being the wrong sort of thing to arouse feelings of approbation and disapprobation).[46] Accordingly, it was natural for the sentimentalists to believe that the faculty of moral judgment is a sense of a sort, and not reason, which is a theoretical faculty that tracks necessary relations. Given this commitment, sentimentalists such as Hutcheson also found it natural to speak of the objects of this faculty as being simply those entities that arouse feelings of approbation and disapprobation.[47]

But the price for this package of views, according to sentimentalism's critics, is too high. Insofar as they claimed that moral qualities are akin to colors, and thus existentially dependent on contingent features of our constitution, the sentimentalists were accused of sacrificing the objectivity of morality.

So rationalists such as Wollaston, Balguy, and Price took a different avenue. In their view, the salient feature of morality is not the motivational force of moral judgments, but the objectivity of moral facts. Accordingly, rationalists claimed that the primary objects of moral judgments are necessary moral norms. And moral norms they considered to be relational entities of a sort whose constituents are universals. It was thus natural for the rationalists to suppose that the faculty of moral judgment is reason – where reason is a capacity for grasping the abstract realm. In this way, the rationalists took themselves to preserve the objectivity of morality; moral facts are not mind-dependent in the way that colors are.

But there is a putative price to pay for this view too. While the rationalists may have preserved the objectivity of morality, they were accused of offering no explanation for the intimate connection between moral judgment and motivation.

Reid thus inherited a tradition of moral philosophy at odds with itself. Neither the sentimentalists nor the rationalists seemed able to fashion a moral epistemology congruent with both the objectivity of morality and the close connection between moral judgment and motivation. Reid's solution to the problem is to erase the heavy line that Lockeans had drawn between the faculties of sense and reason. In contrast to sentimentalists and rationalists alike, Reid suggests that all well-formed persons are endowed with a "moral sense," a faculty or ability to form *both* general and particular moral conceptions and judgments. The Reidian moral sense is thus an ability to grasp both particulars and universals.[48] It is also, as I've already indicated, a capacity to generate moral feelings. To this Reid adds the claim that the moral sense is an "original" or innate faculty. We have reason to believe this because the moral sense is "common to the whole species, in all the varieties of instruction and education" (EAP III.iii.viii: 595a). Nevertheless, Reid is at pains to emphasize that the moral sense develops with maturity, and "may be greatly assisted or retarded, improved or corrupted, by education, instruction, example, exercise, and by the society and conversation of men..." (ibid.).

If the moral faculty is a "moral sense," according to Reid, then it is natural to raise the question to what extent he thought that moral apprehension and judgment are akin to ordinary visual, tactile, olfactory, and auditory perception. Reid's unpublished lectures on jurisprudence indicate that he saw the different types of perception as intimately related:

By our Moral Faculty we have an immediate perception of Right and wrong of Moral Rectitude & Depravity in moral Agents in like Manner as we have a perception of black and white in visible Objects by the Eyes of harmony and Discord by a Musical Ear and of other qualities in objects by means of the several faculties of our Nature as to give us not onely Ideas of such Qualities but an immediate perception of their Existence in certain Subjects. (PE: 144)

To use the terminology I introduced at the outset of our discussion, the moral sense is the faculty by which we can perceive both general and particular moral facts. But how exactly should we understand Reid's talk of "perceiving" here?

In his most systematic discussion of the moral sense in the *Active Powers*, it is clear that Reid mainly has his eye on how we perceive or apprehend general moral facts. This is the overtly "intuitionist" side of Reid's epistemology. Through an a priori act of the moral sense, says Reid, we can "perceive" the necessary first principles of moral-ity.[49] I suggest that we view "perception" of this sort to be a species of what Bertrand Russell called "acquaintance."[50] Moral perception of this variety is a matter of being acquainted with moral reality – or to put it the other way around, of moral reality being present to us in an act of intellection. That said, there's little concern on Reid's part to explain how we can have acquaintance with the abstract realm: "As to the manner how we conceive universals, I confess my ignorance. . . . In all our original faculties, the fabric and manner of operation is, I apprehend, beyond our comprehension, and perhaps is perfectly understood by him only who made them" (EIP V.vi: 394).

Although Reid does not try to explain how we apprehend the prin-ciples of morality, he takes it to be obvious *that* we all do. Indeed, Reid, like Butler, takes it to be clear that the basic principles of moral-ity are evident to all (not radically defective) persons and "immedi-ately perceived without reasoning, by all men come to years of un-derstanding" (EAP III.iii.vi: 591a).[51] By claiming that these principles are "evident" to us, Reid has several things in mind. Most obviously, Reid means to claim that the principles are self-evident in the sense that, if a person believes them, she does not believe them on the evidential basis of other propositions that she accepts.[52] But Reid also indicates that moral principles have what Alvin Plantinga has recently called "impulsional evidence."[53] That is, for a person with a "candid mind," believing moral principles seems to be particularly "fitting" or "attractive," and that person thereby has a felt impulsion to believe it:

Right principles of the conduct have an affinity with a candid mind, which wrong principles have not. When they are set before it in a just light, a well disposed mind recognizes this affinity, feels their authority, and perceives them to be genuine. (EAP III.iii.viii: 596a)

So an agent's "perceiving" general moral facts is, in Reid's view, an act of intellectual intuition that is accompanied by a distinctive phe-nomenology. But what about our grasp of particular moral facts? Is that also a matter of being acquainted with moral reality?

It is here, I suggest, that it is easy to miss the thrust of Reid's view. Throughout his discussion of moral knowledge in the *Active Powers*,

Reid has his eye on the phenomenon of moral *reasoning*. Reid emphasizes that when we engage in moral reasoning, we reason from general moral principles to particular practical conclusions. One might be tempted to believe that, for Reid, we ordinarily grasp particular moral facts by a process of reasoning of this sort. However, Reid clearly indicates that this is not so.[54] In the ordinary case, says Reid, our apprehension of particular moral facts is also noninferential.[55] I want now to suggest that there's a reason for this. Reid's account of our grasp of particular moral facts is modeled on his general account of perception. So, let me say something briefly by way of clarification on this matter.

Underlying Reid's views on the nature of perception is a broad model or "schema" for how human perception works.[56] The schema tells us this: Suppose we let "O" stand for some quality of an object (such as an object's hardness). When S perceives O, there is a sign (such as a pressure sensation) that stands in some type of dependence relation to O (e.g., it is caused by O) and indicates or signifies O. And when all goes well, by a complex physical process that involves certain laws of our constitution, this sign evokes in S the apprehension of O, and the immediate belief about O that it exists (or some belief that entails this). Reid tells us that the signs in question may be anything from sensations (e.g., as in tactile perception) to appearances of certain kinds that are not sensations (e.g., as in perception of visible figure). In an "Essay on Taste," Reid applies the schema to our grasp of moral reality:

> But neither mind, nor any of its qualities or powers, is an immediate object of perception to man. We are, indeed, immediately conscious of the operations of our own mind. . . . Other minds we perceive only through the medium of material objects, on which their signatures are impressed. It is through this medium that we perceive life, activity, wisdom, and every moral and intellectual quality in other beings. The signs of those qualities are immediately perceived by the senses; by them the qualities themselves are reflected to our understanding; and we are very apt to attribute to the sign, the beauty or the grandeur, which is properly and originally in the things signified. (EIP VIII.iv: 602–3)[57]

The basic idea is the following: Particular moral qualities are most fundamentally features of persons and their intentions, beliefs, desires, and so forth. These qualities are manifested in various ways in the countenance and behavior of the persons who instantiate them. As such the countenance and behavior of persons function as natural and artificial signs – natural and artificial signs of qualities to which they stand in the relation of signifying. When all goes well, moral agents with the requisite maturity, conceptual expertise, and training interpret these signs as signifying those qualities.

Of particular interest for our purposes is that Reid sees no conflict between a given case of moral perception's being "theoretically loaded" insofar as it presupposes that a person has extensive background beliefs, assumptions, and conceptual expertise, and its being noninferential. In persons with sufficient maturation and proper experience and habits, awareness of certain types of signs immediately evokes apprehension and belief of the moral qualities they signify. To use an analogy partly borrowed from Reid, the interpretation of signs in perception is more akin to an agent's immediately seeing that a group of letters has a certain meaning, than it is to, say, a detective's sifting through clues to determine whether someone has committed a crime.[58] Part of nature's gift to us is the ability in cases of perception to pass immediately from sign to what is signified.

When we consider what Reid himself says about moral perception of this sort, it is clear that in most cases he has his eye on the way in which we perceive particular evaluative properties of persons and what Reid calls "things in the mind" (EIP I.i: 21). It is worth quoting Reid at length on the point.

Intelligence, design, and skill, are not objects of the external senses, nor can we be conscious of them in any person but ourselves....

A man's wisdom is known to us only by the signs of it in his conduct; his eloquence by the signs of it in his speech. In the same manner we judge of his virtue, of his fortitude, and of all his talents and qualities of mind.

Yet it is to be observed, that we judge of men's talents with as little doubt or hesitation as we judge of the immediate objects of sense.

... We perceive one man to be open, another cunning; one to be ignorant, another very knowing; one to be slow of understanding, another quick. Every man forms such judgments of those he converses with; and the common affairs of life depend upon such judgments. We can as little avoid them as we can avoid seeing what is before our eyes.

From this it appears, that it is no less part of the human constitution, to judge of men's characters, and of their intellectual powers, from the signs of them in their actions and discourse, than to judge of corporeal objects by our senses. (EIP VI.vi: 503–4)

In this passage, we find Reid explicitly applying what I've called his "broad schema" of perception to our perception of character traits of persons.[59] Upon being aware of signs of certain kinds, we find ourselves immediately apprehending and believing of a person that she is wise, benevolent, or wicked as the case may be (or believing something that entails this). Presumably, perception of this sort can take different forms. In some cases in which we perceive moral traits, we're explicitly aware of the signs that evoke apprehension and belief. For instance, a person might be explicitly aware of Sam's having sharply rebuked Melissa for what appears to be a matter of little importance. In this case, we might say that this person is aware of Sam as being morally insensitive by virtue of being aware of his behavior toward Melissa. In other cases, however, the signs that occasion apprehension and belief are not explicitly noticed. Upon interacting with Sam, a person might find herself apprehending and believing of Sam that he is insensitive; he "strikes" her in this way, and she finds herself aware of him under the concept of being morally insensitive. In this case, Sam's striking this person in this way may be the upshot of a variety of extraordinarily subtle signs – the way he looks her over, his tone of voice, his inattention to their conversation, an off-hand remark of his – which she does not explicitly notice. So while this person may be aware of these signs, it is not a case of *noticed* awareness. It is cases such as these that mirror most closely what Reid believes to happen in most instances of our perception of external objects. In such cases, Reid says that we typically take no notice of the signs that suggest apprehension and belief. Indeed, Reid points out that we don't have names for most of the signs that occasion apprehension and belief.[60]

One of the more interesting features of the passage just quoted is that Reid insists that we don't have acquaintance with the character traits of agents; the traits themselves are not present to us in perception. What this strongly suggests is that Reid thinks of our apprehension of moral virtues as being a species of what we might term "conceptual apprehension" – apprehension by way of the apprehensive use of some definite description or singular concept. To be sure, in cases in which we perceive a person to have one or another virtue or vice, we ordinarily are aware of that person (or her behavior) under some moral concept; we see that person (or her behavior) *as* being insensitive, benevolent, or wicked. That is, so to speak, the "representational content" of our perception. But our apprehending that person's trait, in Reid's view, is itself a function of what we might call an "expressive particular concept." We apprehend Sam's insensitivity by virtue of being aware of the behavior that expresses this trait. We grasp it by way of the singular concept of *the insensitivity of which this behavior is an expression.*

Let me close with the following speculation. In various places, Reid endeavors to show that we can trust the deliverances of our moral faculty because they are on the same epistemic footing as the deliverances of our other native faculties.[61] The foregoing suggests, then, one way of developing Reid's view to answer the challenge that moral realism is suspect because it can give no plausible account of how we could have epistemic access to moral qualities.[62] In its most basic form, the argument is this: It seems evident that nonmoral qualities such as being intelligent, frightened, stingy, cheeky, determined, etc., are qualities of persons and their intentions, beliefs, etc. We have, moreover, little doubt that we can grasp these qualities by way of being aware of the behavior that expresses them. But if that's right, then there's no special problem about how we can perceive particular moral qualities. Particular moral qualities are also qualities of persons and things in the mind that are expressed in behavior. So putative perception of moral qualities is simply a special case of perceiving features of persons and things in the mind: We are presented with various signs as experiential inputs, and this gives rise, when all goes well, by a law of our constitution, to apprehension and belief of the appropriate sort.[63]

NOTES

1. EIP VII.ii: 550–1.
2. EIP VI.vi: 494–5.
3. EIP VIII.i: 578. Here Reid has his eye on aesthetic facts. But since Reid views aesthetic facts as analogous to moral ones, I assume he believes that particular moral facts are supervenient facts as well.
4. EAP V.iv: 649a.
5. THN 3.2.2: 314–15.

6. THN 3.2.2: 318.
7. Reid's best formulation of the argument can be found at EIP VI.vi: 494–5 and VII.iii: 549. It is clear from Reid's formulation of the argument at EIP VII.iii: 584 that he has Hutcheson in mind as his main opponent. Variants of this argument can be found in Price 1948: 15–17 and Balguy 1728: 7ff.
8. See Bennett 1993.
9. "Acting" here should be understood to include cognitive acts such as paying attention to certain things. See EAP II.iii: 538a, 541b. See, also, Knud Haakonssen's discussion of virtues and obligations in his introduction to PE: 49ff.
10. EAP V.iii. But see what Reid says in PE: 199.
11. EAP V.v: 651b.
12. Reid's division between general and particular principles is different from the distinction I've drawn between general and particular moral facts.
13. See Reid's discussion in PE for a different, but complementary account of these duties.
14. See Shaftesbury 1999: 182ff; Hutcheson 1999: 126; and Butler 1983: Preface.
15. See EAP III.iii.iii: 584a. It should be emphasized that Reid believes there are severe limitations to deriving one's moral duties from one's self-interest. See EAP III.iii.iv.
16. EAP III.iii.viii: 598a–b.
17. Butler's argument is spread out between *Sermons* I, II, III, and VI.
18. EAP III.iii.iv: 586a.
19. I have been helped here by McGinn 1997, Chap. 5.
20. For Shaftesbury's views, see Shaftesbury 1999: 172–3, and Darwall 1995: 185.
21. EAP V.i: 637b.
22. See Darwall 1995.
23. Darwall 1995: 17.
24. Compare William Paley, who claims that at one time he had supposed that "to be *obligated* to do a thing, was very different from being *induced* only to it," but on reflection concluded that "*obligation* is nothing more than an *inducement* of sufficient strength...." Paley 1991: 260.
25. See Mackie 1977: 40.
26. EAP III.iii.v: 587a–b.
27. I assume that, even though general moral facts have the logical form of being universal generalizations, the propositions that correspond to these facts can be given a subject/predicate form.
28. EIP VIII.i: 577.

29. Reid puts the view thus: "*Moral Approbation or Disapprobation* is not an *Act of the Judgment*, which, like all acts of judgment, must be true or false, it is only a certain *Feeling*, which, from the constitution of human nature, arises upon contemplating certain characters of qualities of mind coolly and impartially" (EAP V.v: 651a).

30. See Price 1948, Chap. 1.

31. See Jensen 1978.

32. I borrow the term from an unpublished essay by William C. Davis, "Thomas Reid on the Role of Moral Feelings in Moral Judgment."

33. See EAP V.vii: 673a–b.

34. It is a little strange that Reid should have conflated these two views; he clearly separates them elsewhere (see EAP V.vii: 671b).

35. EAP V.vii: 671a–2a. In this paragraph, I use the term "feel" in a wider sense than Reid himself does.

36. THN 3.1.2: 302.

37. It is precisely this sort of objection that Reid levels against Hume's way of distinguishing between impressions and ideas. Hume's official view is that the difference between these types of entity lies in their differing degrees of vivacity. Reid objects that the difference is one of kind, and not degree of vivacity. See EIP I.i: 33.

38. That the principle is a prima facie one for Reid is made clear by his willingness to deviate from it when it comes to the analysis of causal language. See EAP IV.ii.

39. It is worth noting that the terms "principle" and "motive" have a double valence for Reid. On the one hand, the term picks out a state of being motivated. On the other, it picks out the object of that state, viz., a proposition or state of affairs. Reid doesn't clearly distinguish the two, and at one point says that the motives of action "don't exist" and, hence, are not causes (EAP IV.iv: 608b). I assume that when Reid says this he has the Clarkean view that the objects of (at least some) motivational states are abstract entities (see Clarke 1998: 134). For Reid, these entities do not exist in space and time.

40. See THN 3.1.1ff.

41. See Price 1948: 42, 186.

42. Reid does point out, however, that the mere fact that we can conceive of normative judgments and affections coming apart does not imply that they can come apart (EIP VIII.iv: 592). In this respect, Reid would resist the arguments offered by Brink 1989 for motivational externalism.

43. See EAP III.iii.ii: 581a, III.iii.iii: 584a, III.iii.vii: 592b, 594a; EIP VIII.ii: 578.

44. EAP V.vii: 673b.

45. In what follows, I've been helped by Davis 1992.

46. See, e.g., Hutcheson 1999: 126–8.
47. See Hutcheson 1999: 142. Although Hutcheson speaks of moral qualities in this way, it is a matter of some controversy whether this is his considered view.
48. Butler is perhaps Reid's inspiration here; see "A Dissertation upon the Nature of Virtue" in Butler 1983.
49. That the operation is a priori is stressed by Reid at EIP VI.vi: 654.
50. See Russell 1997, Chap. 5. Here I draw upon Nicholas Wolterstorff's claim that what Reid calls "conception" is a synonym for "apprehension." See Wolterstorff 2001, Chap. 1.
51. See PE: 192, where Reid offers a justification for the claim that the "rights and obligations of men" are obvious to the plain person.
52. See EIP VI.iv: 452.
53. Plantinga 1993: 192.
54. See EIP VII.ii: 553 and PE: 144, 155, 179.
55. Why then the emphasis on moral reasoning in Reid's discussion? I believe the answer is that Reid is concerned to establish that there must be necessary moral first principles, and he can establish this by way of discussing the nature of moral reasoning.
56. See Wolterstorff 2001, Chap. 5, and Van Cleve's essay in this volume. What follows is treated at more length in Cuneo 2003.
57. See, also, EIP VI.v: 486 and IHM: 191.
58. IHM V.ii: 57.
59. By far and away, Reid talks most frequently about our perceiving character traits, and so I shall focus on this aspect of Reid's thought. For Reid's views on our perception of particular deontic moral qualities, see Cuneo 2003.
60. It is a striking feature of Reid's official account of moral perception that our feelings do not function as signs for moral qualities (see EAP V.vii: 672b). If moral feelings did play this role, then Reid's account of moral perception would exhibit a pleasing parallel with his account of tactile, olfactory, etc., perception. I discuss the issue in an unpublished essay, "Signs of Value: Thomas Reid on the Evidential Role of Feelings in Moral Judgment."
61. See EAP III.iii.vi: 591a–b.
62. See THN 3.1.1 and Mackie 1977, Chap. 1.
63. I thank Alexander Broadie, Rebecca Copenhaver, James Harris, Luke Reinsma, Gideon Yaffe, René van Woudenberg, and my colleagues at Seattle Pacific University and the Vrije Universiteit, Netherlands, for their comments on earlier drafts of this essay. I also thank the National Endowment of the Humanities and the Vrije Universiteit, whose financial support made work on this essay possible.

11   Reid's Philosophy of Art

I

I must begin by stating emphatically what my subject is *not*. My subject is *not* the aesthetics of Thomas Reid: It is his *philosophy of art*.

By "aesthetics" I understand that branch of philosophy that deals with a wide, not clearly demarcated range of familiar questions, among which are the subset of questions that have specifically to do with the nature of the fine arts, their relevant qualities, and our interactions with them either as artists, critics, or audience. Philosophers, since and beginning with Plato, have written in a philosophical vein about what *we* would recognize as art and the aesthetic. But for some well-known reasons that I will adduce in a moment, no philosopher, before the eighteenth century, can really be said to have had a *philosophy of art*. Furthermore, even in the eighteenth century, to have a philosophy of art was an uncommon thing. And if Reid did have one, it would put him in the company of a very small group, perhaps consisting only of Alexander Baumgarten and, of course, Immanuel Kant. It would put him in the company of the pioneer philosophers of art. That Reid was of this number – or, at least, that he came very close to being – is the argument of this chapter.

Why was there no philosophy or philosopher of art, strictly speaking, before the eighteenth century? The answer to this question follows from what has become the standard account of how aesthetics and the philosophy of art came into being.[1] There is a perfectly uncontroversial sense in which Plato did not have a philosophy of art but *did* have philosophies of the "arts." His philosophy of the literary "arts," poetry and drama, was part of his philosophy of "inspiration," which included, also, both the practice of oracles and prophets, and, at least in the *Meno*, the practice of virtue. His philosophy of music, painting, sculpture and architecture was part of his philosophy of "craft" or *techne*. Thus Plato had two philosophies of "arts": a philosophy of the literary arts, and a philosophy of music, painting, sculpture, and architecture.

The reason Plato did not have a philosophy of art is the same as the reason that I put "arts" in scare quotes in describing his philosophies of them. Plato did not have a concept of the arts, the "fine arts," as they came to be called in Britain, in the eighteenth century. He did not think of poetry, drama, music, painting, sculpture, and architecture as species of the same genus. That is, clearly, why he did not have one philosophy of all of them. He had philosophies of what *we* think of as the fine arts. But he did not, could not have had a philosophy of art in the sense of an overarching theory that brought all of the "arts" under a definition and explained why they belonged there and nowhere else. To have *that* kind of philosophy of art one first had to have a concept of the fine arts to begin with: What had to be in place first is what Paul Oskar Kristeller called, in his groundbreaking article on the subject, "the modern system of the arts."[2]

The formation of the modern system of the arts was a gradual process, as Kristeller showed, that only had the finishing touches put on it in the first quarter of the eighteenth century. But even when in place, as it seems to have been by 1725, the year Francis Hutcheson's influential *Inquiry Concerning Beauty, Order, Harmony, Design* was published – arguably the first full-length study in the then newly established discipline of philosophical aesthetics – it was by no means the case that philosophers who contributed to this fledgling field had or felt the need to have a philosophy of art. Hutcheson, for one, did not; nor, for another, did Hume. Yet it is clear that both had a firm grasp on the concept of the fine arts: In the aesthetical writings of both, the modern system of the arts was firmly in place. We know this by observing that in both Hutcheson's *Inquiry* and in Hume's essay "Of the Standard of Taste," when the various fine arts are adduced as examples, they are clearly being adduced as examples of *the same kind of thing*.

At mid-century Alexander Baumgarten's *Aesthetica* can probably be singled out as the first fully fledged philosophy of art. And no one, I think, would demur from the suggestion that Kant's *Critique of*

Aesthetic Judgement presents the first fully worked out philosophy of art by a philosopher of the first rank. What I propose to add to this very short list is the name of Thomas Reid. I do not suggest that Reid's philosophy of art is fully worked out. I do suggest that the basic skeleton is there. Nor do I have any hesitation, at this date, in putting forth Reid as a philosopher of the first rank. The last fifty years of Reid scholarship have established that beyond reasonable doubt.

But at this point the reader is no doubt getting antsy to know just what the requirements are for a *philosophy of art*. By what criteria do I judge Reid and Kant to have one but Hutcheson and Hume not? To that question we must now briefly turn our attention.

II

We already know that the *first requirement* of a philosophy of art is: a firmly established concept of the fine arts. Without that there is nothing for the philosophy of art to be a philosophy of.

Let me suggest that the *second requirement* for a philosophy of art is an adequate analysis of what "art-relevant" or "artistic" features each of the major fine arts possesses. What this means will be gone into more fully when we come to examine Reid's philosophy of art.

Finally, the *third requirement* is what has consistently been referred to in analytic philosophy of art, since the end of the Second World War, if not before, as a "definition" of art or, in lieu of that, a philosophical argument to the effect that such a definition is impossible. Such definitions, in recent times, have taken the form of more or less strict statements of necessary and sufficient conditions. And the philosophical rejection of this project has been based on Wittgensteinian arguments and the notion of family resemblance, as laid out in the well-known passages on defining "game" in *Philosophical Investigations*. But it would, I think, be over-fastidious to insist that for a philosopher to have given a definition of art, she must have displayed and flagged, in numbered propositions, strict necessary and sufficient conditions for "arthood." One finds no such theories until the second half of the twentieth century, certainly not in Kant, Schopenhauer, Hegel, Dewey, or Collingwood, all of whom have left us broadly conceived accounts of the nature of art that are real definitions, in spirit if not in letter. Whether Reid has done so is part of my present topic.

In summary, then, we can think of a genuine philosophy of art as having three necessary (and together sufficient) criteria: (1) a full-fledged concept of the fine arts as an integrated whole; (2) an analysis of the art-relevant features of the individual arts; (3) a definition of art, formal, or at least implied, and, in lieu of that, an argument as to why such definitions cannot be produced.

In the following pages I shall try to show that Reid came very close to fulfilling these criteria: came very close, in other words, to having a full-blown philosophy of art. But before I start doing that I want to make some preliminary remarks as to what *kind* of philosophy of art I think Reid came very close to having.

III

Since the philosophical project of "defining" the work of art came into being, in the eighteenth century, with the formation of the modern system of the arts, there have been various kinds of definitions offered, singling out one or another of the prominent features that *most* works of art exhibit. There have been definitions centering on representation, the concept of the aesthetic, form, organic unity and so on. But in the twentieth century, presaged notably by Hegel, the foremost candidate has been what is now generally called the "expression theory" of art. Croce, Collingwood, and Dewey, as well as numerous lesser lights, have relentlessly pursued the notion that art is, *essentially*, the "expression of emotion," with "expression" and "emotion" broadly enough conceived to evade the more obvious counterexamples.

It is part of my argument in the present chapter that Reid, way ahead of his time, came very close to espousing an "expression theory" of the fine arts. What are the major claims of the "expression theory" that Reid would have to be making, in order to be identified as an expression theorist?

(1) An "expression theory" of art must give an account of how works of art can, in some sense, "express" emotions.

(2) An "expression theory" of art must not only claim that *some* works of art have the expression of emotions as one of their art-relevant features. It must say that expressing emotions is the necessary and sufficient condition for something's being a work of the fine arts.

(3) An "expression theory" of art, in its traditional, authentic form, must be a "self-expression" theory of art. That is to say, it must define expression as a process in which the artist expresses an emotion or emotions in some way or another, through embodying his experience in the work of art, thereby conveying that experience of emotive expression to the perceiver, so that he or she can have something like the experience the artist had. Art, in other words, is, for the expression theorist, a kind of emotive communication between artist and audience.

In 1978 I published an article called "Thomas Reid and the Expression Theory of Art."[3] In it I argued, and will argue again here, that Reid came very close to formulating a bona fide expression theory of art, in the sense just outlined above. But in rereading that essay, by a very much younger version of my present self – almost a philosophical stranger to me in certain respects – I detected various weaknesses and infelicities in my argument there, as well as failures in my interpretation of Reid. This reaction was reinforced by my encounter with the trenchant and insightful criticism of my early attempt by Roger D. Gallie in his recent study *Thomas Reid: Ethics, Aesthetics, and the Anatomy of the Self.*[4]

In some respects, then, what follows will be a kind of three-way dialogue between me, my former self, and Professor Gallie, although I will have both the advantages *and* disadvantages of a dialogue in which the other parties can't answer back.

In what now follows, in the body of my paper, I am going to go through, seriatim, the three requirements I laid out for a genuine philosophy of art and see if I can find them satisfied in Reid's texts. This process will be informed, as well, by the three requirements for an expression theory of art. In the end I hope to show, as I tried to do, but not with complete success, in my earlier paper, that Reid came very close to having a true philosophy of the fine arts, and that that philosophy came very close to being an expression theory of the fine arts in the traditional sense.

IV

As regards the first criterion for a genuine philosophy of art, namely, a concept of the fine arts, there is little need to argue at length that

Reid possessed one. He uses the designation "fine arts" regularly to refer to the same art-categories, more or less, that we do. As well, the title of the manuscript, *Lectures on the Fine Arts by Dr. Reid*, obviously speaks for itself.[5]

From the *Lectures*, and other places in his works where he refers to the fine arts, it can be inferred that among the fine arts Reid recognized the following: literature, stage drama, painting, sculpture, music, architecture, landscape gardening, and oratory. There are no particular surprises on this list, although a couple of points are worth noticing.

Landscape gardening and oratory are not ordinarily thought of, these days, as fine arts. However, no one in eighteenth-century Britain would have been the least bit surprised in Reid's considering them to be. Oratory provided Hume, for instance, in "Of the Standard of Taste," with one of his prime illustrative examples, and Reid, in the *Lectures*, hailed it as "undoubtedly the noblest of all the fine arts, for it unites the beauties of them all" (LFA: 51–2). As well, landscape gardening not only achieved a high degree of aesthetic sophistication, in Britain and the Continent, by Reid's time, but left in its wake a gaggle of treatises that must be considered not merely as practical manuals but as a major contribution to Enlightenment aesthetics and philosophy of art, at least broadly conceived.

What might have raised many eyebrows in Reid's day, but certainly not in ours, was his unequivocal inclusion of *music* among the arts. For music, pure wordless music, at least, was a very difficult case for the aesthetics of the Enlightenment. By the 1770s, if not before, pure instrumental music had gained a social and aesthetic status that made it impossible to ignore as a candidate for "arthood." Yet the reigning principle of the fine arts was representation; and it was very difficult to see music – pure, wordless music, remember – as a representational art. (Vocal music had long been seen as a representation of the passionate speaking voice.)

Thus, in unequivocally including pure instrumental music among the fine arts, Reid was well ahead of his time, in effect, bucking a trend. Both Kant and Hegel, to instance two pretty impressive cases in point, would allow only music with words to qualify, unconditionally. On "absolute" music both of them hemmed and hawed and waffled.

There can be no doubt, then, that Reid fulfilled completely the first criterion for a philosophy of art: a firm concept of the modern system of the arts. It may differ in some particulars from *our* concept. But it is clearly enough recognizable to be beyond any dispute.

V

It will be remembered that the second of the requirements for a bona fide philosophy of art I adduced was an analysis of the art-relevant features of the individual arts. In this section I want to show what Reid's analysis of these features is for what *we* would think of as the three major fine arts (at least of his time): music, literature, and the visual arts (which is to say, painting and sculpture). And I am going to begin with music, because it not only raises some problems for Reid peculiarly its own, but also displays all of the features that are to be found in literature and the visual arts as well. (Interestingly enough, given pure music's low status in the eighteenth century, Reid spends more time on it than on any of the other arts.)

To begin with I want to introduce some terminology, not Reid's own, but in general use in contemporary analytic philosophy of art, that will help me to explain more clearly what I think Reid is saying.

I want to say that a work is "expressive" of an emotion when that emotion is "perceived in" the work as one of its features. Being expressive as I use the term, then, has nothing necessarily to do with the state of mind of the artist. That is to say, an artist may make a work expressive of an emotion without herself being in that emotional state.

I shall say, on the other hand, that a work "expresses" an emotion when some feature of the work is a vehicle for the expression of the artist's emotion (although I shall sometimes use the word "expression," in quotation marks, to refer to Reid's theory, when "expressive" is what is really meant). And I shall assume, although it may not necessarily be the case all of the time, that when an artist expresses her emotion in a work, she expresses it through an expressive property she imparts to the work: Thus she expresses her sadness by making a work of art expressive of sadness. According to this usage, then, it is a necessary condition for being an expression of an emotion, but not for being expressive of an emotion, that the person expressing is in that emotional state. In other words, you can't express an emotion you are not experiencing, although you can make yourself or something else expressive of it.

Finally, it is necessary to distinguish between a work of art's expressing an emotion, being expressive of an emotion, and arousing an emotion. They are logically distinct notions, even though some writers have claimed that when a work is expressive of an emotion it tends to arouse that emotion in perceivers, and other writers have claimed that a work is expressive of an emotion in virtue of its tendency to arouse that emotion in perceivers. What Reid thinks about all of these things I want to now try to determine, beginning, as I said, with the fine art of music, which will be our model, so to speak, for the other major arts.

Reid's most extended and self-contained account of musical aesthetics occurs in Essay VIII, Chapter IV, of the *Essays on the Intellectual Powers of Man*. It consists of eight connected paragraphs, and seems to me to constitute Reid's most mature and considered expression of his musical opinions, and so I shall treat it.

To begin with, it would seem that Reid thinks music has three basic kinds of art-relevant properties, all subsumable under the head of beauty (or, I presume, sublimity). Thus he writes: "In a composition of sounds, or a piece of music, the beauty is either in the harmony, the melody, or the expression" (EIP VIII.iv: 604). And I take it that what Reid calls music's "expression" is what I want to call its "expressive" character or "expressiveness": In other words, what Reid says music "expresses" I say it is "expressive of."

But as it turns out, as far as I can see, there is really only *one* source of beauty in music, namely, "expression." For, in Reid's view, *both* the beauty of harmony and the beauty of melody seem to be in reality the beauty of "expression" after all. Thus he concludes his account of music, in Chapter IV, in this wise: "I leave it to the adepts in the science of music, to determine whether music, composed according to the established rules of harmony and melody, can be altogether void of expression; and whether music that has no expression can have any beauty" (EIP VIII.iv: 605). I take it that the answers to both of these rhetorical questions to "the adepts in the science of music" Reid expects to be "No." And from this I infer that the beauty of music (and, I take it, its sublimity as well) is due, according to Reid, to its "expression," and that its "expression" has two sources: its melody and its harmony.

How is it that melody and harmony both give rise to expressiveness? The answer is through representation, or, as Reid's

contemporaries more usually put it, imitation. Reid thought that
both harmony and melody were expressive of human emotions
through the representation of the human voice when it is expressing a
particular emotion. Harmony in music, Reid seems to be suggesting,
is a representation of amiable human conversation. For "when two
or more persons, of good voice and ear, converse together in amity
and friendship, the tones of their different voices are concordant, but
become discordant when they give vent to angry passions..." (EIP
VIII.iv: 604). Whereas musical dissonance represents conversation
that becomes angry or disputatious. So that

When discord arises occasionally in conversation, but soon terminates in
perfect amity, we receive more pleasure than from perfect unanimity. In
like manner, in the harmony of music, discordant sounds are occasionally
introduced, but it is always in order to give a relish to the most perfect
concord that follows. (EIP VIII.iv: 605)

And melody, more obviously, fulfills the representational function,
for, as Reid puts it: "To me it seems, that every strain in melody that
is agreeable, is an imitation of the human voice in the expression of
some sentiment or passion..." Thus, in effect, "music, as well as
poetry, is an imitative art" (ibid.).

It would seem then that for Reid the beauty of music resides either
in the expressiveness of its melody or in the expressiveness of its harmony, and that the expressiveness of both is the result of their being
representations of the human voice in its expression of the emotions.
(And if music can be sublime, its sublimity would be explained in
the same way.) This, I think, is Reid's settled, mature doctrine.

There is, however, some evidence of an evolution in Reid's view on
musical "expression" well worth mentioning, both for its philosophical and for its historical significance. In the manuscript, *Lectures
on the Fine Arts*, dated 1774, and thus pre-dating the *Essays on the
Intellectual Powers* by more then ten years, at least, Reid places musical expressiveness not in the imitation of the human voice, as he
does in the *Essays*, but in the arousal of the emotions in the listener;
and the enjoyment of music, it would appear, resides solely in our
experiencing these aroused emotions. "There is something in music
called expression and with which we are pleased," Reid begins; and,
he continues, "this expression is nothing but the fitness of certain
sounds to produce certain sentiments in our minds." These "certain

sentiments" are, it becomes clear, as he develops his thought, what I like to call the "garden variety emotions" – hope, anger, sadness, joy, and the like. Indeed, Reid avers, "There is no passion that may not be affected [i.e., caused] by music. It is as much adapted to grief and sorrow as to joy...." Furthermore, it is in this "affecting" of the emotions that music pleasures us. "Whenever it affects any of the passions it is agreeable: the connection of sounds and sentiments is such; and wherever this is performed it is attended with an agreeable sensation" (LFA: 49).

All of this drops out of Reid's final account of music in the *Essays*, and, as we shall see, with good reason. For Reid presents a unitary account of what pleases in *all* of the arts (and other aesthetic domains as well) which is not consistent with his early views on musical pleasure. Nor is there evidence in Reid's mature account of musical "expression" that he thought the arousing of the garden variety emotions had anything to do with it.[6] Rather, what he clearly is suggesting in his account of "expression" in music, as in the rest of the arts, is not that we *feel* the emotions therein but that we *perceive* or become cognizant of them. What we *feel* is something else again.

With Reid's mature views on music before us, we can now move on to the other major arts, painting and sculpture, and literature. I begin with the former.

There is precious little in Essay VIII of the *Essays on the Intellectual Powers* about the visual arts. In one of the few passages devoted to them Reid simply states the not very surprising thesis that the beauty of painting lies in its representational features. "The proper arrangement of colour, and of light and shade, is one of the chief beauties of painting; but the beauty is greatest, when the arrangement gives the most distinct, the most natural, and the most agreeable image of that which the painter intended to represent" (EIP VIII.iv: 606). I take it that the main lesson to be learned from this brief passage is that painting is, in Reid's view, a representational art.

This bare statement can be fleshed out to some extent by appeal to a passage in Chapter VI, Section VIII of the *Inquiry into the Human Mind* (1764), the account of "Painting and Sculpture" in the *Lectures*, and by some judicious surmises.

The passage in the *Inquiry* reads, in part:

An excellent painter or statuary can tell, not only what are the proportions of a good face, but what changes every passion makes in it ... [W]hen he puts his art in practice, and happily expresses a passion by its proper signs, every one understands the meaning of the signs without art, and without reflection.

What has been said of painting, might easily be applied to all the fine arts. (IHM VI.viii: 102)

The first point to note here is that Reid thinks painting and sculpture are on all fours with the other arts regarding "expression." Music, as we have seen, is expressive of the garden variety emotions by representing the sound of passionate human speech and conversation with melody and harmony. Painting and sculpture are expressive of the garden variety emotions by representing the human countenance and "what changes every passion makes in it...." In the *Lectures*, "expression" in the visual arts is extended to the dispositions of the body – "body language," as it has been called – as well. Thus Reid says there that "Painting... derives the chief part of its beauty from the representation of the passion & dispositions of men in the attitudes and countenances." And as this passage is titled "Painting & Sculpture" I am sure we have the right to assume that, as in the *Inquiry*, what Reid says about painting applies *pari passu* to sculpture as well (although he adds as a rider that "A countenance with no expression may be fit for a statue but never a painting: hence portraits are disapproved unless they express some passion" (LFA: 50)).

Furthermore, in the *Lectures*, as in the *Inquiry*, Reid does not fail to make the point that the general manner in which painting and sculpture achieve "expression" can be extended to the other fine arts as well, although in the *Lectures* he mentions literature and music specifically. Thus: "There has always been remarked a great affinity between poetry & painting: poetry speaks & painting acts...." And "Certain attitudes are expressive of certain passions as well as certain conformations of the countenance. This is the main thing to be studied in painting as well as in music, i.e., expression" (ibid.).

Moving on now to literature, or "poetry," rather, which is what Reid consistently refers to, we find repeated at the outset of the discussion in the *Lectures* that its character is to be understood along the same lines as music and the visual arts. "We may observe," he says, "that the beauties of poetry arise from the same principles as those wh[ich] I have formerly explained in music and painting" (LFA: 51). But having said this, Reid goes on, rather unexpectedly, *not* to discuss "expression," which had played such a dominant role in the account of painting, sculpture, and music, but, rather, details of poetic language and structure. It is only toward the end of the passage on poetry in the *Lectures* that he reverts to the major theme of "expression," in direct reference to drama. "In dramatic performances, the beauty of the action lies in the expression" (ibid.).

It is also important to note that just as in the discussion of music in the *Lectures*, the payoff of expression in drama, and, we should assume, in every other form of literature, is said to be in the arousal of the emotions the work is expressive of. Thus: "It is introduced as a sign or expression of the passions, & when this is accomplished, it affects us and causes the same passion in us ..." (ibid.).

But, again, as in the case of music, I think this should be considered part of an early version of Reid's theory, which later drops out of it in its mature form. Unfortunately Reid does not provide any extended discussion of literature, as he does of music, in the *Essays on the Intellectual Powers*. So we can merely surmise that this is the case with literature as well. But it is, I think, a safe surmise, given Reid's oft-repeated assertion that his theory of "expression" applies, *pari passu*, to all of the fine arts.

I said earlier that the dropping out of emotive arousal from Reid's theory had a good reason. It is time, now, in concluding this discussion of Reid's account of art-relevant properties, to suggest what it was. Remember that the work the emotive arousal theory was doing in Reid's early account of musical "expression" was to explain what it is about music that we enjoy. "Whenever it affects any of the passions ... it is agreeable." The arousal of emotion "is attended with an agreeable sensation" (LFA: 49). But this explanation of what we enjoy in music (and the other arts) is redundant. There already is an explanation latent in the recognition that the expressive properties of the arts are their beauties. For it is part of Reid's doctrine of the beautiful that beauty is an objective property, an "excellence" in things that possess it, but that it regularly gives rise in the perceiver to pleasant sensations. And the same is true of the other art-relevant category in Reid's theory, grandeur, or sublimity. This is repeated over and over again throughout Reid's works. Thus beautiful things "produce a certain agreeable emotion or feeling in the mind...." It "is gay and pleasant. It sweetens and humanises the temper, is friendly to every benevolent affection, and tends to allay sullen and angry passions" (EIP VIII.iv: 592), while "The emotion raised by grand objects is awful, solemn and serious." Grandeur "disposes to seriousness, elevates the mind above its usual state, to a kind of enthusiasm, and inspires magnanimity and a contempt of what is mean" (EIP VIII.iii: 582).

Thus there is no need for the hypothesis that music, or any of the other arts provides enjoyment through arousal of the garden variety emotions it is expressive of. It is the possession of the garden variety emotions as perceptual properties that gives the fine arts their beautiful and sublime features. And their beautiful and sublime features arouse in us various enjoyable feelings described above. One unitary account, then, explains why we enjoy the expressive features of all of the arts (and nature as well).

It is now time, at this point, for me to step back, survey what has so far been established, and provide a summary.

The second requirement for a philosophy of the fine arts is an account of the art-relevant features of the individual arts. On Reid's account, the most important art-relevant features of all of what we would think of as the major arts of Reid's time, music, literature, painting, and sculpture, are their expressive properties: properties such as anger, sadness, joy, love, jealousy, and the like – what I have been calling the garden variety emotions. Works of art possess these emotions, as perceptible features of them, in virtue of being, in their various ways, representations of expressive human behavior. Thus, a piece of music might be sad or angry in one place or another in virtue of representing, in its harmony and melody, the sound of the human voice in conversation expressing sadness or anger. A painting might be sad in one place, angry in another in virtue of representing a man with a sad countenance and cast down posture in one place, a woman, in another, with an angry countenance and threatening posture. And an epic poem might be sad in one place, angry in another, in virtue of describing the expressive behavior and appearance of a sad Aeneas in one place, an angry Achilles in another.

Reid repeats over and over again that most of an artwork's beauty or grandeur lies in its "expression." This means that a work's expressive features constitute the major portion of its beauty and grandeur. Its expressive features are ipso facto its beautiful and sublime features. And we enjoy these features because beauty and sublimity arouse in us enjoyable feelings, although of distinctly different kinds.

I think it fair to conclude from all of this that Reid has presented us so far with what might be correctly described as an *expressive* theory of art: that is, a theory of art as, in the main, beautiful and sublime, or, in other words, "successful" *qua* art, in virtue of being expressive of the garden variety emotions. But the question is, did Reid have an *expression* theory of art? For an *expression* theory of art says not only that art is *expressive* of emotions but that it thereby *expresses* the emotions of the artist and arouses or invokes them in the perceiver. To that question we now turn.

VI

It must be said straightaway that Reid was certainly *not* presenting an expression theory of art if one takes that to mean a theory that the artist must feel the garden variety emotions he makes his work expressive of before he creates his work of art, and then expresses those garden variety emotions in the expressive properties of his work: that, in other words, he feels sad and then expresses his sadness by making his work expressive of sadness in one place, feels angry and then expresses his anger by making his work expressive of anger in another place, and so on. As Gallie quite rightly observes: "How it is with the artist in these matters Reid scarcely mentions."[7]

Nor was Reid presenting an expression theory of art if one means by that a theory that requires that the sad features of music make us sad, the happy features of poems make us happy, the angry features of paintings make us angry, and so on. This indeed was what Reid was saying, as we have seen, in his early formulations; but, so far as I can make out, he allowed this view to vanish without a trace in his ripe reflections on art, in Essay VIII of the *Essays on the Intellectual Powers*.

Reid's "expression theory" of art, then, if indeed he has one, is not the theory that artists feel the garden variety emotions and express them in works of art, the perceiving of which, in turn, arouses those garden variety emotions in us. So what form might his expression theory take? To begin to answer this question we must now introduce what is perhaps Reid's most commented upon aesthetic precept, although by no means original with him, to the effect that only *mind*, never matter, can be beautiful or sublime, and that the perceived beauty and sublimity (so-called) of physical objects, among which are counted works of art, is derivative, always, of some beauty or sublimity of mind.

Reid expresses this thesis in many different ways throughout his works. I begin by simply adducing one of the many to serve as an example. It is a passage well off the beaten path, indeed from a letter to the Scottish aesthetician Archibald Alison. And I choose it not only for its pith but for the sense it conveys of the extreme importance Reid placed upon this thesis. He writes to Alison (3 February 1790): "I am proud to think that I first, in clear and explicit terms, and in the cool blood of a philosopher, maintained that all the beauty and sublimity of objects of sense is derived from the expression they exhibit of things intellectual, which alone have original beauty" (C: 209).

Another way Reid frequently puts the point is to say that the beauties and sublimities of physical objects, or "objects of sense," essentially are "signs" of mental excellence. Thus, "When we consider matter as an inert, extended, divisible, and movable substance, there seems to be nothing in these qualities which we can call grand; and when we ascribe grandeur to any portion of matter, however modified, may not it borrow this quality from something intellectual, of which it is the effect, or sign, or instrument, or to which it bears some analogy . . . ?" (EIP VIII.iii: 590). Or, again, "it will be evident that beauty originally is derived from those activities & qualities of mind wh[ich] excite our esteem & that beauty in mat[erial] objects is the sign of these qualities" (LFA: 41–2).

What exactly Reid meant by all of this talk (and more) is very hard to make out. Gallie, in his recent and admirable book on Reid, has devoted ten closely argued pages to the question, has put forward many useful suggestions, and, in the end, has not been able to frame a conclusive answer.[8] Nor is this a task I wish to undertake. (I doubt if I could do a better job on it than Gallie anyway.) What I propose instead is to leave Reid's position with regard to the derivative nature of material beauty and grandeur in the vague state in which I have presented it. And what I hope to be able to do in what follows is to answer *my* questions, Does Reid have a philosophy of art? and Is it an "expression theory" of art? in a manner that will be consistent with a wide range of answers to the question of what exactly Reid may have meant by calling the beauty and grandeur of sensible objects "derivative" of intellectual beauty and grandeur.

Let us return, then, to works of art and their expressive features. Most of the beauty and grandeur of art works, for Reid, resides, let us recall, in their "expression." Works of music are beautiful or sublime in virtue of their harmony and melody representing the emotive expression of human speech. Works of painting and sculpture are beautiful or sublime in virtue of their representations of the faces and postures of men and women expressing the garden variety emotions. And literature achieves beauty and grandeur in its descriptions "representing" the emotively expressive actions and speeches of its characters. But where does the beauty or grandeur come from?

Well, generally speaking, it is an axiom of eighteenth-century philosophy of art, as well as a part of folk wisdom, that the beauty or sublimity of a representation can come from two sources: the beauty or sublimity of the object represented and the beauty or sublimity of the *manner* in which the object is represented. Thus a beautiful rendering in oil paint of a beautiful face will, *qua* representation, gain its beauty *both* from the beauty of the sitter *and* from the beauty of the rendering.

The beauty of "expression" in works of art is really a special case of this general axiom. Thus, Reid says with regard to musical "expression": "The beauty of expression must be derived, either from the beauty of the thing expressed, or from the art and skill employed in expressing it properly" (EIP VIII.iv: 604). And what Reid says here of beauty in musical "expression" we can reasonably conclude applies *pari passu* to sublimity in musical "expression" as well (if music is indeed capable of it), and as well to both beauty and sublimity in the other fine arts. I will not argue this obvious point any further.

The beauties and sublimities of artistic "expression" then must be beauties and sublimities in Reid's "derivative" sense. They are beauties and sublimities of physical objects, sensible objects, and hence can only be beautiful and sublime in that way: as signs, in other words, of the beauties and sublimities of the mental states of the characters represented, be they characters with names, like Hamlet or Hercules in a play or a painting, or the abstract and nameless human voices in music without text, represented by its melody and harmony. Thus in the *Iliad* one part of its sublimity lies in the sublimity of the minds of the characters represented: "the grandeur is properly in HECTOR and ACHILLES, and the other great personages, human and divine, brought upon the stage" (EIP VIII.iii: 587).

The sublimity is the sublimity of their passions, which Homer represented in his descriptions. And, as above, this applies, *pari passu*, to beauty in literature, as well as to beauty and grandeur in the rest of the fine arts. (I shall return to this extremely important passage on the *Iliad* in a moment.)

The eighteenth century, it should be noted, unlike ours, had no problem with the notion of beautiful and sublime states of mind, and it is the beautifully and sublimely passionate states of mind of its represented characters from which works of art get, according to Reid, *part* of their necessarily derivative beauty and grandeur. As representations of beautiful faces or sublime sunsets get part of their beauty and sublimity from these beautiful and sublime objects of representation, so beautiful and sublime "expressions" in art works gain part of their beauty and sublimity from the beautifully and sublimely passionate states of mind of the characters that are the objects of their depictions. The rest of their beauty and sublimity they get from the *manner* in which these states of mind are depicted. And to that *extremely important* source of artistic beauty and grandeur we must now turn our attention. If Reid really did hold an expression theory of art, this is the place we will find it.

The crucial passage in this regard is that concerning the *Iliad*, from which I quoted briefly just a minute ago, and to which I promised to return. I am going to quote it now in full. Here is what Reid says:

By a figure [of speech], we assign to the effect a quality which is inherent only in the cause.

By the same figure, we ascribe to a work that grandeur which properly is inherent in the mind of the author.

When we consider the "Iliad" as the work of the poet, its sublimity was really in the mind of HOMER. He conceived great characters, great actions, and great events, in a manner suitable to their nature, and with those emotions which they are naturally fitted to produce; and he conveys his conceptions and his emotions by the most proper signs. The grandeur of his thoughts is reflected to our eye by his work, and therefore, it is justly called a grand work.

When we consider the things presented to our mind in the "Iliad" without regard to the poet, the grandeur is properly in HECTOR and ACHILLES, and the other great personages, human and divine, brought upon the stage. (EIP VIII.iii: 587)

The grandeur of Homer becomes the "grandeur" of the *Iliad* by a figure of speech. Does that mean the *Iliad* is not grand? If it isn't, what *is* it, anyway? Here is something like what I think Reid might be trying to tell us.

Let me begin with another figure of speech. When we describe such works as the *Iliad*, or the Sistine Ceiling, or Bach's *St. Matthew Passion*, we frequently say that they are "grand" or "massive conceptions": sometimes, grand or massive "in conception." This is a natural way of speaking, not the paradoxical result of philosophical theorizing; and I think it suggests just what Reid's intuition is in the long passage I have just quoted.

What we are trying to express in this second figure of speech is the feeling that such works as the *Iliad*, or the Sistine Ceiling, or the *St. Matthew Passion* are somehow putting us in contact with a mind of massive dimensions: an intellect far beyond our own, and magnificent in its workings and proportions. We are directly communicating with a mind far beyond our own and vicariously experiencing through its creation what the mind itself experienced.

But it is not, I think, as if we are being given "evidence," as it were, of a mind beyond our own, the way we might have indirect evidence of a mouse in the results of its gnawing, or indirect evidence of a virus through a liver function test. The *St. Matthew Passion* is not some kind of symptom of Bach's mental stature, an evidential trace from which we infer his greatness of mind. It *is*, in a manner of speaking, that greatness of mind on display: The work bears the direct imprint of the mind; the mind is immanent in the work. And in experiencing the work we are coming as close as it is possible for us to get to experiencing what Bach experienced. For awhile we are coming as close as we possibly can to *being* Bach. And *that*, let me suggest, is the intuition that *the* "expression theory" of art, in its mature versions, was trying to capture. Whether it is a valid intuition I leave an open question.

Now there *are* passages in Reid where he gives a far more pallid picture of the relationship between the artist's mind and the artist's work than I am giving here; passages where he says, in effect, nothing much more than that a beautiful or sublime work is a "sign" of the artist's talent for producing such works. And Gallie quite rightly observes that such a view holds out little if any hope for an expression theory of art. The way Gallie puts his worry, "as part of a formulation of an expression theory of art, this point would surely rate as a very minimal component, if indeed a genuine component at all. The banality of saying that a fine work of art makes manifest the talent of its producer is clear."[9]

It may well be that the difference between Gallie and me is that he is viewing Reid, to appropriate Reid's own phrase, "in clear and explicit terms, in the cool blood of a philosopher," while I am more like a wild-eyed enthusiast, pursuing in full cry, a perhaps imaginary prey. But I do think more can be said for Reid as an expression theorist than Gallie will allow: There is more room to maneuver.

Let me remind the reader of the vital distinction Reid makes between the beauty (or sublimity) of the thing expressed and the beauty (or sublimity) of the *manner in which it is expressed*. And remember too that it is the expressive properties of a work wherein its beauty and sublimity for the most part lie. Thus Homer makes the *Iliad* expressive of Achilles' anger, Patroklos' love, Hector's fear, by representations of their expressions of anger, love, and fear. But lots of poets can write about an angry Achilles, a loving Patroklos, a fearful Hector. It is the *manner* in which Homer represents the sublime passions of these sublime, larger than life figures that makes him *Homer*. And that he represents their passions *in a sublime manner* makes their passions and the work that much *more* sublime. "He conceived great characters, great actions, and great events, *in a manner suitable to their nature* ...," in a word, in the "grand manner." Furthermore, it is the *manner* in which Homer represents these grand passions, his grand manner, that is his *expression*. And what it expresses is the grandeur of his mind which, Reid argues, is the true repository of the *Iliad*'s grandeur. "The grandeur of his thoughts is reflected to our eye [our mind's eye, of course] by his work, and, therefore, it is justly called a grand work."

There is a word for the particular grand manner in which Homer expresses the grand passions of his characters that we all know: The *manner* is his *style*. What makes Homer the unique artist that he is, is his *style*, and his style resides for the most part in the *manner* in which he represents the passions of his characters, not in the passions themselves. But recognizing this, we can see that there is no need to think Reid's "expression theory" will collapse, as Gallie fears, into the banality of saying that what a work of art expresses is the talent of the artist. What Homer's *Iliad* expresses, and what it thereby puts us in contact and communion with, is the *uniquely* sublime mental states that are Homer's and Homer's alone. It does this through Homer's manner of representation: though his style. This is, in essence, what I think Reid was trying to say; and it is the very essence of the "expression theory" of art.

Do all the sublime artists then express the same thing: sublimity of mind? Not at all. Just as Homer represents the passions of his characters in the *Iliad* in a sublime manner that is uniquely his, so Shakespeare, in *King Lear*, represents the passions of his characters in a sublime manner that is uniquely *his*. *King Lear*, like the *Iliad*, puts us in contact with a sublime mind. But it is a very different kind of mind, and a very different kind of sublimity.

There is no need, I think, to carry out this argument point for point for the concept of beauty, or for the rest of the fine arts. There is no reason to believe that, in this respect as in others, Reid did not think beauty and sublimity susceptible of the same philosophical analysis, and the rest of the arts into the bargain. And that being the case, it seems high time now to make my summary, and make my conclusion.

VII

So, did Reid have a philosophy of art, and was it an "expression theory" of art?

Reid clearly satisfied the first criterion of a philosophy of art. He had a robust conception of the fine arts, much like our own, although somewhat different in detail and emphasis.

Second, Reid clearly had an elaborate account of what *he* considered to be the art-relevant properties of art works, namely, their *expressive* properties: which is to say, garden variety emotions such as anger, fear, love, joy, and the like, as perceived properties of *them*, not dispositions to arouse such emotions in us. Reid did, indeed, recognize other art-relevant properties; but the over-arching importance he placed on the expressive ones is notable, and may indicate both a reflection of the "age of sensibility" as well as an anticipation of the Romantic movement.

Finally, most importantly, and, to be sure, most controversially, I am strongly inclined to conclude that Reid did have a theory of art, broadly conceived, and that it was an "expression theory" of art, broadly conceived. Reid, as I have argued, thought of the relation of artist to work, work to audience, and audience to artist in roughly the same way that such classic expression theorists as Collingwood did. The artist expresses in works of art his beautiful or sublime states of mind in the artistic manner in which he represents the human passions and emotions in his works. The manner is his personal style, so the beautiful or sublime states are uniquely his. His audience, in contemplating his works, comes close to contemplating the beautiful and sublime states of his consciousness: comes close to "experiencing" them; and, at least, in a noncontroversial sense, becomes "aware" of them. I do not say that Reid's theory matches, point for point, *any* twentieth-century version of the "expression theory" of art. But I do say that if I were trying to decide in *which* class of art theories to put Reid's, it would be the class of expression theories, and no other. Only, however, if one additional condition is met. For an "expression theory" of art, as I stated early on, is not merely a theory that art sometimes expresses emotions, in the above sense; it is a theory that says expression in the above sense is a necessary and sufficient condition for arthood. It is, in other words, a real definition of art.

Does Reid offer such a definition? I think not: certainly not in letter. But he *is* trying to tell us *what art is* in some deep philosophical sense. Perhaps that is enough.

One further point. The "expression theory" of art is the theory that art is the expression of emotion (in the sense of expression stated above). But surely, it will be argued, what I have represented Reid as saying art expresses, namely, beautiful and sublime states of mind, are not emotions at all, at least in the ordinary sense.

That's right. But as I pointed out in my earlier article, "Thomas Reid and the Expression Theory of Art,"

the expression theory of art has never been guilty of using "emotion" in its ordinary sense either. If it did, it could never have gotten off the ground, since it is evident that not all of the things we want to call works of art express emotions in the ordinary sense of "emotion" (or in the ordinary sense of "express," for that matter).[10]

So, in effect, *had* Reid held the view that art is the expression of emotion, in the ordinary sense of "emotion," he would not be holding the "expression theory" of art in its classical version at all.

I think, then, that Reid did come to hold, in the last of the *Essays on the Intellectual Powers of Man*, a proto-version of the "expression theory" of art. Am I paying him a compliment or not? The answer, I suppose, is "Yes" and "No."

I think the "expression theory" of art is a deeply flawed theory. It seems hardly a compliment, then, to say that Reid was perhaps the first to embrace it.

On the other hand, the "expression theory" of art evolved in response to the felt need for a better theory of art than was then available. That Reid may have been well ahead of his time in sensing the need, and in framing a response to it, he deserves our praise and admiration. On that positive note I think it best to conclude.

NOTES

1. The "standard account" is found in Kristeller 1992.
2. Ibid.
3. Kivy 1978.
4. Gallie 1998.
5. Reid's *Lectures on the Fine Arts* exists in a manuscript of 1774, not in his own hand.
6. There is one vagrant passage in EIP VI.v: 484 to the effect that music arouses the garden variety emotions. But I am inclined to see this as a vestige of the older theory rather than a functional part of the new one.
7. Gallie 1998: 178.
8. Gallie 1998: 165–74.
9. Gallie 1998: 179.
10. Kivy 1978: 180.

12 Reid's Philosophy of Religion

I. INTRODUCTION

Thomas Reid was a Christian philosopher. He never wavered from his theism or Christian belief, and a temperate, sincere faith pervades his writing and his biography. Apparently orthodox in belief,[1] he wasn't given to theological and ecclesiastical controversies, but he did have a life-long interest in what we now call philosophy of religion issues. From 1751 to 1780 Reid's lectures included the subject of natural theology, or what can be known about God apart from revelation. Reid's notes for these lectures are almost entirely lost, but several student transcriptions from his lectures at Glasgow University (1763–1780) survive.[2]

Reid is a unique anti-medieval early modern theist, perhaps the last great Newtonian theist. An admirer of Samuel Clarke and Joseph Butler, he combines the rationalistic apologetics of the early eighteenth century with an antispeculative bent and a keen eye for human psychology. He doesn't hesitate to employ the tools of philosophy in matters of religion. We shouldn't, he says, be led by "zeal for religion" to defame reason in a rush to exalt revelation (EAP IV.xi: 636a). In this way Calvinism and Bayle, he saw, paved the way for Hume and other critics of religion.[3] Although he continually emphasizes the limits of human understanding, Reid insists that "Revelation was not intended to supersede, but to aid the use of our natural faculties" (EAP V.ii: 641b).

Reid's lectures follow an ancient pattern, treating the existence, attributes, and works of God.[4] Shortly we'll explore some of the more interesting contents of Reid's lectures: arguments for theism (section II), God and epistemology (III), our knowledge of divine attributes

(IV), and the problem of evil (V). One comes to these lectures hoping to see Reid wrestle with Hume's carefully crafted attack on religious theism in his *Dialogues Concerning Natural Religion*. One searches in vain for a reference to this in Reid's published works, though it gets a brief mention in his lectures. It seems Reid dismissed it as old news, a mere rerun of Hobbes' and Bolingbroke's watery theism, that there is a creator of the world but that "we know nothing of his moral attributes or the principles of his actions" (1780: 158; LNT: 95). We can guess that Reid acknowledged the subtlety and philosophical depth of the work (as he did with Hume's other philosophical productions), but he apparently considered it too off-track, too wrong-headed to demand his full attention.[5] Happily, he does wrestle at length with Section XI of Hume's *An Enquiry Concerning Human Understanding*. Reid ignores the celebrated section X "Of Miracles" in his natural religion lectures,[6] but replies to some of what Hume says about miracles in his logic lectures.[7]

Why didn't Reid work this lecture material into a book on natural theology? I suggest four reasons.[8] First, as we'll see, much of this material found its way into Reid's two final books, *Essays on the Intellectual Powers of Man* and *Essays on the Active Powers of Man*. Second, Reid knew he didn't have a critical mass of original, careful philosophical material here.[9] Third, in Reid's eyes, the real danger to theism is from bad epistemology (IHM Dedication: 3–4); once one gets one's theory of knowledge and evidence right, there is no remaining threat to religious belief or natural religion. Hence, Reid put his labor into a big second book on epistemology, *Essays on the Intellectual Powers of Man*. Fourth, Reid worked in an atmosphere of complacent theism.[10] The deist controversy was well behind, and miscellaneous "free thinkers" posed little threat. One has to remember that for thoughtful people natural teleology was a huge barrier to atheism before the general acceptance of Darwin's theory of evolution. Even Hume, patron saint of many a latter-day atheist, declined to espouse atheism, and apparently had beliefs incompatible with it.[11] In this atmosphere, there was no pressing need for an unassailable argument for God's existence, or a carefully wrought free will defense, or the like. Materialism (in the form of materialist philosophies of mind) and skepticism *were* living threats for Reid,[12] but not atheism *per se*. But aside from atheism, there remained a universe of false and unduly speculative claims about the divine, and Reid

was concerned to address these and outline a right-headed natural
theology for his students.

II. ARGUMENTS FOR THE EXISTENCE OF GOD

Before lecturing on theism, Reid gives a twofold diagnosis of "speculative" atheism. Looking to the ancient world for examples of this,
he posits two causes. The first is "false systems of philosophy by
which they thought to account for the formation of the World and
what happens in it without once bringing in a wise and intelligent
maker" (1780: 20; LNT: 3).[13] In Reid's view, these groundless and
pseudoexplanatory hypotheses are cast out by careful attention to
nature, yielding discovery of the manifold marks of design (more on
this shortly). Second, "It was intended ... to free mens minds from
the fear of punishment for their crimes in an after state To free them
from alll reflections on the future or remorse for the past" (1780:
21; LNT: 3).[14] Reid declares this misguided. From atheism, it doesn't
follow that there is no life after death, nor that our fate there doesn't
depend on the lives we lead here. To the contrary, he argues that
dualism is reasonable, and that by analogy with other forms of life,
there is good reason to think that we'll survive death with our character intact.[15] Further, atheism is not conducive to peace of mind,
while theism is.[16]

In his lectures, Reid mentions several lines of argument to God's
existence: (1) a cosmological argument, (2) a design argument, (3)
an argument from the nearly unanimous consent of humans every-
where through the ages, (4) an argument from empirical evidence that
the world is not eternal, and (5) an argument from miracles.[17] Concerning these five Reid pronounces (in a Clarkean tone), "All which
being put together amount to an Absolute certainty and Demonstration that there is a first Cause possessed of all possible perfections,
who must have Existed from all Eternity" (1766: 76).[18] Reid fully
presents only the first two arguments in his natural religion lectures,
spending more energy on the second.

In Reid's eyes, Clarke's cosmological argument is a triumph. It
shows that some one thing "must have existed from all Eternity un-
caused and uncreated" (1775: lect. 57). His argument for this conclusion, mostly a condensation of Clarke's *Demonstration*,[19] is something like the following (in his lectures this is frequently compressed

or scattered in discussions of various divine attributes). The universe either began to exist at some past point, or it has always existed. If it began to exist, then there must have been at least one cause of the universe, as it is a first principle and a necessary truth that what begins to exist has a cause. If the universe had an infinite past, there would be an infinite chain of causes and effects. Though on this supposition the universe never began to exist, there must be an explanation for the fact of its existence, as it is also a first principle that there is a cause or an explanation for the existence of any thing.[20] The supposition of an infinite past chain of causes with no cause of the whole chain is thus impossible. The explanation for this infinitely old universe must be in terms of some other thing, for both the parts and the whole of the universe seem to be metaphysically dependent and non-self-explaining. There must be at least one cause of it, then, which is metaphysically independent.

Reid castigates Hume for calling into question the epistemic status of the first principle,[21] which Reid argues has always been believed, is necessary to common life and the legal system, is as certain as a mathematical axiom, and is believed in common life even by Hume. Hume's theory of knowledge implies that this principle is not self-evident, but so much the worse for his theory.[22]

Whatever is independent must be necessary as well. Every being is either necessary or contingent, and whatever is contingent depends on the will of some other being. An independent being "derives his power and his existence from no other being" (1780: 113; LNT: 66); therefore, an independent being must be necessary as well.

Thus far the argument purports to prove that there's at least one independent and necessary being that is the cause of the cosmos. We can also argue that there is only one such being, both a posteriori and a priori. Observing our law-governed universe, we find the same laws operative at every place and time we know of, and this confirms monotheism over polytheism, which posits many deities each with her own domain of influence and the potential to clash.[23] All too briefly, Reid tries to show a priori the impossibility of more than one independent and necessary being from two angles. First, "When once it's Discovered that the Deity is a necessary, and Self existant being, it's impossible to set bounds to any of his perfections." We must ascribe to him "Every Attribute which can make a Being the Object of our adoration and esteem" (1766: 78).[24] One of these is uniqueness or unity; therefore, there can only be one God.[25] Second, two beings which were omnipresent, eternal, and in possession of all perfections could not differ in any way. But by the principle of the identity of indiscernibles, any numerically distinct individuals must differ in some respect.[26] Therefore, there could not be more than one such being.[27]

The cosmological argument produces one more significant conclusion. "The same light of reason that convinces us that there can be no existence without a cause, convinces us that every cause cannot produce every effect" (1780: 34; LNT: 13). To produce this sort of world, the first cause must have certain features itself. "Every real excellence in the effect is to be found in the cause" (1780: 142; LNT: 84).[28] The upshot is this: Given that the cosmos contains creatures with life, power, intelligence, and moral virtue, the first cause must have those features as well.[29]

One wonders why the Clarkean cosmological argument, which plays such a crucial role in his natural religion lectures, makes no appearance in the *Intellectual Powers* or the *Active Powers*.[30] One hypothesis would be that after he stopped lecturing, a reading of Hume's *Dialogues* section IX persuaded him that the argument had some defect or at least raised serious doubts in Reid's mind about it. Three considerations rule this out. First, some of Hume's objections there depend on controversial epistemological claims that Reid rejects.[31] Second, as recent research has shown, Hume's chapter lands few (if any) blows against a Clarkean cosmological argument; rather, it shows that Hume had no clear grasp of it.[32] Third, in a late letter (dateable to between the summer of 1789 and some time in 1792) Reid gives a compressed version of the core of the Clarkean argument.[33] The answer to our puzzle is simply this: Had Reid's main aims in his books included arguing for divine eternality, independence, necessity, perfection, or uniqueness, he would have included the extended cosmological argument. Those claims simply weren't at issue there.

Reid belongs to the still living tradition which supplements a cosmological argument with a teleological argument.[34] His final statement of the latter is as follows:

1. Design and intelligence in the cause, may, with certainty, be inferred from marks or signs of it in the effect.

2. There are in fact the clearest marks of design and wisdom in the works of nature.
3. The works of nature are the effects of a wise and intelligent Cause.[35]

The truth of 2, he thinks, is apparent to any unprejudiced and careful observer of nature. "As to final Causes, they stare us in the face wherever we cast our Eyes" (C: 143). In his lectures Reid goes through numerous examples of natural teleology, emphasizing what is useful to humankind, in something like this sequence: stars, solar system, gross features of the earth, plant life, animal bodies, animal instincts, human bodies, and the human mind.[36] The most interesting and original of these observations are the final ones, where Reid displays his skill at observing the human faculties, instincts, natural affections, developmental stages, and tendencies, which make individual and corporate human life as we know it possible.[37] The advance of science, he says, only strengthens the design argument, as it uncovers more examples of apparent design.[38] Reid defends 1 as a first principle, something which we know, but not by reasoning or experience, and claims that it is a necessary truth.[39]

Initially, there are two ways to understand his first premise.[40]

1a. Necessarily, if anything exhibits marks of design, then it was caused to exist by at least one intelligent agent.
1b. Necessarily, if anything exhibits marks of design, we can infer with a high degree of certainty that it was caused to exist by at least one intelligent agent.

Several factors suggest 1a. 1 occurs in Reid's list of the first principles which are necessary truths in the realm of metaphysics, not about principles of evidence or inference. A necessary truth is one whose contrary is impossible;[41] thus 1a says that it is absolutely impossible that something not designed exhibit marks of design. If this is his claim, we must know what he means by "marks of design." He seems to think of these as regularity and variety of structure, and fitness of structure to some end.[42] With Cicero, he agrees that some degree of regularity can come from an unintelligent cause, but claims it is obviously absurd to assert that a complex thing like a sentence or four hundred aces thrown on a die in a row came about by chance.[43] On the present reading, this is absurd because the thing is impossible: "An effect produced without design can never manifest design" (1769: 64). 1 can't be known by experience, Reid says, in part because experience can never reveal a necessary connection, here between a property in the object and a property in its maker (*not* between the fact of apparent design and the appropriateness of an inference to a designer).[44] Again, this reading of 1 seems to sit well with the causal excellence principle, which is presented as a necessary truth about causal relations. Finally, on this reading, the argument is valid and purports to prove God's existence.

Charity urges a way around this reading, however, for 1a is false. Some examples of apparent design do come from unintelligent causes; pebbles on some beaches are nicely arranged according to size, yet the arranger was merely the waves. And though it has never happened, surely it is possible that an avalanche occurs and the rocks fall to perfectly spell out "Eat at Joes!" Fortunately for Reid, other passages militate against the interpretation of 1 as 1a. For one thing, Reid phrases 1 as a necessarily true rule of inference, not a description of what must be, a metaphysical principle.[45] For another thing, some of Reid's remarks in his lectures seem inconsistent with 1a.

If a scratch be made upon the sand, it is infinite to one, if it be a circle, or a parabola, an undesigning cause could never have rounded much less have properly placed a single wheel in a machine But if the parabola or a wheel ... properly placed be presented to us it immediately shaeks our belief to hear that either of them proceeded from undesigning chance. We may therefore with certainty conclude that the world which evidences so much wisdom and design must have been formed by a designing cause. (1769: 64–5)

By saying the odds are infinite to one against the marks of design having arisen without an intelligent cause, Reid seems to say that this scenario is not impossible but only overwhelmingly unlikely.[46] There is also Reid's repeated claim that

there is as much reason to believe that there is a supreme being, as that there are minds besides our own. From the actions of a human being conducted with wisdom and design we conclude that this being has an intelligent mind, and this is all the evidence we have of it. . . . even in the formation of a human body, there is much more design displayed than in any human action In both cases we see not the cause, but trace it out by the effects. (1769: 65)[47]

It is not, we may suppose, a contradiction that our fellow humans act as they do and are nonetheless automata; all the same, we have extremely strong grounds for our belief that they are conscious, intelligent beings like ourselves. The evidence is conclusive without implying the conclusion – similarly with marks of design and the designer hypothesis. In what sense is the evidence in the two cases (God and other minds) supposed to be "the same"? Is it the kind or the amount that is at issue? The main point is that there is the same kind of evidence for each, so that it is arbitrary to recognize it in one and not the other. As to amount, we have either more or the same amount of evidence for God's existence as we have for the existence of other minds![48] Thus,

the man who maintains, that there is no force in the argument from final causes, must, if he will be consistent, see no evidence of the existence of any intelligent being but himself. (EIP VI.vi: 512)

Against this second reading of the argument is the fact that the argument (1b, 2, 3) would be invalid. But this is easily remedied, if we revise 3 to 3a by adding the preface, "We may believe that...." This remedy, however, comes with a price; on this reading, the argument is not for God's existence, but for that rationality of belief in God's existence. Interesting though this argument may be, it doesn't seem to represent what Reid is up to. He means to be exploring the grounds for believing and knowing that God exists, not the grounds for believing and knowing that our belief in God is rational.

Thus far we haven't found a satisfying reading of Reid's design argument. I suggest there is a third reading. If 3 (not 3a) is really what is at issue, then perhaps the argument shouldn't really be read as a valid deductive argument, but rather probabilistically, so that the premises support without implying the conclusion. The occurrence of "certainty" in 1 should perhaps be read in light of Reid's belief that "many things are certain for which we have only that kind of evidence which Philosophers call probable" (EIP VII.iii: 562). Perhaps what he wants to say is that

1c. Necessarily, if anything exhibits marks of design, then it is overwhelmingly probable that it was caused to exist by at least one intelligent agent.

Perhaps this is what Reid is getting at; this would be what makes 1b true. Combined with 2, he would have an argument that gives strong support to 3. As Reid is a fallibilist, he can say that in this way we *know* 3 and are entitled to be certain about 3.

Several things can be said in favor of reading 1 as 1c. First, 1c is a plausible candidate for being a first principle, as it deals with things,[49] not inferences or beliefs about them, and it arguably has all of Reid's marks of a first principle.[50] Second, the argument on this reading (1c, 2, 3) seems to properly mirror the natural belief-formation that Reid has in mind. One confusing thing about this discussion is that Reid is blending psychology and argument. He is manifestly giving an argument reflective folk can use to argue for the claim that God exists. But he is also describing a process of belief-formation that occurs in most people, whether or not they ever get into the game of offering philosophical arguments. That process is: We carefully observe the intricate and wonderful web of apparent design in nature, and this triggers an overwhelmingly strong propensity to believe that this is the product of intelligence. Hence we find ourselves with a firm belief in 3. The strength of the propensity is matched with the strong objective likelihood of at least one designing cause's involvement. Just as one can form false beliefs via this belief-forming process, so the premises of the argument don't imply the conclusion. Both the tendency to believe and the proposition 1c couldn't not be, so to speak; both are "necessary," though in different senses. The first is unavoidable given our nature, and the second is true with metaphysical necessity. Third, this reading, though it clashes with his syllogism terminology, fits his discussion quite well, namely: The passages cited above in my rejection of 1a, his quotations from Cicero and Tillotson, and his declining to follow other philosophers in mounting an argument for the first principle.[51] What he says in this last passage is revealing. What is it that those authors try to argue for that Reid thinks need not be argued for? It is "how improbable it is that a regular arrangement of parts should be the effect of chance, or that it should not be the effect of design" (EIP VI.vi: 507). Gone is the talk of inference, and in its stead we have a proposition equivalent to 1c. I suggest that the phrase "may, with certainty, be inferred" is used by Reid to soften the connection between actual and apparent design. He means to say something weaker than 1a, and misleadingly suggests 1b, though what he's really interested in is the objective unlikelihood of apparent without actual design, as in 1c. While this reading has its own problems,[52] I offer it as a reading of what Reid is up to, and a thesis worthy of further discussion. It may well be that Reid was simply not clear about what he wanted his design argument to be, so there may be no unambiguous interpretation which captures what Reid really thought. Even if that is so, we can consider whether the preceding is what he should have said given his commitments, aims, and intuitions.

On this reading, does Reid tragically offer a design argument which has already been refuted by Hume? Though the matter deserves a full discussion, on the face of it, it seems that Hume does no damage, for the argument is neither an inductive generalization, nor based on an analogy between objects, nor supposed to stand all by itself.[53] The point that Elliot Sober makes about William Paley's design argument applies equally well to Reid's.[54] Rather than comparing things (artifacts and natural things, or artifacts and the whole world), Reid is comparing inferences or belief-acquisitions. It is not to the point to play up the overall dissimilarity of natural things and artifacts, for the argument's strength doesn't depend on that, but only on the inferences or belief-acquisitions involved having similar grounds.

If therefore from seeing a curious engine we conceive that it had a wise and skillfull Maker, must we not in a much higher degree apply these qualities to [the] contriver and maker of the curious fabric of the human body. (1780: 75–6; LNT: 41)[55]

Just as we form the belief upon seeing a watch that it was designed, or upon observing a course of action that it results from the decisions of a conscious agent like ourselves, or upon observing certain actions we form the belief that there is an actor carrying them out who is brave, so when we carefully observe the sky, the earth, the animal and plant kingdoms, and the human body and mind, we form the belief that these are the product of at least one exceptionally wise and good agent. Reid views both inferences or belief-acquisitions as issuing from a single built-in tendency. Had he gone on to argue that apparent design is probable given theism but improbable given atheism, then he would have had an inference to the best explanation argument for theism. While he veers near this approach in his lectures by considering theism in relation to competing theories,[56] in the end he rests content with his claim 1c. It is a first principle, something we all naturally believe and know, unless love for some cherished hypothesis causes us to lose or never form the belief.[57]

It seems that if Hume refutes this design argument, it is only by putting forth a superior account of what things we are entitled to remain certain about even though we can't argue for them.

III. GOD AND EPISTEMOLOGY

Contemporary readers wonder: Is Reid a proto-Reformed-Epistemologist? One has to answer that question negatively, with an important qualification. On this Reid agrees with Reformed Epistemology: More people than can understand various tricky metaphysical arguments can know that a good and intelligent designer of the world exists. This is by way of the quick and natural reasoning process mirrored by the design argument. But on other things, he disagrees. First, by the amount of time he spends on two arguments for God's existence, it is evident that he doesn't hold, as at least some radical forebears of Reformed Epistemology did, that such arguments are useless, wrong-headed, or morally objectionable. Thus he has no sympathy for what Plantinga calls the Reformed objection to natural theology.[58] Second, while it can be known by all without benefit of any lengthy reasoning process that a good and intelligent designer of the world exists, this belief is not, as Plantinga says, "properly basic," because for Reid it is not basic, but believed on the basis of other beliefs (in 1c and 2 of Section II above). Third, Reid doesn't posit a *sensus divinitatis* – a natural faculty of forming true beliefs about God in various circumstances – though his faculty approach to epistemology and rejection of what Plantinga calls classical foundationalism have provided considerable inspiration to those who do.[59] We don't need any such extra faculty, for we already have an inbuilt tendency to detect intelligence behind apparent design; the tendency that (upon carefully noticing the intricate apparent design in the natural world) yields belief in God is the same one that (upon certain social experiences) yields belief in other conscious humans.[60] Fourth, even if belief in God were basic for Reid, that belief lacks most of Reid's marks of a first principle. It isn't necessary to everyday life, doesn't appear too early to come from education or reasoning, isn't as universally believed as most of his first principles, and can't be argued for by showing that denying it leads to practical absurdities.[61] I take it that for Reid, what is not a first principle is not properly basic.

There is another strategy that Reid mentions for arguing that
something is a first principle – a kind of parity argument. A Reformed Epistemologist in search of an ally could quote Reid back at
him, "It is a good argument *ad hominem*, if it can be shewn, that
a first principle which a man rejects, stands upon the same footing
with others which he admits" (EIP VI.iv: 463). And, turning to his
account of our knowledge of other minds, "The very same argument
applied to the works of nature, leads us to conclude, that there is an
intelligent Author of nature, and appears equally strong and obvious
in the last case as in the first" (EIP VI.v: 483). How can Reid deny
that the theistic proposition is a first principle, if it is supported by
the same kind of argument, and issues from the same innate belief-
forming tendency in us as belief in other minds?

Reid can reply that no matter how certain, firmly held, or well-
grounded the theistic belief is once formed (and perhaps reinforced
by habit, further experience, and argument) it is not "automatic"
enough to be a first principle. Belief in other minds is forced on us
very early in our lives by our social experiences, and we can't shake
it thereafter (short of insanity). By contrast, belief in God isn't automatically formed; it isn't inevitable given the normal course of
human life. We have deliberately to pay attention to the structure of
the natural world for the God/other minds belief-forming tendency
to be triggered. Moreover, these triggering experiences can be perma-
nently avoided or short-circuited by adherence to hypotheses inconsistent with theism. And as we know, theistic belief is loseable. So
far, Reid has principled reasons for resisting any claim that the existence of a good and intelligent maker of the world is a first principle
or a properly basic belief.

A serious difficulty remains.[62] Isn't testimony a source of properly basic belief, and thus immediate knowlege, perhaps even the
source of the majority of what we know?[63] A number of witnesses
tell us throughout our lives that God exists, so can't we know that
he exists by accepting their testimony? If so, belief in God will be
properly basic after all. As we've seen, Reid casts a friendly glance at
an argument for God's existence based on miracles, so apparently he
wouldn't take a Humean stance on religious testimony.[64] Further, in
his logic lectures, he asserts that solid testimony can give us knowledge that a miracle happened, a deviation in the normal course of
nature wrought by the hand of God.[65] If testimony tells me that God

did X, doesn't it thereby tell me that God exists? Reid's interest in our natural propensities to tell the truth and to believe what others say is largely psychological and developmental; for this reason his theory of knowledge is underdeveloped on a crucial point: What is the scope of what we can know through testimony? Still, he does claim that testimony is a distinct source of knowledge. If Reid can find no principled grounds for discounting the mass of testimony concerning God's existence, then his epistemology of testimony clashes with his religious epistemology as interpreted in this section and the preceding one.

IV. DIVINE ATTRIBUTES

There are three ways we can determine the divine attributes: (1) reasoning from the marks of certain attributes in the cosmos, (2) recognizing what attributes are implied by God's necessary existence, and (3) reasoning from God's unlimited perfections.[66] The Clarkean cosmological argument establishes that there is a necessary and unlimited being, legitimating the second and third ways.

Reid divides God's attributes into the natural and moral. The former are eternity (everlastingness, not timelessness), necessity, independence, immensity (omnipresence), unlimited power, unlimited perfection, perfect knowledge and wisdom, spirituality, unity (uniqueness), and immutable happiness. The latter are goodness, mercy, forbearance, veracity, love of virtue, hatred of vice, justice, and freedom.[67] One can argue for each of these divine attributes from either reason alone or revelation.[68]

Commentators note that in Hume's *Dialogues* a common sort of theist is conspicuous by her absence: one who neither puts all of her eggs in the basket of the design argument nor "is so skeptically pious that she ascribes no properties to God."[69] As we've seen, Reid is such a theist. When it comes to knowing the divine attributes, Reid complains that Hume in *Enquiry* XI arbitrarily limits us to the first method of determining divine attributes. Hume claims, in Reid's paraphrase, that

... we have no reason to [attribute to] the Supreme Being wisdom, power, or inteligence, in a higher degree than what we see Manifested ... in his works; a conclusion evidently grounded on this, that a cause is exactly proportioned to its effect. as therefore these marks of wisdom and [etc.] are limited, so we must conclude that this cause, that is, the perfections of the Deity are limited. (1780: 151–2; LNT: 91)[70]

Reid makes two replies. First, contrary to Hume's restriction, we can prove many divine perfections "reasoning from the Necessary Existence of Deity and his unlimited perfections" (1780: 153; LNT: 93). Second, Hume's proportionality principle

... may perhaps be true of natural causes, but as to intelligent causes which operate freely and voluntary, this maxim is not founded on reason.... Suppose I should ask a man, on a journey, pray which is the road to Edinburgh? And ... he returns me a pertinent answer.... Am I therefore to conclude that his understanding just enabld him to answer my question and neither more nor less? surely this would be absurd – the natural conclusion is, that he has such a degree, how much more I do not know.... this maxim of Mr. Humes, when applied to voluntary causes is neither selfevident nor consistent with our reasoning about causes in common Life. (1780: 153–4; LNT: 92–3)[71]

Reid attributes another objection regarding knowledge of divine attributes to Hobbes, Bolingbroke, and Hume in his *Dialogues*. These philosophers admit

that there must be a first cause posessed of power, wisdom, and the other natural attributes we have ascribed to him, but maintained that we know nothing of his moral attributes or the principles of his action; when we talk of his goodness, Mercy, or justice, we use, says he,[72] words without meaning. (1780: 158; LNT: 95)[73]

Reid replies that "We ... have the same reason to ascribe justice and goodness to the Deity as power and inteligence nor is there the least ground to think his moral ... attributes More incomprehensible than his natural attributes" (1780: 158–9; LNT: 95). Further, moral truths are necessary, so it make no sense to suppose that God "thinks morally ill what we think morally good and the contrary" (1780: 159; LNT: 97). God's moral knowledge exceeds but includes ours.

V. EVIL

Reid is interested in evil as a source of objections against "a good government of the World," and as an invitation to speculative mischief, in the form of baseless schemes designed to explain its presence.[74]

Good but vain or overzealous people concoct bad theodicies, and bad people use evil as an excuse for atheism.[75] The chief failed theodicies in view are Leibniz's and the "Manichean" scheme explored by Bayle.[76] "The Manichean System ... supposes that there are 2 eternal intelligent powerful beings so that the one can not prevent the actions of the other and the one good the other the author of all the evils in the world" (1768: 90). Bayle argues that traditional believers cannot refute this rival hypothesis, which is part of his larger case that reason can't dispel important objections to religious belief.[77] Reid has little patience for Bayle's fideism, alleging that Bayle "advances this System rather to show his talents, than from any conviction" (1768: 91). Moreover, this system can be disproved. If one of the two ultimate principles were more powerful, he'd banish the other from any influence in the world. And if they were equally powerful and had

contrary wills they would perfectly ballance one another, and could produce nothing. The Phenomena of nature do not support this hypothesis, for there is evidently more good than evil, Besides there is no occasion to have recourse to two principles, because we can account for evil more Phylosophically and more simply from one.... (1769: 97)

In Reid's view, theism accounts for evil better that her rivals, and no sort of evil provides significant evidence against the world being ruled by a good God.

Reid distinguishes three kinds of evil: evils of imperfection, natural evil, and moral evil.[78] "Evils" of imperfection are not really evils, but merely the lack of some good (e.g., humans being limited in knowledge and power). "Imperfection must cleave to every order of created beings tho' the Oyster were as high as the Seraph" (1769: 92). No matter how perfect the creation, there would still be an infinite distance between God and creatures. Reid assumes that God has no duty to refrain from creating, and further, that creation implies some lack of goodness in the product. Thus in all possible universes creatures can complain about their limits – "even the Worm, may thus put in it's claim for greater perfection" (1766: 87)[79] – but these seem to be unjustified complaints about something which is unavoidable, if there is to be any creation.

Reid makes four points about natural evils. First, given the present constitution of humans and their environment, natural evils are necessary for us to develop virtues such as prudence, wisdom, patience, and fortitude. Some of this suffering, then, serves a purpose, as it is the discipline of a loving Father. We can't tell whether it is metaphysically possible for there to be creatures who develop these virtues without suffering.[80] Second, with some exaggeration, Reid comments:

We ought to consider how far natural evil may be a punishment of moral evil ... Many of the most grevious natural evils are the consequences of Vices, and indeed if all vice were removed there would be little pain at all, and this earth would be a paradise. Almost all the evils we are liable to are consequences either of our own folly or of some other persons. (1769: 93–4)[81]

Third, "... as far as we perceive they [natural evils] are necessary consequences of good general laws," and "without these they [rational creatures] could never pursue any means to the attainment of an end" (1780: 168; LNT: 102).[82] Further, these laws "are infinitely more useful, than the Evils are hurtful which flow from them" (1766: 87).[83] If philosophers claim there could be laws which bring along fewer natural evils, "this is swimming beyond our Depth" (1766: 87). Fourth, while in "the present Establishment ... Happiness is far more prevalent than misery" (1766: 88), "we cannot determine what proportion this evil bears to the sum of the enjoyment of God's creatures. We see a small part and can't judge of the whole of the Universe" (1780: 168; LNT: 102). "We are better judges of evil as it respects individuals than as it respects the whole universe" (1769: 93).

Like many theists, Reid believes that human free will is the key to defusing arguments from evil. If there is no free will, "then every event good or bad is to be considered as Gods doing...." But if we do have free will, "then the actions done in consequence of this [exercise of our power] are Mens only and not Gods. There is no maxim more evident than that ... the action of one agent cannot be the action of another" (1780: 169; LNT: 102).[84] God "gave the power, but they [injurious actions] proceed from an abuse of that power. All moral evil then is not properly the doing of God but of men" (1780: 170; LNT: 103).[85]

This strategy of Reid's immediately raises three issues. First, even if God isn't the agent of sin, the evildoer, might he not be morally responsible for making that sin possible, by giving individuals power which he knew they would misuse? Second, isn't it false that no event can be the action of two agents, for example, the destruction of a plane by a squad of four terrorists? Third, why didn't God just arrange the circumstances so that even though all humans have free will, they only use it for good?

While Reid explicitly answers only the first question, he has philosophical resources to answer, or attempt to answer the remaining two. To the first, Reid makes the insightful reply that knowledge of the future is providentially useless. What will be, will be, and it is contradictory to suppose that God sees something will be, and based on that knowledge prevents it.[86] Middle knowledge *would* be providentially useful, but Reid, because of his theory of human freedom, denies that there is such a thing.[87] Still, on any theist's views, God would know or reasonably believe this prior to creating: *Probably, were I to create a world of such and such kind, someone or other would abuse my gift of liberty*. Thus the difficulty remains.

To the second, Reid can say the following: An action is an event which has its ultimate origin in some one agent, the agent which exercised her active power to produce that event, or to start a chain that leads inexorably to it (he may require that the agent will or intend the event as well). Thus willing to shoot a man, grabbing the gun, pulling the trigger, and firing the gun at him are all actions. If these events have their ultimate origin in some one agent, they can't *also* have it in some other agent. Unfortunately for Reid, one can be praiseworthy and blameworthy for more that one's own actions in the present sense. I can be to some degree responsible for *your* freely committed crimes if I aid or motivate you in certain ways, or even if I'm culpably negligent in your upbringing. The sense of "action" Reid is interested in, whereby it is impossible for the action to belong to more than one agent, is not the only morally relevant kind of event. It is not necessary for an agent to be blameworthy for an event that it originate by an exercise of her active power, or that she intend or will the event to occur. Reid's "God didn't do it" strategy fails to contribute to a workable defense or theodicy. Even if God didn't commit the sins, it is conceivable that he is blameworthy for others committing them.

To the third objection Reid should but doesn't say that it is contradictory to suppose that God guarantees that everyone always freely does what is right, because it is contradictory to suppose that anyone can force or cause an exercise of active power to happen.[88] While it is logically possible that everyone freely does what is right, it is not possible that even an omnipotent being singlehandedly makes this happen. In sum, Reid has at best some materials for a free will defense, but not a theodicy. Not surprisingly, he consistently expresses pessimism about the prospects for a theodicy.[89]

VI. CONCLUSION

A famous Reid scholar once remarked to me that when it came to philosophy of religion, he thought Reid "never really put his head to it." This is half true. Reid did think seriously about these things over a long period of time, but as his main research interests lay elsewhere, he often only pushed his discussions as far as they needed to go for the benefit of his students. Reid's lectures on natural theology had a pastoral purpose, as is not suprising coming from an older pious man who was a father and former minister. He normally ended his natural theology lectures by expounding on the many practical benefits of theism and the unfortunate effects of atheism.[90] Reid was convinced that this information would improve his students' lives and society as a whole. Fully developed or not, Reid's philosophy of religion consistently clashes with our current fashions in philosophy. Because of this, we can use Reid's philosophy of religion as an occasion to examine what we take as obvious and beyond dispute.[91]

NOTES

1. "Orthodox," that is, in a broad sense. He was quite out of step with the Calvinism of eighteenth-century Scotland. (See C: 38, 40, 97.)
2. I use the following abbreviations for the student transcriptions, citing original page numbers except where noted.

   1780: Baird, George. "Notes from the Lectures of Dr. Thomas Reid," MS A104929, 8 vol., Mitchell Library, Glasgow. I have used my own transcriptions of this, but I also give the page numbers for the Duncan 1981 edition using the abbreviation LNT. At lecture number 86 (LNT: 123f) the pagination restarts with a change of volume. Quotations made by the permission of Enda Ryan, Senior Librarian of Archives and Special Collections, Mitchell Library.

   1775: Jack, Robert. "Dr. Reid's Lectures," MS Gen 117, Glasgow University Library. As this manuscript is not paginated, I cite it by lecture number. Quotations made by permission of the Special Collections Department, Glasgow University Library.

   1769: Anonymous. "Notes of Thomas Reid's lectures on pneumatology, 1769," MS Gen 760, Glasgow University Library. Quotations made by permission of the Special Collections Department, Glasgow University Library.

1768: Anonymous. "Dr. Reid's Lectures," New College Library, University of Edinburgh. Quotations made by permission of the New College Library, University of Edinburgh.

1766: Anonymous. "Reid's Essays" [Student notes on pneumatology, natural theology, moral and political philosophy] 1766–1767, Aberdeen University Library MS 2131/8/VII. Quotations made by permission of Dr. Iain Beavan, Senior Curator, Special Libraries and Archives, Historic Collections, Aberdeen University.

Some of these were jotted down (at times in shorthand) as Reid slowly read his lectures. Others were re-expanded from shorthand versions some time after being written. As a reminder of the low quality of this material compared to Reid's published writings and manuscripts in his own hand, I have not corrected spelling or punctuation, though I have silently expanded common abbreviations, replaced certain eighteenth-century conventions (such as using "M^r" for "Mr."), and occasionally inserted a word in brackets for clarity.

3. Stewart 2003b, section 2; EAP IV.xi: 636a; Popkin 1965: xxii–xxxii; Bayle 1965, Clarifications I–III: 395–435.

4. Reid says he has taken this idea from Francis Hutcheson's *Synopsis Metphysicae* (1744), which he recommends to his students. (1780: 19; LNT: 2; 1775 lect. 55; 1769: 49; 1766: 60–1.) This sort of sequence goes back to the Stoics. (See Cicero 1998, II: 47–8.)

5. Judging by the delayed response to Hume's *Dialogues*, it would seem that many of Reid's contemporaries were similarly underwhelmed. According to M.A. Stewart, the first substantial common sense response to Hume's *Dialogues* is by Dugald Stewart in 1828. (See Stewart 2003b n.43; Stewart 1828, III.ii.)

6. Reid probably thought his fellow Aberdeen Philosophical Society members George Campbell and Alexander Gerard had adequately refuted those arguments. See Campbell 1983; Gerard 1766; Broadie 2002b, section 5; McCosh 1875, Chaps. 25 and 30; Stewart 2003b.

7. These student notes are partially transcribed in Stewart 2003a and Michael and Michael 1987: 520–6.

8. For other such speculations, see Duncan's comments in LNT: xx–xxiii.

9. See Stewart 1803: 10.

10. The difference between his intellectual climate and ours can be seen in his addressing a concern we wouldn't think worth mentioning:

> Some have dowbted if ever any one was sincerly an Atheist, but this is an idle doubt, for there is no doctrine that may not be disbelieved. One would, indeed, imagine that to a thinking man, there must appear ... much design in the universe, that all the objections to it cannot even make it dowbtfule, but passion

and prejudices may lead a man not only to doubt of this, but even to believe transubstantiation (1769: 49–50)

11. Gaskin 1988: 6–7, 217–23; Gaskin 1993: 319–22; Popkin 1965: ix–xiv.

12. PRLS: 30–56, 125–241.

13. Cf. 1775: lect. 55–6; 1766: 77, 86.

14. See 1775: lect. 55; 1768: 58; 1766: 61–2.

15. For Reid's full arguments on dualism and the afterlife, see his "Lectures on the Nature and Duration of the Soul" in EIP: 618–31; 1780 lect. 71–2; 1775 lect. 52–4; 1769: 43–4; 1768: 51–7; 1766: 54–9. This discussion comes at the end of his pneumatology lectures, just before the natural theology lectures, and is clearly inspired by the first chapter of Joseph Butler's *Analogy*.

16. 1780: 21–31; LNT: 4–9; 1775 lect. 55–6; 1769: 50–2; 1768: 58–9; 1766: 62–3.

17. (3) and (4) are mentioned at 1780: 104; LNT: 58; 1769: 70–1; 1766: 76 and (5) is mentioned at 1766: 76.

18. Cf. Clarke 1998, I, III, XII: 8, 15–16, 91–2. According to Reid's mature views, these can't amount to a strict demonstration (EIP VII.i: 545–6), but "many things are certain for which we have only that kind of evidence which Philosophers call probable"(EIP VII.iii: 562).

19. M.A. Stewart points out in correspondence that several authors contemporary with Reid were propagating various cosmological arguments. I take it that Clarke is Reid's main source because he recommends to his students "Dr Clarke upon the Being and atrebutes of God" (1768: 78), doesn't mention other sources in these contexts, shows in several places that he's aware of what Clarke calls his argument a priori, and uses many of Clarke's metaphors, supporting claims, and language.

20. Reid doesn't clearly distinguish this first principle from the previous one, or from the claim that all events have causes, all changes have causes, all modes of existence have causes, or (sometimes) the tautological formula that all effects have causes. He seems to use these interchangeably (e.g. EIP VI.vi: 497–8, 501–2; EAP IV.ii: 603a; C: 143, 174, 250; 1780: 34; LNT: 13; 1775 lect. 56; 1768: 60–1), yet to be valid the argument clearly requires the two different principles. On such principles and Reid's theory of free will, see Tuggy 2000: 15–16. For evaluation of this first stage of the Clarkean argument, see Rowe 2002 and Rowe 1998.

21. THN 1.3.3: 56–8. See previous note.

22. 1780: 32–7; LNT: 10–5; 1775 lect. 56–7; 1769: 73–4; 1768: 61–4. The clarified and developed final version of this response to Hume, with an argument that the causal principle is a first principle, is in EIP VI.vi: 497ff.

23. 1780: 136–7; LNT: 81; 1768: 82–3; 1766: 81.
24. Cf. 1780: 125–6; LNT: 73; 1769: 76–7. The manuscript has two pages numbered "78"; the quotation is from the second of these.
25. 1780: 137; LNT: 81.
26. See Leibniz 1989: 32.
27. 1780: 137–8; LNT: 81–2; 1769: 81–2; 1768: 83. This part of Reid's cosmological argument doesn't derive from Clarke, who offers different a priori means to prove divine uniqueness. (See Clarke 1998 VII: 35–8.) In the earliest extant set of notes, Reid argues that the supposition of two deities implies the existence of two eternities and two immensities, which is impossible (1766: 81). Presumably, this assumes the Clarkean identification of time and space with those divine attributes, an identification which Reid later declines to follow.
28. Cf. 1769: 77 and 1768: 84. Reid rules out bodily traits as being "perfections" (e.g., having shapely calves or beautiful eyes): "It is only what belongs to Man as a rational creature that we must ascribe to Deity" (1780: 141; LNT: 84). He believes that there is a common sense distinction between properties that do and don't contribute to greatness, or perhaps glory, or moral goodness. (See 1780: 126–7; LNT: 73–4.) Unlike Reid, Clarke tries his hand at an argument for the causal excellence principle. (Clarke 1998, VIII: 38–46; for criticism see Rowe 1998: 238–42.) Reid also makes the stronger claims that "we cannot help thinking that there is more perfection in the cause than in the effect" (1780: 156; LNT: 94; see also Clarke 1998, VIII: 38) and "every perfection or real excellence which we perceive in the creation belongs in a much higher degree to the Creator" (1780: 127; LNT: 74). For Descartes' use of such principles, see Clatterbaugh 1999: 17–45.
29. 1775 lect. 57; 1780: 142; LNT: 84.
30. At one point in EIP III.iii: 260–1, Reid mentions without endorsing the argument in the context of disavowing Clarke's speculations that space and time are divine attributes.
31. Gaskin 1988: 77–8.
32. Stewart 1985 and Yandell 1990: 227–40.
33. C: 254–5.
34. E.g., Willard 1990: 201–13.
35. EIP VI.vi: 508ff; 1780: 96; LNT: 54. For some puzzling features of this short form of Reid's argument, see Stewart 2003a.
36. 1780: 39–90; LNT: 16–49; 1775 lect. 57–9; 1769: 52–62; 1768: 62–75; 1766: 63–73.
37. This material is recast and expanded in Reid's last book. See EAP I.viii: 529, II.ii: 533–4, III.i.ii: 545–9, III.ii.iii–vi: 558–75a, III.iii.viii: 594b–9, V.vi: 666.

38. EIP VI.vi: 509.
39. EIP VI.vi: 503–8.
40. For language that alternately suggests each of these readings, see EIP VI.vi: 508.
41. EIP VI.v: 468.
42. EIP VIII.iv: 606–7; 1769: 63.
43. 1780: 92; LNT: 52.
44. EIP VI.vi: 498.
45. EIP VI.vi: 509; 1780: 95, 97; LNT: 53, 55.
46. EIP VI.vi: 507.
47. Cf. EIP VI.vi: 511–12; 1780: 99–100, 129; LNT: 56, 75; 1766: 73–4. See also Reid's logic lectures transcribed in Stewart 2003a, Michael and Michael 1987: 523–5.
48. 1780: 129; LNT: 75; EIP VI.v: 483.
49. On the present suggestion, the conception of probability in 1c is one of proportion. 1c shorn of the initial "Necessarily" is true just because, of all the things great and small that exhibit apparent design, most of them are in fact designed. 1c as written will be true just in case of all things in all possible worlds that exhibit apparent design, most of them are designed.
50. EIP VI.iv: 462–5.
51. EIP VI.vi: 504–7.
52. Among them: Can 1c be a necessary truth?
53. That is, it is part of a two-pronged approach with the extended cosmological argument above.
54. Sober 1993: 30–3.
55. See 1780: 46; LNT: 21; EAP IV.viii: 623a.
56. Reid had nothing like post-Darwin evolutionary theory to contend with, but only various fantastic flights of speculation on the origins of the world, which he rightly saw as intellectually worthless (1766: 77, 86; C: 77–8). For the relevance of Darwin to inference to the best explanation design arguments, see Sober 1993: 30–54. If Clarke's and Reid's causal excellence principle were defensible, they would have an a priori argument against evolutionary theory understood as not including intelligent agency. Unfortunately, Reid merely asserts this principle, Clarke gives a compressed and unconvincing argument for it (Clarke 1998, VIII: 38–46), and many apparent counterexamples threaten it (e.g., two unmusical parents produce a Mozart; an essentially incorruptible God produces virtuous agents who can resist real temptation).
57. EIP VI.vi: 510ff.
58. Plantinga 1983: 63–71. Plantinga mentions without endorsing this objection, and is on record as rejecting it in Plantinga 1986.

59. Alston 1991: 149–65; Plantinga 2000: 170–9; Plantinga 1983: 48ff; Wolterstorff 1983a: 148–55.

60. The Reformed Epistemologist can reply that faculty individuation is difficult and perhaps somewhat arbitrary, but there's no barrier to her admitting that one natural tendency is the source of belief in both God and other minds, and that it results not in properly basic theistic belief but rather nonbasic, warranted belief, or a premise of a quick argument for or inference to theism. (See Plantinga 2000: 176; Alston 1991: 165–7.) Something like this sort of *sensus divinitatis* is one Reid could accept.

61. EIP VI.iv: 463ff.

62. I thank Terence Cuneo for pressing this objection in correspondence.

63. IHM VI.xxiv: 193; EIP VII.iii: 557–8.

64. EHU X: 169–86.

65. Michael and Michael 1987: 525.

66. 1780: 107, 155; LNT: 62–3, 93, 1769: 72–3, 1768: 78, 1766: 77. See also the different list relating to moral attributes at EAP IV.xi: 633b.

67. 1780: 32–9, 75–7, 104–51; LNT: 10–16, 41–2, 61–91; 1775 lect. 56–7; 1769: 72–90; 1768: 78–9; 1766: 75–83; EAP IV.viii: 623–4.

68. 1780: 138–47; LNT: 82–7.

69. Yandell 1990: 166. In the earlier *Enquiry* discussion Hume also has a Cleanthean believer in his sights, who thinks that "the chief or sole argument for a divine existence . . . is derived from the order of nature" (EHU XI: 189).

70. Cf. 1769: 66–71 and 1766: 84.

71. Cf. 1766: 84.

72. From the context this evidently refers to Bolingbroke.

73. Cf. 1768: 86. This 1780 passage suggests that Reid didn't spend much energy on Hume's *Dialogues*, as nothing there suggests that Hume believes in a being with all of what Reid calls the natural divine attributes (see IV below). Reid's misinterpretation may be based on a less than careful reading of *Dialogues* XI–XII: 74–8.

74. 1780: 166; LNT: 101.

75. 1769: 90–2, 98; 1766: 84–5.

76. Leibniz 1951; Bayle 1965 "Manicheans," "Paulicans": 144–63, 166–93. Bayle is quoted and discussed at length by Leibniz.

77. Bayle 1965 "Clarifications": IV, "Second Clarification": 397, 409–20.

78. 1780: 166–7; LNT: 101; 1769: 92; 1768: 87; 1766: 85–6.

79. Cf. 1769: 85; 1780: 167; LNT: 101.

80. 1780: 168; LNT: 101–2; 1769: 93; 1768: 88.

81. Cf. 1780: 15–16; LNT: 118–19.

82. Cf. 1780: 3–7; LNT: 112–14; 1769: 93; 1768: 87.

83. Cf. 1769: 85–6; 1768: 88.

84. Cf. 1766: 86.

85. Reid also makes but doesn't develop the claim that "we cannot suppose any being made so high as not to be capable of abusing his liberty" (1766: 88).

86. 1766: 88–9; 1769: 96.

87. EAP IV.x: 631a; 1780: 132; LNT: 76; 1769: 79; 1766: 81.

88. EAP IV.iii: 607b and Tuggy 2000: 6. See Peterson et al. 1998: 118–21 for a summary of how this sort of reply has been used in recent discussions.

89. 1766: 84–5; IHM Introduction: 12; EAP IV.xi: 634.

90. 1780: 22–7; LNT: 125–8; 1769: 103–9; 1766: 92–3. See also 1780: 30–1; LNT: 8–9; EAP III.ii.vii: 577a.

91. I wish to thank Terence Cuneo, Knud Haakonssen, Michael Pace, William Rowe, James Van Cleve, René van Woudenberg, Paul Wood, and especially M.A. Stewart for either helpful correspondence, access to valuable unpublished work, or critical comments on previous drafts. Thanks are also due to Maria Rosa Antognazza, the Reid Project at the University of Aberdeen, and Alexander Broadie for their help with research travel arrangements, the New York State/UUP Professional Development Program and the SUNY Fredonia Professional Development Committee for travel funds, and my wife Candise for her support and patience during this project.

13 Reid's Influence in Britain, Germany, France, and America

The philosophy of Thomas Reid has exercised an enormous influence on Western thought from the publication of his *Inquiry* in 1764 until the present day. Reid's thought appeared on the world stage as at once amenable to science, Christian beliefs, the rise of a modern public sphere, and democratic politics. Exercising its most profound impact in postrevolutionary France and America, it promised to combine progress and stability by establishing links between common sense experience and philosophical and scientific thought in an era of rapid sociopolitical, religious, and scientific change. Reidian thought, moreover, had a significant impact on the development of higher education in both countries and was an important undercurrent in the broad expanse of nineteenth-century intellectual culture, an undercurrent that fed and mingled with other streams of Enlightenment thought. And although an identifiable school of "common sense philosophy" began to wane around the middle of the nineteenth century, Reid's thought proved to be a multivalent and fertile influence on subsequent philosophical developments in Britain, France, and America such as positivism and pragmatism. Reid's impact in German-speaking lands was slight but worth considering, since it has been claimed that his thought was highly influential there, and Kantianism became an important alternative – and at times bedfellow – to it.

I. BRITISH INFLUENCE

Reid's thought gained an immediate following in Britain upon publication of his *Inquiry* in 1764. Among the first to appropriate Reid's work was James Oswald (1703–93), a Scottish minister who

313

published *An Appeal to Common Sense in Behalf of Religion* in two volumes (1766, 1772). Although he cited Reid sparingly, Oswald seized upon Reid's ideas to defend the faith from "the assertions of sceptics and infidels,"[1] opposing the common sense principles that ordinary people take for granted to the labored and drawn-out reasonings of the learned, the latter threatening to confound the instinctive moral and religious impulses possessed by all human beings.

A somewhat more substantial defense of religion and traditional morality soon followed from the pen of James Beattie (1735–1803), appointed Professor of Moral Philosophy and Logic at Marischal College in 1760. Beattie joined the Aberdeen Philosophical Society in that year and thus came into personal contact with Reid during the formative stage of Reid's *Inquiry*. In his *Essay on the Nature and Immutability of Truth* (1770), Beattie mounted a vociferous attack on Hume, using arguments drawn from Reid but with little of Reid's characteristic subtlety or depth. In Beattie's view, nothing less than the existence of truth itself was at stake in the debate with Hume (and other skeptics and infidels). Religion, morality, and civilized behavior were teetering on the edge of the abyss, and it was time to rise up and put a stop to the nonsense before all was lost. Echoing Reid, Beattie emphasized the public nature of all forms of higher knowledge and their roots in the common sense of humankind. Just as mathematical reasoning falls to the ground if one doubts the axioms of geometry, so also if one supposes that "the dictates of common sense are erroneous or deceitful, all science, truth, and virtue are vain."[2]

Beattie combined a dire sense of imminent cultural collapse with enough of an understanding of Reid's ideas to produce what amounted to a literary blockbuster. All initial reviews of the book were favorable, the work being praised by Samuel Johnson, Thomas Percy, David Garrick, and Edmund Burke, among others. It even merited praise from George III, who granted Beattie a royal pension of £200, while Joshua Reynolds painted a portrait of Beattie with the *Essay* under his arm and the Angel of Truth hovering nearby. The *Essay* became an important conduit through which Reidian thought was made known outside of Scotland, going through fourteen English editions by the end of the century, and being translated into German, French, and Dutch.[3]

Reid attained deeper and more lasting influence through another disciple, Dugald Stewart (1753–1828). Entering the University of

Edinburgh in 1765, Stewart was inspired by Newtonian physics and
the Baconian inductive method. He attended Reid's lectures at Glasgow in 1771–2, and Reid's impact on Stewart is evident in nearly all
of Stewart's writings. In 1785, Stewart was appointed to the Chair of
Moral Philosophy at Edinburgh, a position he held until his retirement in 1810. His works included *Elements of the Philosophy of the
Human Mind* in 3 volumes (1792, 1814, 1827), *Outlines of Moral Philosophy* (1793) and *Philosophical Essays* (1810). These works (especially the *Elements*), which were extensively reprinted in France and
America, sought to develop the scientific and practical applications
of Reid's thought while placing it in a broad social and intellectual
context.

In Volume One of the *Elements*, Stewart attempted to demonstrate how an inductive science of the mind is relevant to improvements in education, science, politics, and the arts. For example,
Stewart asserts that education will be improved by clarifying the
distinctions between basic features of the mind and acquired associations and prejudices. Science will benefit from a clear understanding
of the relationship between the principles of our nature and the phenomena of physical nature, an understanding that will discourage
unwarranted hypotheses and encourage a focus on verifiable facts
and laws of nature. Political and economic thought must also be
grounded in common experience and understandings, if it is going to
be useful. The arts similarly gain by an understanding of the formative role played by basic human propensities (including the power of
association) in poetry, painting, eloquence, and other fine arts.[4]

In his discussion of modern social and political developments,
Stewart looks with favor on the rise of the commons and public
opinion, chiding the French monarchy for having ignored the latter
for so long that it finally exploded in its face.[5] In Stewart's discourse,
the common people, endowed as they are with what he would later
call "fundamental laws of belief," appear as the foundational units
of the whole social structure, yet they must be educated and enlightened by the right sort of scientific philosophy if they are to be put
on an appropriate path.

Stewart's second volume, appearing more than twenty years after
the first, is taken up with more strictly philosophical topics. Stewart uses the example of mathematics to critique Reid's language of
"principles of common sense," arguing that what Reid was talking

about were neither "principles" nor "common sense," as both are commonly understood. Voicing what was to become a common criticism, Stewart argued that the term "common sense" is problematic because it is loose and ambiguous and implies "common opinion" or even "prejudice."[6] Stewart's solution was to drop the term entirely, and urge the less ambiguous "fundamental laws of human belief" on his readers. Thus if the first volume of the *Elements* argued for the utility of Reid's philosophy, the second volume sought, albeit via changes in terminology, to assure its respectability.

Stewart was influential not only through his writings but also through his students, many of whom went on to become significant politicians, religious leaders, and men of letters, including Sir Walter Scott, Thomas Chalmers, James Mill, and Thomas Brown.[7] Brown assumed Stewart's chair in moral philosophy from 1810 until Brown's death in 1820. A medical doctor, Brown continued to follow the "scientific," psychological method of his predecessors (adding his own physiological elements), and he argued strenuously for the existence of intuitive beliefs or principles of the mind. Brown's lectures were clearly indebted to Reid, and he often cited Reid's works, but he also argued that Reid's critique of "the theory of ideas" was misguided, and he criticized Reid's account of perception.[8] In his *Inquiry into the Relation of Cause and Effect* (1818) Brown criticized Reid's identification of "power" with agent power, arguing that a relation of uniform antecedents and consequents is all that the term "cause" really means. At the same time, he argued that our belief in such notions is intuitive rather than derived from custom or experience. Brown, who was widely read in America, thus staked out something of a middle position between Reid and Hume on the issue of causality.[9]

As time passed, Reid's ideas were subjected to critical scrutiny, amended, and joined to other ideas and doctrines, while remaining a central undercurrent of nineteenth-century British thought. One figure who took Reidian thought in a new direction was William Hamilton (1788–1856), who became Professor of Logic and Metaphysics at Edinburgh in 1836 and was a dominating figure in British philosophy until his death in 1856. Thomas Carlyle, Clerk Maxwell, and James Lorimer were among the members of Hamilton's circle, "a seed-bed of cultural resurgence" in the 1830s and 1840s.[10] It was through Hamilton's heavily annotated and oft-reprinted edition of Reid's works that many in Britain and America were exposed to Reid's philosophy in the second half of the nineteenth century. Hamilton, like a number of others at the time, assimilated Reid's ideas to Kantian philosophy, and he used Reidian notions, including the existence of first principles of mind and the need for critical analysis of the contents of consciousness, as a starting point for his own metaphysical inquiries. His "philosophy of the unconditioned" led to a kind of agnosticism and phenomenalism in the eyes of some,[11] while others saw it "as a mean between the one extreme of a thoroughgoing scepticism and the other extreme of the monistic omniscience of gnosticism."[12]

James Ferrier (1808–64) was a friend and admirer of Hamilton who, after an unsuccessful bid to assume Hamilton's Chair at Edinburgh, became Professor of Moral Philosophy at St. Andrews. Ferrier's thought was described by contemporaries as "German philosophy refracted through a Scottish medium"[13] and as such signaled the end of Reidian hegemony and the turn towards various forms of idealism in British universities during the second half of the nineteenth century. Ferrier was highly critical of Reid's thought, arguing that Reid had accepted a premise central to the ideal theory, namely, the existence of an object of thought separate from the thinking subject. Ferrier believed that this distinction between inquiring subject and observed object is violated in the very act of introspective analysis, for in this case subject and object are identical. To treat the mind as both inquiring subject and observed object was a "radical defect" in Reid's psychological method and the science of the human mind, Ferrier argued, and was based on the importation of the methods and assumptions of physical science into philosophy. But whereas Brown clearly had Reid's texts in front of him while leveling his criticisms, Ferrier did not; rather, he seems to have been responding primarily to a vague (and rather distorted) memory of Reid's ideas, Brown's reductive, "scientific" approach to mental phenomena, and the growing hegemony of natural science in general.[14]

By the middle of the nineteenth century, then, Reid's thought had sustained critiques from both physical reductionist (Brown) and idealist (Ferrier) perspectives, while Hamilton had effected an idiosyncratic adaptation of Reid's thought to Kantianism. Hamilton's thought was itself subjected to devastating criticism by J. S. Mill in 1865, an attack that contributed to the decline of the common sense tradition, by then strongly associated with Hamilton, in Britain as well as in America.[15] Mill's frontal assault on Hamilton can be seen as one more episode in a long struggle between an optimistic scientism, which held that scientific specialization and technical education were the keys to the future, and the Reidian notion "that the scientific and technical expertise required by modern civilization will turn into an unintelligible and lifeless routine if it is allowed to develop in a departmentalised way, out of touch with the common sense of the lay populace."[16]

Just as, in the latter decades of the nineteenth century, the Reidian thread was becoming attenuated in Scotland, in England it was being woven into the thought of Henry Sidgwick and his student G. E. Moore. Sidgwick (1838–1900) was probably exposed to Reid as a student at Cambridge under William Whewell. Sidgwick's early writings on epistemology "suggest a common-sense approach to problems he was later happy to associate with Reid," and his own ethical position "incorporates much of the substance of Reid's [ethical position]."[17] That Sidgwick felt strong affinities for Reid was made clear in an 1895 lecture delivered to the Glasgow Philosophical Society, titled "The Philosophy of Common Sense." In this lecture, Sidgwick rebutted Kant's critique of Reid (discussed below) and praised Reid's psychological method and, in particular, his separation of sensation from perception. Sidgwick "[could] not think Reid wrong in holding that the propositions he is most concerned to maintain as first principles are implicitly assented to by men in general." This was not to say that such beliefs are always correct. Reid's "essential demand . . . on the philosopher, is not primarily that he should make his beliefs consistent with those of the vulgar, but that he should make them consistent with his own."[18]

George Edward Moore (1873–1958) studied under Sidgwick at Cambridge, and in giving his own stamp to Reidian thought, influenced a whole generation of British intellectuals.[19] Moore is widely seen to have spearheaded the attack on idealism and to have turned British philosophy away from questions about whether ordinary claims concerning the external world and morality are true or meaningful toward the analysis of such claims.[20] Despite the fact that Moore rarely referred to Reid, it is clear that he had studied Reid's works, writing approvingly of Reid on occasion, and the connections and affinities between the two have been noted by scholars.[21] In

"A Defense of Common Sense," Moore employed his careful analytical method to defend the truth of common sense convictions such as "There exists at present a living body, which is *my* body,"[22] arguing that denials of such truisms are false. Moore was thus led to say that "I am one of those philosophers who have held that the 'Common Sense view of the world' is, in certain fundamental features, *wholly* true."[23] Thus despite going out of fashion during the latter decades of the nineteenth century in Britain, Reid's thought played a significant role in the rise of the analytic movement in the twentieth century.

II. GERMAN INFLUENCE

Although German philosophers became aware of Reidian thought early on, Reid's thought did not have much of an impact on the mainstream of German philosophy. The paradox of the "German reception" of Reid is that most sympathetic Germans did not accept two of the essential elements of Reid's thought: the rejection of the theory of ideas, and the claim that the principles of common sense are not themselves amenable to any type of (noncircular) rational justification.[24] If Reid, Beattie, and Oswald helped to focus German interest on the first principles of mind and the role of sense experience in cognition, they were also widely seen to be advocating a perspective antithetical to philosophy itself, a "misology, reduced to principles" in Kant's words.[25] The rationalistic tradition of German philosophy, coupled with the absence of sociopolitical conditions that made recourse to common sense understandings attractive,[26] contributed to the generally tepid response to Reid's thought in the Germanies.

There were a number of avenues by which Germans could become aware of the works of Reid, Beattie, and Oswald. French and German journals reviewed Reid's *Inquiry*, which was translated into French in 1768 and German in 1782. Oswald's *Appeal* and Beattie's *Essay* were widely reviewed in German periodicals, and Beattie's *Essay* was quickly assimilated after being translated into German in 1772.[27] Reid's thought, more often than not, was made known through the writings of Beattie, Oswald, and Priestley, whose *An Examination of Dr. Reid's Inquiry into the Human Mind on the Principles of Common Sense, Dr. Beattie's Essay on the Nature and Immutability of Truth, and Dr. Oswald's Appeal to Common Sense in Behalf of*

Religion was published in 1774 and was reviewed in the *Göttingsche Anzeigen*. The latter work helped to fix the notion in German minds of an interchangeable triad "Reid, Oswald, and Beattie." No friend of Reidian thought, Priestley argued that the Reidian approach put up barriers to scientific research into mental phenomena, ascribing too much importance to intuition and instinct, and too little to reason and education.[28]

Yet Reidian thought did spark some interest in German lands. Beattie's work had an influence on the Göttingen thinkers Christoph Meiners and Georg Lichtenberg, while the writings of Johann Feder (1740–1821) exhibit the impact of both Beattie and Reid – Feder having warmly praised both Reid's *Inquiry* and *Intellectual Powers*.[29] In *Logik und Metaphysik* (1770), Feder follows Reid and Beattie in arguing for the existence of "first principles that reasoning does not clarify and illuminate, rather confuses." And in his discussion of "The sources of truth and the grounds of the reliability of perception," he argues for the reliability of sense perception in Reidian terms and cites Reid and Beattie for further reading.[30] *Logik und Metaphysik* thus contains one of the most straightforward presentations of Reidian ideas in German letters, yet as a whole it is an eclectic and synthetic work, Feder citing many modern philosophers – Reid only rarely, while Hume is cited more often than Reid, and Locke more often than both of them.[31] Feder furthermore did not reject the theory of ideas, and "[He] never became a follower of the Scots in the sense of accepting all or even most of Reid's theory of knowledge."[32]

Johann August Eberhard (1739–1809) propounded a Reidian distinction between sensation and perception, but he accepted only a few very basic principles of common sense such as the principle of noncontradiction, and he felt, as most German thinkers did, that the Reidian insistence that such principles were not open to rational scrutiny represented a turning-away from scientific and philosophical analysis.[33] Eberhard's notion that principles of common sense required clarification and rectification by rational analysis was further developed by Johann Nicolaus Tetens (1736–1807), whom Kuehn calls "the German philosopher most influenced by the Scots."[34] But Tetens argued that Reid's response to Hume was "not wrong, only unphilosophical" – not much different than if a natural scientist were to explain the phenomenon of magnetism by saying that "the magnet drew the iron to it by instinct."[35]

There is not much evidence that Reid exercised a significant influence on Immanuel Kant (1724–1804). If Kant's dismissive attack on Reid and his epigones in the *Prolegomena to Any Future Metaphysics* (1783) indicates that Scottish common-sensism was a part of the intellectual climate in which Kant's works were formulated,[36] it also indicates that Kant most likely had not studied Reid and that instead he was basing his understanding of Reid on Priestley's *Examination*, or perhaps on Oswald's *Appeal* or Beattie's *Essay*.[37] Whatever the case, if one wants to argue that Kant read Reid in any depth, then one must also assert that Kant either did not understand him, or that he willfully misrepresented him, arguing as he did that Reid missed the point of Hume's problem and that "Seen clearly, this appeal [to common sense] is nothing but a call upon the judgment of the multitude, whose applause embarrasses the philosopher, while the popular wiseacre glories and boasts in it."[38] In his discussion of common sense philosophy, Kant uses four different German expressions in referring to common sense, none of which approximates Reid's own more precise notion of "principles" of common sense, again throwing into doubt Kant's familiarity with Reid's thought.[39]

Two of Kant's principal opponents, J. G. Herder and Friedrich Nicolai, freely and uncritically appealed to common sense in their works, albeit without reference to Reid. Both thinkers ascribed to a populist conception of Enlightenment, and Herder, in contrast to Kant, grounded his philosophical perspective in the understandings, language, and traditions of the German *Volk*.[40] F. H. Jacobi, another critic of Kantian thought, appealed to a primordial certainty about what is real "that animates our experiences from the beginning and pervades all levels of language." Jacobi called this certainty "faith," and in clarifying what he meant by it, made reference to Reid's *Intellectual Powers*, although it is unclear whether he had actually read Reid's works himself.[41] J. G. Hamann, another swimmer against the German metaphysical current, appears to have read Reid, and espoused ideas of natural language and original perceptions similar to Reid's.[42]

Kant's own remarks and lack of familiarity with Reid, along with the fact that his opponents freely appealed to a faculty of common sense, highlights the overall lack of affinity between Reidian thought and the more rationalistic mainstream of German metaphysics. In his *Lectures on the History of Philosophy*, G. W. F. Hegel exhibited a better understanding of Reid than did Kant, yet it appears that he too was not directly familiar with Reid's work.[43] It is more than a little ironic that over the course of the nineteenth century many individuals came to see Reid and Kant as having been engaged in similar enterprises (with some fundamental differences between them). For it is hard not to sense in Kant's vehement attack on common sense a defensive reaction to the Reidian suggestion that rational analysis of the a priori conditions for the possibility of knowledge – conditions akin to Reid's principles of common sense – is misguided.

III. FRENCH INFLUENCE

Reid had a major impact on French thought in the first half of the nineteenth century, particularly on the so-called "Eclectics"(or "Spiritualists"), who forged a position between conservatives horrified by the Revolution and radicals who felt that its aims had not been fully realized. Although Reid's *Inquiry* had been translated into French in 1768, it was not until the first decades of the nineteenth century that Reid's thought aroused significant interest in France, as some individuals – including "Traditionalists" such as de Maistre and de Bonald – began calling into question the legacy of the French Enlightenment, including particularly its materialist currents. The way had been cleared as early as 1804, when Joseph Marie de Gérando included a section on "the Scottish School" in his *Histoire comparée des systémes de philosophie*, giving a mixed review of Reid while reserving heartier praise for Stewart, whose *Elements of Philosophy* appeared a few years later (1808) in French translation.[44] Soon thereafter, Maine de Biran (1766–1824), who read and praised Reid,[45] developed an influential notion of metaphysics "as the science of principles ... found in the primitive facts or basic data of intuition."[46]

The story of Reid's reception in France usually begins, however, with Paul Royer-Collard (1763–1845), a political figure appointed by Napoleon to the chair of philosophy at the Sorbonne in 1811. It was through Royer-Collard's lectures there that Reid became widely known in France. In his opening lectures to the Course in the History of Philosophy, as well as in his other literary remains, Royer-Collard recapitulated some of Reid's central insights into the nature of perception and the philosophical basis for scientific knowledge of the world. He reiterated Reid's critique of modern philosophy, and gave Reid credit for "utterly destroying" the theory of ideas.[47] Royer-Collard furthermore provided a detailed Reidian answer to Hume's "problem of induction," arguing that we are enabled to grasp causal relations in nature by the "primitive facts" of consciousness and memory.[48] "When one goes against [such] primitive facts, one misunderstands both the constitution of our intelligence and the goal of philosophy," which like all the other sciences, is to attend to facts and avoid hypotheses. The result of the interaction of sense, consciousness, and memory is that "order shines on the universe and man learns to read in the great book of nature."[49]

Generally speaking, Royer-Collard employed Reid's theory of perception to affirm our ability to have knowledge of ourselves, of the physical world, and of "a first and necessary cause ... whose power and extension is equal to the magnificence and harmony of the effects it produces before our eyes."[50] Royer-Collard, and those who followed in his footsteps, thus found a way around the tradition of French philosophy stretching from Descartes through Condillac, which, in Royer-Collard's view, was overly hypothetical and had led to a skepticism and materialism with destructive consequences: "When all existence is in question, what authority remains in the relationships that unite it? Yet on these relationships depend all the laws of societies, all the rights, all the obligations that constitute public and private morality."[51]

When Royer-Collard stepped down from his teaching post in 1814, Victor Cousin (1792–1867), a student of Royer-Collard's, took over his lectures in the history of philosophy, quite consciously seeing himself to be "continuing the investigations of our illustrious predecessor."[52] *Du vrai, du beau et du bien* (1836, 1853) was drawn from course lectures delivered starting in 1817 and contains representative doctrines that Cousin reaffirmed late in life.[53] In the book, Cousin claims to expound "a sound and generous philosophy" which, "setting out modestly from psychology, from the humble study of the human mind," eventually reaches "the highest regions," traversing "metaphysics, aesthetics, theodicea, morals, and politics."[54] In so doing, Cousin builds an eclectic philosophy of the true, beautiful, and good on foundations laid by Reid and, to a lesser degree, Kant. Highest praise is reserved for Reid, of whom Cousin declares himself a disciple: "We regard Reid as common sense itself, and ... common sense is to us the only legitimate point of departure, and the constant and inviolable rule of science. Reid never errs; his method is true, [and] his general principles are incontestable."[55]

Cousin argues at length that "universal and necessary principles" of mind (or common sense) such as space, time, and causality "are encountered in the most common experience"[56] and undergird all the sciences, while also leading to the perception of "ideal truths" (i.e., Platonic Forms) and the existence of God. As such, Cousin presents his "philosophical science" as a form of "idealism rightly tempered by empiricism," that is, a reconciliation of the empiricist claim that we apprehend reality through sense experience with the broadly Platonic thesis that we apprehend Ideas, or Forms, by reason:

From empiricism we have retained the maxim ... that the conditions of science, of art, of ethics, are in experience, and often in sensible experience. But we profess at the same time this other maxim, that the foundation of science is absolute truth, that the direct foundation of art is absolute beauty, that the direct foundation of ethics and politics is the good, is duty, is right, and that what reveals to us these absolute ideas of the true, the beautiful, and the good, is reason.[57]

Thus absolute "ideas" or "truths" that ultimately find their source in God are revealed in experience (but are not reducible to it) and grasped by reason, a "spontaneous" faculty that "discovers" universal and necessary principles of common sense without "passing through analysis, abstraction, and deduction."[58]

"Spiritualism" was Cousin's term for this doctrine, whose "character in fact is that of subordinating the senses to spirit, and tending, by all the means that reason acknowledges, to elevate and ennoble man." Eclectically drawing on Plato, the Gospels, and Descartes, "It teaches the spirituality of the soul, the liberty and responsibility of human actions, moral obligation, disinterested virtue, the dignity of justice, the beauty of charity; and beyond the limits of this world it shows a God ... who ... will not abandon [man] in the mysterious development of his destiny." Such an all-encompassing doctrine was needed when, "following the great wars of the Revolution, and after the downfall of the Empire, the constitutional monarchy still poorly established, left the future of France ... [in doubt]."[59]

Cousin in fact became a dominant figure in French political and educational life under the July Monarchy. He had achieved public

fame in the late 'teens and 'twenties as an innovator in philosophy
and a champion of liberty who had spent time in a Prussian prison for
his views. Once restored to his teaching post at the École Normale in
1828 (it was closed in 1820), his lectures were reportedly printed and
sold to the tune of 3000 copies.[60] In the decade after the accession of
Louis-Phillipe in 1830, he rose to become a member of the Superior
Council of Public Instruction, President of the National Teacher's
Examination in Philosophy, Director of the École Normale, Minister
of Public Instruction, and President of the Academy of Moral and
Political Sciences, finally retiring from public life amid the tumult
of 1848.

In these various capacities Cousin played a major role in the institutionalization of philosophy instruction at secondary and university levels, establishing "Eclecticism," "University Philosophy," or
"New French Philosophy" – all synonyms for Cousin's school – as the
standard philosophy curriculum of higher education. According to
Patrice Vermeren, "Cousin's sweep into hegemony in the 1830s and
1840s represents the first time philosophers became men of state in
France, and his model for the place and role of institutions of knowledge would determine their course ever since."[61] If Cousin imposed
a philosophical orthodoxy on French institutions of higher learning,
he was also an intermediary and catalyst in the transition from an
elitist social system to a modern merit-based society. Through the
institutionalization of philosophy, Cousin helped to make the university, rather than the salon, the focal point and training ground of
liberal society.[62]

Cousin's many followers were also for the most part followers of
Reid. Most prominent among them was Théodore Jouffroy (1796–
1842). Jouffroy had studied under Cousin at the École Normale, and
during the 1820s he hosted an influential salon in his own apart-
ments, before being appointed Professor of Ancient Philosophy at
the Collège de France in 1833. Jouffroy's writings included philosophical essays and courses on natural law and aesthetics, and he
translated Dugald Stewart's *Outlines of Moral Philosophy* (1826)
and the complete works of Reid (1828–36), attaching lengthy, influential prefaces to both works outlining his own views. Jouffroy
was concerned with establishing a "philosophical science" on a par
with the physical sciences, both in terms of establishing fundamental facts and laws of the mind, and in achieving public stature and

credibility comparable to that of natural scientists. If Cousin had paid lip-service to science, Jouffroy, who for the most part rejected Cousin's spiritualism,[63] intended to flesh out the potentialities of Reid's thought for putting philosophy onto a firmly scientific – yet antireductionist – footing.[64] For example, in Jouffroy's view, the common sense judgment that mind and body are of a fundamentally different nature provides a point of departure for psychological research, underwriting the notion that the object of psychology is empirical study of the self-conscious life-force or soul.[65]

For Jouffroy, then, Reidian thought had put philosophy onto a scientific footing, helping to lift it out of its "impotent" state and paving the way for philosophical science to assume a public stature on par with the natural sciences.[66] And there can in fact be little doubt that Royer-Collard, Cousin, and Jouffroy became arbiters of public opinion to a degree that philosophers rarely attain, common sense philosophy receiving acceptance by a large part of society and dominating higher education in France until it began a slow decline around 1870.[67] To which it should be added that attaining this public status was abetted by the fact that Reidian thought exercised influence in the fine arts by informing the aesthetic theories of Cousin, Jouffroy, and those who followed in their footsteps, including Adolphe Garnier, Charles Lévêque, René Sully-Prudhomme, and C.A. Sainte-Beuve.[68]

The extent of Reid's impact on nineteenth-century French intellectual life is indicated by the fact that the positivism of August Comte, which was gathering adherents by the middle of the century, was firmly grounded in what Comte variously called "universal good sense," "vulgar wisdom," "common reason," and "simple good sense." According to Comte, "Science, properly speaking, is simply a methodical extension of universal good sense. Far, therefore, from treating as questionable what has been truly decided by it, healthy philosophic speculation must always be indebted to common reason."[69] Comte, who lectured in Paris during the years of Cousinian hegemony, advanced a view of the relationship between common sense and science clearly in tune with that of the common sense school. He characterized Eclecticism as a useful if rather impotent "stationary" school of thought, and positivism as the way forward in the ongoing effort to reconcile order with progress.[70] This had been precisely the attraction of Reidian thought in the first place, providing, according to Charles Rémusat, a scientific foundation on which to rebuild philosophy and social order in an age when "One only hears about ... the uncertainty of theories, the vices of institutions, the instability of governments, the decadence of the arts and letters, the lowering of character, the rarity of talent, the weakness of mores, the loss of convictions, [and] the dangers of industry."[71]

IV. AMERICAN INFLUENCE

Translations of works by Cousin and Jouffroy were published in the United States starting in the early 1830s, contributing to the pervasive influence of Reidian thought in nineteenth-century America. Reid's thought played an important role in the conservative evangelicalism of Princeton and the American South, the Unitarianism and Transcendentalism of the New England states, and the institutionalization of science and science education in universities throughout the country. A profusion of textbooks ensured that Reidian thought, in the guise of mental and moral "science," spread far and wide, while at the end of the century it was assimilated into the "pragmaticism" of C. S. Peirce. Common sense philosophy was thus one of the primary conduits by which the perspectives of the new science and the Enlightenment were received in America, and it had an impact on many subsequent developments in American philosophy and higher thought.[72]

Reid's impact on American thought was already evident in the eighteenth century. Thomas Jefferson was familiar with Reid's *Inquiry*, and a number of Jefferson's key ideas can be traced to the influence of Reid.[73] Another founding father, the visionary legal scholar James Wilson, was deeply influenced by Reid. Wilson gave a celebrated series of lectures at the College of Philadelphia in 1790–1 in which he criticized Locke and praised Reid, maintaining that while the skepticism of Hume was subversive of liberty and responsibility, Reid's philosophy of common sense offered a scientific confirmation of an innate moral sense that could be relied upon to serve as a secure egalitarian basis for law and politics in the new republic.[74]

Another early proponent of Reidian thought was John Witherspoon (1723–1794), a respected minister in the Church of Scotland who became President of the College of New Jersey in 1768. In America, Witherspoon became a prominent Presbyterian leader and supporter of American independence, serving in the Continental Congress from 1776 to 1782. At Princeton, he broadened the curriculum on the pattern of the Scottish universities, encouraging the study of natural philosophy and introducing many of the leading lights of the Scottish Enlightenment to his students. Under Witherspoon's watch the College assumed a national stature as a training ground for public leaders.[75]

As was the norm for American college presidents, Witherspoon taught the course in moral philosophy. In his lectures he revealed himself to be an eclectic follower of Hutcheson and other British moralists, concerned to harmonize the claims of revelation, reason, and conscience. Witherspoon introduced Reid and Beattie to students and propounded a philosophical response to idealism and skepticism that was similar in broad outlines to Reid's philosophy, and he thus helped prepare the way for the American appropriation of Reid's thought.[76] Many of Witherspoon's students rose to prominence, assisting the spread of the Scottish Enlightenment – and Reid's ideas – in America. They included over 100 ministers, thirteen college presidents and many more college educators, a U.S. President (Madison), a Vice President (Burr), and twenty U.S. Senators.[77]

It was, however, under Witherspoon's successor, Samuel Stanhope Smith (1750–1819), that the college came fully under the influence of Reid and the philosophy of common sense. Smith developed the more liberal and progressive intellectual tendencies of his father-in-law Witherspoon, and worked to expand and deepen the natural science curriculum at the college, purchasing scientific instruments and appointing the first Professor of Chemistry in America, John Maclean, in 1795.[78]

Smith's wide-ranging *Lectures ... On Moral and Political Philosophy* (1812) was the first major exposition and application of Reid's thought written and published in America. Based on class lectures spanning the previous thirty years, the two volumes indicate that Smith had adopted Reid's perspective and terminology in forging a *rapprochement* between science and religion. Modern Newtonian science had banished hypotheses and concentrated on the formulation of general rules of nature's effects by inductive analysis; similarly, through inductive analysis of the powers of mind, as well as from external evidence, we can discern the laws of our constitution and the intentions of our creator. Smith recapitulates Reid's critique that the theory of ideas was an unsound hypothesis, preferring a view according to which we "form judgments [based] on experience and fact, interpreted by plain common sense." Accordingly, he lauds Reid for having placed philosophy on the proper foundation, "that common sense which it had deserted."[79]

The *Lectures*, in essence, apply a Reidian perspective to the broad expanse of moral philosophy, featuring chapters on everything from sense perception to volition to language (where Reid's view on natural language is presented), to natural theology, duty, aesthetics, economics, and politics. Smith's scientific proclivities are evident throughout – the lecture on internal sense perception, for example, culminates in a discussion of Hartley's theory of "vibratiuncles" as a way to account for madness and nervous diseases (Lecture VII). When it came to natural theology, Smith rehearsed a Reidian critique of Hume's position on causality, asserting that an instinctive inductive principle is a basic feature of our constitution that makes all forms of knowledge possible and leads us to infer the existence of God from the effects we see in the world (Lecture XV).

Smith was widely seen in his day as a progressive educator and eloquent speaker, and many of his students went on to assume leading roles in American churches and universities.[80] He and Witherspoon were thus in many respects responsible for bringing the philosophy of Reid into wide circulation in America, including the American South.[81] But Princeton proved not to be conducive to Smith's kind of liberalism, and he resigned under pressure in 1812, ushering in a more conservative, evangelical era at the College, dominated by men who employed common sense philosophy for primarily religious and didactic ends. Archibald Alexander, who occupied the Chair of Didactic and Polemic Theology at the seminary from 1812 to 1851, published *Outlines of Moral Philosophy* in 1852, a distillation of four decades of lectures. Although focusing on religious considerations, Alexander cites Reid at several points and the book exhibits a basic common sense orientation in the tradition of Oswald.[82] In later years, Charles Hodge, longtime professor at Princeton and founder of the *Princeton Review*, published the highly influential *Systematic Theology* (1872–73), a book pervaded by common sense teachings.[83]

James McCosh (1811–94) became President of the college in 1868. Before coming to America from Scotland, McCosh had published *The Intuitions of the Mind, Inductively Considered* (1860), in which he sought to clarify and delimit the nature and mode of operation of Reid's principles of common sense, although like Stewart he felt that the term was too loose and ambiguous to merit use in philosophical discussion. McCosh saw himself to be charting a middle way between transcendentalism/idealism on the one hand, and radical empiricism/utilitarianism on the other. He indicated his indebtedness to Hamilton, but was clearly wary of the latter's Kantianism, and wished to return philosophy to the sound and secure foundation of inductive observation of the laws of consciousness as revealed through experience of the world – the observation of facts rather than a priori speculation.[84]

Earlier in the century, just as Princeton was turning to a conservative interpretation of Reid, the considerably more liberal Harvard Unitarians had begun their own appropriation of Reidian thought. Upon the foundation laid by Scottish common sense philosophers, "Harvard professors were able to construct a durable consensus, containing room for both Enlightenment aspirations and Christian principles."[85] Levi Frisbie, Levi Hedge, James Walker, and Francis Bowen, successive holders of the Alford Professorship of Natural Religion, Moral Philosophy, and Civil Polity, all subscribed to common sense philosophy, forming an unbroken chain of Reidian thought at Harvard from the turn of the century to the 1870s. Students passing through Harvard in those years were exposed to Reid's thought in classroom lectures and texts, including texts written by Reid himself and Harvard professors.[86]

Levi Frisbie (1784–1822) became the first Alford Professor in 1817, and his inaugural address in November of that year set the tone for the next half century of instruction in moral philosophy at Harvard. According to Frisbie, moral philosophy is the "science of the principles and obligation of duty." The "unremitting labours of the moralist" are required "to relieve the sentiments of mankind, from those associations of prejudice, of fashion, and of false opinion, which have so constant an influence in perverting the judgment and corrupting the heart, and to bring them back to the unbiassed dictates of nature and common sense."[87] Levi Hedge (1766–1844) replaced Frisbie as Alford Professor in 1827. Hedge was the author of *Elements of Logick* (1816), a short, lucid book heavily indebted to Reid and Stewart that became an oft-reprinted college text in the following decades. Reid and Stewart receive citation on a number of topics throughout the book, and at the end Hedge makes a general recommendation of the writings of Locke, Reid, Stewart, and Brown as "compris[ing] in themselves a complete system of intellectual philosophy."[88]

James Walker (1794–1874), a Harvard-educated pastor and editor of American editions of Reid and Stewart, replaced Hedge in the Alford Chair in 1839, becoming one of Harvard's most popular teachers before assuming the presidency of Harvard in 1853. In 1834, Walker published a sermon which exhibited affinities for Reidian thought as well as Cousinian Spiritualism.[89] Walker made three points in the widely-reprinted sermon, which was entitled "The Philosophy of Man's Spiritual Nature in Regard to the Foundations of Faith." First, an inspection of consciousness reveals the existence of spiritual faculties in man. Second, "religion in the soul" is as much of a reality as our rational faculties. And third, the "spiritual world" is just as real as the material one. "These three propositions being established, it will follow that our conviction of the existence and reality of the spiritual world is resolvable into the same *fundamental law of belief* as that on which our conviction of the existence and reality of the sensible world depends."[90]

The sermon distills the potentialities of Reidian thought for religious apologetics, but there were also other factors contributing to the popularity of common sense philosophy among Harvard Unitarians, including its provision of a politics and educational philosophy that consolidated the gains of the Revolution while assuring social stability and a dominant position for them (at least for a while) in American intellectual life.[91] In sermons delivered while President of Harvard, Walker outlined a social and educational philosophy that was rooted in common sense and public opinion, yet was firmly convinced of the need for the work of enlightenment and education to correct the vagaries of public opinion.[92]

Francis Bowen (1811–1890) employed Reidian thought as a basis for maintaining a sound moral and religious perspective in the face of the rise of modern science and democratic politics. His Lowell Lectures in 1848–9 reveal a desire to harmonize religion and science on common sense principles and to combat the infidelity and social disorder that seemed to be growing daily. Bowen endeavored to demonstrate in his lectures "that the fundamental doctrines of religion rest upon the same basis which supports all science, and that they cannot be denied without rejecting also the familiar truths, which we adopt almost unconsciously, and upon which we depend for the conduct of life and the regulation of our ordinary concerns."[93]

One offshoot of Scottish common sense philosophy at Harvard was the rise of New England Transcendentalism.[94] Several types of thought helped to form Transcendentalism, but in many respects Reidian thought was the rock from which the movement sprang. Most of the main figures in the movement were schooled in common sense philosophy at Harvard, and Emerson in particular seems to have been influenced by Reid and Stewart. He studied their works under Frisbie and Hedge, and asserted in a prize-winning essay in 1821 that the reasonings of Reid's school "yet want the neatness and conclusiveness of a system," but "the first advance which is made must go on in the school in which Reid and Stewart have labored."[95] Emerson's thought in turn "aided Thoreau in his movement from the empirical, rationalistic version of Common Sense taught at Harvard to the espousal of idealism and the intuitive grasping of Transcendentalism."[96]

Richard Petersen identifies a "moderate" school of Reidian thought, represented by Eliphalet Nott, President of Union College from 1804 to 1866, and Francis Wayland, who had been a student and a faculty member under Nott before becoming President of Brown in 1827. Both Nott and Wayland were exponents of common sense philosophy in their schools, and both "were early advocates for broadening the appeal and usefulness of a college education," offering programs that were precursors of the elective system.[97] Wayland (1796–1865) wrote one of the most successful textbooks in the Reidian tradition, *Elements of Moral Science* (1835), which went through four editions in two years and by 1890 had sold 200,000 copies.[98] Although the book does not mention Reid by name, it has a clear Reidian stamp, confirmed by the fact that Wayland's *Elements of Intellectual Philosophy* (1854) was basically a gloss on Reid, citing Reid a total of 72 times.[99] *Elements of Moral Science* is divided into two "books," theoretical and practical ethics, and the argument is framed, typically, in an analogy to the natural sciences. Wayland suggests that just as there is a pre-established physical order in the universe, so also is there a pre-established moral order that we are constitutionally equipped to make sense of.[100] The book presents a view of the world as a relatively unchanging entity created by God for certain ends, and as such is a prime example of how common sense philosophy was often transmuted into an ethics that, except in evangelical circles,[101] would find it difficult to withstand the onslaught of Darwinism.

Wayland's textbooks reflected the trend in American higher education, beginning around 1820, of dividing what had been called "moral philosophy" into two components – moral and mental science (or philosophy) – that reflected the faculty psychology and empirical methodology of Reid and Stewart.[102] Ezra Stiles Ely's *Conversations on the Science of the Human Mind* (1819), which recommended an inductive approach to the study of the mind on the model of Reid and Stewart, is an early example of the new "science of the mind," as is Frederick Beasley's *A Search of Truth in the Science of the Human Mind* (1822). In attempting to rehabilitate Locke, Beasley advanced one of the more searching critiques of Reid's thought to appear in early nineteenth-century America, and the book's polemical tone is indicative of the pervasive influence of Reid by the second decade of the century.[103]

The first major American textbook in mental philosophy was Francis Upham's *Elements of Intellectual Philosophy* (1827). Herbert Schneider calls it a work of "empirical psychology rather than a philosophical system," and the work has been seen by others as opening "the era of American textbooks" in psychology.[104] Upham himself saw the work to be "eclectic in character," and it in fact cites a wide range of thinkers, including Buffier, Cousin, Jouffroy, and Kant. But Upham's heaviest debt is to Reid and Stewart, and he follows their ideas closely throughout the work.[105] In the decades that followed, a number of textbooks on mental philosophy were published in America. Although most of these texts were in the Reidian tradition, Schneider suggests that only McCosh "adhered closely to the Scottish school," and that as time went on, German, French, and British thought made serious inroads on Reidian mental and moral philosophy.[106] And indeed, by the time of Noah Porter's *Human Intellect* (1868), Reid appears as but one figure in a much larger constellation of thinkers (many of them German), even though a number of Porter's ideas can be traced to Reid.[107]

But lest one assume that Reidian thought had run its course in American intellectual life, it was to be reborn once more in the pragmaticism of Charles Sanders Peirce (1839–1914), which Peirce also called "critical common-sensism." Peirce, who had been a student of Bowen at Harvard, explicitly acknowledged his debt to Reid in an era when the traditional formulations of common sense philosophy were hardly fashionable among philosophers adjusting to the rise of Darwinism and the shattering experience of the Civil War.[108] What Peirce did, in effect, was to place at least some elements of Reidian thought into a Darwinian framework, making explicit its pragmatic elements and potentialities.

In published and unpublished manuscripts, Peirce dealt at length with the relationship between Reid's thought and his own. In a 1905 article published in *The Monist*, Peirce wrote about the doctrine of original beliefs maintained by "the old Scotch philosophers":

Before any waft of the air of evolution had reached those coasts, how could they think otherwise? When I first wrote, we were hardly orientated in the new ideas, and my impression was that the indubitable propositions changed with a thinking man from year to year.... It has been only during the last two years that I have completed a provisional inquiry which shows me that the changes are so slight from generation to generation, though not imperceptible even in that short period, that I thought to own my adhesion, under inevitable modification, to the opinion of that subtle but well-balanced intellect, Thomas Reid, in the matter of Common Sense (as well as in regard to immediate perception, along with Kant).[109]

Peirce saw Reid's principles of common sense to be "the instinctive result of human experience" – vague instincts or "innate cognitive habits" adapted to a primitive environment – that serve as a foundation for higher forms of judgment and decision-making.[110] The "pragmaticist's" doctrine "essentially insists upon the close affinity between thinking in particular and endeavour in general. Since, therefore, action in general is largely a matter of instinct, he will be pretty sure to ask himself whether it be not the same with belief."[111] To be sure, critical common-sensism subjects instinctive beliefs to doubt, but to do so is really not that easy – the "real metal" (as opposed to "paper doubts") can only be discovered after arduously subjecting doubts to the test of practical experience.[112] Given Reid's appeal to the fruits of everyday human experience – language, common beliefs and behaviors, habits of mind – to test the claims of philosophy, it is easy to see why Peirce felt a particular affinity for Reid. In the end, Peirce finds that a critical sifting of experience "invariably leaves a certain vague residuum [of instinctive beliefs] unaffected."[113]

V. CONCLUSION

Reid's thought led in many directions. If it served the needs of Christianity in its confrontation with modernity, it simultaneously played an important role, during the nineteenth century, in the expansion of higher education and the propagation of the perspectives and methods of modern science. Reidian thought promoted a vision of human nature and society that was particularly appealing to French and American educators in the aftermath of their respective political revolutions, providing a coherent and stable foundation for philosophical and scientific education in modernizing politically fragile nation-states. In the Germanies, by contrast, Reid's philosophical perspective clashed with the rationalistic tenor of German philosophy, seeming to offer little to thinkers writing in polities with weak middling classes and entrenched hierarchies and lacking republican institutions and a common public sphere of social and political interaction.[114] It would seem that there needs to be a "commons" for common sense philosophy to have any resonance, and for this reason it is not surprising that it initially emerged and gained a foothold in Britain before spreading abroad.

By the middle of the nineteenth century, varieties of idealism, transcendentalism, positivism, and empiricism had begun to compete with Reidian thought, but in more than a few cases these intellectual trends occurred in tandem with, or grew from, Reidian premises. Reid himself took "removing rubbish" and "digging for a foundation" to be among his primary tasks (IHM I.ii:15), and thus it is not surprising that Reidian thought has proven to be fertile ground for the growth of new ideas and perspectives – if one or the other offshoot has withered, others remain. Peirce's placement of Reid's philosophy into an evolutionary framework, a view which anticipated the emerging consensus of cognitive scientists, indicates that Reid's thought is not exhausted by pre-Darwinian and/or theistic understandings of the world.[115] Moore's influential development of common sense philosophy similarly indicates the enduring importance of Reid's response to skepticism and idealism. Of course given that the gap between common sense and scientific thinking is now greater than ever, and that postmodernist philosophies have updated Hume's skeptical challenge to both science and common sense, one wonders if Reid's thought will continue to exhibit the same type of vitality it has in the last several hundred years. The signs are promising, however. And one suspects it will.

NOTES

1. Oswald 1766: 312.
2. Beattie 1773: 141.
3. Robinson 1996: xxix–xxx.
4. Stewart 1814: 15–53, 61–80, 188–95, 252–73, and 403–49.
5. Stewart 1814: 207–9.
6. Stewart 1818: 39–40, 51–7.
7. McCosh 1875: 283; Laurie 1902: 221.
8. Brown 1851, Vol. 1: 325–9, 457–9; Vol. 2: 22–90.
9. See Brown 1835: *passim*; 244–9, 273–3. For a recent discussion of Reid's differences with Hume on the issue of causality, see Redekop 2002.
10. Davie 1961: 261.
11. Laurie 1902: 291.
12. See Davie 1961: 260–80; quote from 271.
13. The remark was made by Ferrier's contemporary De Quincey. See Thomson 1985: x.
14. See Ferrier 1866: 9–19, 82–9, 407–59. For affinities between Ferrier and Reid, see Davie 1961 and Graham 1999.
15. Mill 1865.
16. Davie 1991: 62.
17. Schneewind 1977: 63.
18. Sidgwick 1905: 418, 415.
19. See Broad's comments in Moore 1962: 6.
20. See Klemke 1995; Warnock 1995.
21. Moore 1951: 57–8, 86–9; Passmore 1957: 212; Beanblossom 1983: xliii–xlvii.
22. Moore 1962: 33.
23. Moore 1962: 44.
24. Kuehn argues that Reid's thought exerted a significant impact on eighteenth-century German philosophy, yet admits this very point. See Kuehn 1987: 243–4. For a recent critique of Kuehn's argument, see Wright 1998.
25. Quoted in Kuehn 1987: 173.

26. This point is discussed further in the Conclusion.
27. Kuehn 1987: 52–64.
28. Priestley 1774.
29. Kuehn 1987: 70–5.
30. Feder 1783: 130–58; quote from 117.
31. I could find only two references to Reid in the book. See Feder 1783: 50, 158.
32. Kuehn 1987: 76–80; quote from 76.
33. Kuehn 1987: 104–13; Eberhard 1776.
34. Kuehn 1987: 119.
35. Tetens 1777: 393, 375–6.
36. Kuehn 1987: 208.
37. Sidgwick 1905: 408–10; Kuehn 1987: 170.
38. Kant 1783: 12.
39. They are *gemeinen Menschenverstand, gesunden Verstand, geraden* or *schlichten Menschenverstand*, and *gemeinen Verstand*. See Kant 1783: 11–12.
40. For more, see Redekop 2000 and Knudsen 1982.
41. Giovanni 1998: 44; Jacobi 1994: 266.
42. Kuehn 1987: 145–52.
43. Hegel 1986: 140–6, 376–7.
44. Gérando 1847: 191–209; Boutroux 1897: 417–20.
45. Moore 1985.
46. Copleston 1985, Vol. IX: 19–36; quote from 29.
47. Royer-Collard 1913; quote from 196.
48. Royer-Collard 1913: 181–8. For discussion of the "problem of induction" as advanced by Hume, and Reid's response, see Redekop 2002.
49. Royer-Collard 1913: 182, 189.
50. Royer-Collard 1913: 188.
51. For Royer-Collard's critique of "modern philosophy," see Royer-Collard 1913: 25–40, 81–105, 213–49; quote from 105.
52. Cousin 1870: 33.
53. See the Author's Preface in Cousin 1870.
54. Cousin 1870: 37.
55. Cousin 1870: 347.
56. Cousin 1870: 40.
57. Cousin 1870: 354–5.
58. Cousin 1870: 49, 353–62; quote from 358; Cousin 1857: 395–7.
59. Cousin 1870: 9–10; 31.
60. Vermeren 1995: 95.
61. Vermeren 1995: 191.
62. Vermeren 1995; Boutroux 1897: 438–9.

63. Goblot 1997.
64. See Jouffroy 1833 "Translator's Forward" and i–lxvii; Jouffroy 1872: 1–155; Jouffroy 1994.
65. Jouffroy 1872: 141–2, 151–5.
66. See Jouffroy 1833: i–ii, lxiv–lxvii; Jouffroy 1836: *passim*; Jouffroy 1872: 74; Jouffroy 1994: 72–4.
67. Boutroux 1897: 440–3.
68. Manns 1994; Garnier 1840.
69. Comte 1995: 128.
70. See Comte 1995: 126–48.
71. See Rémusat 1842, Vol. 1: 176–247; Vol. 2: 408–48; quote from Vol. 2: 589–90.
72. Flower and Murphey 1977, Introduction; Chaps. 4–6.
73. Wills 1978: 175–91.
74. Conrad 1984; May 1976: 205–7, 348–9.
75. Sloan 1971.
76. Petersen 1964, Chap. III; Sloan 1971, Chap. IV; Miller 1990: 152–73, 229–30.
77. Petersen 1964: 63.
78. Sloan 1971, Chap. V; Petersen 1964, Chap. IV.
79. Smith 1812, Vol. I: 10–16, 20, 138–9.
80. Sloan 1971: 148–9n.7, 182–3.
81. Holifield 1978; Come 1945.
82. Alexander 1854.
83. Hodge 1873; Bozeman 1977.
84. McCosh 1860; Hoeveler 1981.
85. Howe 1988: 27.
86. Rand 1928: 46; Petersen 1964: 146.
87. Frisbie 1817: 10–11.
88. Hedge 1833: 170.
89. Cousin was in fact the only thinker cited in the sermon. See Walker 1877: 60.
90. Walker 1877: 39–40.
91. Howe 1988.
92. See Walker 1877: esp. 205–6, 223–31.
93. Bowen 1855: vi.
94. Petersen 1964, Chap. VIII; Kern 1953; Davis 1944.
95. Quoted in Davis 1944: 226.
96. Petersen 1964: 176.
97. Petersen 1964: 117.
98. Schneider 1946: 242.
99. See Wayland 1868.

100. See Wayland 1856.
101. Noll 1985: 232.
102. Schneider 1946, Chaps. 19–21.
103. See Beasley 1822: esp. 51–65.
104. Schneider 1946: 241; Fay 1939: 91.
105. For example, Upham 1856, Vol. 1: 59–134; quote from iii.
106. Schneider 1946: 241.
107. See, for example, Porter 1890: 103, 198, 391–440.
108. See Menand 2001. Menand unfortunately neglects to consider the role played by common sense philosophy in the rise of Pragmatism.
109. Peirce 1934: 296–7.
110. Peirce 1934: 297, 347, 354–66.
111. Peirce 1934: 348.
112. Peirce 1934: 295–7, 305, 347, 361–2.
113. Peirce 1934: 355.
114. For more on eighteenth-century German sociopolitical conditions, see Redekop 2000.
115. See Pinker 1997 and Redekop 1999.

BIBLIOGRAPHY

This bibliography provides information concerning the books and articles referred to in this volume and a selected offering of work on Reid not referred to in this volume. For a more extensive bibliography that canvasses both editions of Reid's work and work on Reid, see Squillante 1998a, 1998b, and 2000.

REID'S OWN WORKS

Reid, Thomas. 1748. An Essay on Quantity; occasioned by reading a Treatise, in which Simple and Compound Ratios are applied to Virtue and Merit. *Philosophical Transactions of the Royal Society of London* 45: 505–20. Reprinted in *The Works of Thomas Reid*: 715–19.

Reid, Thomas. 1863. *The Works of Thomas Reid*. 6th ed. Ed. Sir William Hamilton. Edinburgh: MacLachlan and Stewart. Reprint Bristol: Thoemmes Press, 1994.

Reid, Thomas. 1863. *Essays on the Active Powers of Man*. In Sir William Hamilton, ed., *The Works of Thomas Reid*, 6th edn. Edinburgh: MacLachlan and Stewart. Reprint Bristol: Thoemmes Press, 1994.

Reid, Thomas. 1973. *Lectures on the Fine Arts*. Ed. Peter Kivy. The Hague: Martinus Nijhoff.

Reid, Thomas. 1981. *Lectures on Natural Theology (1780)*. Ed. Elmer Duncan. Washington: University Press of America.

Reid, Thomas. 1989. *The Philosophical Orations of Thomas Reid*. Ed. D. D. Todd. Carbondale: Southern Illinois University Press.

Reid, Thomas. 1990. *Practical Ethics*. Ed. Knud Haakonssen. Princeton: Princeton University Press.

Reid, Thomas. 1995. *Thomas Reid on the Animate Creation: Papers Relating to the Life Sciences*. Ed. Paul Wood. Edinburgh: Edinburgh University Press.

341

Reid, Thomas. 1997. *An Inquiry into the Human Mind on the Principles of Common Sense*. Ed. Derek R. Brookes. Edinburgh: Edinburgh University Press.

Reid, Thomas. 2001. "On Power." Ed. John Haldane. *Philosophical Quarterly* 51: 3–12.

Reid, Thomas. 2002a. *Essays on the Intellectual Powers of Man*. Ed. Derek R. Brookes, with annotations by Derek R. Brookes and Knud Haakonssen. Edinburgh: Edinburgh University Press.

Reid, Thomas. 2002b. *The Correspondence of Thomas Reid*. Ed. Paul Wood. Edinburgh: Edinburgh University Press.

Reid, Thomas. forthcoming a. *Thomas Reid on Logic, Rhetoric and the Fine Arts*. Ed. Alexander Broadie. Edinburgh: Edinburgh University Press.

Reid, Thomas. forthcoming b. *Reid on Society and Politics*. Ed. Knud Haakonssen and Paul Wood. Edinburgh: Edinburgh University Press.

OTHER

Aepinus, F. U. T. 1979. *Essay on the Theory of Electricity and Magnetism*. Ed. R. W. Home, trans. P. J. Connor. Princeton: Princeton University Press.

Alexander, Archibald. 1854. *Outlines of Moral Science*. New York: Charles Scribner.

Alston, William. 1985. Thomas Reid on epistemic principles. *History of Philosophy Quarterly* 2: 435–52.

Alston, William. 1989. Reid on perception and conception. In Dalgarno and Matthews 1989.

Alston, William. 1991. *Perceiving God: The Epistemology of Religious Experience*. Ithaca: Cornell University Press.

Alston, William. 1993. *The Reliability of Sense Perception*. Ithaca: Cornell University Press.

Angell, R. B. 1974. The geometry of visibles. *Noûs* 8: 87–117.

Armstrong, D. M. 1968. *A Materialist Theory of the Mind*. London: Routledge & Kegan Paul.

Anstey, Peter. 1995. Thomas Reid and the justification of induction. *History of Philosophy Quarterly* 12: 77–93.

Austin, John L. 1961. *Philosophical Papers*. Oxford: Oxford University Press.

Bach, Kent. 1987. *Thought and Reference*. Oxford: Oxford University Press.

Balguy, John. 1728. *The Foundation of Moral Goodness*. London. Facsimile edition 1976, New York: Garland.

Barker, Stephen and Beauchamp, Tom, eds. 1976. *Thomas Reid: Critical Interpretations*. Philadelphia: Temple University Philosophical Monographs, no. 3.

Bayle, Pierre. 1965. *Historical and Critical Dictionary: Selections*. Trans. Richard H. Popkin. New York: Bobbs-Merrill Company.

Beanblossom, Ronald E. 1983. Introduction. In Ronald E. Beanblossom and Keith Lehrer, eds., *Thomas Reid's Inquiry and Essays*. Indianapolis: Hackett Publishing Company.

Beanblossom, Ronald E. 2000. James and Reid: Meliorism vs. metaphysics. *American Catholic Philosophical Quarterly* 74: 471–90.

Beasley, Frederick. 1822. *A Search of Truth in the Science of the Human Mind*. Philadelphia: J. Maxwell.

Beattie, James. 1773. *An Essay on the Nature and Immutability of Truth*. Edinburgh: Kincaid & Creech.

Bennett, Jonathan. 1993. The necessity of moral judgment. *Ethics* 103: 458–72.

Berkeley, George. 1710. *A Treatise Concerning the Principles of Human Knowledge*. Dublin: Aaron Rhames, for Jeremy Pepyat.

Berkeley, George. 1979. *Three Dialogues between Hylas and Philonous*. Ed. Robert M. Adams. Indianapolis: Hackett Publishing Company.

Bergmann, Michael. 2002. Commonsense naturalism. In James Beilby, ed., *Naturalism Defeated? Essays on Plantinga's Evolutionary Argument against Naturalism*. Ithaca: Cornell University Press.

Blackburn, Simon. 1993. Hume and thick connexions. In *Essays in Quasi-Realism*. Oxford: Oxford University Press.

Boutroux, Emile. 1897. *Etudes de l'histoire de la philosophie*. Paris: Germer Bailliére et Cie.

Bowen, Francis. 1855. *The Principles of Metaphysical and Ethical Science Applied to the Evidences of Religion*. Boston: Hickling, Swan and Brown.

Bozeman, Theodore. 1977. *Protestants in an Age of Science: The Baconian Ideal and Antebellum Religious Thought*. Chapel Hill: University of North Carolina Press.

Brink, David. 1989. *Moral Realism and the Foundations of Ethics*. Cambridge: Cambridge University Press.

Broad, C. D. 1959. *Scientific Thought*. Patterson: Littlefield, Adams.

Broadie, Alexander. 1998. Reid making sense of moral sense. *Reid Studies* 1, no. 2: 5–16.

Broadie, Alexander. 2000a. *Why Scottish Philosophy Matters*. Edinburgh: The Saltire Society.

Broadie, Alexander. 2000b. George Campbell, Thomas Reid, and universals of language. In Paul B. Wood, ed., *The Scottish Enlightenment: Essays in Reassessment*. Rochester: Rochester University Press.

Broadie, Alexander. 2000c. The Scotist Thomas Reid. *American Catholic Philosophical Quarterly* 74: 385–407.

Broadie, Alexander. 2002a. The association of ideas: Thomas Reid's context. *Reid Studies* 5, no. 2: 31–53.

Broadie, Alexander. 2002b. Scottish philosophy in the 18th century. *The Stanford Encyclopedia of Philosophy*. Available online at http://plato.stanford.edu/entries/scottish-18th/.

Broadie, Alexander, ed. 2003a. *The Cambridge Companion to the Scottish Enlightenment*. Cambridge: Cambridge University Press.

Broadie, Alexander. 2003b. The mind and its powers. In Broadie 2003a.

Brody, Baruch. 1971. Reid and Hamilton on perception. *The Monist* 55: 423–41.

Brody, Baruch. 1976. Hume, Reid, and Kant on causality. In Barker and Beauchamp 1976.

Brody, Baruch. 1980. *Identity and Essence*. Princeton: Princeton University Press.

Brown, Thomas. 1835. *Inquiry into the relation of cause and effect*. London: Henry G. Bohn.

Brown, Thomas. 1851. *Lectures on the Philosophy of the Mind*, vols. 1 and 2. Edinburgh: Adam & Charles Black.

Brun-Rovet, Etienne. 2002. Reid, Kant and the philosophy of mind. *The Philosophical Quarterly* 52: 495–510.

Buras, J. Todd. 2002. The Problem with Reid's direct realism. *Philosophical Quarterly* 52: 457–94.

Burge, Tyler. 1979. Individualism and the mental. In Peter French et al., eds. *Midwest Studies in Philosophy*, vol. 4. Minneapolis: University of Minnesota Press.

Butler, Joseph. 1975. Of identity. In John Perry, ed., *Personal Idenity*. Berkeley: University of California Press.

Butler, Joseph. 1983. *Five Sermons*. Ed. Stephen Darwall. Indianapolis: Hackett Publishing Company.

Callegard, Robert. 1999. The hypothesis of ether and Reid's interpretation of Newton's first rule of philosophizing. *Synthese* 120: 19–26.

Campbell, George. 1983. *A Dissertation on Miracles*. New York: Garland Publishing.

Cantor, G. N. 1977. Berkeley, Reid, and the mathematization of mid-eighteenth-century optics. *Journal of the History of Ideas* 38: 429–48.

Cantor, G. N. 1983. *Optics after Newton: Theories of Light in Britain and Ireland, 1704–1840*. Manchester: Manchester University Press.

Chappell, Vere. 1989. The theory of sensations. In Dalgarno and Matthews 1989.

Charlevoix, Pierre-François-Xavier de. 1744. *Histoire et description générale de la Novelle France*, 3 vols. Paris: Ganeau.

Chisholm, Roderick M. 1957. *Perceiving*. Ithaca: Cornell University Press.

Chisholm, Roderick M. 1966. *Theory of Knowledge*. Englewood Cliffs: Prentice-Hall.

Chisholm, Roderick M. 1976. *Person and Object: A Metaphysical Study*. LaSalle: Open Court.

Chisholm, Roderick M. 1991. On the simplicity of the soul. In James Tomberlin, ed., *Philosophical Perspectives 5, Philosophy of Religion*, Atascadero, CA: Ridgeview Publishing Company.

Cicero, Marcus Tullius. 1998. *The Nature of the Gods*. Trans. P. G. Walsh. New York: Oxford University Press.

Clarke, Samuel. 1738. *The Works of Samuel Clarke, D. D. Late Rector of St James's Westminster*, 4 vols. London: John and Paul Knapton.

Clarke, Samuel and Leibniz, G. W. 1956. *The Leibniz–Clarke Correspondence*, Ed. H. G. Alexander. Manchester: Manchester University Press.

Clarke, Samuel. 1998. *A Demonstration of the Being and Attributes of God and Other Writings*, Ed. Ezio Vailati. Cambridge: Cambridge University Press.

Clatterbaugh, Kenneth. 1999. *The Causation Debate in Modern Philosophy*. New York: Routledge.

Coady, C. A. J. 1992. *Testimony: A Philosophical Study*. Oxford: Oxford University Press.

Coady, C. A. J. 2000. Contract, justice and self interest: Reid and modern feminism. *American Catholic Philosophical Quarterly* 74: 519–39.

Come, D. R. 1945. The influence of Princeton on higher education in the South before 1825. *The William and Mary Quarterly*: 362–94.

Comte, August. 1995. *Discours sur L'Esprit Positif*. Paris: Librairie Philosophique J. Vrin.

Conrad, Stephen. 1984. Polite foundation: Citizenship and common sense in James Wilson's republican theory. *The Supreme Court Review*: 359–88.

Copenhaver, Rebecca. 2000. Thomas Reid's direct realism. *Reid Studies* 4, no. 1: 17–34.

Copleston, Frederick. 1985. *A History of Philosophy*, vols. IV–IX. New York: Doubleday.

Cousin, Victor. 1857. *Philosophie Ecossaise*. Paris: Librairie Nouvelle.

Cousin, Victor. 1870. *Lectures on the True, the Beautiful, and the Good*. New York: Appleton & Co.

Coutts, James. 1909. *A History of the University of Glasgow, from Its Foundation in 1451 to 1909*. Glasgow: James Maclehose and Sons.

Craig, Edward. 1987. *The Mind of God and the Works of Man*. Oxford: Clarendon Press.

Craig, William L. 2002. The Kalam Cosmological argument. In William L. Craig, ed., *Philosophy of Religion: A Reader and Guide*. New Brunswick: Rutgers University Press.

Crawford, Adair. 1788. *Experiments and Observations on Animal Heat, and the Inflammation of Combustible Bodies; Being an Attempt to Resolve These Phenomena into a General Law of Nature*, 2nd ed. London: J. Johnson.

Cummins, Phillip. 1974. Reid's realism. *Journal of the History of Philosophy* 12: 317–40.

Cummins, Phillip. 1976. Reid on abstract general ideas. In Barker and Beauchamp 1976.

Cummins, Phillip. 1990. Pappas on the role of sensations in Reid's theory of perception. *Philosophy and Phenomenological Research* 50: 755–62.

Cuneo, Terence. 2003. Reidian moral perception. *Canadian Journal of Philosophy* 33: 229–258.

Dalgarno, Melvin. 1984. Reid's natural jurisprudence – The language of rights and duties. In Vincent Hope, ed., *Philosophers of the Scottish Enlightenment*. Edinburgh: Edinburgh University Press.

Dalgarno, Melvin, and Matthews, Eric, eds. 1989. *The Philosophy of Thomas Reid*. Dordrecht: Kluwer Academic Publishers.

Daniels, Norman. 1989. *Thomas Reid's 'Inquiry': The Geometry of Visibles and the Case for Realism*. Stanford: Stanford University Press.

Darwall, Stephen. 1995. *The British Moralists and the Internal 'Ought' 1640–1740*. Cambridge: Cambridge University Press.

Davie, George. 1961. *The Democratic Intellect: Scotland and Her Universities in the Nineteenth Century*. Edinburgh: Edinburgh University Press.

Davie, George. 1981. *The Democratic Intellect: Scotland and Her Universities in the Nineteenth Century*, 2nd ed. Edinburgh: Edinburgh University Press.

Davie, George. 1991. *The Scottish Enlightenment and Other Essays*. Edinburgh: Polygon.

Davis, Merrell. 1944. Emerson's "reason" and the Scottish philosophers. *The New England Quarterly* 17: 209–28.

Davis, William C. 1992. Thomas Reid on moral epistemology and the moral sense. Ph.D. dissertation, University of Notre Dame.

de Bary, Philip. 2000. Thomas Reid's metaprinciple. *American Catholic Philosophical Quarterly* 74: 373–83.

de Bary, Philip. 2001. *Thomas Reid and Scepticism: His Reliabilist Response*. London and New York: Routledge.

DeRose, Keith. 1989. Reid's anti-sensationalism and his realism. *The Philosophical Review* 98: 313–48.

Desaguliers, J. T. 1763. *A Course of Experimental Philosophy*, 3rd ed., 2 vols. London: A. Millar.

Descartes, René. 1971–75. *Oeuvres de Des Cartes*. Ed. Charles Adam and Paul Tannery. 11 vols. Paris: Vrin.

Donovan, Arthur L. 1975. *Philosophical Chemistry in the Scottish Enlightenment: The Doctrines and Discoveries of William Cullen and Joseph Black*. Edinburgh: Edinburgh University Press.

Dretske, Fred. 1981. *Knowledge and the Flow of Information*. Cambridge: MIT Press.

Duggan, Timothy. 1960. Thomas Reid's theory of sensation. *Philosophical Review* 69: 90–100.

Duggan, Timothy. 1976. Active power and the liberty of moral agents. In Barker and Beauchamp 1976.

Eberhard, Johann. 1776. *Allgemeine Theorie des Denkens und Empfindens*. Berlin: Voß.

Emerson, Roger L. 1992. *Professors, Patronage and Politics: The Aberdeen Universities in the Eighteenth Century*. Aberdeen: Aberdeen University Press.

Emerson, Roger L. 1994. The "affair" at Edinburgh and the "project" at Glasgow: The politics of Hume's attempts to become a professor. In M. A. Stewart and John P. Wright 1994.

Emerson, Roger L. 1995. Politics and the Glasgow professors, 1690–1800. In Andrew Hook and Richard B. Sher, eds., *The Glasgow Enlightenment*. East Linton: Tuckwell Press.

Emerson, Roger L. and Wood, Paul. 2002. Science and enlightenment in Glasgow, 1690–1802. In Charles W. J. Withers and Paul Wood, eds., *Science and Medicine in the Scottish Enlightenment*. East Linton: Tuckwell Press.

Falkenstein, Lorne. 1994. Intuition and construction in Berkeley's account of visual space. *Journal of the History of Philosophy* 32: 63–84.

Falkenstein, Lorne. 1995. Hume and Reid on the simplicity of the soul. *Hume Studies* 21: 25–45.

Falkenstein, Lorne. 1997. Hume on manners of disposition and the ideas of space and time. *Archiv für Geschichte der Philosophie* 79: 179–201.

Falkenstein, Lorne. 2000a. Reid's critique of Berkeley's position on the inverted image. *Reid Studies* 4, no. 1: 35–51.

Falkenstein, Lorne. 2000b. Reid's account of localization. *Philosophy and Phenomenological Research* 61: 305–28.

Fay, Jay. 1939. *American Psychology before William James*. New Brunswick: Rutgers University Press.

Feder, Johann. 1783. *Logik und Metaphysik*. Vienna: Trattnern.

Ferrier, James. 1866. *Lectures on Greek Philosophy and Other Philosophical Remains*, vol. II. Edinburgh: William Blackwood & Sons.

Fischer, John Martin. 1994. *The Metaphysics of Freedom*. Oxford: Blackwell.

Flower, Elizabeth, and Murphey, Murray. 1977. *A History of Philosophy in America*, vol. 1. New York: Capricorn Books.

Frankfurt, Harry G. 1969. Alternate possibilities and moral responsibility. *Journal of Philosophy* 66: 829–39.

Fraser, A. Campbell. 1898. *Thomas Reid*. Edinburgh and London: Oliphant, Anderson & Ferrier.

Friedman, Michael. 1992. Causal laws and the foundations of natural science. In Paul Guyer, ed., *The Cambridge Companion to Kant*. Cambridge: Cambridge University Press.

Frisbie, Levi. 1817. *Inaugural Address*. Cambridge: Hilliard and Metcalf.

Gallie, Roger D. 1989. *Thomas Reid and "The Way of Ideas."* Dordrecht: Kluwer Academic Publishers.

Gallie, Roger D. 1998. *Thomas Reid: Ethics, Aesthetics and the Autonomy of the Self*. Dordrecht: Kluwer Academic Publishers.

Gallie, Roger D. 2000. Reid, Kant and the doctrine of the two standpoints. *American Catholic Philosophical Quarterly* 74: 409–24.

Garnier, Adolphe. 1840. *Critique de la Philosophie de Thomas Reid*. Paris: Hachette.

Gaskin, J. C. A. 1988. *Hume's Philosophy of Religion*, 2nd ed. London: Macmillan.

Gaskin, J. C. A. 1993. Hume on Religion. In David F. Norton, ed., *The Cambridge Companion to Hume*. Cambridge: Cambridge University Press.

Gérando, Joseph. 1847. *Histoire comparée des systémes de philosophie*, vol. IV. Paris: Librairie philosophique de Ladrange.

Gerard, Alexander. 1766. *Dissertations on subjects relating to the genius and evidences of Christianity*. Edinburgh: A. Millar.

Gibson, J. J. 1966. *The Senses Considered as Perceptual Systems*. New York: Houghton Mifflin.

Ginet, Carl. 1975. *Knowledge, Perception, and Memory*. Dordrecht: Reidel.

Giovanni, George di. 1998. Hume, Jacobi, and common sense. *Kant Studien* 89: 44–58.

Goblot, Jean-Jacques. 1997. Jouffroy et Cousin. In Eric Fauquet, ed., *Victor Cousin, Homo Theologico-politicus*. Paris: Editions Kimé.

Gracyck, Theodore. 1987. The failure of Thomas Reid's aesthetics. *The Monist* 70: 465–82.

Graham, Gordon. 1999. The Scottish tradition in philosophy. *The Aberdeen University Review* 58, no. 1: 1–13.

Grave, Selwyn. 1960. *The Scottish Philosophy of Common Sense*. Oxford: Clarendon Press.

Greco, John. 1995. Reid's critique of Berkeley and Hume: What's the big idea? *Philosophy and Phenomenological Research* 55: 279–96.

Greco, John. 2000. *Putting Skeptics in Their Place*. Cambridge: Cambridge University Press.

Greco, John. 2002. How to Reid Moore. *The Philosophical Quarterly* 52: 544–63.

Greig, J. Y. T., ed. 1932. *The Letters of David Hume*, 2 vols. Oxford: Clarendon Press.

Guicciardini, Niccoló. 2001. Thomas Reid's mathematical manuscripts: A survey. *Reid Studies* 4, no. 2: 71–86.

Haldane, John. 1993. Whose theory? Which representations? *Pacific Philosophical Quarterly* 74: 247–57.

Haldane, John. 2000a. Thomas Reid: Life and work. *American Catholic Philosophical Quarterly* 84: 317–44.

Haldane, John. 2000b. Thomas Reid and the history of ideas. *American Catholic Philosophical Quarterly* 84: 447–69.

Hedge, Levi. 1833. *Elements of Logick*. Boston: Hilliard, Gray and Co.

Hegel, G. W. F. 1975. *Hegel's Logic: Being Part One of the Encyclopaedia of the Philosophical Sciences (1830)*. Trans. William Wallace. Oxford: Clarendon Press.

Hegel, Georg. 1986. *Vorlesungen über die Geschichte der Philosophie*, vol. 4. Hamburg: Felix Meiner Verlag.

Heilbron, John. 1979. *Electricity in the Seventeenth and Eighteenth Centuries: A Study of Early Modern Physics*. Berkeley, Los Angeles, and London: University of California Press.

Hodge, Charles. 1873. *Systematic Theology*, vol. 1. New York: Charles Scribner.

Hoeveler, J. David. 1981. *James McCosh and the Scottish Intellectual Tradition*. Princeton: Princeton University Press.

Holifield, E. Brooks. 1978. *The Gentleman Theologians: American Theology in Southern Culture, 1795–1860*. Durham: Duke University Press.

Holland, A. J., ed. 1985. *Philosophy, Its History and Historiography*. Dordrecht and Boston: D. Reidel.

Houston, Joseph, ed. 2003. *Thomas Reid: Context, Significance and Influence*. Edinburgh: Scottish Academic Press.

Howe, Daniel. 1988. *The Unitarian Conscience: Harvard Moral Philosophy, 1805–1861*. Middletown: Wesleyan University Press.

Hume, David. 1980. *Dialogues Concerning Natural Religion*. Ed. Richard H. Popkin. Indianapolis: Hackett Publishing Company.

Hume, David. 1998. *An Enquiry concerning the Principles of Morals*. Ed. Tom L. Beauchamp. Oxford: Oxford University Press.

Hume, David. 1999. *An Enquiry concerning Human Understanding*. Ed. Tom L. Beauchamp. Oxford: Oxford University Press.

Hume, David. 2001. *A Treatise of Human Nature*. Ed. David Fate Norton and Mary J. Norton. Oxford: Oxford University Press.

Hutcheson, Francis. 1971. *Synopsis Metaphysicae, Ontologiam et Pneumatologiam complectens*. Hildesheim: Georg Olms Verlag.

Hutcheson, Francis. 1999. *On the Nature and Conduct of the Passions*. Ed. Andrew Ward. Manchester: Clinamen Press.

Hutton, Charles. 1795–96. *A Mathematical and Philosophical Dictionary*, 2 vols. London: J. Johnson and G. G. and J. Robinson.

Iltis, Carolyn. 1973. The Leibnizian–Newtonian debates: Natural philosophy and social psychology. *The British Journal for the History of Science* 6: 343–77.

Immerwahr, John. 1978. The development of Reid's realism. *The Monist* 61: 245–56.

Jackson, Frank. 1977. *Perception*. Cambridge: Cambridge University Press.

Jacobi, Friedrich. 1994. *The Main Philosophical Writings*. Montreal and Kingston: McGill–Queen's University Press.

Jardine, George. 1825. *Outlines of Philosophical Education, Illustrated by the Method of Teaching the Logic Class in the University of Glasgow*, 2nd ed. Glasgow: For Oliver and Boyd.

Jensen, Henning. 1978. Common sense and common language in Thomas Reid's ethical theory. *The Monist* 61: 299–310.

Jensen, Henning. 1979. Reid and Wittgenstein on philosophy and language. *Philosophical Studies* 36: 359–76.

Jouffroy, Théodore, ed. and trans. 1833. *Esquisses de philosophie morale*. Paris: A Johanneau.

Jouffroy, Théodore, ed. and trans. 1836. *Œuvres Complètes de Thomas Reid*, vol. 1. Paris: Victor Masson.

Jouffroy, Théodore. 1872. *Nouveaux mélanges philosophiques*. Paris: Hachette.

Jouffroy, Théodore. 1994. De la philosophie et du sens commun. In Stéphane Douaillier et al., eds., *Philosophie, France, XIXème siècle: écrits et opuscules*. Paris: Librairie Générale Française.

Kames, Henry Home, Lord. 1774. *Sketches of the History of Man*, 2 vols. Edinburgh: W. Creech.

Kant, Immanuel. 1783. *Prolegomena zu einer jeden künftigen Metaphysik*. Riga: Hartknoch.

Kant, Immanuel. 1910- . *Gesammelte Schriften*, 27+ vols. Berlin: Royal Prussian Academy of the Sciences (and successors).

Kant, Immanuel. 1950. *Prolegomena to Any Future Metaphysics*. Ed. Lewis White Beck. Indianapolis: Bobbs-Merrill Company.

Kant, Immanuel. 1998. *Critique of Pure Reason*. Ed. and trans. Paul Guyer and Allen W. Wood. Cambridge: Cambridge University Press.

Kern, Alexander. 1953. The rise of transcendentalism 1815–1860. In Harry Clark, ed., *Transitions in American Literary History*. Durham: Duke University Press.

Kivy, Peter. 1976. The logic of taste: Reid and the second fifty years. In Barker and Beauchamp 1976.

Kivy, Peter. 1978. Thomas Reid and the expression theory of art. *The Monist* 61: 167–83.

Kivy, Peter. 1989. Seeing is believing: On the significance of Reid in the history of aesthetics. In Delgarno and Mathews 1989.

Klemke, E. D. 1995. G. E. Moore. In Robert Audi, ed., *The Cambridge Dictionary of Philosophy*. Cambridge: Cambridge University Press.

Klemme, Heiner. 2003. Scepticism and common sense. In Broadie 2003a.

Knudsen, Jonathan. 1982. Friedrich Nicolai's "wirkliche Welt": On common sense in the German enlightenment. In *Mentalitäten und Lebensverhältnisse: Beispiele aus der Sozialgeschichte der Neuzeit*. Göttingen: Vandenhoeck and Ruprecht: 77–91.

Kristeller, Paul Oskar. 1992. The modern system of the arts, parts I and II. In Peter Kivy, ed., *Essays in the History of Aesthetics*. Rochester: University of Rochester Press.

Kuehn, Manfred. 1987. *Scottish Common Sense in Germany, 1768–1800*. Kingston and Montreal: McGill–Queen's University Press.

Kuflik, Arthur. 1998. Hume on justice to animals, Indians and women. *Hume Studies* 24: 53–70.

Laudan, Larry L. 1968. The *vis viva* controversy, a postmortem. *Isis* 59: 131–43.

Laudan, Larry L. 1970. Thomas Reid and the Newtonian turn of British methodological thought. In Robert E. Butts and John W. Davis, eds., *The Methodological Heritage of Newton*. Oxford: Blackwell.

Laurie, Henry. 1902. *Scottish Philosophy in its National Development*. Glasgow: Maclehose.

Lehrer, Keith. 1989. *Thomas Reid*. London: Routledge.

Lehrer, Keith and Warner, Bradley. 2000. Reid, God and epistemology. *American Catholic Philosophical Quarterly* 74: 357–72.

Leibniz, G. W. 1951. *Theodicy: Essays on the Goodness of God and the Freedom of Man and the Origin of Evil*. Ed. Austin Farrar, trans. E. M. Huggard. London: Routledge and Kegan Paul.

Leibniz, G. W. 1989. Primary truths. In Roger Ariew and Daniel Garber, eds., *Philosophical Essays*. Indianapolis: Hackett Publishing Company.

Levy, Sanford. 1999. Thomas Reid's defence of conscience. *History of Philosophy Quarterly* 16: 413–35.

Loar, Brian. 1988. Social content and psychological content. In Robert Grimm and Daniel Merrill, eds., *Contents of Thought*. Tucson: University of Arizona Press.

Locke, John. 1975. *An Essay concerning Human Understanding*. Ed. Peter H. Nidditch. Oxford: Clarendon Press.

McCosh, James. 1860. *The Intuitions of the Mind Inductively Investigated*. New York: Carter & Bros.

McCosh, James. 1875. *The Scottish Philosophy: Biographical, Expository, and Critical*. London: Macmillan and Company.

McDermid, Douglas. 1999. Thomas Reid on moral liberty and common sense. *British Journal for the History of Philosophy* 7: 275–303.

McGinn, Colin. 1997. *Ethics, Evil and Fiction*. Oxford: Oxford University Press.

McGregor, Joan. 1987. Reid on justice as a natural virtue. *The Monist* 70: 483–95.

McInerny, Ralph. 2000. Thomas Reid and common sense. *American Catholic Philosophical Quarterly* 74: 345–55.

MacIntyre, Alasdair. 1966. *A Short History of Ethics: A History of Moral Philosophy from the Homeric Age to the Twentieth Century*. New York: Collier Books.

MacIntyre, Alasdair. 1988. *Whose Justice? Which Rationality?* Notre Dame: University of Notre Dame Press.

McKitrick, Jennifer. 2002. Reid's foundation for the primary/secondary quality distinction. *Philosophical Quarterly* 52: 476–94.

Mackie, John L. 1977. *Ethics: Inventing Right and Wrong*. New York: Penguin.

Maclaurin, Colin. 1737–38. An observation of the eclipse of the sun, on Feb.18.1737 made at Edinburgh. *Philosophical Transactions of the Royal Society of London* 40: 177–95.

Maclaurin, Colin. 1742. *A Treatise of Fluxions in Two Books*, 2 vols. Edinburgh: T. W. and T. Ruddimans.

Malcolm, Norman. 1963. *Knowledge and Certainty*. Ithaca: Cornell University Press.

Manns, James. 1994. *Reid and His French Disciples: Aesthetics and Metaphysics*. Leiden: E. J. Brill.

May, Henry. 1976. *The Enlightenment in America*. New York: Oxford University Press.

Melvill, Thomas. 1756. Observations on light and colours. *Essays and Observations, Physical and Literary* 2: 12–90.

Menand, Louis. 2001. *The Metaphysical Club*. New York: Farrar, Straus and Giroux.

Michael, Fred, and Michael, Emily. 1987. Reid's Hume. *The Monist* 70: 508–26.

Michael, Emily. 1999. Reid's critique of the Scottish logic of ideas. *Reid Studies* 2, no.2: 3–18.

Mill, John Stuart. 1865. *An Examination of Sir William Hamilton's Philosophy*. London: Longmans, Green and Co.

Miller, Thomas, ed. 1990. *The Selected Writings of John Witherspoon*. Carbondale and Edwardsville: Southern Illinois University Press.

Moore, F. C. T. 1985. Une copie mal déguisée. *Victor Cousin, les idéologues et les Ecossais.* Paris: Presses de l'Ecole Normale Supérieure.

Moore, G. E. 1951. *Philosophical Studies.* New York: The Humanities Press.

Moore, G. E. 1962. *Philosophical Papers.* New York: Collier Books.

Morton, the Earl of, et al. 1748. An eclipse of the sun, July 14. 1748. *Philosophical Transactions of the Royal Society of London* 45: 582–97.

Muir, James. 1950. *John Anderson, Pioneer of Technical Education and the College He Founded.* Ed. James M. Macaulay. Glasgow: John Smith and Son.

Nadler, Steven M. 1986. Reid, Arnauld, and the objects of perception. *History of Philosophy Quarterly* 3: 165–174.

Nauckhoff, Josefine. 1994. Objectivity and expression in Thomas Reid's aesthetics. *The Journal of Aesthetics and Art Criticism* 52: 183–91.

Newton, Sir Isaac. 1952. *Opticks: Or, a Treatise on the Reflections, Refractions, Inflections and Colours of Light,* 4th ed. Reprint with a preface by I. Bernard Cohen. New York: Dover Publications.

Newton, Sir Isaac. 1999. *The Principia: Mathematical Principles of Natural Philosophy.* Trans. I. Bernard Cohen, Anne Whitman, and Julia Budenz. Berkeley, Los Angeles, and London: University of California Press.

Nichols, Ryan. 2002a. Reid on fictional objects and the way of ideas. *The Philosophical Quarterly* 52: 582–601.

Nichols, Ryan. 2002b. Learning and conceptual content in Reid's theory of perception. *British Journal for the History of Philosophy* 10: 49–79.

Nichols, Ryan. forthcoming. Visible figure and Reid's theory of visual perception. *Hume Studies,* 28.

Noll, Mark. 1985. Common sense traditions and American evangelical thought. *American Quarterly* 37: 216–38.

Norton, David Fate. 1966. From moral sense to common sense: An essay on the development of Scottish common sense philosophy, 1700–1765. Ph.D. diss., University of California at San Diego.

Norton, David Fate, and Stewart-Robertson, J. C. 1984. Thomas Reid on Adam Smith's theory of morals. *Journal of the History of Ideas* 41: 381–98.

O'Connor, Timothy. 1994. Thomas Reid on free agency. *Journal of the History of Philosophy* 32: 605–22.

Olson, Richard. 1975. *Scottish Philosophy and British Physics, 1750–1880: A Study in the Foundations of the Victorian Scientific Style.* Princeton: Princeton University Press.

Oswald, James. 1766. *An Appeal to Common Sense in Behalf of Religion.* Edinburgh: Kincaid & Bell.

Pakaluk, Michael. 2002. A defence of Scottish common sense. *The Philosophical Quarterly* 52: 564–81.

Paley, William. 1991. Selection from *Principles of Moral and Political Philosophy*. In D. D. Raphael, ed., *The British Moralists 1650–1800*. Indianapolis: Hackett Publishing Company.

Palmer, Stephen E. 1999. *Vision Science: Photons to Phenomenology*. Cambridge, MA: MIT Press.

Pappas, George S. 1989. Sensation and perception in Reid. *Noûs* 23: 155–67.

Pappas, George S. 1990. Causation and perception in Reid. *Philosophy and Phenomenological Research* 50: 763–66.

Passmore, John. 1957. *A Hundred Years of Philosophy*. London: G. Duckworth.

Pederson, Kurt Møller. 1980. Roger Joseph Boscovich and John Robison on terrestrial aberration. *Centaurus* 24: 335–45.

Peirce, Charles. 1934. *Collected Papers of Charles Sanders Peirce*, vol. 1. Cambridge, MA: Harvard University Press.

Peterson, Michael, et al., eds. 1998. *Reason and Religious Belief*, 2nd ed. New York: Oxford University Press.

Petersen, Richard. 1964. Scottish common sense in America, 1768–1850: An evaluation of its influence. Ph.D. dissertation, American University.

Pinker, Steven. 1997. *How the Mind Works*. New York: Norton.

Pitcher, George. 1971. *A Theory of Perception*. Princeton: Princeton University Press.

Plantinga, Alvin. 1983. Reason and belief in God. In Plantinga and Wolterstorff 1983.

Plantinga, Alvin. 1986. Two dozen (or so) theistic arguments. Unpublished lecture notes from the 33rd Annual Philosophy Conference, Wheaton College, October 23–24, 1986. Available online at http://philofreligion.homestead.com/files/Theisticarguments.html and http://www.homestead.com/philofreligion/files/Theisticarguments.html.

Plantinga, Alvin. 1993. *Warrant and Proper Function*. Oxford: Oxford University Press.

Plantinga, Alvin. 2000. *Warranted Christian Belief*. Oxford: Oxford University Press.

Plantinga, Alvin, and Wolterstorff, Nicholas, eds. 1983. *Faith and Rationality: Reason and Belief in God*. Notre Dame: University of Notre Dame Press.

Popkin, Richard. 1965. Introduction. In *Historical and Critical Dictionary: Selections*. New York: Bobbs–Merrill Company.

Porter, Noah. 1890. *The Elements of Intellectual Science*. New York: Charles Scribner's Sons.

Price, H. H. 1932. *Perception*. London: Methuen.

Price, Richard. 1948. *A Review of the Principal Questions in Morals*. Ed. D. D. Raphael. Oxford: Clarendon Press.

Priestley, Joseph. 1774. *An examination of Dr. Reid's Inquiry into the human mind on the principles of common sense, Dr. Beattie's Essay on the nature and immutability of truth, and Dr. Oswald's Appeal to common sense in behalf of religion*. London: J. Johnson.

Priestley, Joseph. 1976. *The Doctrine of Philosophical Necessity Illustrated*. New York: Garland Publishing.

Pritchard, Michael. 1978. Reason and passion: Reid's reply to Hume. *The Monist* 61: 283–98.

Putnam, Hilary. 1975. The meaning of "Meaning." In *Mind, Language and Meaning: Philosophical Papers*, vol. 2. Cambridge: Cambridge University Press.

Rand, Benjamin. 1928. Philosophical instruction in Harvard University from 1636 to 1906. *The Harvard Graduates Magazine* 37: 25–46.

Redekop, Benjamin. 1999. Common sense and science: Reid then and now. *Reid Studies* 3, no. 1: 31–47.

Redekop, Benjamin. 2000. *Enlightenment and Community: Lessing, Abbt, Herder, and the Quest for a German Public*. Montreal and London: McGill–Queen's University Press.

Redekop, Benjamin. 2002. Thomas Reid and the problem of induction: From common experience to common sense. *Studies in History and Philosophy of Science* 33A: 33–54.

Rémusat, Charles. 1842. *Essais de philosophie*, 2 vols. Paris: Librairie philosophique de Ladrange.

Robinson, Daniel. 1976. Thomas Reid's *Gestalt* psychology. In Barker and Beauchamp 1976.

Robinson, Daniel. 1989. Thomas Reid's critique of Dugald Stewart. *Journal of the History of Philosophy* 27: 405–22.

Robinson, Roger. 1996. Introduction. In James Beattie, *An Essay on the Nature and Immutability of Truth*. London: Routledge.

Robison, John. 1790. On the motion of light, as affected by refracting and reflecting substances, which are also in motion. *Transactions of the Royal Society of Edinburgh* 2: 83–111.

Robison, John. 1797. Simson, Robert. In *Encyclopaedia Britannica*, 3rd ed., vol. 17. Edinburgh: A. Bell and C. Macfarquhar.

Rowe, William. 1989. Causing and being responsible for what is inevitable. *American Philosophical Quarterly* 26: 153–9.

Rowe, William. 1991. *Thomas Reid on Freedom and Morality*. Ithaca: Cornell University Press.

Rowe, William. 1998. *The Cosmological Argument*. New York: Fordham University Press.

Rowe, William. 2000. The metaphysics of freedom: Reid's theory of agent causation. *American Catholic Philosophical Quarterly* 74: 425–46.

Rowe, William. 2002. The cosmological argument. In Joel Feinburg and Russ Shafer-Landau, eds., *Reason and Responsibility*, 11th ed. Belmont: Wadsworth.

Royer-Collard, Paul. 1913. *Les Fragments philosophiques de Royer-Collard*. Paris: Félix Alcan.

Russell, Bertrand. 1997. *The Problems of Philosophy*. New York: Oxford University Press.

Russell, Paul. 1997. Wishart, Baxter and Hume's *Letter from a Gentleman*. *Hume Studies* 23: 245–76.

Rysiew, Patrick. 1999. Reid's (mis)characterization of judgment. *Reid Studies* 3, no. 1: 63–8.

Rysiew, Patrick. 2002. Reid and epistemic naturalism. *The Philosophical Quarterly* 52: 437–56.

Schneewind, J. B. 1977. *Sidgwick's Ethics and Victorian Moral Philosophy*. Oxford: Clarendon Press.

Schneewind, J. B. 1998. *The Invention of Autonomy*. Cambridge: Cambridge University Press.

Schneider, Herbert. 1946. *A History of American Philosophy*. New York: Columbia University Press.

Schuhmann, Karl, and Smith, Barry. 1990. Elements of speech act theory in the work of Thomas Reid. *History of Philosophy Quarterly* 7: 47–66.

Schulthess, Daniel. 1983. *Philosophie et Sense Commun chez Thomas Reid*. Berne, New York: Peter Lang.

Shaftesbury, Anthony Ashley Cooper, 3d Earl of. 1999. *Characteristics of Men, Manners, Opinions, Times*. Ed. Lawrence E. Klein. Cambridge: Cambridge University Press.

Sher, Richard B. 1985. *Church and University in the Scottish Enlightenment: The Moderate Literati of Edinburgh*. Edinburgh: Edinburgh University Press.

Sidgwick, Henry. 1905. *Lectures on the Philosophy of Kant*. London and New York: Macmillan and Company.

Sloan, Douglas. 1971. *The Scottish Enlightenment and the American College Ideal*. New York: Teachers College Press.

Smellie, William. 2001. *The Philosophy of Natural History*, 2 vols. Bristol: Thoemmes Press.

Smith, J-C. 1986. Reid's functional explanation of sensation. *History of Philosophy Quarterly* 3: 175–94.

Smith, Samuel. 1812. *The Lectures, Corrected and Improved, Which Have Been Delivered for a Series of Years, in the College of New Jersey; on the Subjects of Moral and Political Philosophy*, 2 vols. Trenton: Daniel Fenton.

Sober, Elliott. 1993. *Philosophy of Biology*. Boulder: Westview Press.

Sorabji, Richard. 1983. *Time, Creation, and the Continuum: Theories in Antiquity and the Early Middle Ages.* Ithaca: Cornell University Press.

Sosa, Ernest, and Van Cleve, James. 2001. Thomas Reid. In Steven M. Emmanuel, ed., *The Blackwell Guide to the Modern Philosophers.* Oxford: Blackwell.

Squillante, Martino. 1998a. Thomas Reid: An updated bibliography, part I. *Reid Studies* 1, no. 2: 71–81.

Squillante, Martino. 1998b. Thomas Reid: An updated bibliography, part II. *Reid Studies* 2, no. 1: 57–78.

Squillante, Martino. 2000. Thomas Reid: A bibliographical update. *Reid Studies* 4, no. 1: 93–96.

Stecker, Robert. 1992. Does Thomas Reid reject/refute the representational theory of mind? *Pacific Philosophical Quarterly* 73: 174–84.

Stewart, Dugald. 1803. *Account of the Life and Writings of Thomas Reid, D. D. F. R. S.Edin. Late Professor of Moral Philosophy in the University of Glasgow.* Edinburgh: William Creech.

Stewart, Dugald. 1814. *Elements of the Philosophy of the Human Mind,* vol. 1. Boston: Wells & Lilly.

Stewart, Dugald. 1818. *Elements of the Philosophy of the Human Mind,* vol. 2. Boston: Wells & Lilly.

Stewart, Dugald. 1828. *The Philosophy of the Active and Moral Powers of Man.* Edinburgh: Adam Black.

Stewart, Dugald. 1834. *Philosophie des Facultés de l'homme.* Trans. Léon Simon. Paris: Alexandre Johanneau.

Stewart, John. 1745. *Sir Isaac Newton's Two Treatises of the Quadratures of Curves, and Analysis by Equations of an Infinite Number of Terms, Explained.* London: John Nourse and John Whiston.

Stewart, M. A. 1985. Hume and metaphysical argument a priori. In Holland 1985.

Stewart, M. A. 1987. George Turnbull and educational reform. In Jennifer J. Carter and Joan H. Pittock, eds., *Aberdeen and the Enlightenment.* Aberdeen: Aberdeen University Press.

Stewart, M. A. 2003a. Rational religion and common sense. In Houston 2003.

Stewart, M. A. 2003b. Religion and rational theology. In Broadie 2003a.

Stewart, M. A. forthcoming. George Turnbull. In the *New Dictionary of National Biography.* Oxford: Oxford University Press.

Stewart, M. A. and Wright, John P., eds. 1994. *Hume and Hume's Connexions.* Edinburgh: Edinburgh University Press.

Strawson, Galen. 1989. *The Secret Connexion.* Oxford: Clarendon Press.

Strawson, Galen. 1990. What's so good about Reid? *London Review of Books,* February 22: 14–16.

Strawson, Peter F. 1968. Freedom and resentment. In *Studies in the Philosophy of Thought and Action*. Oxford: Oxford University Press.

Suderman, Jeffrey M. 2002. *Orthodoxy and Enlightenment: George Campbell in the Eighteenth Century*. Montreal and Kingston: McGill–Queen's University Press.

Tapper, Alan. 2002. Reid and Priestley on method and the mind. *The Philosophical Quarterly* 52: 511–25.

Tetens, Johann. 1777. *Philosophische Versuche über die menschliche Natur*, vol. 1. Leipzig: Weidmanns Erben u. Reich.

Thomson, Arthur. 1985. *Ferrier of St. Andrews: An Academic Tragedy*. Edinburgh: Scottish Academic Press Ltd.

Thomson, George. 1950. Robert Cleghorn, M. D. In Andrew Kent, ed., *An Eighteenth-Century Lectureship in Chemistry*. Glasgow: Jackson, Son, and Company.

Todd, D. D. 2000. An inquiry into Thomas Reid. *Dialogue* 39: 381–8.

Tootell, R. B. H., Silverman, M. S., Switkes, E., and DeValois, R. L. 1982. Deoxyglucose analysis of retinotopic organization in primate striate cortex. *Science* 218: 45–75.

Tuggy, Dale. 2000. Thomas Reid on causation. *Reid Studies* 3, no. 2: 3–27.

Turnbull, George. 1740. *The Principles of Moral and Christian Philosophy*, 2 vols. London: A. Millar.

Turnbull, George. forthcoming. *The Principles of Moral and Christian Philosophy*. Ed. Alexander Broadie. Indianapolis: Liberty Fund.

Ulman, H. Lewis. 1990. *The Minutes of the Aberdeen Philosophical Society, 1758–1773*. Aberdeen: Aberdeen University Press.

Upham, Thomas. 1856. *Elements of Mental Philosophy*, 2 vols. New York: Harper and Brothers.

Van Cleve, James. 1999. Reid on the first principles of contingent truths. *Reid Studies* 3, no. 1: 3–30.

Van Cleve, James. forthcoming a. Review of Nicholas Wolterstorff's *Thomas Reid and the Story of Epistemology*. *Mind*.

Van Cleve, James. forthcoming b. Thomas Reid's geometry of visibles. *The Philosophical Review*.

Van Woudenberg, René. 1999. Thomas Reid on memory. *Journal of the History of Philosophy* 37: 117–33.

Van Woudenberg, René. 2000. Perceptual relativism, scepticism, and Thomas Reid. *Reid Studies* 3, no. 2: 65–85.

Van Woudenberg, René. 2003. Kant and Reid against the sceptic. In Houston 2003.

Vermeren, Patrice. 1995. *Victor Cousin: Le jeu de la philosophie et de l'état*. Paris: L'Harmattan.

Walker, James. 1877. *Reason, Faith, and Duty: Sermons*. Boston: Roberts Brothers.

Warnock, Geoffrey. 1995. George Edward Moore. In Ted Honderich, ed., *The Oxford Companion to Philosophy*. Oxford: Oxford University Press.

Wayland, Francis. 1856. *The Elements of Moral Science*. Boston: Gould and Lincoln.

Wayland, Francis. 1868. *The Elements of Intellectual Philosophy*. New York: Sheldon & Company.

Weinstock, Jerome A. 1975. Reid's definition of freedom. *Journal of the History of Philosophy* 13: 335–45.

Weldon, Susan. 1978. Thomas Reid's theory of vision. Ph.D. dissertation, McGill University.

Weldon, Susan. 1982. Direct realism and visual distortion: A development of arguments from Thomas Reid. *Journal of the History of Philosophy* 20: 355–68.

Willard, Dallas. 1990. Language, being, God, and the three stages of theistic evidence. In J. P. Moreland and Kai Nielson, eds., *Does God Exist? The Great Debate*. Nashville: Thomas Nelson Publishers.

Wills, Garry. 1978. *Inventing America: Jefferson's Declaration of Independence*. Garden City: Doubleday.

Wilson, Alexander. 1769. Observations of the transit of Venus over the sun. *Philosophical Transactions of the Royal Society of London* 59: 333–8.

Wilson, Patrick. 1782. An experiment proposed for determining by the aberration of the fixed stars, whether the rays of light, in pervading different media, change their velocity according to the law which results from Sir Isaac Newton's ideas concerning the cause of refraction; and for ascertaining their velocity in every medium whose refractive density is known. *Philosophical Transactions of the Royal Society of London* 72: 58–70.

Wittgenstein, Ludwig. 1969. *On Certainty*. Ed. G. E. M. Anscombe and G. H.von Wright. Oxford: Basil Blackwell.

Wolterstorff, Nicholas. 1983a. Can belief in God be rational if it has no foundations? In Plantinga and Wolterstorff 1983.

Wolterstorff, Nicholas. 1983b. Thomas Reid on rationality. In Hendrik Hart, Johan van der Hoeven, and Nicholas Wolterstorff, eds., *Rationality in the Calvinian Tradition*. Lanham, MD: University Press of America.

Wolterstorff, Nicholas. 1987. Reid and Hume. *The Monist* 70: 398–417.

Wolterstorff, Nicholas. 2000. Reid on common sense, with Wittgenstein's assistance. *American Catholic Philosophical Quarterly* 74: 491–517.

Wolterstorff, Nicholas. 2001. *Thomas Reid and the story of epistemology*. Cambridge: Cambridge University Press.

Wood, Paul B. 1984. Thomas Reid, natural philosopher: A study of science and philosophy in the Scottish enlightenment. Ph.D. dissertation, Leeds University.

Wood, Paul B. 1985. The hagiography of common sense: Dugald Stewart's *Account of the life and writings of Thomas Reid*. In A. J. Holland 1985.

Wood, Paul B. 1987. Buffon's reception in Scotland: The Aberdeen connection. *Annals of Science* 44: 169–90.

Wood, Paul B. 1989. Reid on hypotheses and the ether: A reassessment. In Dalgarno and Matthews 1989.

Wood, Paul B. 1993. *The Aberdeen Enlightenment: The Arts Curriculum in the Eighteenth Century*. Aberdeen: Aberdeen University Press.

Wood, Paul B. 1994. Hume, Reid, and the science of the mind. In M. A. Stewart and John P. Wright 1994.

Wood, Paul B. 1997. "The fittest man in the kingdom": Thomas Reid and the Glasgow Chair of Moral Philosophy. *Hume Studies* 23: 277–313.

Wood, Paul B. 1998. Reid, parallel lines, and the geometry of visibles. *Reid Studies* 2, no. 1: 27–41.

Wood, Paul. B. 2000a. Marginalia on the mind: John Robison and Thomas Reid. In Paul B. Wood, ed., *The Culture of the Book in the Scottish Enlightenment*. Toronto: Thomas Fisher Rare Book Library: 89–119.

Wood, Paul B. 2000b. Chi era Thomas Reid? In Antonio Santucci, ed., *Filosofia e cultura nel Settecento britannico*, vol. 2. Bologna: Mulino.

Wood, Paul B. 2001. Who was Thomas Reid? *Reid Studies* 5, no. 1: 35–51.

Woozley, A. D. 1987. Reid on moral liberty. *The Monist* 70: 442–52.

Wright, John P. 1987. Hume versus Reid on ideas: The new Hume letter. *Mind* 76: 392–8.

Wright, John P. 1998. Critical notice of Manfred Kuehn's *Scottish Common Sense in Germany, 1768–1800*. *Reid Studies* 2, no.1: 49–55.

Yaffe, Gideon. 2002. Reconsidering Reid's geometry of visibles. *The Philosophical Quarterly* 52: 602–20.

Yaffe,Gideon. forthcoming. *Manifest Activity: Thomas Reid's Theory of Action*. Oxford: Oxford University Press.

Yandell, Keith. 1990. *Hume's Inexplicable Mystery: His Views on Religion*. Philadelphia: Temple University Press.

Yolton, John. 1984. *Perceptual Acquaintance from Descartes to Reid*. Minneapolis: University of Minnesota Press.

INDEX OF NAMES AND SUBJECTS